The New Politics of Energy Security in the European Union and Beyond

"A cogent and highly readable book about the politics of energy security in Europe and beyond. Analyzing oil and particularly natural gas developments in a wide area stretching from the Baltic to the Mediterranean sea, Andrea Prontera convincingly demonstrates that energy security is neither a matter of geopolitics, or of markets, but rather of both."

–**Thijs Van de Graaf**, *Assistant Professor of International Politics at the Department of Political Science at Ghent University in Belgium*

Combining theoretical reflections and empirical insights from paradigmatic case studies in the area of external energy governance, pipeline politics, Liquefied Natural Gas development and offshore petroleum policy and politics, this groundbreaking study demonstrates that a distinctive and new politics of energy security is definitively emerging in the European Union. Innovative not only in regard to the case studies presented (which include the Caspian region, the Baltic, Mediterranean countries, Central Asia and EU-Russia relations), but also in regard to the analytical framework adopted – an International Political Economy approach informed by an historical institutional perspective – the book challenges the common view of the 'depoliticisation' of energy security supported by the mainstream market approach and the power politics and 'zero-sum game' view supported by the geopolitical perspective. This book places the study of EU energy politics in the broader, evolving context of global energy markets and explores the complex interactions between EU and national political dynamics and between energy security and environmental concerns at the local level.

Andrea Prontera is Assistant Professor of International Relations and EU Institutions and Policies in the Department of Political Science, Communication and International Relations at the University of Macerata, Italy. His main research interests and publications lie in the areas of international political economy, comparative public policy and energy policy.

The New Politics of Energy Security in the European Union and Beyond

States, Markets, Institutions

Andrea Prontera

Routledge
Taylor & Francis Group

LONDON AND NEW YORK

First published 2017
by Routledge
2 Park Square, Milton Park, Abingdon, Oxon OX14 4RN

and by Routledge
605 Third Avenue, New York, NY 10017

First issued in paperback 2021

Routledge is an imprint of the Taylor & Francis Group, an informa business

British Library Cataloguing-in-Publication Data
A catalogue record for this book is available from the British Library

Library of Congress Cataloging-in-Publication Data
Names: Prontera, Andrea, author.
Title: The new politics of energy security in the European Union and
    beyond : states, markets, institutions / Andrea Prontera.
Description: Abingdon, Oxon ; New York, NY : Routledge, 2017. | Includes
    bibliographical references and index.
Identifiers: LCCN 2016054860 | ISBN 9781472476920 (hardback) |
    ISBN 9781315555126 (e-book)
Subjects: LCSH: Energy security—Political aspects—European Union
    countries. | Energy development—Political aspects—European Union
    countries. | Energy policy—European Union countries.
Classification: LCC HD9502.E852 P76 2017 | DDC 333.79094—dc23
LC record available at https://lccn.loc.gov/2016054860

Publisher's Note
The publisher has gone to great lengths to ensure the quality of this reprint but points out that some imperfections in the original copies may be apparent.

ISBN 13: 978-1-03-209683-4 (pbk)
ISBN 13: 978-1-472-47692-0 (hbk)

Typeset in Times New Roman
by Apex CoVantage, LLC

Contents

Figures and Tables

Figures

Tables

Acknowledgments

The idea of this book emerged in 2013–14 when I first thought to organise the different research I was doing on energy politics and energy security in Europe into one coherent work. Over the next two years, the original idea developed thanks to the help of many individuals and institutions who have generously supported my efforts with time, resources and advice. The colleagues, staff and friends at the Department of Political Science, International Relations and Communications at the University of Macerata have provided the best environment possible for this work. I would like to thank Luca Lanzalaco in particular for drawing my attention to the importance of the states-markets nexus in political science and discussing many of the theoretical arguments presented in the book with me.

This book has also greatly benefitted from the research periods I spent at the Centre for Energy, Petroleum and Mineral Law and Policy (CEPMLP) at the University of Dundee (2015) and the Oxford Institute for Energy Studies (OIES) at the University of Oxford (2016). In both cases, I enjoyed incredible support from colleagues, experts and staff and was able to discuss my work with them and improve it. I am particularly grateful to Peter Cameron of the Centre for Energy, Petroleum and Mineral Law and Policy and Jonathan Stern, Bassam Fattouh, Howard Rogers and all the members of the Natural Gas Research Programme at the Oxford Institute for Energy Studies for hosting me during my project. I would also like to offer special thanks to Jonathan Stern, who dedicated much of his valuable time to read all the drafts of the book and offer thoughtful comments. I would also like to offer special thanks to Katja Yafimava for her generous support and comments on important sections of the work.

Many empirical and theoretical arguments in the book have also been presented and discussed during several conferences at the University of Glasgow (2014), the University of Duesto, Bilbao (2015), and Queen Mary University of London (2016). I would like to thank all the organisers and participants at these events for their comments and suggestions. I would also like to thank the coordinators of the *UACES Collaborative Research Network on European Energy Policy* for providing an effective and excellent platform for exchanging ideas and research on energy-related issues in the European Union.

Any errors or misjudgements that are still present in this final text, notwithstanding all this support and advice, are my sole responsibility.

1 Introduction

At the very beginning of the 2000s, in a context of rising oil prices and global energy demand, the European Commission raised concern about the increasing energy dependence of the European Union (EU) and sketched out the main pillars for a long-term strategy aimed at reducing the risks of such dependence, especially in the gas sector. Since then, the enhancement of the Internal Energy Market (IEM) and the development of the EU's external energy policy have begun to challenge the long-standing European approach to security of supply, mainly based on a combination of national champions and bilateral foreign energy policy.

What have been the main effects of these reforms on the politics of energy security in the EU and beyond? How have these transformations affected the traditional politics of energy security in the EU member states? How does the continuous, large EU dependence on energy from abroad affect EU external actions and the foreign policy and diplomacy of the EU member states? How can we assess the effectiveness of the EU energy security strategy? What roles do EU member states and European energy companies play in the emerging EU security of supply governance structure? Are national governments losing their importance in the new context of liberalised energy markets? How does the nexus between energy security and environmental protection practically affect the EU strategy aimed at the diversification of energy sources and routes?

EU energy security challenges have changed dramatically in the past 15 years. On one hand, the tensions between Russia and the EU, aggravated by the annexation of the Crimea, are undermining their historical partnership on energy; on the other hand, deep transformations in the structure of global energy supply and demand, triggered by technological advances and geopolitical and economic dynamics – e.g. the US shale gas revolution and the development of Liquefied Natural Gas worldwide – are leading the EU to rethink its energy security strategy. This begs the additional question of whether European countries will be able to respond to these new challenges while remaining in a complex process of transformation that is redefining the structure of EU energy markets and the institutional arrangements which preside over their functioning.

This book aims to answer all of these questions by combining theoretical reflections from an International Political Economy (IPE) approach to energy policy, informed by a historical institutional perspective, and empirical insights from illustrative case studies in the area of external energy governance (with a focus on the Caspian region and Central Asia), pipeline politics (with a focus on the East-West corridor and Southern Gas Corridor), Liquefied Natural Gas (LNG) development (with a focus on the Baltic and Mediterranean countries), and offshore petroleum policy and politics (with a focus on the Central and Eastern Mediterranean Sea) in order to show that, in fact, a distinctive and new politics of energy security is definitively emerging in the EU.

More broadly, the main argument of this book is that the traditional understanding of the politics of energy security in Europe is based on two oversimplified views that prevent a true appreciation of the current political dynamics. The first view seems to confine energy security only to matters of high politics, or overt geopolitical confrontations among states, and the second view assumes that energy security in a liberalised market context means a 'depoliticisation' of energy dependence and energy matters. This dichotomy hampers the capacity of the observer to focus on what is a common and constitutive element of energy security, the combination of high and low politics. In other words, by overly stressing the high (geopolitical) vs. low (economic) aspects of energy security, these views risk missing the large part of political dynamics that indeed take place in the 'middle' zone between these two opposite poles, where politics, security and economics intertwine. Moreover, these views tend to neglect the importance of the institutional and ideational context in which interactions among states' policies and market dynamics are embedded. They also tend to consider single aspects of European energy security as indicative of the overall pattern of evolution of the politics of energy security in the EU and beyond. Thus, the foreign energy policy of member states towards Russia or their emphasis on national interests indicates that 'geopolitics return', whereas the move towards liberalised energy markets shows the 'economisation' of the international energy dynamics (Youngs 2011, 47–49). Finally, these views also produce a distortive effect that hampers a true appreciation of the degree and scope of the changes that have occurred in the European politics of energy security in the last few decades. For the high politics, geopolitical-oriented perspective, nothing seems really changed, since the basics of European energy security are driven by the geopolitical considerations of the major European countries. On the opposite side, for the low politics, market-oriented perspective, everything is changing since, with the spread of the market approach to energy policy in Europe, there will be an 'economisation' of energy politics that will make the old world of inter-state competition obsolete.

In contrast to these views, three main theses are specifically supported in this book: first, that states still play a fundamental role in the practice of EU energy security governance and that energy resources still have an inescapable political significance in the liberalised EU market structure; second, that the interactions among states, markets and institutions must be put into specific, national and regional contexts for a true understanding of energy security politics; and third, that the current politics of energy security in the EU and beyond involve a meshing of some old and new dynamics.

With regard to the first thesis, this book demonstrates that while the construction of the EU internal energy market has shifted the balance in the institutional structure of European energy security from states to markets, this does not mean that governments are losing their importance; even if their functions are changing today, security of supply, diplomacy and foreign policy are strictly interconnected, as they were in the past. The book thus clarifies that the liberalisation and privatisation of EU energy markets do not imply a 'depoliticisation' or 'economisation' of energy issues. Rather, the new market principles and the new role that EU institutions play in energy security governance have led to a reconfiguration of energy politics and diplomacy that have challenged the previous system in different policy areas, but that have left the basic political significance of energy dependence for foreign and domestic politics unchanged.

With regard to the second thesis, the book demonstrates how and why the interactions between states and markets should be put in specific geographical, historical and institutional contexts to understand the dynamics of energy security. Global and EU-wide developments cannot explain the patterns of transformation in energy security politics, which are shaped by the combination of these developments with the specific nature and meaning that the energy security challenge assumes in different sectors and contexts. The interactions between supranational dynamics and regional and domestic dynamics are also crucial to understanding the effectiveness of the EU energy security strategy. Finally, with regard to the third thesis, by providing an empirical analysis of different areas and contexts of European energy security, the book demonstrates how the developments of recent decades have led to a 'reconfiguration' of the politics of energy security in the EU and beyond. In contrast to the approaches that envisage the emergence of an entire new politics of energy security – due to the recent economic and institutional transformations at the international and EU level – and the approaches that, instead, emphasise a substantial continuity with past experiences, the book shows that the current politics of energy security in the EU is better mirrored by a particular and context-specific combination of new and old dynamics.

Before presenting the empirical research that supports these theses, the goals of this introductory chapter are first to discuss and clarify the basic definition of energy security used in the book, and thus to specify and delimit the field of the analysis. This point is important. Energy security is a wide-ranging concept that includes different issues related to energy politics, policy and governance, while this book focuses only on a limited subset of this wider ensemble. Then, a brief overview of the development of the competences of the EU in the areas of energy policy and energy security will be provided, highlighting recent innovations and their implications for traditional European politics of energy security. Thirdly, a critical review of the existing literature will be offered, and the building blocks of the IPE analytical framework that will be used to study the changing patterns of energy security politics in the EU and beyond will be presented. The goal is not to offer a theoretical model capable of explaining the specific outcomes in particular cases of energy politics, but to sketch an analytical framework that can be adapted to different issue areas and contexts of the politics of energy security and that can serve to highlight the emerging patterns of interactions and the changes and continuities in respect to the previous system. This IPE framework will be integrated with a conceptual analysis, based on the concept of *forms of state* that will serve to better collocate recent European developments in a historical and comparative perspective and elaborate hypotheses on current dynamics. Fourth, the main pillars of the EU energy security strategy and a broad overview of the current and future challenges that affect EU security of supply are presented. In this introduction, only some general data on the EU energy dependence, especially in the gas sector, are provided, whereas more specific data will be presented and discussed in each empirical chapter. Finally, the specific policy areas and case studies that will be analysed in greater detail in the empirical chapters of the book are introduced. The criteria for the selection of the case studies and other methodological issues are also discussed.

Energy Security, Energy Dependence and Foreign Policy

Energy security has been a practical concern for almost a century. It has periodically emerged as a prominent area for scholarly attention in political science and international relations, mainly in conjunction with the occurrence of oil price shocks or supply disruptions, or during periods of tight energy market conditions (Shaffer 2009; Hughes and Lipscy 2013). Political and economic developments combine to produce these events, which catalyse the attention of policymakers, experts and analysts and trigger different sets of responses, depending on the specific geographical, economic and political situation in each country or region. The last wave of attention traces back to the beginning of the 2000s, when rising oil prices and the prospect of a structural shift in energy demand towards emerging economies, mainly China and India, coupled with the instability instilled in the international system by the terrorist attacks of 11 September 2001, brought this old issue back onto the international agenda. In Europe, this trend received additional reinforcement from the 2006 and 2009 gas disputes between Russia and Ukraine, which especially highlighted the vulnerability of some new eastern members of the EU and raised concern about the reliability of Russian energy supplies at a time when energy policies in Europe were moving towards liberalised and de-monopolised energy markets.

Traditionally, by adopting the perspective of the consumer states, 'energy security' has been considered synonymous with security of supply: the ability to secure adequate amounts of energy – principally oil and later natural gas – at prices that enable the normal functioning of the economies of industrialised countries and that sustain the way of life of an affluent, mobile consumer society. This perspective is well represented by the definition still used by the International Energy Agency (IEA), which defines energy security as 'the uninterrupted availability of energy sources at an affordable price'.[1]

With the last wave of scholarly attention, the analysis of energy security has become more sophisticated, and different dimensions of the concept have been scrutinised (Yergin 2006; Sovacool 2011a; Dyer and Trombetta 2013). The perspective of the producer countries and concerns related to security of demand have been integrated into the analysis of energy security. Other common dimensions included in the concept of energy security are environmental stewardship – related to the nexus between fossil fuel consumption and climate change and the negative externalities linked to the production, transportation and consumption of energy sources – and questions of social and human security, including issues such as energy poverty, equity and access to energy services. The concept of energy security has been also extended to include other sectors than oil and gas, such as nuclear energy and electricity, and to cover a wide range of risks, from the traditional manipulation and cartelisation of markets by producer states to terrorist attacks and natural disasters.

The broadening of the concept of energy security has been instrumental in highlighting the many interconnections between the various faces of the current global energy challenge. Moreover, these analyses have the merit of clarifying that the concept of energy security is not a fixed object: its meaning changes over time, and it is dependent on specific contexts and sectors, on the place that states have in energy supply chains, and on the theoretical and cognitive frames applied by observers and policy actors. New models to assess and measure energy security have also been developed, combing qualitative and quantitative methods (e.g. Sovacool 2011b). Long lists of indicators have been formulated, and a better integration of social science, engineering, natural science etc. has been advocated to make sense of a such complex phenomenon (Cherp and Jewell 2011). However, the contribution of this literature towards untangling one of the classical issues of energy security, i.e. the international political implications of the management of energy dependence, is not entirely clear. Reviewing the International Relations literature on the subject, scholars can easily conclude that the two main approaches used to analyse this issue are still the traditional realist-geopolitical and market-liberal perspectives, and that few attempts to explicitly theorise international energy relations depart from these alternatives (Cherp and Jewell 2011; Stoddard 2013; Svyatets 2016; Van de Graaf and Colgan 2016).

This situation is particularly unwelcome because the challenge of meeting national energy demand by securing adequate (with regard to price and quantity) supplies of oil and gas remains a policy priority of the governments of consumer countries – a priority that today, as in the past, implies a close linkage between domestic energy governance, foreign policy and diplomacy.

The interactions between energy dependence and international politics have been manifest since the famous decision of Winston Churchill, as First Lord of the Admiralty, to shift the power source of the British navy's ships from coal to oil: a switch that meant that the Royal Navy would rely, not on coal from Wales, but on insecure oil supplies from what was then Persia (Yergin 2006). The role of oil in modern warfare and international security was confirmed by the events of World War I and World War II. However, it was with the oil shocks of the 1970s that the important implications of energy dependence for the practical functioning of the economies and societies of industrialised countries in times of peace were more clearly manifested.

The oil shocks signalled the end of the so-called 'first oil regime' (Frank 1985). This regime was based on the political and strategic predominance of the hegemonic powers in the Middle East – first the UK and later the US – and on the control exercised by a small group of Western energy companies – the so-called 'seven sisters' – over the production and commercialisation of oil products. When the political and economic foundations of this system began to shift, partly as a result of the actions of OPEC members, energy security rose to the top of the agenda of consumer countries. In the following years, various strategies were developed to manage energy dependence and to prevent energy crises and supply disruptions. Strategic and military involvement of the hegemonic power, the US, in the Middle East and other producing regions has remained an important component of global energy security (Stokes and Raphael 2010). And this strategic dimension of energy security, where energy resources may become the object of military competition among major powers, remains an important aspect of today's global security dynamics (e.g. Klare 2009; Moran and Russel 2009; O'Sullivan 2013). However, an entire set of additional measures have been developed since the oil shocks. These measures, such as those intended to reduce oil dependence by promoting new technologies – e.g. nuclear energy – or by diversifying suppliers and routes, have not changed the significance of the relationship between energy security and foreign policy, although they have created new patterns of domestic and international energy politics, with some variations from state to state and region to region. In Western Europe, for example, natural gas from Russia came to partially replace Middle Eastern oil, paving the way for the subsequent development of the East-West energy interdependence that still represents one of the major concerns of many European policymakers today.

Since the 1970s, a common set of measures have become the standard toolkit that consumer countries use to manage their energy dependence on hydrocarbon resources, i.e. oil and natural gas. A simple distinction can be made between measures designed to ensure long-term and short-term security of supply. Although these types of measures interact with each other and, like any classification, this one has limits and shortcomings, this distinction can be used to specify the main sectors in which the politics of energy dependence can be practically analysed. Short-term measures include mainly the set of tools intended to respond rapidly to supply disruptions, such as strategic reserves, storage capacity, emergency plans, contingency plans, mechanisms of solidarities among consumer countries etc. These measures can guarantee the continuation of economic and social activities in consumer countries for a limited time, giving their governments time to resolve the problems responsible for the crisis. Long-term measures include interventions intended mainly to prevent energy crises related to supply disruption or excessive price increases. Long-term measures may include diversification of suppliers and supply routes, promotion of domestic energy sources, promotion of the functioning of international energy markets and support for the investments necessary to develop adequate resources and infrastructure to match energy demand. These measures aim at assuring adequate energy supply to sustain the economic development of consumer countries in the long term, and many of them imply some form of interaction, dialogue and cooperation among consumer and producer states and between governments and market actors. Long-term security of supply also has an internal dimension; energy infrastructure and diversification, for example, have important effects on domestic politics. However, long-term measures are the privileged area in which the international implications of energy dependence show their main structural effects.

To sum up, rather than offering the umpteenth definition of energy security – in a review of the concept, Sovacool (2011b, 3) listed forty-five definitions of energy security – in this book I use the term to mean its traditional definition: long-term security of supply and its connection to international politics in the areas of diversification, infrastructure, investments and market governance. That is to say, in this book, the term energy security refers to the politics of energy in specific areas that contribute to the EU's strategy of long-term security of supply. Since the book is focused on the EU and EU member states, the perspective of consumer countries will be highlighted, and since natural gas has recently become a major concern of European countries, I focus mainly on this energy source.

To be sure, a discussion of security of supply in the EU can also include coal, uranium and electricity (Talus 2011; Schubert, Pollak and Kreutler 2016). However, coal is far less politicised than oil and gas, and it is also less important from the perspective of international and foreign policy. Coal resources are less concentrated than oil and gas, several alternative sources and supply routes are available and its storage is relatively easier and cheaper. Uranium also poses fewer problems than oil and gas because supplies are stable and reliable, as are the means to ship this source into the EU market. Unlike uranium, oil, gas and coal, electricity is not a primary fuel, and security of electricity supply is generally associated with domestic issues and technical failures (e.g. infrastructure availability, sufficient investment in generation and transmission etc.) rather than geopolitical or external problems. Finally, security of gas supply is additionally complicated by the fact that, unlike oil, natural gas is not easy to store. While creating strategic oil reserves is a common practice for consumer countries, gas storage is much more problematic and relies also on favourable geological conditions in each country. The EU and the IEA require member states to maintain a minimum of strategic oil reserves, but no similar requirements exist regarding strategic reserves of natural gas.

The focus on natural gas is also justified because so far, this primary fuel has attracted less attention than oil in the literature of international political economy, although it is becoming a crucial component of energy security worldwide (Hancock and Vivoda 2014). Natural gas is widely considered the 'fuel of choice' for the decades to come because is comparatively cleaner than other fossil fuels – especially coal – and is abundant. It is also more and more available since increasing unconventional gas production has boosted global reserve-to-production ratios for more than two hundred years (Hulbert and Goldthau 2013, 98). Moreover, for the governance and security of international oil trade, the EU is largely a 'free-rider on the USA' (Andersen, Goldthau and Sitter 2016, 52). The US uses its hard power tools to oversee global oil markets (for example the US Fifth Fleet keeps the Straits of Hormuz open and the oil flowing). In the case of natural gas, however, the EU and EU member states play a more important role in energy security and trade, especially at the regional level. Indeed, unlike oil, which is a global commodity that is mostly distributed by long-distance tankers, sold in spot markets and negotiated on a day-to-day basis, natural gas trade is much more rigid and more regional (Proedrou 2012; Hulbert and Goldthau 2013). Natural gas runs principally through pipelines – global LNG trade in more significant quantities is a recent phenomenon – and it is mainly sold (except in the North American market) according to long-term contracts, which usually cover one or two decades. This promotes mutual dependence between partners, rather than diversification and flexibility. As a result, there is no unified global gas market, but there are a number of regional markets (the North American, the East Asian, the South American and the Eurasian gas markets) with only limited connections through LNG trade (although these connections are growing with the development of LNG worldwide). The Eurasian gas market, spanning from Russia and the North Sea to the Mediterranean Sea and North Africa, Caucasus and Central Asia and including the entire EU, can thus be studied as a quite coherent system with its own peculiarities, dynamics and regional politics, although, obviously, it is influenced by developments in global energy markets.

In a similar system, the strategies adopted by the EU and the EU member states have implications beyond Europe, especially in the neighbouring regions of the Eurasian gas market that are the main targets of those activities. Although this book focuses on the perspective of European consumers, it tries to integrate and show the perspective of the producer countries as well when analysing specific issues and to examine how the balance between security of supply and security of demand is practically constructed and maintained. Where it is necessary, the energy security concerns of transit states will also be considered. These concerns usually revolve around ensuring a reliable flow of revenue either from transit fees or through a percentage of gas shipped as payment in kind. The importance of revenues generated from transit is well illustrated by the often-difficult negotiations between Belarus, Ukraine and Russia over the transit fees for natural gas destined for Europe (De Jong, Wouters and Sterkx 2013, 141). In general, an important part of a transit state's energy security policy is the consolidation, enhancement and utilisation of its strategic geographical position between suppliers and consumers (De Jong, Wouters and Sterkx 2013, 141).

The book also tries to integrate the environmental dimension attached to the development of hydrocarbon resources in the study of energy security. Rather than focusing on the wider global nexus between fossil fuel consumption and climate change, or on mitigation measures such as energy efficiency and renewable, the book focuses on the environmental problems and risks related to upstream, midstream and downstream activities in the specific territories and regions in which they take place.[2] Those problems and risks trigger additional political dynamics that can link the local and international dimensions of energy security politics.

Energy Security in the EU and Beyond: States, Markets and Institutions

Setting the Stage: Navigating EU and Member States Competences from States to Markets and Back

As is well known, energy management was a key factor in the European integration accomplished through the European Coal and Steel Community and the European Atomic Energy Community. Nevertheless, the European response to the 1970s oil shocks, rather than being handled within the framework of the European Community, was played out in the framework proposed by the US through the International Energy Agency (France was the exception). Security of supply and foreign energy policy were matters of poor cooperation among European countries, as demonstrated by the unilateral responses to the 1973–74 oil embargo (Turner 1975).

Following the oil shocks, the European Community adopted ambitious long-term goals for energy production, consumption and import, but it was never able to agree on concrete steps for achieving them (Duffield and Birchfield 2011). Competences over the formulation and implementation of energy policy remained firmly in the hands of member states. National governments continued to decide the structure of their energy mix and the pace and timing of the diversification of sources and routes. Major European consumers also continued to develop their national foreign energy policies, supporting their state-owned energy companies – or national champions – abroad. They did this through active *energy diplomacy*, that is, through using various forms of state power to secure access to energy supplies, to flank energy contracts and energy companies, and to promote (mostly bilateral, i.e. government-to-government) cooperation in the energy sector (Goldthau 2010, 26–28). Domestic energy policies were also based on direct state intervention and traditional policy instruments of command and control. And, in many European countries, state ownership of energy companies was an additional way to strengthen the control of government on energy policymaking.

During the 1980s, the international energy landscape changed radically compared to the previous decade. Oil prices dropped, and the power of OPEC producers was no longer a particular concern for Western countries. In Europe, important energy resources were now guaranteed by the Soviet Union, and the UK, Norway and the Netherlands secured additional oil and gas supplies, while several major countries established nuclear programmes. In a similar context, characterised also by the diffusion of neoliberal thought, the European Commission embraced the idea to promote a closer integration among the energy markets of the member states, liberalisation and limited competition. This development was consistent with – and supported by – the important paradigm shift occurring in the realm of energy policy, which challenged the existing state-controlled system of governance in favour of a more market-oriented approach (Helm 2005; Goldthau 2012).

In 1988, after the adoption of the Single European Act, the European Commission, relying on its competences over market integration, launched an ambitious project: the construction of the Internal Energy Market (IEM). The aim was to overcome the 'energy exception' and start to treat the energy sector like any other economic sector, handling it according to common market principles and rules. The electricity and gas sectors were the main targets of this project. Oil markets in Europe, like in other industrialised consumer countries, began to move towards greater liberalisation and a market-based approach by the mid-1980s. This occurred partly in response to international dynamics and competitive forces (Hughes 2014). But the electricity and gas sectors were relatively sheltered from these pressures. In these sectors, the move towards a market-oriented approach should have been promoted by actively dismantling the previous state-controlled system of governance. Electricity and gas were still firmly organised around national monopolies with little or no integration among member states, and they were still managed according to principles of direct state intervention and public planning rather than market principles. In the view of the European Commission, a 'more integrated energy market' was 'a significant additional factor as regards the security of supply for all Member States', since 'greater interconnections' would have made it possible to increase 'the solidarity between Member States' in the event of a crisis (European Commission 1988). It would also have fortified the European energy industries, allowing them to play a bigger role in an environment of greater international competition. Moreover, in the view of the European Commission, the IEM project should have been accompanied by the achievement of common external energy objectives (Maltby 2013).

The IEM project and the implementation of the market paradigm in energy policymaking was opposed by many member states and the energy industry, and it took a decade for the Commission to finalise the original proposals (McGowan 1989; Matlary 1997; Schmidt 1998; Cameron 2007). The first directives to open up national electricity and gas markets were adopted in the late 1990s. However, the development of an external and common dimension of energy policy proved to be even more difficult to achieve. During negotiations for the Treaty of Maastricht, in the early 1990s, the inclusion of a new chapter on energy was proposed but not accepted. The Maastricht Treaty only gave the EU competences to improve cross-border energy infrastructures through a programme known as the Trans-European-Networks (TENs). In 1996, the Council adopted two decisions on Trans-European energy networks of 'common interest', later termed TEN-E projects. With these decisions, the European Commission gained some competences to promote supplier diversification and concede limited financial assistance (mainly for the feasibility studies) to projects proposed by energy companies and backed by national governments. Although the transformation of the national energy markets in response to the IEM project, especially in the gas sector, was starting to challenge the traditional institutional and ideational structure of European energy security, the establishment of a common external strategy as envisaged by the European Commission still lacked substantive legislation. This legislation was also not included in the Amsterdam (1997) or Nice (2001) Treaties.

Apart from the construction of the internal energy market and the first competences in the area of energy infrastructures, another one of the pillars that would later constitute the EU energy security strategy was established in the 1990s. This pillar also provided the initial manifestation of the EU's external energy dimension. In the wake of the end of the Cold War, an important opportunity arose, enabling the EU to expand the rules of the internal energy market beyond its borders and externally promote an agenda of liberalisation. In 1990, the Energy Charter process, which supports the adoption of market rules in producer and transit countries, was launched by the Dutch Prime Minister Ruud Lubbers. The project was embraced by the other heads of state, and the European Council mandated that the European Commission design the Energy Charter Treaty (ECT). The ECT went into force in 1998; its aim was to integrate the energy system of the former Soviet Union into the European and global energy markets by promoting common rules and standards and by encouraging investments in upstream and midstream activities. From the European perspective, this measure should have ensured continuous and reliable long-term security of supply.

Russia was one of the main targets of the ECT, as this legally binding treaty promised to have a more profound impact than the political cooperation established by the EU and Russia with the 1994 Partnership and Cooperation Agreement and the energy-focused cooperation established in 2000 with the EU-Russia Energy Dialogue. Although these expectations did not materialise – in 2009 Russia eventually refused to ratify the ECT – since that first initiative, a large portion of the EU's activities in external energy relations has been focused on promoting the rules of the internal energy market beyond the EU's borders.[3] This approach – commonly referred as the external 'energy governance' dimension of European energy policy (Herranz-Surrallés 2015a, 912) – paralleled the market-oriented approach pursued internally by the European Commission. At the beginning of the 2000s, the Energy Community Treaty was established, and several other regional initiatives were proposed to extend the EU's regulatory space beyond its borders (Prange-Gstöhl 2009). These efforts would result in a fragmented set of institutions – bilateral and multilateral, legally binding and not legally binding – that became the concrete and complex manifestation of the external governance dimension of the EU energy policy (e.g. Cameron 2011; Padgett 2011).

This external energy governance, mainly promoted by the European Commission, is a very different kind of external energy relations than the traditional practice of energy diplomacy (Herranz-Surrallés 2015b, 3–4). External energy governance views energy security as an economic problem related to lack of transparency, regulatory gaps and market failures. Rather than relying on bilateral intergovernmental agreements, state-owned energy companies (or private companies that have close relationships with their host country) or state-backed strategic infrastructural projects, external governance is mainly grounded in multilateral institutions and frameworks to promote regulatory harmonisation (including transgovernmental networks), and in positive/negative incentives to induce third countries to adopt liberal market energy reforms.

In the first decade of the twenty-first century, the relative neglect of energy policy underwent a profound change (Duffield and Birchfield 2011, 5–6). A large number of proposals, communications, directives and regulations touching almost every aspect of energy policy were formulated and enacted. The IEM project was completed with the Second and Third Legislative Energy Packages. Many measures were also adopted to strengthen the environmental side of energy policy, such as those intended to promote renewable sources or energy efficiency and schemes to reduce greenhouse gas emissions. These measures began to indirectly affect the structure of member states' energy supplies and their energy mix. Furthermore, principles attached to sustainable development and environmental protection gained prominence throughout the European system of governance. This latter development, coupled with a trend towards the decentralisation of energy decision-making in many member states, enhanced the role of regional and local governments and communities in the policymaking process (e.g. Marcou and Wollmann 2007).

In the area of energy security, the decade opened in 2000 with the first Green Paper on security of supply (*Towards a European Strategy for the Security of Energy Supply*) published by the European Commission (European Commission 2000). Concerns about EU security of supply were then reaffirmed in 2006 with the second Green Paper on energy, *A European Strategy for Sustainable, Competitive and Secure Energy*. During this period, as a result of the 2004 and then 2007 enlargement, and of the 2005–06 Russian-Ukrainian gas dispute, natural gas definitely emerged as the major area of concern in Brussels and other national capitals. Many new member states in Eastern Europe and the Baltic were overly dependent on a single gas supplier: Russia. Moreover, at the time of the gas dispute, about 80 percent of Russian gas supplied to the European markets passed through Ukraine. When Russian supplies to Ukraine were cut off on 1 January 2006, several member states (i.e. Hungary, Austria, Slovakia, France, Poland, Italy and Germany), experienced a reduction in Russian gas flows. The dispute ended on 4 January, and there have been no reports that this four-day event caused any significant disruption of EU gas supplies (Stern 2006). However, it finally brought the EU's attention to security of gas supply from Russia and transit issues, and it reinforced the perception of vulnerability among European decision makers. The 2006 Green Paper called for greater solidarity among member states to ensure an uninterrupted energy supply in case of crisis or supply disruption. Although the European Commission reaffirmed that 'opening up the markets is one way of guaranteeing a secure energy supply', it stressed the necessity for more coordination of EU and member states' actions in external energy policy to ensure a more coherent and consistent approach towards key producer and transit countries and promote energy diversification (European Commission 2006).

In the mid-2000s, as a result of a combination of internal and external factors – i.e. the 2004 and 2007 enlargements and the first Russia-Ukraine gas crisis – a window of opportunity was open to anchor this strategy more firmly into the institutional architecture of the EU (Maltby 2013). With the energy chapter included in the Lisbon Treaty, to 'ensure security of energy supply' and 'promote the interconnection of energy networks' became formal aims of EU energy policy (Treaty on the Functioning of the European Union, Art. 194). According to the Lisbon Treaty, which entered into force in 2009, those aims should be pursued in the context of an established and functioning internal market, with regard for the need to protect the environment and in a 'spirit of solidarity' among member states. The reference to the principle of solidarity, in particular, was finally included in the new Treaty after strong lobbying from Poland[4] (Roth 2011). However, the same Article 194 reaffirms that 'such measures shall not affect a member state's right to determine the conditions for exploiting its energy resources, its choice between different energy sources and the general structure of its energy supply'. Thus, the Lisbon Treaty, while enhancing the power and competences of the EU and, in theory, facilitating a more common mode of decision-making on energy policy and energy security, did not reduce the autonomy that member states traditionally enjoyed.

The redesign of the EU competences over energy security and the call made by the European Commission, the High Representative and some member states to better embed energy matters in the EU's foreign policy was supported by the perception that the existing external governance approach had not effectively tackled important aspects of energy security, especially the issue of diversification of gas supply, and that a more proactive approach was needed to manage energy dependency. Since then, the European Commission has pushed for more competence to act in respect to external energy relations (Talus 2013). In the 2008 *Second Strategic Energy Review – An EU Energy Security and Solidarity Action Plan,* the European Commission proposed to diversify gas supplies through the creation of a Southern Gas Corridor. Moreover, the Commission asked not only for better coordination among member states but for the EU to 'speak with one voice' in foreign energy affairs. This position was further recalled in the 2011 Communication *On Security of Energy Supply and International Cooperation,* in which the Commission called for the 'EU to speak with a common voice when it comes to external energy relations' and stated that this idea must be 'further exploited and transformed into a systematic approach' (European Commission 2011a, 3). But these innovations were also supported by a retreat of the market paradigm of energy policy. Indeed, as the liberalisation agenda pursued by the EU at the end of the 1980s was strengthened by the spread of the market paradigm, the push to reassert more direct public control on energy affairs in the mid-2000s has to be understood in the context of the simultaneous general retrenchment of the market paradigm of energy matters in consumer countries (Helm 2005; Goldthau 2012). The move back towards major state involvement in energy governance was driven worldwide by the tightening of global energy markets and the subsequent improvement of the position of producer countries and their state-controlled energy companies.[5] In the EU, this perspective – which had never completely disappeared, as it was largely supported by many member states – was reinforced by the specific events occurring in the Eurasian gas market: Moscow's military intervention in Georgia in 2008 and the second Russian-Ukrainian gas crisis of 2009. All in all, worries about security of supply were now bringing states back into energy governance and undermining the EU liberal model in which energy supplies were approached as 'a matter for private companies rather than government command' (Youngs 2011, 51).

As a result, starting in the late 2000s, the EU began to complement its external governance approach with more direct financial, political and diplomatic involvement, supporting infrastructure projects to diversify gas supply routes and speaking with producer countries. That is to say, the EU, and especially the European Commission, was moving from a more market-oriented approach based on multilateral energy governance towards a greater focus on an *EU-level energy diplomacy* (Herranz-Surrallés 2015b). This development was, however, constrained by two different factors (Herranz-Surrallés 2015b). On one hand, the European Commission, while it embraced the discourse of energy diplomacy, was more cautious in departing from its traditional role of defendant of the internal energy market and external promoter of the *acquis communautaire*. On the other hand, the EU's departure from its traditional market approach has also been constrained by the prevailing practices in the energy business sector and member states' opposition to reviewing the traditional rules of the game of *national energy diplomacy*. In fact, member states had already clearly manifested their attachment to national sovereignty in energy matters, allowing only shared competences to be included in the Lisbon Treaty and, in practice, continuing to develop their bilateral relations with producers.

Despite these problems, and despite the fact the European Commission obviously lacked one of the traditional complements of energy diplomacy – a national energy company – it took on a more proactive and political role in the diversification of gas supply. The Commission actively supported the Nabucco pipeline project to open the Southern Gas Corridor, and it also proposed the establishment of a single purchasing mechanism – the so-called Caspian Development Corporation – to aggregate gas demand of member states and convince Caspian producers to commit their resources to the EU. At the beginning of 2011, the European Council embraced this new activism of the European Commission. The Council invited the Commission to 'continue its efforts to facilitate the development of strategic corridors (. . .) such as the Southern Corridor', and it supported the proposal to grant EU funding to infrastructure projects that were unable to attract market-based financing but 'justified from a security of supply/solidarity perspective' (European Council 2011). This view was later incorporated in the new 2013 TEN-E guidelines with Regulation 347/2013, which expands the options for so-called 'Projects of Common Interest' (PCI), allowing them to profit from EU grants not only for studies but also, under certain conditions, for works. On the same occasion, the European Council also invited the Commission to formulate a proposal for granting major transparency into the field of bilateral energy Intergovernmental Agreements (IGAs), a traditional *domaine réservé* of national diplomacy[6] (and in 2012 an information exchange mechanism was established by decision No. 994/2012/EU). Finally, in September 2011, the Council adopted a decision authorising the Commission to negotiate an agreement with Azerbaijan and Turkmenistan on a legal framework for a Trans-Caspian natural gas pipeline system, thus granting the Commission its first mandate to negotiate external diversification infrastructure on behalf of member states.

It is worth noting that during this period, a general rethinking of the state-markets nexus also affected the internal market project. Indeed, with growing fears of an investment gap in energy infrastructure, essential for diversification and security of supply, the Third Energy Package departed from the pure market-based mechanism formulated with the First and Second Packages and moved towards a regime where the role of the state was increasingly important (Talus 2015, 208). This was not, however, a return to the previous system of direct state control and public sector planning; in line with market-oriented methods of energy governance, the new EU infrastructural planning system can be described as 'regulation of self-regulation' (Del Guayo and Pielow 2012, 358). Moreover, while the pre-liberalisation system was driven by national governments, the new scheme was marked by the importance of the European Commission's role.

Although resistance to the EU's involvement in energy diplomacy and infrastructure development did not disappear, especially from larger member states, the move towards a more proactive role for the European Commission continued in the following years and received a boost after war broke out in eastern Ukraine and Russia annexed the Crimea. In the wake of these new crises, the 2015 Communication on the *Energy Union Package – A Framework Strategy for a Resilient Energy Union with a Forward-Looking Climate Change Policy* again stressed the need for the European Commission to play a proactive role in the diversification of gas supply, in promoting strategic partnerships with key producer and transit countries, and in monitoring the IGAs. The Communication also once again proposed the establishment of 'demand aggregation mechanisms for collective purchasing of gas' (European Commission 2015). The same year, on 20 July, the EU Foreign Affairs Council endorsed the first *EU Energy Diplomacy Action Plan*, which reiterated support for more incisive energy diplomacy at the EU level.

To sum up, since the late 2000s, the traditional 'division of labour' (Herranz-Surrallés 2015b, 15) in European energy security – EU-level external energy governance and national energy diplomacies – has begun to change. The development of EU-level energy diplomacy has started to directly challenge the national energy diplomacy of member states and their original approach to energy security. This approach, however, had already been challenged indirectly by the enhancement of the internal energy market – with its focus on the liberalisation and de-monopolisation of national energy systems and new market-oriented methods of energy governance – and the spread of environmental and sustainable principles and practices that were transforming the institutional, market and ideational background in which the traditional European politics of energy security were played out.

Approaches to EU Energy Security and Their Limits

The late-2000s also represent a turning point with regard to scholarly attention to European energy security. Since then, much research has been done on the political, institutional and legal dimensions of EU energy security and the evolution of the EU's approach to security of supply in respect to specific foreign countries or regions, especially with regard to the gas sector and EU-Russia relationships (e.g.

Correljé and Van der Linde 2006; Haghighi 2007; Aalto 2008; McGowan 2008; Bilgin 2009; Youngs 2009; Umbach 2010; Cameron 2011; Proedrou 2012; Kuzemko 2014). If, in 2009, in one of the pioneering books exploring European energy security, Youngs could reasonably affirm that this issue 'has remained virtually absent from studies of EU foreign policy' (Youngs 2009, 5), in 2015 a review on the subject could equally realistically assert that scholarly research had 'started to keep pace with this fast-moving target' (Herranz-Surrallés 2015a, 911).

However, apart from a few notable examples (e.g. Keating et al. 2012; Aalto and Korkmaz Temel 2014; Belyi and Talus 2015; Boersma 2015; Herranz-Surrallés 2015b), the bulk of the literature on the EU's energy security is based on the traditional division between the realist-geopolitical and the liberal-market approaches (e.g. Correljé and Van der Linde 2006; Finon and Locatelli 2008; McGowan 2008; Umbach 2010). As a result, European energy security has typically been conceptualised as oscillating between 'multilateral governance and geopolitics' (Westphal 2006), between 'geopolitics and the market' (Youngs 2009), or between geopolitics and a 'liberal model of energy security' (Youngs 2011). The EU has usually been described as more committed to a multilateral market-governance approach and the EU member states more inclined to lean towards 'geopolitical behaviour', with their governments mainly interested in backing their respective national champions and signing bilateral deals (Youngs 2009, 174). In particular, the European Commission is portrayed as the main actor championing a liberal approach to international energy affairs in a world of energy that is becoming more realist (Goldthau and Sitter 2014).

Looking at the last decade's literature on European energy security, the gap between the growing number of empirical research and the poor conceptual development is particularly striking, although developing a conceptual framework is especially important in the area of energy policy/energy security, an extremely complex subject matter (Prontera 2009; Aalto 2012; Aalto 2015). The main problem with realist-geopolitical and liberal-market approaches is that they tend to view politics and economics as discrete analytical areas, and they fail to effectively explore the potential interrelationships that are crucial for understanding the dynamics of energy security (Keating et al. 2012, 3). This is particularly true regarding the role of the state in energy markets. The geopolitical approach tends to assume that states can manipulate energy markets and transactions without constraints (consider the idea of the 'energy weapon') and are always in the midst of a 'zero-sum' competition with other states. In contrast, the market approach tends to equate energy security with 'free markets' and to limit government intervention to market failures, criticising other strategies as 'political interference' or 'statism' (Keating et al. 2012, 3).

Liberal-market approaches also seem poorly equipped to address the question of change in the energy security realm, since they tend to view any form of state intervention in energy markets as the return to an 'old world' of energy affairs, and they view market governance-based strategies as the only manifestation of new politics and a 'new world' of energy (e.g. Hayes and Victor 2006). That is to say, they seem to overlook the fact that energy security has always been a combination of market forces and political and geopolitical dynamics. The way in which those elements combine and the equilibrium they form in different periods and contexts is, in fact, the real question scholars must address. As Stoddard (2013) has recently pointed out, energy security is typically provided by a nexus of market actors and political authorities that are mutually dependent on each other's resources. Companies provide the bulk of the production knowledge, production capacity and financing necessary to exploit energy resources, and political authorities provide security and political support for companies and shape the institutional and legal framework in which market actors operate.

Moreover, both realist-geopolitical and liberal-market schools derive from the traditional scholarship of International Relations (IR): they focus mainly on the external dimension of energy security, and they are less interested in – and less equipped for – an analysis of the interactions between domestic energy governance and politics and foreign energy affairs (Svyatets 2016). But the transformations in national energy markets and methods of governance and in the domestic politics of energy have an important effect on external energy relations, just as transformations in global or regional energy markets and international energy affairs affect the domestic choices and strategies both of states and market actors.

Finally, both approaches do not properly address the interactions between concerns about security of supply and concern for the environment, especially at the local level. Modern energy systems are large, complex socio-technical systems composed of materials and cognitive, symbolic and institutional elements (Mayntz and Hughes 1988; Rip and Kemp 1998). Those systems perform important functions at the macro-level, as they provide energy services for citizens and for the economic activities of entire countries or regions. However, upstream and midstream hydrocarbon activities in particular have an important infrastructural component – e.g. oil and gas exploration and production facilities, pipelines, LNG terminals etc. – that impact specific territories and socio-economic areas on the micro-level. At this micro-level, important spaces for contestation and political mobilisation can open, producing resistance against macro-level political or economic dynamics. This is particularly true when different visions and forms of political legitimacy can be mobilised to oppose the cognitive and symbolic elements of the predominant socio-technical systems. In the last decades, particularly in the industrialised energy consumer countries, principles and practices such as those attached to the concept of sustainable development or environmental protection have challenged the long-standing association between fossil-fuel-based energy systems and notions of development or modernisation. Alternative views based on decentralised energy systems, conservation practices, substitution of fossil fuels, energy efficiency etc. have gained legitimacy and are normally at work in any debate on energy security, not only at the global but also at the local level.

All these limits are particularly important when realist-geopolitical and liberal-market approaches are applied to the analysis of energy security politics in the EU and beyond, i.e. in the EU and in the regions influenced by the European energy security strategy. Energy security is the outcome of a continuous tension between states and markets, among subnational, national and supranational interests, and between multilateral institutions and bilateral energy diplomacy, particularly in the EU. Indeed, the main effect of the integration process in Europe is to challenge the traditional equilibrium between states and markets and trigger a redefinition of the institutional balance between different layers of governance and governance principles.

Especially in the gas sector, the development of the internal energy market has implied the break-up of national monopolies and the progressive dismantling of the vertically integrated national champions that have greatly contributed, backed by their respective national governments, to the management of energy dependence and the realisation of the importing infrastructure supplying the European markets. On one hand, this process has contributed to a more integrated continental gas market, but on the other hand, this economic integration is confronted with a growing fragmentation of political authority, preventing an effective decision-making process and hindering the projection of political influence beyond EU borders (Verda 2015, 28). In other words, when the institutional and market structure underpinning the traditional European security of supply is under a process of transformation, different political authorities are competing to offer, on different basis and only on partially overlapping agendas, their political and diplomatic support to market actors.

With their focus on the external dimension of energy policy, both schools are also less capable of analysing the close linkage between the changing politics of energy security at the national level and the evolution of the EU's energy security strategy, although the latter is strongly connected to the transformation of energy security in the EU member states. This optical distortion can result in the paradox of looking at and assessing the strategies of member states and EU's institutions, such as the European Commission, as if they were completely separate and separable. In fact, they are embedded into the same multi-level political-institutional system, the EU, in which authority, competences and resources are divided and/or disputed among different layers of government, and in which interactions, conflicts and/or convergences of interest and ideas along and among those layers are the norm rather than the exception.

Finally, especially in the EU, the new principles and practices questioning the traditional fossil-fuel-based energy systems are important, as they are embedded in the overall European institutional and legal system and in energy policy and environmental policy in particular. As a result, it is not surprising that the new institutional and ideational milieu of EU energy politics is also characterised by an 'increasing local opposition to energy infrastructure projects all over Europe' that that is 'leading to ever more complex permitting procedures'.[7] These dynamics reveal that energy security is not only the result of the interactions between states and markets or between national and supranational interests, but also encompasses different political and normative cleavages, such as those between the centre and the periphery or between different conceptions of economic development, which lie at the very heart of the relationship between energy and society. The traditional paradigm of centralisation and large technical systems, around which the current structure of the EU's security of supply has been built (with its physical manifestation in pipelines, LNG terminals etc.), is more and more contested by the emergence of new principles of energy policy. Although, in theory, the EU energy policy should coherently and simultaneously pursue security of supply and environmental goals, in the short-term and with regard to specific decision-making processes, clashes of views, interests and objectives are more and more common.

A Framework for the Analysis

Traditional IR approaches demonstrate their limits in the study of European energy security. According to these perspectives, European energy security is usually conceptualised as something oscillating 'in between' markets and geopolitics without further specification. A similar problem has characterised research by scholars who focus on EU energy security from the perspective of European integration, securitisation approaches or policy ideas and narratives. Rather than elaborating new concepts to grasp the EU situation, they have underlined the tensions *between* national sovereignty and supranational integration, *between* member states and EU institutions, *between* multilateral and bilateral diplomacy, *between* national manoeuvres and common energy policy, or *between* energy diplomacy and external governance (e.g. Belkin and Morelli 2007; Natorski and Herranz-Surrallés 2012; Kirchner and Berk 2010; Maltby 2013; Kuzemko 2014; Herranz-Surrallés 2015b). In other words, in this case as well, European energy security has been portrayed as something oscillating 'between' two poles, but few conceptual efforts to analyse the current phase with more precision, or to compare it with the previous period, have been developed.

To overcome these limitations and shortcomings, this book adopts an IPE approach informed by a historical institutional perspective. Notwithstanding the quite long tradition of IPE analysis of energy policy (e.g. Bromley 1991; Strange 1994; Harald Claes 2001), this approach has been practically absent in the study of EU energy security (Keating et al. 2012; Herranz-Surrallés 2015a). This situation is particularly unwelcome since an IPE approach can offer important advantages for the analysis of energy security politics in Europe and beyond (Keating et al. 2012, 4–5). IPE traditionally focuses on the state-market nexus, engages with a multiplicity of actors and institutions, and seriously considers the linkages and interdependences between global, regional and domestic dynamics and policy processes. It openly discusses a wide range of normative and substantive questions and is multi-disciplinary in character and scope.

In what follows, first, the building blocks of the IPE analytical framework adopted in this book will be presented. Then, the notion of *forms of state* will be elaborated in order to advance a conceptual distinction capable of describing the main features of the equilibrium in the state-market nexus and in the modes of external energy policy emerging in the multi-level European context. This conceptual analysis also serves to provide a historical and comparative perspective on European energy security politics and offer a general scheme for better organising the empirical research carried out in the next chapters.

IPE and Energy Security: The Building Blocks

The importance of focusing on the state-market nexus and adopting an IPE view-point on energy issues to avoid the shortcomings of a simplistic distinction between politics and economics was recognised years ago by Susan Strange. She considered energy a topic in need of 'some analytical framework for relating the impact of states' actions on the markets for various sources of energy, with the impact of these markets on the policies and actions, and indeed the economic development and national security of the states' (Strange 1994, 195). In her historical analysis of the 'oil business game', Strange stressed the centrality of governments, companies and markets as three key players and characterised each period by a different balance in the complex triangle of state-market-company (Strange 1994, 190–203).

Bressand (2013, 18–19) has recently sketched out a multidimensional framework for studying state-market interactions in the energy realm that can be applied for a dynamic analysis of energy security. This framework is composed of four building blocks: a) the analysis of the development of the energy markets, their logics and functioning, which is also influenced by the physical characteristic of energy resources and technology (geographical distribution, vectors of transportation etc.); b) the study of the institutional structures and governance mechanisms that preside over the functioning of energy markets; c) the study of the power structures that determine which actors are in a position to exercise control over production or transit of energy resources and which actors can influence the governance of institutions setting the stage for energy market transactions; d) the study of the transactions relating to energy assets, products and services across the entire value chain – upstream, midstream and downstream (these transactions can happen in traditional commodities markets or they can unfold in state-to-state relations). These four building blocks represent a useful starting point for an IPE approach to energy security that takes the interactions between market dynamics and states' policies seriously. However, additional specification and integration of the relevant actors and actor constellations are required. Moreover, an institutional historical perspective seems particularly suitable for the study of the institutional structures, market dynamics and their development.

With regard to actors and actor constellations, a contemporary IPE approach, while reasserting the state's role in energy governance, does not necessarily view states as centralised actors – as sub-state, inter-state, and supra-state actors must be considered – nor as the sole relevant actors (Keating et al. 2012). In other words, a broader range of players must be included in the analysis than the traditional ones outlined by Susan Strange, i.e. governments and companies. Today, in the oil business game, 'actors of influence include states, national energy companies, international energy companies, large-user groups, legislator and political organisations such as the EU', and also various civil society groups that are 'in a position to bring their values to bear onto energy arena' (Bressand 2013, 19). Similarly, as shown in recent research on European (and Eurasian) gas markets, states and companies remain crucial, but a broader range of actors – e.g. international organisations, international financial institutions, non-governmental organisations (NGOs), EU's institutions, subnational governments etc. – take part in the natural gas business game (e.g. Keating et al. 2012; Aalto and Korkmaz Temel 2014; Aalto 2015; Belyi and Talus 2015). NGOs, along with sub-state actors, have become important players, especially with regard to energy infrastructure localisation (e.g. Van de Graaf and Sovacool 2014). With the growing attention of public opinion on environmental issues and the spread of principles of sustainable development, these actors are gaining influence over the transit and production of energy resources and along the entire energy value chain.

The wider range of actors considered represents a common trend of the new economic diplomacy practices amid the growing liberalisation of commercial and trade relations, the fragmentation of the state, and the spread of regional and global supranational governance structures (Jayasuriya 2005; Lee and Hocking 2010). This changing context has resulted in new patterns of diplomatic interactions that go beyond the traditional bilateral diplomacy and government-to-company negotiations. These new patterns have been highlighted by terms such as 'multi-stakeholder diplomacy', 'network diplomacy' or 'catalytic-diplomacy' (Hocking 1999; Lee and Hocking 2010). Similar concepts provide new tools to not only recognise a greater constellation of actors involved in diplomatic practices but also to highlight the changing character of the bargaining processes, which are no longer confined to inter-state negotiations and now involve social, economic and political interactions that break down the barriers between domestic and international relations (Lee and Hocking 2010). These concepts are especially important within the 'EU multi-layered political-diplomatic environment' generated by the interactions of EU institutions, member states' governments, subnational interests and extra European actors (Hocking 2004). Rather than eroding the role of traditional bilateral diplomacy and government-to-company negotiations, European integration has promoted a meshing of bilateral negotiations with those conducted by a wider set of public and private actors (Hocking 2004).

With regard to the analysis of institutional structures and market dynamics, adopting an historical, institutionalist perspective seems quite obvious *prima facie*: due to their technological, economic and institutional fundamentals, energy markets are biased towards a strong path-dependent pattern of evolution. Once a power plant, pipeline, LNG facility etc. has been built, sunk costs, scale economies, long-term commitments and interest group politics are powerful forces that are capable of triggering self-reinforcing processes. The oil and gas sector is not only a dynamic business driven by technological innovation, but 'it has also much inertia: once solutions are identified and are materialised in fixed assets they continue working for decades' (Kryukov 2016, 83). In particular, the construction of pipelines creates sunk costs for investors that can only yield returns on the basis of long-term and stable energy relations. As pointed out by Victor and Victor (2006, 147), pipelines are the 'gas industry's equivalent of the standard QWERTY keyboard; once infrastructures are in place it is costly to move far from the main line'. Thus, pipeline route selection and construction is usually an issue of intense political debate: pipelines can strengthen the energy security of some states but at the same time undermine that of others (Müller-Kraenner 2008, 22–24). Moreover, pipelines bind exporters and importers into an interdependent trade partnership that incorporates a long-term perspective and can potentially pave the way for the exploitation of asymmetric relationships among the countries involved (Shaffer 2013).

Path dependence is not limited to sunk costs and physical assets; it is also felt with in contractual relations and prices regimes governing energy trade. The business of natural gas is currently witnessing a fundamental shift from a system characterised by regional markets and oil-indexed long-term contracts to one of liquid spot trading, gas-to-gas competition and global price interconnections (Hulbert and Goldthau 2013). But the historical legacy of the past system will not simply disappear overnight. It is still shaping current dynamics, resulting in a 'hybrid' model in Europe that combines oil-indexed long-term deals and spot-traded prices (Hulbert and Goldthau 2013).

On a broader analytical level, a path-dependent pattern of evolution means that understanding energy security policy and politics at time-1 is impossible without analysing the choices made at time-0 and their effects: the main characteristics of the energy system that scholars examine at any point in time, and which importantly constrain policy actors' choices, are the result of decisions taken ten, fifteen or more years previously. Therefore, a long-term perspective is necessary to accurately understand the transformations occurring in the politics of energy security. Only by analysing an appropriate period of time is it possible to assess whether the current dynamics represent something new, and to what degree, or if they have simply replaced the previous structures and processes, or, as much institutional literature suggests (e.g. Lanzalaco 1995; Streeck and Thelen 2005), if they can be better conceptualised as a combination of old elements with the most recent ones.

Adoption of a historical institutional perspective also means considering both the way actors shape institutional structures and the way institutional structures shape actors' behaviours and strategies (Steinmo 2008). Institutional structures refer to formal institutions and decision-making procedures as well as informal institutions (e.g. the traditional pattern of company-government relations) and ideational structures, that is, the ideas and 'guiding principles' (Sovacool and Sidorstov 2013) that frame energy security policymaking and influence actors' choices.

The different forms of the institutional structures have also to be considered. They can range from centralised institutional systems to more complex and fragmented systems of governance – regime complexes or governance architectures (Biermann et al. 2009; Keohane and Victor 2011) – with overlapping rules, principles and decision-making arenas. Institutional proliferation, complexity, coherence and interplay is a matter to address both with regard to the feature of the EU system of governance and the international system of governance in which EU and member states initiatives and strategies are incorporated.

Lastly, a historical institutionalist perspective means recognising that any analysis of energy security politics should focus strongly on the interactions among political, economic and natural (resource endowment, geography etc.) elements in specific contexts. The very meaning of energy security and the perceptions of the main risks associated with this term can be truly appreciated only by contextualising the concept and the practice of energy security. Quantitative data – such as those on energy dependence, production, reserves etc. – are important starting point for the analysis, but only as long as they are interpreted in a specific context (for example, and for obvious reasons, dependency on Russian gas supplies can have a very different meaning in Eastern and Western Europe).

Forms of State and a Comparative Historical Perspective on European Energy Security

The illustrated IPE building blocks – integrated with the historical institutional perspective – constitute an appropriate framework for a dynamic analysis of energy security politics in Europe and beyond. However, it would be also useful to take a snapshot of the current situation and to explain some concepts that allow it to be systematically compared with the previous phase or other geopolitical contexts. The concept of *forms of state* can contribute to these tasks. This concept has a long tradition in IPE (and political science) scholarship and in the historical institutional perspective (e.g. Clift 2014). It has been widely used – especially by the transformationalist branch of globalisation literature (Held et al. 1999) – to understand the transformations of the state and of the interactions among state and market actors in the wake of complex changes in the ideational, institutional and market structures in which they operate (e.g. Cox 1987; Cerny 1997). The concept of forms of state has been also used to highlight crucial political transformations promoted by the development of EU integration and changes in the institutional structures in which governmental agents are embedded (e.g. Caporaso 1996; Majone 1996, 1997). In particular, the traditional literature on forms of state in Europe has mainly explored – with the concept of the regulatory state – the relationship between structural changes promoted by European integration and actors' interactions and strategies by underlining the emergence of new modes of policymaking at both the *EU level* and the *national level* of government (e.g. Majone 1996, 1997; Eberlein and Grande 2005; Lodge 2008). Here, the focus will be on the emergence of new patterns of energy diplomacy, and attention will be paid to the changing relationship between market actors and political authorities.

In the realm of energy policy, the concept of forms of state was originally adopted in research on the oil sector. With regard to producer states, the characteristics of the rentier state have been widely studied (e.g. Beblawi and Luciani 1987). With regard to consumer countries, Randall (2005) describes the US experience from World War II (WWII) to the 1990s using the term *associational (or associative) state*. In an associational state, energy companies are in private hands and pursue their own direct, short-term commercial interests. The government works with and for the companies and supports their business activities abroad. Nevertheless, the government does not just serve the oil industries, but rather seeks to balance the companies' commercial interests with the country's long-term interest in energy security.

The model of the associational state is closely related to the peculiar history of the US oil sector and the 'guiding principles' behind the US domestic approach to economic and energy governance. Unlike in Western Europe, those factors prevented the development of something like a 'US National Oil Company' (Wälde 2008). The associational state model is also closely related to the US's peculiar role as a global hegemonic power, with its diplomatic and military involvement in the world's major oil-rich regions, especially the Middle East (Bromley 1991; Bahgat 2003; Stokes and Raphael 2010). According to this stylized state model, energy security is grounded basically on bilateral energy diplomacy and special strategic partnerships – such as those between Washington and Riyadh – rather than on multilateral efforts.[8] Governments prefer to rely mainly on their national economic, diplomatic and political resources, and they consider multilateral practices, rule-based governance structures and international cooperation ineffective, especially because these measures can limit the government's freedom to manoeuvre.[9] In the US experience, the militarisation of energy security is another important feature. The attempt at secure control over global oil supplies has traditionally been part of the US grand strategy, and to manage its energy security, Washington has even applied coercive instruments and used, or threatened to use, its military power (Peters 2004; Stokes and Raphael 2010).

After WWII, the militarisation of energy security and the use of force progressively disappeared as an option for Western European governments. They relied on bilateral relations to manage their oil dependency. Unlike in the US, however, the major European consumers have traditionally assigned the state a more direct role in the governance of national energy markets. Many countries, such as France, Italy and the UK, established state-owned companies to directly promote their energy security interests abroad. The model of *partner state* can describe this situation: national governments create and protect domestic national champions and use diplomacy and foreign policy to support those champions' negotiations with producer states and their companies abroad.[10] This approach – in which energy diplomacy is an integral part of national foreign policy – was also based on competition between European consumers. On one hand, European governments protected their domestic markets, and, on the other hand, they competed for access to the energy resources in producer states.

However, the partner state model is not confined to the past experience of Western Europe. This approach has also been taken by new energy consumers, such as China. The turning point in the Chinese history of energy security is generally placed in 1993–94, when the country became a net oil importer for the first time. This development – which was reinforced over the next two decades, transforming China into the world's largest net importer of oil in 2014 – triggered a reorganisation of the Chinese energy sector that resulted in the creation of three giant, vertically integrated, state-controlled oil companies: the China National Petroleum Corporation (CNPC), the China Petroleum and Chemical Corporation (Sinopec) and the China National Offshore Oil Company (CNOOC). The Chinese government has supported the internationalisation of these companies abroad with active, bilateral energy diplomacy backed by the state and firmly coordinated with other foreign policy goals. With this approach, the Chinese government aims to establish strategic partnerships with important producer states in the Middle East (like Saudi Arabia and Iran), Africa, Latin America and Central Asia and secure supply contracts and energy imports (Liu 2006; Yetiv and Lu 2007; Kong 2009; Proedrou 2012). China's strategy, however, is not limited to contracts with exporters; it also involves active engagement with infrastructure projects. In the gas sector, China has worked in partnership with its national energy companies to develop LNG facilities and international pipelines to promote imports and diversification, such as in the case of the infrastructures built in Central Asia.[11]

In the gas sector, the models of the positive state (or interventionist state) and regulatory state have already been applied to highlight some important characteristics of the energy governance of European countries (Majone 1996, 1997). Gas, along with other public utilities such as electricity, water, railways, telephone etc., was the quintessence of the post-WWII European positive state: public ownership, long-term planning, centralisation of the decision-making process and direct government intervention in the industrial organisational structure were the norm. Western European governments considered these sectors so strategically important that the state needed to retain the power to protect the public interest against powerful private interests. Progressive liberalisation and privatisation and the establishment of new methods of regulation in these sectors confirmed the rise of the regulatory state in Europe (Majone 1996). To be sure, both models capture important features of the post-WWII European organisation of energy governance and of its transformation, which started in the 1980s, partially in response to the deepening of integration within the EU. However, both models have been used to describe the general modes of national economic governance, but they cannot account for all the peculiarities of the energy sector, especially in the area of security of supply. Their focus is mainly on domestic policymaking, while security of supply has an important international and foreign policy dimension. In addition, both models neglect the role of energy companies in international energy markets and the crucial relationships between them and national governments.

The model of the partner state is better equipped than the positive state to include this external dimension, even when discussing the traditional organisation of the gas sector. However, in the oil sector, the partner state has assumed an essentially competitive position, but in the gas sector, the need to develop pipeline routes to supply Western European markets with Russian resources has paved the way for an increasingly multilateral form of energy diplomacy. The model of the *cooperative partner state* – as opposed to the *competitive partner state* – describes this situation: governments protect their national champions domestically and still support their activities abroad, but they collaborate rather than compete with other governments to develop resources and build the infrastructure necessary to physically link producers and consumers. Thus, in Europe, with regard to security of gas supply, the partner state model has assumed two different forms, with more cooperation and multilateral energy diplomacy along the East-West energy corridor (*cooperative partner state*), and a more competitive stand in energy relations between Western Europe and North Africa (*competitive partner state*).[12]

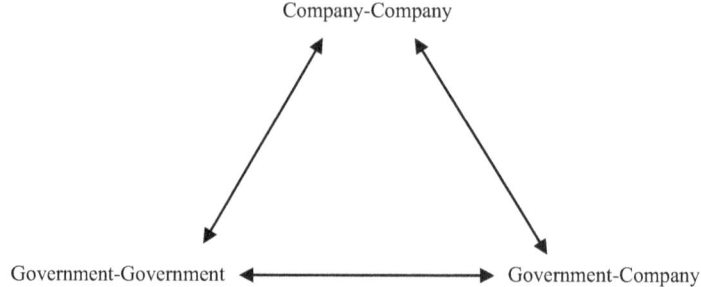

Figure 1.1 The 'triangular diplomacy' framework.
Sources: Adapted from Stopford and Strange (1991).

Despite these differences, the patterns of energy diplomacy in both competitive partner states and cooperative partner states are easily captured by the so-called 'triangular diplomacy' framework (Stopford and Strange 1991), as the most important agreements in the gas sector were the outcome of government-to-government, government-to-company and company-to-company negotiations (Figure 1.1). In particular, governments were at the centre of all the agreements for infrastructure development: they actively supported the construction of international pipelines and LNG terminals with state-backed finance and by creating gas demand at the national level to match the rigid structure of supply from abroad.

All in all, the models of the competitive and cooperative partner state, with their patterns of triangular diplomacy, are better at describing the specificity of traditional European energy security politics than the positive state model. Similarly, two alternative state-models can better illustrate the equilibrium emerging from the breakdown of the original system and the different types of political interactions embedded in the new institutional, ideational and market environment of EU energy security than the regulatory state. These models are the *provider state* and the *catalytic state*.[13] The provider state is based on the market approach to energy policy, assigns a limited role to public intervention and is characterised by multilateral patterns of energy diplomacy. On the other hand, the catalytic state underlines the combination of market-oriented instruments with more direct and *ad hoc* forms of state intervention. It also emphasises the active role of governmental agents as strategic decision makers in a liberalised market structure and their wide participation in a networked pattern of energy diplomacy.

These new models can be conceptually collocated and compared with each other and the others previously described in a two-dimensional space. The horizontal axis represents the major/minor role of the state or the market in domestic energy governance, and the vertical axis indicates the prevalence of bilateralism/multilateralism in external energy relations (Figure 1.2). In what follows, the general contours of these two new state-models are presented first, and then their possible applications to the current European context are discussed and specified.

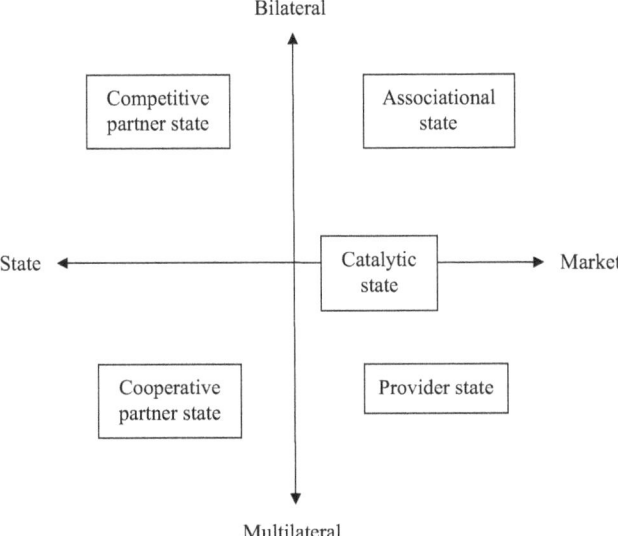

Figure 1.2 Forms of state and energy security: a conceptual model.

As anticipated, the first model – the provider state – is in line with the market-oriented approach to energy policy. According to this perspective, the state is essentially a provider of market institutions that create the context for private firms to take risks and reap rewards from investment in costly energy and infrastructural projects (Hayes and Victor 2006, 322). The guiding principles of this approach rest on the assumption that market forces can fulfil the energy needs of citizens and companies and that public authorities should concentrate their efforts on designing and enforcing the regulatory framework that allows the market to operate properly, taking particular care to avoid market failures. Market failures and an inability to produce 'public goods', such as security of supply, justify public intervention. However, this intervention is inspired by new methods of energy governance and focuses on market design, independent regulatory agencies and regulatory incentives for investments in infrastructure projects rather than planning, state-owned companies and other instruments of direct state intervention. The market approach also stresses the role of institutions at the international level, where interactions among market players should be governed by effective multilateral arrangements (e.g. Goldthau and Witte 2010; Goldthau 2012). Rather than negotiating ad hoc bilateral deals for specific projects, or supporting particular energy companies, the provider state concentrates its diplomatic efforts on setting up, ex ante, multilateral governance structures that prevent market failures, lower transaction costs and set rules and standards for market exchanges (Goldthau and Witte 2010, 7–8).

In Europe, the emergence of this model must be understood as a two-step process. The first step is strictly connected with a structural move from state to market through the intertwined processes of deregulation, liberalisation and privatisation. These processes began by the mid-1980s, first in the oil sector, and then in the gas (and electricity) sectors through the three energy legislative packages (1998, 2003 and 2009) that implemented the IEM and established national and supranational regulatory structures in line with new methods of energy governance (Boussena and Locatelli 2013; Talus 2015). In the gas sector, these transformations have challenged the traditional institutional and power structures underpinning the European politics of energy security. The opening to market dynamics means that supply and demand play a more important role than government decisions in determining gas volumes, routes and prices. And, although state-owned enterprises still operate in the markets of many member states, they no longer have a monopoly and have to compete with other private or state-owned companies for market share and government support. Finally, these transformations have strengthened the rule-making and rule-enforcing role of EU-level institutions. The European Commission in particular has acquired important regulatory powers regarding oversight of the internal energy market and the development of energy networks.

The second step towards the provider state is connected to European Commission's efforts to internationally promote a market approach to energy policy by projecting the internal market rules beyond EU borders. As we saw, this approach is widely manifested in the external governance dimension of EU energy policy. External governance is based on various policy tools, which range from multilateral legally binding treaties, such as the Energy Charter Treaty and the Energy Community Treaty, to less institutionalised international agreements – in the form of Partnership and Cooperation Agreements, which typically include chapters related to energy – or regional initiatives, such as the Inogate and Traceca programmes, which were intended to develop the Eurasian gas network and the Caspian Sea pipeline infrastructures (Goldthau and Sitter 2014, 1463–1467). With these tools, the European Commission seeks to provide stable and predictable legal frameworks and/or transnational dispute resolution mechanisms to support energy companies in upstream and midstream activities beyond EU borders, and to push producer and transit countries to align their domestic energy governance with EU principles, rules and standards.

To sum up, the transformation towards the provider state in Europe has mainly involved the EU level of government. Member state governments have implemented liberalisation and privatisation agendas and have established national regulatory agencies in the energy sector, but in contrast to the European Commission's focus on market governance and multilateral diplomacy, they have never stopped playing a more active and direct role in energy security and in supporting energy companies abroad. That is to say, the reconfiguration of the state-market nexus according to the provider state model seems to mainly describe developments at the EU-level, and it cannot be applied at the national level.[14] In order to promote security of supply, this model requires, internally, that public authorities – i.e. EU institutions directly, or by coordinating and overseeing member states' regulators – focus on making and enforcing rules, leaving the external tasks of promoting ex ante international institutional arrangements to prevent market failures and setting rules and standards for market exchanges and market governance to the European Commission. In this respect, the provider state differs from the associational state. Unlike in the US, in Europe the move towards market governance has been paralleled by a progressive multilateralisation of energy diplomacy, with a growing role for EU-level institutions. But this process has not resulted in a complete delegation of power over external energy policy to the EU. Member states have granted the European Commission the power to promote external energy governance structures and some competences over security of supply, but at the same time they have not renounced their autonomy in foreign energy matters. That is to say, the EU as a whole – as an *international state* (Caporaso 1996) – cannot be considered an associational state. This outcome is also prevented by the fact that the EU has primarily promoted a multilateral and rule-based approach to energy security. And it is additionally constrained by the lack of a coherent and common EU foreign and security policy, and by the fact that the militarisation of energy security has been largely rejected by European policymakers (Young 2009).

The move towards the provider state, with its focus on market governance and multilateral energy policy pursued at the EU level by the European Commission, has characterised the recent period of European integration in energy matters, particularly its first phase – that is, approximately from the mid-1990s to the late 2000s. But, as mentioned in the previous section, since the late 2000s, the pendulum of energy policy has swung back from market to state. In the European multilevel system of governance, however, this move back does not mean simply a return to the previous phase of triangular diplomacy and partner states, nor that the EU as a whole is becoming similar to the original European partner state. The move back towards more direct public intervention in energy affairs means a major role for the European Commission – particularly with regard to diversification of gas supply – but also a greater focus by member states on their foreign energy policies, albeit in the context of the now-liberalised European markets. The final result of these processes can be described by the concept of a *catalytic state*. Like the provider state, the catalytic state is committed to the new methods of energy governance, and it is concerned with avoiding and preventing market failures. However, in a more specific sense, its actions are oriented towards supporting market actors and facilitating their efforts to realise specific investment projects. The idea that the state acts as a facilitator to promote and support market actors in order to realise specific goals emphasises the role of governmental agents as strategic actors in a liberalised market environment (Schmidt 2009; Colli, Mariotti and Piscitello 2014). According to this perspective, liberalisation and privatisation do not necessarily imply a linear shift from direct government action (*faire*) to market action (*laissez-faire*), nor only the emergence of forms of *faire-faire*, with private actors taking on the state's former responsibility and public authorities relegated to setting guidelines and incentives for market actions. Indeed, in many cases, states have adopted a wider set of policy instruments and have begun to engage in *faire-avec* by collaborating with market actors to pursue their objectives (Colli, Mariotti and Piscitello 2014).

The notion of the catalytic state, first introduced by Lind (1992), was developed by Linda Weiss to stress the crucial role that states still have in the face of globalisation, liberalisation and the spread of regional, supranational governance structures (Weiss 1998, 2010). According to Weiss, states have lost many of their traditional instruments for controlling economic activities, but they are not merely engaged in setting the stage for markets to operate by providing rules and institutions; they have also been able to develop new strategies to more actively pursue their goals. In particular, catalytic states seek to achieve their goals less by relying on their own resources than by working with a wider range of actors; in other words, the catalytic state tries to balance the loss of some of its power by forging coalitions with other (state and non-state) actors to realise its objectives (Weiss 1998, 209–210). These strategies include new forms of government-company cooperation and the establishment of national and transnational public-private partnerships or consortia to promote policy implementation (Weiss 1998, 2010). Such institutional arrangements are becoming more and more common in the energy realm, where new modes of public *involvement* in ownership are replacing the traditional forms of public ownership (Haney and Pollitt 2013; Pollitt 2016). The latter tended to take the form of a large state-owned company or local municipally utility that were 100 percent owned by the central government or local authorities whereas the new modes of public involvement take many different forms, from partly privatised companies to hybrid types of ownership at national and local levels.

Drawing from Weiss, Hocking (1999) uses the notion of 'catalytic diplomacy' or 'network diplomacy' to reconceptualise the new practice of diplomacy in the current international economic environment, which is characterised by the growing liberalisation of commercial and trade relations and the fragmentation of the state.[15] That is, states have lost powers in favour of markets and supranational and subnational layers of governance, and governments are increasingly involved in bargaining relationships at different levels, with a greater number of both private and public actors, in order to pursue their policy goals. Accordingly, not only is the catalytic state characterised by a *faire-avec* approach, which combines market-oriented policy tools with direct forms of state intervention and new modes of public involvement in ownership, but it also embraces a specific pattern of energy diplomacy. This pattern is different from the ex ante multilateral diplomacy of the provider state, but it also cannot be encompassed by Susan Strange's triangular diplomacy framework. Triangular diplomacy rests on classical, bilateral, government-to-government and company-to-government interactions. It does not take into account the relevance of the supranational level (e.g. the EU) or the complex negotiations involving networks of actors that transcend domestic-international frontiers. These dynamics can be better taken into account by the concept of network diplomacy, which, as anticipated, is particularly suitable for the peculiar combination of international and transnational interactions taking place in the European 'multi-layered political-diplomatic environment' (Hocking 2004).

Indeed, in the emerging *régime constitutionnel* of European energy policy, member states have granted some powers to EU institutions, especially the

European Commission, in matters of external energy policy and infrastructure, while retaining the right to conduct their own bilateral (energy) relations with non-EU countries and to determine the structure of their own energy supply (Braun 2011). Consequently, in the 'politics of energy under the Lisbon Treaty' (Braun 2011), member states' governments must negotiate with EU institutions and create interstate coalitions to support or defend their preferred energy security agendas. Moreover, owing to the new political climate and the growing local opposition to infrastructure localisation, when negotiating at the EU level, governments should also take action to minimise opposition from subnational actors, which can challenge the implementation of the projects. Additionally, while negotiating with other companies, energy companies as well must obtain political support at the EU and local levels.

These new political-diplomatic layers – supra- and subnational – coexist with more traditional components of energy diplomacy, i.e. government-to-government and government-to-company negotiations. In particular, states continue to depend on energy companies for the practical realisation of their energy security agendas, and they must balance the interests of the companies with their own political interests (Aalto and Korkmaz Temel 2014). However, in the liberalised and competitive European market structure, these relationships are becoming more complex than in the partner state tradition. Governments are losing their long-term strategic connections to national champions, and they should be prepared to actively support different energy companies on an ad hoc basis if those companies' projects are consistent with their energy strategy. That is to say, in the partner state, the relationships between public authorities and energy companies were mutually supportive – the government directly protected the domestic market (for example by establishing monopolies) and supported the internationalisation of national champions with the aim of ensuring energy security, whereas in the catalytic state, governments are indirectly supportive. Energy companies are interested in backing government strategies if they can expect sufficient financial returns and political and diplomatic support. Owing to their huge financial burdens and risks, large infrastructure energy projects, such as pipelines or LNG facilities, cannot be developed without political and institutional commitments (Walker 2000). In the partner state, the contributions of public authorities to the implementation of such projects were related to their capacity to create demand at the national level, which, along with state-backed financing, constituted a sufficient guarantee for the operators. In the provider state, the capacity and credibility of public authorities as rule-makers and enforcers provide the necessary legal stability and the adequate regulatory incentives to guarantee private operators and finance projects. Rule-making and enforcing and regulatory incentives are also important in the catalytic state, but governments must play a more active and strategic role in facilitating the implementation of projects by engaging in political negotiations at the EU, international and local levels, adopting more direct forms of state intervention and/or creating partnerships with market actors. The establishment of public-private partnership is important not only for spreading risks among market and state actors – a traditional function of these policy instruments (e.g. Skelcher 2005) – but also to signal to the companies involved the political commitment of public authorities towards specific projects.[16] This is an important issue, considering the significant domestic and foreign policy implications of energy business. On the other hand, by cooperating with public authorities, companies can increase their legitimacy in the perception of local communities, speed up authorisation processes and/or reduce the political and legal risks.

Energy companies' involvement in local politics for large infrastructure energy projects is not new, but the nature of this participation is quite different in the new environment. In the past, the national champions were usually regarded as a branch of the state, committed to the country's modernisation and development, whereas current private companies lack this public perception and must devote more attention to building positive relationships with local communities.

In summary, according to the catalytic state model, a *hexagonal diplomacy* framework seems better equipped to describe the current pattern of (network) energy diplomacy in the new institutional and regulatory environment of European energy security politics (Figure 1.3).

The model of the catalytic state and its related networked-hexagonal diplomacy framework provide an alternative set of criteria to those offered by the market approach and the traditional practice of the partner state for understanding the reconfiguration of the state-market nexus in European energy security (Table 1.1). In particular, while the partner state model stresses the direct action of public authorities (*faire*) in assuring energy security, and the provider state model highlights the role of public authorities in setting the regulatory framework and overseeing market actors so they can assure energy security (*faire-faire*), the catalytic state model emphasises the role of public authorities as facilitators of market actors' activities (*faire-avec*) with the aim of promoting energy security.

Finally, whereas the model of the provider state can mainly describe transformations at the EU level of government, the catalytic state model can be applied to the national level of the member states. To be sure, on some occasions, the European

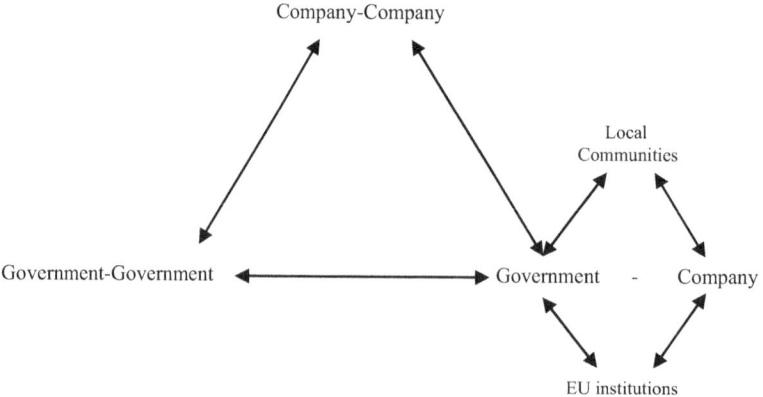

Figure 1.3 The hexagonal diplomacy in European energy security politics.

Table 1.1 Partner state, provider state, catalytic state and European energy security politics.

	Partner state	*Provider state*	*Catalytic state*
European institutional and regulatory structures in energy governance	Underdeveloped	Developed	Developed
European Commission's involvement in foreign energy relations	No	Yes	Yes
Public authorities' role in the implementation of energy investment projects	Demand creator/ state-backed financing	Rule-making and enforcing	Rule-making and enforcing/ facilitator
Guiding principles	Defending/ promoting public interest	Avoiding/preventing market failures	Supporting/ facilitating market actors
Relationships between public authorities and energy companies	Mutually supportive	Neutral	Indirectly supportive
Policy instruments (internal)	Direct forms of state intervention (e.g. planning, ownership)	Market and regulatory instruments (e.g. regulatory and financial incentives, independent regulatory agency)	Market and regulatory instruments/ direct forms of state intervention/ public-private partnership
Energy diplomacy	Triangular diplomacy	Ex ante diplomacy (to promote multilateral international agreements and institutions)	Network (hexagonal) diplomacy

Commission has tried to play a more active and direct role in promoting specific energy projects, coordinating member states and market actors and negotiating with producers. However, its approach has remained focused mainly on avoiding and preventing market failures rather than supporting energy companies or secure supplies through bilateral deals (Goldthau and Sitter 2014, 2015). Member states, instead, normally compete in the new liberalised market structure by supporting their preferred energy projects or national company in order to promote their energy security agenda or other specific goals in the area of industrial policy or foreign policy. Moreover, the European Commission lacks many important instruments that are still in the hands of national governments, notably authority on various energy-related and foreign policy issues, financial resources and ownership, or strong connections with energy companies (e.g. Andersen, Goldthau and Sitter 2016). On the other hand, it is worth noting that since the Russian annexation of the Crimea and the launch of the Energy Union in 2015, the European Commission has been trying to strengthen its presence in energy diplomacy and adopting a more proactive approach to security of supply. Therefore, although, to date, the catalytic state model seems especially appropriate for describing transformation at the national level of the member states, it remains to be seen if, in the future, the EU as a whole might move towards a similar path. A similar evolution would require more systematic action by EU-level governmental agents, i.e. the European Commission, not only in the areas of rule-making, rule-enforcing, market oversight and competition policy, but also in negotiating with producers, facilitating and supporting market actors and, overall, acting as the most important node in the emerging network model of energy diplomacy.

The stylised state-models presented here, particularly the provider state and the catalytic state, will serve as broad conceptual tools to organise the empirical analysis in this book and better explain the general contours of the emerging politics of energy security in Europe and beyond. These models also represent competing hypotheses about the outcome of the recent transformations. These hypotheses highlight different combinations of ideational factors, state-market patterns of interactions and political dynamics in the EU multi-level system. It is worth noting, however, that drawing from Caporaso, each state form illustrated should be considered less as a discrete category and more as an emphasis, i.e. 'something to be accented rather than something to sort into categories' (Caporaso 1996, 31). This perspective has traditionally characterised the adoption of the forms of state's concept. Forms of state should not be considered as settled realities, but as ideal-typical characterisation of emergent processes of transformation (Clift 2014, 172; see also Jessop 2002). Besides, the state forms approach must be deployed in a manner sensitive to particular national legacies and ideational context through historically contextualised qualitative analysis that can capture the changes in state-market relations in their complexity (Clift 2014, 197).

Current and Future Energy Security Challenges for the EU

The Contour of the EU Energy Security Question and the EU Multi-Pillar Energy Security Strategy

In 2015, the EU imported 53 percent of its energy, at a cost of around 400 billion euros, which made it the largest energy importer in the world (European Commission 2015). Compared to other world regions, the EU has few hydrocarbon resources: EU's proven oil reserves amount to only 0.4 percent of global reserves and natural gas reserves to 0.9 percent. Between the mid-1990s and the beginning of the 2010s, the EU's primary energy production decreased by almost one-fifth: natural gas production dropped by 30 percent, and production of crude oil and petroleum went down by 56 percent. On the other hand, EU energy dependency has constantly grown: in 2014, oil dependency almost reached 90 percent and gas dependency passed the 65 percent mark.[17] Supplies are also very concentrated, especially in the gas sector, where Russia, Norway and Algeria account for about the 70–80 percent of the total (although Norwegian gas does not pose political concerns for the EU). Gas dependency has grown in parallel with the steady increase of the share of natural gas in the EU's total primary energy consumption, which has risen from about 5 percent at the end of the 1960s to 25 percent in the

2000s. Moreover, although many European countries have developed LNG import capacity in the last decade, gas is supplied to EU markets mainly through pipelines, which account for about 80–85 percent of total EU gas imports.[18]

Each member state, however, has a specific situation regarding energy and natural gas dependence (Table 1.2). Each state's situation depends on the long-term

Table 1.2 Energy dependency, gas dependency and percentage of gas imported from Russia in EU countries (2006 and 2012).

Country (EU-28)	2006			2012		
	Energy dependence (all fuels) (%)	Energy dependence (natural gas) (%)	Percentage (%) of gas imports from Russia	Energy dependence (all fuels) (%)	Energy dependence (natural gas) (%)	Percentage (%) of gas imports from Russia
Austria	72,3	87,2	82 ·	63,6	86,3	62,7
Belgium	79,5	100,2	4	74	98,6	0
Bulgaria	45,6	89,9	100	36,1	83,3	100
Croatia	54	8	No data	53,6	37,1	0
Czech Republic	27,8	104,4	73,9	25,2	89	100
Cyprus	102,2	0 (*)	0	97	0 (*)	0
Denmark	− 35,5	− 103,1	0	− 3,4	− 54	0
Estonia	29,3	100	100	17,1	100	100
Finland	53,5	100	100	45,4	100	100
France	51,5	99,6	16	48,1	96,6	13,6
Germany	60,8	82	44	61,1	85,7	36,9
Greece	71,9	99,1	81	66,6	100,3	55,1
Hungary	62,7	82,2	80	52,3	72,9	90
Ireland	91	91,5	0	84,8	95,6	0
Italy	87,1	91,2	30	80,8	90,2	26,7
Latvia	66,7	108,8	100	56,4	113,8	100
Lithuania	62	101	100	80,3	100,1	100
Luxembourg	98,1	100	0	97,4	99,7	24
Malta	99,9	0 (*)	0	100,5	0 (*)	0
Netherlands	36,8	− 61,6	0	30,7	− 74,5	11,2
Poland	19,5	70,7	68	30,7	73,8	80 ([a])
Portugal	84	100,6	0	79,5	99,7	0
Romania	29,4	33,7	94	22,7	21,2	85,6
Slovakia	63,8	96,6	100	60	89,8	100
Slovenia	52,1	99,6	52	51,6	99,8	42
Spain	81,2	101,2	0	73,3	99,6	0
Sweden	36,8	95,5	0	28,7	99,1	0
UK	21,2	11,8	0	42,2	47	0

Sources: Eurostat Pocketbooks 2014, Energy, transport and environment indicators.

Note: (*) No natural gas consumption for Cyprus and Malta. Energy dependency = net imports/ (gross inland consumption + bunkers). On gas imports from Russia: European Commission (2008); European Commission (2014b).

([a]) Data from IEA (2011).

structure of its energy supply and its energy infrastructure, resource endowment and geographical location. In particular, gas dependence on Russia – which is the major EU supplier, providing about the 35–40 percent of EU imports – varies among EU regions; the Eastern European member states, the Baltic countries and Finland are highly dependent on Moscow, whereas Western member states have a more diversified gas-supply structure.[19]

Similarly, the volume of gas imported from Russia varies greatly for each member state.[20] The biggest EU markets for Russian gas are, by far, Germany and Italy (importing, respectively, about 39 bcm/y and 20–25 bcm/y), followed by France (7–8 bcm/y) in Western Europe and Poland (8–9 bcm/y) in Eastern Europe. Other important markets in terms of gas volume imported are Hungary (5–6 bcm/y), the Czech Republic (5–6 bcm/y), Slovakia (4–5 bcm/y) and Austria (4–5 bcm/y). Outside the EU, Turkey represents another crucial market for Russia, with 26 bcm/y, and Russian gas accounts for about 55 percent of Turkey's total gas imports. Turkey – a candidate country in the context of the EU enlargement policy – is also important for the diversification of EU gas supplies owing to its involvement in the development of the Southern Gas Corridor. In the Balkans, Serbia and the Former Yugoslav Republic of Macedonia (FYROM), (all EU candidate countries and members of the Energy Community) and Bosnia and Herzegovina (a potential candidate and member of the Energy Community) import minor volumes of Russian gas, respectively about 2, 0.2 and 0.1 bcm/y (Dickel et al. 2014). However, Bosnia and Herzegovina and FYROM are totally dependent on Russian pipeline gas, and Serbia is significantly dependent on Moscow as well. Bosnia and Herzegovina and Serbia suffered some of the most severe consequences of the 2009 Russo-Ukraine gas disputes, along with some EU member states such as Bulgaria, Romania, Slovakia and Hungary (Pirani, Stern and Yafimava 2009).

Confronted with this situation and as a result of internal dynamics as well as external transformations in the global and regional energy landscape, the EU energy security strategy has been focused on four main pillars in recent years: i) the completion of the internal energy market; ii) the extension of the EU 'regulatory space' beyond EU borders; iii) the diversification of supply (especially in the gas sector), including the promotion of energy infrastructures (both pipelines and LNG receiving terminals) and a more common foreign energy policy; and iv) the development of domestic energy sources (both hydrocarbons and renewables) and the promotion of energy efficiency. These pillars were first sketched in the 2000 and 2006 Green Papers on energy. They were later reaffirmed in the 2007 European Commission's Communication *An Energy Policy for Europe* and in the 2008 *EU Energy Security and Solidarity Action Plan* issued after Russia's conflict with Georgia and the gas dispute between Russia and Ukraine. In these Communications, the EU paid special attention to the new member states that are dependent on one single gas supplier (i.e. Russia) in the Baltic region and Eastern Europe (see Table 1.2) and on the diversification of gas supplies and routes through the Southern Gas Corridor and the development of LNG facilities. These proposals were embraced by the Council of the European Union held on 19 February 2009, the first since the second Russian-Ukrainian gas crisis. In the view of the Council, this crisis 'confirmed that the EU urgently needs to continue the development of the internal market, to improve energy interconnections for security of supply, to reinforce its emergency mechanisms and to strengthen its negotiating position vis-à-vis major suppliers' (European Council 2009).

In 2009, a new directive on oil stock obligations was also enacted (Directive 2009/119/EC), and in 2010, the Gas Security Directive (Directive 2004/67/EC) was reviewed with Regulation 994/2010. This new Regulation aimed at strengthening the EU's responses to short-term security of supply in case of crisis or supply disruption and at improving cross-border capacities by pursuing the development of new infrastructure with permanent bi-directional capacity (physical 'reverse flows'). It also introduced the so-called 'N-1 formula' to assess each member state's security of gas supply.[21]

In 2010, a new Communication on energy policy was released – *Energy 2020: A Strategy for Competitive, Sustainable and Secure Energy* – amid the new legal and institutional context provided by the entry of the Lisbon Treaty into force. This Communication recalled that the central goals for the EU energy policy (security of supply, competitiveness and sustainability) were now laid down in the treaties and that this new situation spelled out clearly what was expected of Europe in the energy realm. In the area of security of supply, the European Commission admitted that, although the Russo-Ukraine gas disputes acted as a wake-up call, highlighting Europe's vulnerability, there was still no common approach towards supplier or transit countries (European Commission 2010a). The Communication again called for diversification of suppliers and routes; development of energy infrastructures; and completion of the internal energy market, including better connections for the most isolated member states; as well as strengthening the external dimension of the EU energy market and establishing privileged partnerships with key partners.

Meanwhile, in 2011, the Nord Stream pipeline, directly connecting Russia and Germany, came online. With this new route, the share of Russian natural gas exported to Europe through Ukraine fell from about 80 percent to about 50 percent. In the same year, the key role that natural gas was expected to play in the following decades in the EU climate policy and in the transition towards a low-carbon economy was recalled in the *Energy Roadmap 2050* (European Commission 2011b). Although the 2008 economic crisis had already begun to show its impact on EU energy consumption, the *Energy Roadmap 2050* expected gas to replace coal and oil in the power sector and demand for gas to remain high over a longer period, requiring continuous action to better integrate the gas market and diversify supply sources.

In 2012, Decision No. 994/2012/EU established the information exchange mechanism for intergovernmental agreements between member states and third countries. And, in 2013, a new regulation for the Trans-European energy infrastructure was enacted (Regulation 347/2013) to promote diversification of external routes and supplies and improve the integration of the internal energy networks. Regulation 347/2013 reflected previous concerns about the isolation of member states in the Baltic region, Southeastern Europe and the Adriatic and Aegean Sea basins and included a new area of potential diversification of supply, such as the

Eastern Mediterranean basin, where important gas discoveries had just been realised off the coast of Israel and Cyprus.

The focus on energy infrastructure as a way to improve EU energy security was further developed in the 2013 Communication *Long-term Infrastructure Vision for Europe and Beyond*, which set out the list of energy infrastructure projects of common interest (PCIs). This Communication affirmed the importance of improving diversification of gas supplies so that no member state would be dependent on a single supply source and the need for the EU to be able to benefit from recent developments in the LNG markets (European Commission 2013). Promotion of on-shore and off-shore indigenous energy resources, diversification through the Southern Gas Corridor, and development of the new discoveries in the eastern Mediterranean were once more highlighted as priority actions for improving long-term EU security of supply. In this Communication, the European Commission estimated that about 200 billion euros should be invested by 2020 to upgrade and expand European energy networks. To this end, the Commission assigned the Connecting Europe Facility (CEF), a mechanism established by Regulation No. 1316/2013, a key role in leveraging the necessary private and public funding.

Post-2014 Developments and Future Perspectives

In 2014, the landscape of the European energy security was additionally complicated by the war in the eastern Ukraine, the Russian annexation of the Crimea and the shutting off of Russian supplies to Ukraine. In the wake of these events, on 21 March, the EU Council tasked the European Commission with conducting an indepth study of EU energy security and presenting a comprehensive plan for the reduction of EU energy dependence, to be completed by June 2014. Based on this study, a new *European Energy Security Strategy* was proposed (European Commission 2014a, 2014b). This strategy was confirmed and endorsed at the next summit of the European Council in June 2014.

The *European Energy Security Strategy* recognised that, despite the progress made in the previous years, the EU remained vulnerable to external energy shocks[22] (European Commission 2014a). The most pressing issue was still the strong dependence of six member states (Finland, Slovakia, Bulgaria, Estonia, Latvia and Lithuania) on Russia as their only external supplier and the scarce diversification in Southeastern Europe and the Balkans.[23] In the wake of the crisis in eastern Ukraine, the European Commission also worked to prevent gas supply disruptions by engaging in bilateral and trilateral negotiations with Kiev and Moscow. These negotiations resulted in the so-called winter package of 2014/2015 (and later the winter package of 2015/2016), which guaranteed supplies and transit through Ukraine.

The *European Energy Security Strategy* also reflected the effect of growing worldwide energy demand on EU energy security; worldwide demand was expected to increase by 27 percent by 2030. In the gas sector, consumption was expected to remain stable until 2020 and then increase slightly, to about 340–350 bcm/y, by 2025–2030. Against this backdrop, the European Commission prioritised supporting the development of LNGs in order to access the new supplies expected from North America, Australia, Qatar and East Africa, supporting the development and further expansion of regional gas supply infrastructures through the Southern Gas Corridor as well as the Mediterranean gas hub, completing the internal energy market, and increasing domestic energy production, both in traditional production areas (e.g. the North Sea) and in newly discovered areas (e.g. the Eastern Mediterranean). In the *Energy Security Strategy*, the European Commission also expressed its support for the calls made by some member states for an 'Energy Union'.

The idea of an Energy Union was proposed by the Polish Prime Minister Donald Tusk in April 2014, just after his appointment as President of the European Council and before the European Commission's indepth study on the EU's energy security challenges. Originally, Poland's proposal was intended mainly to address external energy security issues. However, the concept of the Energy Union was eventually embraced – at beginning of 2015 – by the Junker's Commission with a broader policy focus (European Commission 2015). In its Communication on the Energy Union Package (*A Framework Strategy for a Resilient Energy Union with a Forward-Looking Climate Change Policy*), the European Commission conceived the Energy Union strategy as a holistic approach with five principles and fundamental pillars: energy security, completion of the internal energy market, energy efficiency, climate policy and research (Umbach 2015). With regard to energy security, the Energy Union builds on the European Energy Security Strategy and its approach to security of supply by stressing traditional objectives, such as the diversification of gas supplies – focusing on the Southern Gas Corridor, the southern Caucasus, Central Asia, the Eastern Mediterranean region and LNG infrastructures – and a stronger European role in global energy markets, enhancing regional cooperation within a common EU framework, and improving the situation in the most vulnerable regions of the EU, i.e. the Baltic region and Southeastern Europe.

As a follow-up to the Communication on the Energy Union, an *EU Energy Diplomacy Action Plan* was issued to strengthen and monitor the external dimension of the Energy Union. The *EU Energy Diplomacy Action Plan* was endorsed by the Foreign Affairs Council held 20 July 2015 (Council of the European Union 2015). By endorsing this plan, the Council reaffirmed the need to improve coordination and cooperation between EU institutions and EU member states in order to allow the EU to speak with one voice and improve its diplomatic support for the energy goals set out in the Energy Union. At the same time, the Council reaffirmed the rights of the member states to decide on their own energy mix and stressed that the *Energy Diplomacy Action Plan* should be implemented by the High Representative, the European Commission and the member states in accordance with their respective roles and mandates as determined by the treaties. At the beginning of 2016, the European Commission, in line with the Energy Union agenda, also presented an energy security package which included legislative proposals (a revised Regulation on Security of Supply and a revision of the Intergovernmental Agreements decision to include a provision for ex ante compatibility assessment by the European Commission) and a Communication on *An LNG and Storage Strategy*.

To be sure, neither the actual implications of the Energy Union on the politics of EU energy security are yet entirely clear, nor is the willingness of the major member states to really move towards a more common approach. In addition, in 2016, other events have drawn attention in the EU agenda, like the refugee crisis and the 'leave' victory in the Brexit referendum. The effects of the Brexit on the EU and the EU energy policy, in particular, are not yet clear, although possible negotiations between the UK and the EU will probably occupy an important part of Brussels's agenda in the next few years.

However, the Energy Union has had an important indirect effect on the long-term perspective on European security of supply. Indeed, it confirmed the commitment to climate change policy made by member states in the European Council of October 2014, which introduced a target of a 40 percent reduction in greenhouse gas emissions by 2030 from 1990 levels. This target, coupled with the EU's Emission Trading System and efficiency measures, confirms a trend replacing high-emission fuels, such as coal, with lower emission fuels, such as natural gas (Verda 2015). As a result, natural gas is expected to be the only fossil fuel that will remain stable in the long-term European energy mix. At the same time, domestic production of natural gas is expected to continue to decline, owing to the gradual exhaustion of mature fields in the North Sea and the Netherlands, resulting in an increasing dependence on gas imports: 65 percent in 2020, 70 percent in 2025 and 73 percent in 2030 (Verda 2015). According to the projections of the International Energy Agency, the EU's gas imports are expected to increase in all possible scenarios: in the 'current policies scenario' (no changes in current policies), EU's import requirements will be 338 bcm in 2020 and 386 bcm in 2040; in the 'new policies scenario' (with greenhouse gas emission targets effectively implemented at national levels), EU's import requirements will be about 300 bcm in 2030 and 2040; and in the so-called '450 scenario' (policies consistent with the goal of limiting the global increase in temperature to two degrees Celsius), EU imports will peak at 242 bcm in 2030 and decrease over the next decade (European Commission 2014b).

All in all, the projected increase in gas dependency is consistent, and gas dependency will continue to be a structural feature of the EU energy system for the foreseeable future. However, expected import levels for 2030 are generally similar to 2010 levels, so probably only a limited expansion of import capacity will be required. With this in mind, it is worth noting that, in 2015, of the total EU pipeline import capacity (about 422 bcm), only 58 percent was actually utilised, and of the total regasification capacity (about 183 bcm), the utilisation rate was only 32 percent (Tagliapietra and Zachmann 2016). In this context, mobilising the investments required to develop new infrastructures to diversify gas suppliers and route is particularly complicated, especially due to the competition from Asian markets, where gas prices are traditionally higher than in the EU. Market actors may also be discouraged by the 2014–15 drop in energy prices, so political factors – such as the 'willingness to pay' of consumer states to achieve specific energy security objectives (Belyi 2015) – continues to be crucial and to shape European energy security politics.

Plan of the Book

In the following chapters, by applying the overarching IPE theoretical framework sketched in this introduction to specific and relevant case studies in different policy areas, this book highlights the important change that is underway in the politics of energy security in the EU and beyond. The stylised state models – i.e. partner state, provider state and catalytic state – will help in understanding the transformations that have occurred and framing the new equilibrium emerging from the reconfiguration of states, markets and institutions. However, it is necessary to keep in mind that the way in which states, markets and institutions combine is context-dependent, with regard to both specific issues and the geographical area under consideration.

The policy areas considered are: the external energy governance of the EU (i.e. the EU's strategies for promoting energy security by creating institutional arrangements that extend EU rules and principles beyond its borders); the politics of pipeline and LNG development, related to the diversification of gas suppliers and routes; and the politics and policies of offshore hydrocarbon exploration and exploitation, related to the development of indigenous energy resources. These policy areas are important both for their practical importance in the future evolution of EU energy security, since they cover three out of four of the main pillars of the EU's energy security strategy (again, those four pillars are the completion of the internal energy market, diversification of supply, promotion of the EU rules beyond EU borders and promotion of indigenous energy resources and energy efficiency), and because they directly call into question the international and foreign policy dimensions of European energy dependence. For each policy area, illustrative case studies that are substantively important to EU energy security, cover different geographical areas and represent relatively unexplored subjects will be examined.

In particular, mainly due to the role of Russian energy resources in the EU and the recent Russian-Ukrainian disputes and crisis, books on EU energy security in general tend to emphasise the northern dimension of EU external energy dependence and the politics of pipelines (e.g. Aalto 2008, 2012; Kuzemko et al. 2012; Proedrou 2012; Svyatets 2016), with less attention to the southern and Mediterranean regions and other issues. Although the relationships between the EU, the member states and Russia and many aspects of the northern dimension of EU energy security and pipeline politics will also be addressed in the empirical chapters of this book, the southern and Mediterranean dimensions and a broader set of issues will be considered. This book does not directly address the EU-Russia energy relationship (e.g. Aalto 2008; Belyi 2015), but it examines the role of Russia and Russian energy companies in different contexts, regions and issues areas relevant to EU energy security.

Chapter 2 examines the politics and institutions of EU energy security beyond its borders and assesses the potential and limitations of EU external energy governance. This aspect of the EU energy security strategy well represents the external face of the provider state, based on the European Commission's activism in promoting a multilateral and market-oriented system of governance. First, the chapter illustrates the complex mix of policy tools that the EU has built, beginning in the mid-1990s, to create a regulatory space in its wider neighbourhood and export EU principles and rules. The chapter then goes on to analyse in greater detail the institutional subsystem formed by the EU in the Caspian Sea Basin and in Central Asia, a region that is crucial for EU strategies of diversification of supply. This subsystem is composed of an intricate and overlapping set of institutions (e.g. the Baku Initiative, the Eastern Partnership, the Central Asia Strategy etc.), which have created a fragmented and complex governance architecture. This complexity is the result of the competition between different member states and the internal political dynamics of the region, and it is also shaped by important external players, such as Russia and China. The origins, rationale, goals and development of this institutional structure will be considered, underlining the roles of the aforementioned actors and their political interactions. The chapter then analyses and discusses the coherence and effectiveness of this institutional structure at the output level (i.e. procedures and organisational arrangements created to move the governance architecture from paper to practice) and at the outcome level (i.e. its practical capacity to produce changes in the behaviour of the relevant non-EU actors). Finally, the chapter discusses the limits and potential of EU external energy governance in light of domestic constraints and competition with other major powers.

Chapters 3 and 4 deal with a very important issue for EU energy security: the politics of gas infrastructures (pipelines and LNG facilities), on which diversification of gas suppliers and routes depends. Unlike oil, because of the physical characteristics of natural gas, transportation costs – whether for pipeline gas or LNG – constitute a significant fraction of the total delivered cost of gas trade and are a crucial component of the international political economy of the sector (MIT 2011). Although there are some important differences grounded in the specific international political economy of pipeline and LNG development, both chapters demonstrate the shift from the partner state model to the catalytic state model rather than the emergence of a provider state in these policy areas.

Chapter 3 analyses the important changes that have occurred in the institutional settings, market structures, power structures and policymaking processes related to the politics of gas pipelines in Europe. The chapter demonstrates how the establishment of the internal energy market and the development of the EU's external energy policy has first challenged the traditional institutional structure of the European gas market – in which the traditional partner state model was embedded – and then has supported the emergence of a new politics of pipeline in line with the catalytic state hypothesis. This gradual transformation is illustrated by analysing from a historical perspective the politics of pipelines in the various gas corridors that supply European markets. A special focus will be devoted to the case of the Southern Gas Corridor, the most important EU strategy for diversification of gas supply routes. Through this analysis, this chapter shows that, due to the resistance of the previous structure, the transformation has been incremental, partial and mediated by different national institutions, regional political dynamics and policy legacies. This chapter also shows how important external events, such as the war in the eastern Ukraine and the deterioration of EU-Russia relations, have combined with EU internal dynamics to foster this change, with important effects for the energy strategies of both the EU and its member states.

Chapter 4 illustrates the basic features of the politics of LNG, focusing on specific cases in Eastern and Western Europe. In particular, the politics of LNG development in the EU will be considered in the broader context of the evolution of the international LNG markets, but attention will also be paid to national and local politics, since gas infrastructure development is highly influenced by international market dynamics, the national energy security strategy of each member state and the environmental concerns of local communities. In Eastern Europe, the focus will be on the Baltic States (Estonia, Latvia and Lithuania), the so-called 'energy islands' where LNG development is primarily intended to reduce their strong dependence on Russian pipeline gas. In Western Europe, where the gas infrastructure is more diversified and the gas market is more mature, the focus will be on France, Italy and Spain. These three Mediterranean countries together represent the largest LNG contribution to the European continental gas market. Through these case studies, the chapter demonstrates that the politics of LNG is strongly shaped by the national institutional, political and market context. But the chapter also demonstrates the important role of governments in promoting LNG development and diversification of supply. Although government strategies have not always been effective, the empirical analysis, in particular, supports the thesis of an overall move towards the catalytic state model in this sector as well.

Chapter 5 sheds light on another important and innovative theme for European energy security with significant effects on international politics: the development of offshore hydrocarbon resources in the Mediterranean Sea. This chapter first illustrates some basic features of offshore petroleum policies and politics in the EU and also describes some specific characteristics of this energy business regarding the delimitation of international sea borders and protection of the marine environment. The dynamic processes of offshore petroleum politics and policies are then explored with regard to two specific sub-regions of the Mediterranean Sea which involve both EU and non-EU countries and have recently seen a relaunch of those activities: the Central and Eastern Mediterranean. Indeed, due to the hydrocarbon resources located in the Adriatic, Ionian and Levantine Seas, these two areas are the most promising in terms of offshore hydrocarbon development. Particularly, the gas resources recently discovered off the coasts of Cyprus, Israel and Egypt can contribute to the diversification of European gas supply. However, these two areas are also associated with the highest number of – and the most severe – unresolved maritime disputes between EU member states (e.g. Slovenia-Croatia) and between member states and non-member states (e.g. Croatia-Montenegro, Greece-Turkey, Cyprus-Turkey etc.). Furthermore, offshore hydrocarbon development is also affected by the international regimes and governance structures for the protection of the ecosystem of the Mediterranean Sea. Although the peculiarities of the offshore sector complicate the application of the state models presented in this introduction to this policy area – a problem that will be further discussed in

Chapter 5 – this chapter demonstrates that, like the situations described in the previous chapters, the emerging politics of offshore development mirror a combination of 'old' and 'new' dynamics, a fragmentation of national sovereignty and a reconfiguration of states' diplomatic practices towards forms of networked diplomacy. However, this transformation has occurred mainly in the case of the Adriatic and Ionian Seas – portions of the wider Mediterranean Sea surrounded mostly by EU member states –, but in the Eastern Mediterranean region, traditional dynamics and security considerations are still prominent.

Finally, Chapter 6 returns to the questions raised in the opening pages of this introduction. In this concluding chapter, the empirical findings provided in the other chapters are coherently and briefly reorganised to discuss the three main overarching themes and theses of the book: the fundamental role that states still play in the practice of EU energy security governance and the inescapable political significance that energy resources have even in the liberalised EU market structure; the need to put the interactions among states, markets and institutions into specific, national and regional contexts for a true understanding of energy security politics; and the meshing, in the current politics of energy security in the EU and beyond, of some old and new dynamics.

In combining analytical reflections with the exploration of diverse policy areas and case studies, this book attempts to make a modest contribution toward a better appreciation of the emerging politics of energy security in Europe and beyond, in a period in which the study of these issues seems mostly driven by events rather than by coherent research programmes and broad analytical frameworks. By applying an IPE perspective to EU energy security, this book also attempts to make a modest contribution to the emerging literature on the international political economy of energy, a particularly promising field of research with important ramifications on International Relations, Public Policy, Comparative Politics and other disciplines interested in the intersection between energy research and society (e.g. Hancock and Vivoda 2014; Sovacool 2014; Van de Graaf and Colgan 2016; Van de Graaf et al. 2016).

Notes

1 See 'What is energy security?', available at: www.iea.org/topics/energysecurity/subtopics/whatisenergysecurity/ [accessed 20 February 2016].
2 Although now it is quite common to include climate change in the study of energy security, I agree with Luft et al. (2011), who argue that, owing to the trade-offs and complementarities between energy and climate security, the two issues should not be mixed, and climate change should not be factored into the energy security debate (see also Bardazzi et al. 2016).
3 The Russian decision not to ratify the ECT will be discussed further in Chapter 2.
4 After the 2006 Russo-Ukrainian gas crisis, Poland, in a letter to all EU and NATO member states, proposed the establishment of a European Energy Security Treaty based on the idea of solidarity and common responses to energy threats. Although this proposal was refused by the EU countries, the principle of solidarity was later included in the Lisbon Treaty.
5 Environmental concerns also played a role in this paradigm shift (see, e.g. Helm 2005).

6 In autumn 2010, the European Commission was involved, with the consent of Warsaw, in the negotiation of a Poland-Russia bilateral intergovernmental gas agreement.

7 See European Energy Infrastructure Package. Roadmap, CWP, DG ENER, Brussels, November 2010.

8 On the US-Saudi Arabia strategic partnership, which, however, is not limited to energy diplomacy, see, e.g. Bahgat (2003) and Bronson (2006).

9 The difference between bilateral and multilateral practices is not always so clear: often, a government's foreign policy choices – and this is also the case for US energy security – can be more easily collocated along a continuum in which the two terms are only the extremes (Nye 2003).

10 The model of a partner state is derived from Andersen (1993).

11 China's involvement in Central Asian gas markets and pipeline politics is further explored in Chapter 2.

12 These differences are further explored and discussed in Chapter 3.

13 For a preliminary discussion of these two models in the energy realm, see Prontera (2015).

14 The UK, traditionally considered the member state most committed to a market approach to energy policy, has also framed security of supply as a strategic issue for government intervention and foreign policy support (see, e.g. 'Energy security strategy', Department of Energy and Climate Change, November 2012, London).

15 On the concept of network diplomacy see also Heine (2006, 2013).

16 It is worth noting that although the concept of public-private partnership has been widely debated and discussed in the public administration and public policy literature, a clear and accepted common definition of its specific features and contents is still lacking (e.g. Skelcher 2005, 2010; Zarco-Jasso 2005). For the purpose of this book, public-private partnerships are considered those institutional arrangements in which public actors and private firms cooperate in order to realise specific projects by sharing a certain degree of ownership, funding and control (e.g. Zarco-Jasso 2005).

17 'Data from Eurostat statistics', available at: http://ec.europa.eu/eurostat/statistics-explained/index.php/Energy_production_and_imports [accessed 20 January 2016].

18 'Eurogas Statistical Report 2015', available at: www.eurogas.org/statistics [accessed 21 February 2016].

19 It is worth noting that, as with many geopolitical definitions, there is no consensus on the precise area referred to by the terms Eastern and Western Europe. In this book, Western Europe refers mainly to those 'old' EU members that were NATO members during the Cold War, and Eastern Europe refers mainly to the 'new' member states that joined the EU in the 2004 and 2007 Eastern enlargement, i.e. the Czech Republic, Estonia, Hungary, Latvia, Lithuania, Poland, Slovakia, Slovenia, Romania and Bulgaria. This group of countries (many of which were previously Warsaw Pact/COMECOM members) partially overlap with the Baltic countries, which I consider to include the former Soviet Baltic republics: Estonia, Latvia and Lithuania. However, to avoid confusion, in the following chapters I will specify the particular countries or regions considered when I depart slightly from these classifications.

20 The following data are from the BP Statistical Review of World Energy 2014 and 2015.

21 The N-1 formula describes the ability of the technical capacity of the gas infrastructure to satisfy total gas demand in the calculated area (a member state or a region) in the event of disruption of the single largest gas infrastructure during a day of exceptionally high gas demand. The EU Infrastructure Regulation of 2013, which provided a detailed process for defining and implementing infrastructure priority projects of common interest (or PCIs), later included the N-1 formula as one of the key benchmarks in the attribution of PCI status.

22 In particular, according to the country-by-country assessment by the European Commission (2014b), the supplier concentration index (SCI) in the gas sector for the Baltics and Finland was, in 2012, at or above 100, indicating that their entire consumption was covered by a single supplier, i.e. Russia (a number above 100, as in Latvia, indicates the role of storage). Austria, the Czech Republic and Slovakia had SCIs above or close to

80. Moreover, in 2013, five member states (Bulgaria, Greece, Lithuania, Estonia and Slovenia) failed to meet the N-1 standards in regard to their dependence on Russian gas (European Commission 2014b).

23   See European Commission, 'On the short-term resilience of the European Gas System: Preparedness for a possible disruption of supplies from the East during the Fall and Winter of 2014/2015', Brussels, 16 November 2014, COM (2014) 654 final. The situation in Lithuania changed soon after with the opening of the LNG terminal at Klaipeda (the recent LNG developments in the Baltics will be analysed in Chapter 4).

References

Aalto, P. (ed.) 2008. *The EU-Russian Energy Dialogue: Europe's Future Energy Security.* Farnham: Ashgate Publishing.

Aalto, P. (ed.) 2012. *Russia's Energy Policies: National, Interregional and Global Levels.* Cheltenham: Edward Elgar Publishing.

Aalto, P. 2015. States and Markets in Energy Policy, in Belyi, A. V., Talus, K. (eds.), *States and Markets in Hydrocarbon Sectors*, pp. 40–60. Basingstoke: Palgrave Macmillan.

Aalto, P., Korkmaz Temel, D. 2014. European Energy Security: Natural Gas and the Integration Process. *Journal of Common Market Studies* 52(4): 758–774.

Andersen, S. S. 1993. *The Struggle over North Sea Oil and Gas: Government Strategies in Denmark, Britain and Norway.* Oslo: Scandinavian University Press.

Andersen, S. S., Goldthau, A., Sitter, N. 2016. The EU Regulatory State, Commission Leadership and External Energy Governance, in Godzimirki, J. M. (ed.), *EU Leadership in Energy and Environmental Governance: Global and Local Challenges and Responses*, pp. 51–68. London: Palgrave Macmillan.

Bahgat, G. 2003. *American Oil Diplomacy in the Persian Gulf and the Caspian Sea.* Gainesville, FL: University Press of Florida.

Bardazzi, R., Pazienza, M. G., Tonini, A. (eds.) 2016. *European Energy and Climate Security: Public Policies, Energy Sources, and Eastern Partners.* Cham, Heidelberg, New York, Dordrecht, London: Springer.

Beblawi, H., Luciani, G. (eds.) 1987. *The Rentier State.* London: Croom Helm.

Belkin, P., Morelli, V. L. 2007. *The European Union's Energy Security Challenges.* Washington, DC: Library of Congress, Congressional Research Service.

Belyi, A. V. 2015. *Transnational Gas Markets and Euro-Russian Energy Relations.* Basingstoke: Palgrave Macmillan.

Belyi, A. V., Talus, K. (eds.) 2015. *States and Markets in Hydrocarbon Sectors.* Basingstoke: Palgrave Macmillan.

Biermann, F., Pattberg, P. H., Asselt, H. van, Zelli, F. 2009. The Fragmentation of Global Governance Architectures: A Framework for Analysis. *Global Environmental Politics* 9(4): 14–40.

Bilgin, M. 2009. Geopolitics of European Natural Gas Demand: Supplies from Russia, Caspian and the Middle East. *Energy Policy* 37(11): 4482–4492.

Boersma, T. 2015. *Energy Security and Natural Gas Markets in Europe: Lessons from the EU and the United States.* New York: Routledge.

Boussena, S., Locatelli, C. 2013. Energy Institutional and Organisational Changes in EU and Russia: Revisiting Gas Relations. *Energy Policy* 55: 180–189.

Braun, J. F. 2011. *EU Energy Policy under the Treaty of Lisbon Rules: Between a New Policy and Business as Usual.* CEPS/EPIN Working Paper 31.

Bressand, A. 2013. The Role of Markets and Investment in Global Energy, in Goldthau, A. (ed.), *The Handbook of Global Energy Policy*, pp. 15–29. West Sussex, UK: John Wiley & Sons.

Bromley, S. 1991. *American Hegemony and World Oil: The Industry, the State System and the World Economy*. University Park, PA: Pennsylvania State Press.

Bronson, R. 2006. *Thicker Than Oil: America's Uneasy Partnership with Saudi Arabia*. Oxford: Oxford University Press.

Cameron, P. D. 2007. *Competition in Energy Markets: Law and Integration in the European Union*. 2nd ed. Oxford: Oxford University Press.

Cameron, P. D. 2011. The EU and Energy Security: A Critical Review of the Legal Issues, in Antoniadis, A., Schütze, R., Spaventa, E. (eds.), *The European Union and Global Emergencies: A Law and Policy Analysis*, pp. 125–140. Oxford: Hart Publishing.

Caporaso, J. 1996. The European Union and Forms of State: Westphalian, Regulatory or Post-Modern? *Journal of Common Market Studies* 34(1): 29–52.

Cerny, P. 1997. Paradoxes of the Competition State: The Dynamics of Political Globalization. *Government and Opposition* 32(2): 251–274.

Cherp, A., Jewell, J. 2011. The Three Perspectives on Energy Security: Intellectual History, Disciplinary Roots and the Potential for Integration. *Current Opinion in Environmental Sustainability* 3(4): 202–212.

Clift, B. 2014. *Comparative Political Economy: States, Markets and Global Capitalism*. London and New York: Palgrave Macmillan.

Colli, A., Mariotti, S., Piscitello, L. 2014. Governments as Strategists in Designing Global Players: The Case of European Utilities. *Journal of European Public Policy* 21(4): 487–508.

Correljé, A. F., Linde van der, J. G. 2006. Energy Supply Security and Geopolitics: A European Perspective. *Energy Policy* 34(5): 532–543.

Council of the European Union, 2015. *Council Conclusions on Energy Diplomacy*. Foreign Affairs Council, Brussels, July 20, 2015.

Cox, R. W. 1987. *Production, Power, and World Order: Social Forces in the Making of History*. New York: Columbia University Press.

De Jong, S., Wouters, J., Sterkx, S. 2013. The EU in Multilateral Security Governance: The Case of the 2009 Russian-Ukrainian Gas Dispute, in Lucarelli, S., Van Langenhove, L., Wouters, J. (eds.), *The EU and Multilateral Security Governance*, pp. 140–165. London: Routledge.

Del Guayo, I., Pielow, J.-C. 2012. Electricity and Gas Infrastructure Planning in the EU, in Roggenkamp, M. (ed.), *Energy Networks and the Law: Innovative Solutions in Changing Markets*, pp. 353–370. Oxford: Oxford University Press.

Dickel, R., Hassanzadeh, E., Henderson, J., Honoré, A., El-Katiri, L., Pirani, S., Rogers, H., Stern, J., Yafimava, K. 2014. *Reducing European Dependence on Russian Gas: Distinguishing Natural Gas Security from Geopolitics*. Oxford Institute for Energy Studies, NG-92, October 2014.

Duffield, J. S., Birchfield, V. L. 2011. The Recent Upheaval in EU Energy Policy, in Duffield, V., Birchfield, L. (eds.), *Toward a Common European Union Energy Policy*, pp. 1–13. New York: Palgrave Macmillan.

Dyer, H., Trombetta, M. J. (eds.) 2013. *International Handbook of Energy Security*. Cheltenham: Edward-Elgar.

Eberlein, B., Grande, E. 2005. Beyond Delegation: Transnational Regulatory Regimes and the EU Regulatory State. *Journal of European Public Policy* 12(1): 89–112.

European Commission, 1988. *The Internal Energy Market*. COM(88) 238 final.

European Commission, 2000. *Towards a European Strategy for Security of Energy Supply*. COM(2000) 769 final.

European Commission, 2002. *Final Report on the Green Paper towards a European Strategy for the Security of Energy Supply*. COM(2002) 321 final.

European Commission, 2006. *A European Strategy for Sustainable, Competitive and Secure Energy.* COM(2006) 105 final.

European Commission, 2008. *Europe's Current and Future Energy Position Demand - Resources - Investments.* SEC (2008) 2871.

European Commission, 2010. *Energy 2020 a Strategy for Competitive, Sustainable and Secure Energy.* COM(2010) 639 final.

European Commission, 2011a. *On Security of Energy Supply and International Coopera-tion: The EU Energy Policy: Engaging with Partners beyond Our Borders.* COM(2011) 539 final.

European Commission, 2011b. *Energy Roadmap 2050.* COM(2011) 885 final.

European Commission, 2013. *Long Term Infrastructure Vision for Europe and beyond.* COM(2013) 711 final.

European Commission, 2014a. *European Energy Security Strategy.* COM(2014) 330 final.

European Commission, 2014b. *In-Depth Study of European Energy Security.* SWD(2014) 330.

European Commission, 2015. *Energy Union Package: A Framework Strategy for a Resil-ient Energy Union with a Forward-Looking Climate Change Policy.* COM(2015) 80 final.

European Council, 2009. *Second Strategic Energy Review: Council Conclusions.* Press Release Brussels, 19 February 2009.

European Council, 2011. *European Council Conclusions on Energy.* Brussels, 4 February 2011.

Finon, D., Locatelli, C. 2008. Russian and European Gas Interdependence: Could Contrac-tual Trade Channel Geopolitics? *Energy Policy* 36(1): 423–442.

Frank, L. P. 1985. The First Oil Regime. *World Politics* 37(4): 586–598.

Goldthau, A. 2010. Energy Diplomacy in Trade and Investment of Oil and Gas, in Gold-thau, A., Witte, J. M. (eds.), *Global Energy Governance: The New Rules of the Game,* pp. 25–47. Washington, DC: Brooking Institution Press.

Goldthau, A. 2012. From the State to the Market and Back: Policy Implications of Chang-ing Energy Paradigms. *Global Policy* 3(2): 198–210.

Goldthau, A., Sitter, N. 2014. A Liberal Actor in a Realist World? The Commission and the External Dimension of the Single Market for Energy. *Journal of European Public Policy* 21(10): 1452–1472.

Goldthau, A., Sitter, N. 2015. A Liberal Actor in a Realist World: The European Union Regulatory State and the Global Political Economy of Energy. Oxford: Oxford Univer-sity Press.

Goldthau, A., Witte, J. M. (eds.) 2010. *Global Energy Governance: The New Rules of the Game.* Washington, DC: Brooking Institution Press.

Haghighi, S. 2007. *Energy Security: The External Legal Relations of the European Union with Major Oil and Gas Supplying Countries.* Oxford: Hart.

Hancock, K. J., Vivoda, V. 2014. International Political Economy: A Field Born of the OPEC Crisis Returns to Its Energy Roots. *Energy Research & Social Science* 1: 206–216.

Haney, A. B., Pollitt, M. G. 2013. New Models of Public Ownership in Energy. *Interna-tional Review of Applied Economics* 27(2): 174–192.

Harald Claes, D. 2001. *The Politics of Oil-Producer Cooperation.* Boulder, CO: Westview Press.

Hayes, M. H., Victor, D. G. 2006. Politics, Markets, and the Shift to Gas: Insights from the Seven Historical Case Studies, in Victor, D. G., Jaffe, A. M., Hayes, M. H. (eds.), *Natural*

Gas and Geopolitics: From 1970 to 2040, pp. 319–353. Cambridge: Cambridge University Press.

Heine, J. 2006. *On the Manner of Practicing the New Diplomacy*, CIGI Working Paper, No. 11.

Heine, J. 2013. From Club to Network Diplomacy, in Cooper A. F., Heine, J., Thakur, R. (eds.), *The Oxford Handbook of Modern Diplomacy*, pp. 54–69. Oxford: Oxford University Press.

Held, D., McGrew, A. G., Goldblatt, D., Perraton, J. 1999. *Global Transformations: Politics, Economics and Culture*. Cambridge: Polity Press.

Helm, D. 2005. The Assessment: The New Energy Paradigm. *Oxford Review of Economic Policy* 21(1): 1–18.

Herranz-Surrallés, A. 2015a. European External Energy Policy: Governance, Diplomacy and Sustainability, in Aarstad, A. K., Drieskens, E., Jørgensen, K. E, Laatikainen, K., Tonra, B. (eds.), *Sage Handbook of European Foreign Policy*, pp. 911–925. London: Sage.

Herranz-Surrallés, A. 2015b. An Emerging EU Energy Diplomacy? Discursive Shifts, Enduring Practices. *Journal of European Public Policy*: 1–21, doi: 10.1080/13501763.2015.1083044. 23 Sep 2015.

Hocking, B. 1999. Catalytic Diplomacy: Beyond 'Newness' and 'Decline', in Melissen, J. (ed.), *Innovation in Diplomatic Practice*, pp. 97–116. London: Palgrave Macmillan.

Hocking, B. 2004. Diplomacy, in Carlsnaes, W., Sjursen, H., White, B. (eds.), *Contemporary European Foreign Policy*, pp. 91–110. London: Sage.

Hughes, L. 2014. *Globalizing Oil*. Cambridge: Cambridge University Press.

Hughes, L., Lipscy, P. Y. 2013. The Politics of Energy. *Annual Review of Political Science* 16: 449–469.

Hulbert, M., Goldthau, A. 2013. Natural Gas Going Global? Potentials and Pitfalls, in Goldthau, A. (ed.), *The* Handbook *of Global Energy Policy*, pp. 98–112. West Sussex, UK: Wiley-Blackwell.

IEA, 2011. Energy Policies of IEA Countries, Poland 2011 Review. Paris: International Energy Agency.

Jayasuriya, K. 2005. Breaking the 'Westphalian' Frame: Regulatory State, Fragmentation and Diplomacy, in Robertson, J., East, M. A. (eds.), *Diplomacy and Developing Nations: Post-Cold War Foreign Policy-Making Structures and Processes*, pp. 39–54. London: Routledge.

Jessop, B. 2002. *The Future of the Capitalist State*. Cambridge: Polity Press.

Keating, M. F., Kuzemko, C., Belyi, A. V., Goldthau, A. 2012. Introduction: Bringing Energy into International Political Economy, in Kuzemko, C., Belyi, A. V., Goldthau, A., Keating, M. F. (eds.), *Dynamics of Energy Governance in Europe and Russia*, pp. 1–19. Basingstoke: Palgrave Macmillan.

Keohane, R., Victor, D. G. 2011. The Regime Complex for Climate Change. *Perspectives on Politics* 9(1): 7–23.

Kirchner, E., Berk, C. 2010. European Energy Security Co-Operation: Between Amity and Enmity. *Journal of Common Market Studies* 48(4): 859–880.

Klare, M. 2009. *Rising Powers, Shrinking Planet: The New Geopolitics of Energy*. London: Palgrave Macmillan.

Kong, B. 2009. *China's International Petroleum Policy*. Santa Barbara, CA: Praeger.

Kryukov, V. A. 2016. Russia's Oil Dilemmas: Production: To Go North-East or to Go Deep? Exports: Is a Compromise Between Westward and Eastward Directions Possible?, in Bardazzi, R., Pazienza, M. G., Tonini, A. (eds.), *European Energy and Climate Security: Public Policies, Energy Sources, and Eastern Partners*, pp. 81–112. London: Springer.

Kuzemko, C., Belyi A. V., Goldthau, A., Keating, M. F., (eds). 2012. *Dynamics of energy governance in Europe and Russia*. Basingstoke: Palgrave Macmillan.

Kuzemko, C. 2014. Ideas, Power and Change: Explaining EU–Russia Energy Relations. *Journal of European Public Policy* 21(1): 58–75.

Lanzalaco, L. 1995. *Istituzioni, organizzazioni, potere. Introduzione all'analisi istituzionale della politica*. Rome: Nuova Italia Scientifica.

Lee, D., Hocking, B. 2010. Economic Diplomacy, in Denemark, R. A. (ed.), *The International Studies Encyclopedia*, vol. 2, pp. 1216–1227. West Sussex, UK: Wiley-Blackwell.

Lind, M. 1992. The Catalytic State. *The National Interest* 27 (Spring): 3–12.

Liu, X. 2006. *China's Energy Security and Its Grand Strategy*. Policy Analysis Brief, no. 3. Muscatine, USA: The Stanley Foundation, September.

Lodge, M. 2008. Regulation, the Regulatory State and European Politics. *West European Politics* 31(1–2): 280–301.

Luft, G., Korin, A., Gupta, E. 2011. Energy Security and Climate Change: A Tenuous Link, in Sovacool, B. K. (ed.), *The Routledge Handbook of Energy Security*, pp. 43–55. New York: Routledge.

McGowan, F. 1989. The Single Energy Market and Energy Policy: Conflicting Agendas? *Energy Policy* 17(6): 547–553.

McGowan, F. 2008. Can the European Union's Market Liberalism Ensure Energy Security in a Time of 'Economic Nationalism'? *Journal of Contemporary European Research* 4(2): 90–106.

Majone, G. 1996. *Regulating Europe*. London: Routledge.

Majone, G. 1997. From the Positive to the Regulatory State: Causes and Consequences of Changes in the Mode of Governance. *Journal of Public Policy* 17(2): 139–167.

Maltby, T. 2013. European Union Energy Policy Integration: A Case of European Commission Policy Entrepreneurship and Increasing Supranationalism. *Energy Policy* 55: 435–444.

Marcou, G., Wollmann, H. (eds.) 2007. *Les collectivités territoriales et l'énergie*. Paris: CNRS éditions.

Matlary, H. J. 1997. *Energy Policy in the European Union*. London: Palgrave Macmillan.

Mayntz, R., Hughes, T. P. 1988. *The Development of Large Technical Systems*. Frankfurt: Westview Press.

MIT, 2011. *The Future of Natural Gas*. Cambridge, Massachusetts: MIT Energy Initiative.

Moran, D., Russel, J. A. (eds.) 2009. *Energy Security and Global Politics: The Militarization of Resources Management*. London: Routledge.

Müller-Kraenner, S. 2008. *Energy Security: Re-Measuring the World*. London: James & James Earthscan.

Natorski, M., Herranz-Surrallés, A. 2012. The European Energy Policy towards Eastern Neighbors: Rebalancing Priorities or Changing Paradigms?, in Morata, F., Sandoval, I. S. (eds.), *European Energy Policy: An Environmental Approach*, pp. 132–155. Cheltenham: Edward Elgar.

Nye, J. S. 2003. *The Paradox of American Power: Why the World's Only Superpower Can't Go It Alone*. Oxford: Oxford University Press.

O'Sullivan, M. L. 2013. The Entanglement of Energy, Grand Strategy, and International Security, in Goldthau, A. (ed.), *The Handbook of Global Energy Policy*, pp. 30–48. West Sussex, UK: Wiley-Blackwell.

Padgett, S. 2011. Energy Co-Operation in the Wider Europe: Institutionalizing Interdependence. *Journal of Common Market Studies* 49(5): 1065–1087.

Peters, S. 2004. Coercive Western Energy Security Strategies: 'Resource Wars' as a New Threat to Global Security. *Geopolitics* 9(1): 187–212.

Pirani, S., Stern, J., Yafimava, K. 2009. *The Russo-Ukrainian Gas Dispute of January 2009: A Comprehensive Assessment*. Oxford Institute for Energy Studies, NG-27, February 2009.

Pollitt, M. G. 2016. New Models of Public Ownership in Energy, in Picot, A., Florio, M., Grove, N., Kranz, J. (eds.), *The Economics of Infrastructure Provisioning: The Changing Role of the State*, pp. 387–405. Cambridge, MA: MIT Press.

Prange-Gstöhl, H. 2009. Enlarging the EU's Internal Energy Market: Why Would Third Countries Accept EU Rule Export? *Energy Policy* 37(12): 5296–5303.

Proedrou, F. 2012. *EU Energy Security in the Gas Sector: Evolving Dynamics, Policy Dilemmas and Prospects*. Farnham: Ashgate Publishing.

Prontera, A. 2009. Energy Policy: Concepts, Actors, Instruments and Recent Developments. *World Political Science Review* 5(1): 1–30.

Prontera, A. 2015. Italian Energy Security, the Southern Gas Corridor and the New Pipeline Politics in Western Europe: From the Partner State to the Catalytic State. *Journal of International Relations and Development*, doi: 10.1057/jird.2015.31. 14 August 2015.

Randall, S. J. 2005. *United States Foreign Oil Policy since World War I: For Profits and Security*. Montreal: McGill-Queen's Press-MQUP.

Rip, A., Kemp, R. 1998. Technological Change, in Rayner, S., Malone, E. L. (eds.), *Human Choice and Climate Change*, vol. 2, pp. 327–399. Columbus: Battelle Press.

Roth, M. 2011. Poland as a Policy Entrepreneur in European External Energy Policy: Towards Greater Energy Solidarity vis-à-vis Russia? *Geopolitics* 16(3): 600–625.

Schmidt, S. K. 1998. Commission Activism: Subsuming Telecommunications and Electricity under European Competition Law. *Journal of European Public Policy* 5(1): 169–184.

Schmidt, V. A. 2009. Putting the Political Back into Political Economy by Bringing the State Back in Yet again. *World Politics* 61(3): 516–546.

Schubert, S. R., Pollak, J., Kreutler, M. 2016. *Energy Policy of the European Union*. London: Palgrave Macmillan.

Shaffer, B. 2009. *Energy Politics*. Philadelphia: University of Pennsylvania Press.

Shaffer, B. 2013. Natural Gas Supply Stability and Foreign Policy. *Energy Policy* 56: 114–125.

Skelcher, C. 2005. Public-Private Partnerships and Hybridity, in Ferlie, E., Lynn, L. E., Pollitt, C. (eds.), *The Oxford Handbook of Public Management*, pp. 347–370. New York: Oxford University Press.

Skelcher, C. 2010. Governing Partnerships, in Hodge, G., Greve, C., Boardman, A. (eds.), *International Handbook on Public-Private Partnerships*, pp. 292–304. Cheltenham: Edward Elgar.

Sovacool, B. K. (ed.) 2011a. *The Routledge Handbook of Energy Security*. New York: Routledge.

Sovacool, B. K. 2011b. Introduction: Defining, Measuring, and Exploring Energy Security, in Sovacool, B. K. (ed.), *The Routledge Handbook of Energy Security*, pp. 1–43. New York: Routledge.

Sovacool, B. K. 2014. What Are We Doing Here? Analyzing Fifteen Years of Energy Scholarship and Proposing a Social Science Research Agenda. *Energy Research and Social Science* 1: 1–29.

Sovacool, B., Sidorstov, R. 2013. Energy Governance in the United States, in Goldthau, A. (ed.), *The Handbook of Global Energy Policy*, pp. 435–456. West Sussex, UK: Wiley-Blackwell.

Steinmo, S. 2008. Historical Institutionalism, in Della Porta, D., Keating, M. (eds.), *Approaches and Methodologies in the Social Sciences: A Pluralist Perspective*, pp. 118–138. Cambridge: Cambridge University Press.

Stern, J. 2006. *The Russian–Ukrainian Gas Crisis of 2006*. Oxford Institute for Energy Studies, January 2006.

Stoddard, E. 2013. Reconsidering the Ontological Foundations of International Energy Affairs: Realist Geopolitics, Market Liberalism and a Politico-Economic Alternative. *European Security* 22(4): 437–463.

Stokes, D., Raphael, S. 2010. *Global Energy Security and American Hegemony*. Baltimore: Johns Hopkins University Press.

Stopford, J., Strange, S. 1991. *Rival States, Rival Firms: Competition for World Market Shares*. Cambridge: Cambridge University Press.

Strange, S. 1994. *States and Markets*. London: Pinter.

Streeck, W., Thelen, K. 2005. *Beyond Continuity: Institutional Change in Advanced Political Economies*. Oxford: Oxford University Press.

Svyatets, E. 2016. *Energy Security and Cooperation in Eurasia: Power, Profits and Politics*. London: Routledge.

Tagliapietra, S., Zachmann, G. 2016. *Rethinking the Security of the European Union's Gas Supply*. Bruegel Policy Contribution, Issue 2016/01, Brussels.

Talus, K. 2011. *Vertical Natural Gas Transportation Capacity, Upstream Commodity Contracts and EU Competition Law*. Alphen aan den Rijn: Wolter Kluwer.

Talus, K. 2013. *EU Energy Law and Policy: A Critical Account*. Oxford: Oxford University Press.

Talus, K. 2015. European Union Energy: New Role for States and Markets, in Belyi, A., Talus, K. (eds.), *States and Markets in Hydrocarbon Sectors*, pp. 198–213. Basingstoke: Palgrave Macmillan.

Turner, L. 1975. The European Community: Factors of Disintegration: The Politics of Energy Crisis. *International Affairs* 50(3): 404–415.

Umbach, F. 2010. Global Energy Security and the Implication for the EU. *Energy Policy* 38(3): 1229–1240.

Umbach, F. 2015. Strategic Perspectives of the EU's Energy Union and the Southern Gas Corridor. *Caspian Report* Spring 2015(9): 11–25.

Van de Graaf, T., Colgan, J. 2016. Global Energy Governance: A Review and Research Agenda. *Palgrave Communications* 2, doi: 10.1057/palcomms.2015.47. 26 January 2016.

Van de Graaf, T., Sovacool, B. K. 2014. Thinking Big: Politics, Progress, and Security in the Management of Asian and European Energy Megaprojects. *Energy Policy* 74: 16–27.

Van de Graaf, T., Sovacool, B. K., Ghosh, A., Kern, F., Klare, M. T. (eds.) 2016. *The Palgrave Handbook of the International Political Economy of Energy*. London: Palgrave.

Verda, M. 2015. The EU Energy Union and the Role of the Southern Gas Corridor. *Caspian Report* Spring 2015(9): 27–34, Caspian Strategy Institute, Istanbul.

Victor, N. M., Victor, D. G. 2006. Bypassing Ukraine: Exporting Russian Gas to Poland and Germany, in Victor, D. G., Jaffe, A. M., Hayes, M. H. (eds.), *Natural Gas and Geopolitics: From 1970 to 2040*, pp. 319–353. Cambridge: Cambridge University Press.

Wälde, T. W. 2008. US Foreign Oil Policy since World War I: For Profits and Security. *The Journal of World Energy Law & Business* 1(1): 113–117.

Walker, W. 2000. Entrapment in Large Technology Systems: Institutional Commitment and Power Relations. *Research Policy* 29(7–8): 833–846.

Weiss, L. 1998. *The Myth of the Powerless State*. Ithaca: Cornell University Press.

Weiss, L. 2010. Globalization and the Myth of the Powerless State, in Ritzer, G., Ataly, Z. (eds.), *Readings in Globalization: Key Concepts and Major Debates*, pp. 166–175. West Sussex, UK: Wiley-Blackwell.

Westphal, K. 2006. Energy Policy between Multilateral Governance and Geopolitics: Whither Europe? *Internationale Politik und Gesellschaft* 2006(4): 44–62.

Yergin, D. 2006. Ensuring Energy Security. *Foreign Affairs* 85(2): 69–82.

Yetiv, S., Lu, C. 2007. China, Global Energy, and the Middle East. *The Middle East Journal* 61(2): 199–218.

Youngs, R. 2009. *Energy Security: Europe's New Foreign Policy Challenge*. London: Routledge.

Youngs, R. 2011. Foreign Policy and Energy Security: Markets, Pipelines and Politics, in Duffield, J. S., Birchfield, V. L. (eds.), *Toward a Common European Union Energy Policy*, pp. 41–60. New York: Palgrave Macmillan.

Zarco-Jasso, H. 2005. Public–Private Partnerships: A Multidimensional Model for Contracting. *International Journal of Public Policy* 1(1–2): 22–40.

2 The Politics of EU External Energy Governance

The Caspian Sea Basin and Central Asia

As we saw in Chapter 1, the external governance dimension is an important pillar of the wider EU energy security strategy aimed at exporting the principles and rules of the internal energy market beyond the borders of the EU. This dimension represents the external face of the provider state model, which is based on a market approach to energy policy and security of supply and (mainly) multilateral frameworks promoted by the European Commission. Scholars have also referred to this aspect of EU energy policy as the external dimension of the EU regulatory state (see, e.g. Goldthau and Sitter 2014, 2015). This idea has some points in common with the concept of the provider state and its external face. However, I prefer to use the latter term for two main reasons. First, one of the main powers of the EU as a regulatory state in energy matters is related to market oversight and competition policy, but both these aspects do not apply outside the EU borders, where the European Commission cannot force actors' compliance (although its internal regulatory powers can greatly affect the strategies of external players). Second, by using the concept of the provider state – and thus by focusing on the provision of institutional structures beyond EU borders – I can easier connect my analysis with the existing literature on EU external governance (from EU studies) and regime complexes and governance architectures (from IR theories). That is to say, by integrating those different strands of literature and paying attention to the international political economy of energy, it is possible to offer a more accurate account of the politics of EU external energy governance. This politics includes: developments within the EU, where member states and EU institutions seek to promote their energy agendas; developments outside the EU, where the institutional structures promoted by the EU interact with external players which, in turn, affect their forms and effectiveness; and developments within the institutional system created by the EU itself, where different institutional arrangements and transnational networks interact and overlap.

In order to offer this type of analysis, this chapter focuses on the complex institutional subsystem created by the EU in the Caspian Sea Basin and Central Asia. As explained in Chapter 1, this region has always been very important for the EU's energy security strategy, especially with regard to diversification of supply and the development of the Southern Gas Corridor. In particular, the chapter focuses on the five Central Asian states (Tajikistan, Uzbekistan, Kyrgyzstan Turkmenistan and

Kazakhstan) and the three Caucasian states (Azerbaijan, Armenia and Georgia) that have been included in different European energy initiatives since the end of the 1990s. Although the chapter focuses mainly on the hydrocarbon sector, the electricity sector will be considered too, as electricity and gas have been both targeted by EU efforts to promote the rules of the internal energy market in this region and because of the practical relations between these two sectors in the wider process of national energy governance reform in third countries.

The chapter is organised as follows. In the first section, the analytical framework for the study of EU external governance is presented and discussed. The framework of the EU's external governance recognises the EU's peculiarity as an international actor, and it is useful to understand and assess the institutional dimension of the EU energy security strategy beyond EU borders (i.e. the external face of the provider state), its mechanisms and its impact in third countries. The second section briefly presents the overall mix of external policy instruments and regional initiatives that the EU has progressively established and describes the way these instruments have resulted in a complex and fragmented institutional system, which the EU is now adopting to extend its sphere of influence in regions that are crucial for European energy supply. The third section describes the specific political and energy context of the Caspian Sea Basin and Central Asia and then analyses the institutional subsystem of this region in detail. The main focus of the analysis is not the single institutions established by the EU, nor the bilateral relationships between the EU and the third countries of the region, but the EU institutional subsystem as a whole. The origins of this subsystem and its main features will be addressed first. Then its internal dynamics, coherence and effectiveness will also be taken into account. To continue this analysis, the framework of external governance, which is mainly based on EU studies, will be integrated by using the approach to governance architectures and regime complexes derived from IR scholarship and regime theory (Biermann et al. 2009; Keohane and Victor 2011).

In particular, in the third section of the chapter, the approach of governance architectures is used to analyse and assess the internal dynamics of the complex institutional subsystem created by the EU in the Caspian Sea basin and Central Asia and its coherence and effectiveness at the *output level*. Meanwhile, the external governance framework is applied to assess the effectiveness of this institutional subsystem at the *outcome level*. Effectiveness at the output level refers to the regulatory and organisational infrastructures created to move an international institution from paper to practice; on the other side, effectiveness at the outcome level refers to the changes in the behaviour of actors relevant to the problem at hand (Underdal 2004). In the case of EU external energy governance, outcome level effectiveness refers to the way in which third states share, adopt and apply EU principles and rules. Although these dimensions of effectiveness cannot completely assess every aspect of the institutional subsystem established by the EU, they provide a first set of useful information on the potential and limitations of EU external energy security governance.[1] Through this analysis, the chapter illustrates how, on one hand, the EU has been able to develop a complex governance architecture which extends well beyond its traditional sphere of influence but, on the other hand, EU institutional arrangements are poorly equipped to promote important changes in the political and administrative structures of the countries of the region.

Finally, some factors explaining the poor performance of EU external energy security governance will be discussed in the fourth section of the chapter. Two main categories of factors will be considered: domestic energy politics, especially in the main producer states where revenues from hydrocarbon resources are a crucial component of the post-Soviet regime stability and survival; and the influence of major international players, such as Russia and China, which can offer alternative institutional settings, sources of legitimacy and revenues. In other words, to present a complete study of the politics of EU external energy governance, the chapter analyses both the internal dynamics and effectiveness of the EU system of governance and the political- and energy-related domestic and international contexts in which it operates.

EU External Action and Energy Security

The external governance approach aims to analyse the complex and variegated set of institutional processes that allow the diffusion of principles, norms and rules from the EU towards non-EU countries or other international organisations (Lavenex 2004, 2008; Lavenex and Schimmelfening 2009; Lavenex, Lehmkuhl and Wichmann 2009). By adopting a similar perspective and by focusing on those macro frameworks or institutional architectures which structure the interactions between EU actors and external actors and which allow the EU to broaden its organisational and regulatory space beyond its borders, this approach has contributed to a better understanding of the EU's external actions, including many specific features such as the fragmentation and differentiation among various policy sectors, issue areas and regions (Lavenex 2011). Three main aspects are particularly important in the study of external governance: i) how EU external institutional architectures emerge and the roles of EU institutions, member states and external actors in this process; ii) the specific forms assumed by these institutional architectures, i.e. the different ways in which the EU structures its interdependence with third countries and by which it tries to extend its regulatory space in neighbouring regions; iii) the effectiveness of EU external governance, or, more broadly, how to evaluate and measure the effects of the processes triggered by EU external governance and the way in which they are able to produce the desired changes or not.

With regard to the first point, i.e. how the institutional architectures of external governance are created, important factors are policy developments within the EU – as they are promoted by EU institutions in response to new challenges – and the roles played out by member states. Indeed, in many cases, European integration and EU external action develop in parallel: the EU's internal innovations in a policy area precede the efforts to externalise and diffuse abroad the agreements and equilibrium reached within the EU. Member states seek to direct EU external governance according to their preferences and interests, juxtaposing the more functionalist perspective supported by EU institutions with a perspective that is more sensitive to the political significance that external governance can assume in different regional contexts. Internal EU policy development and the dynamics of cooperation and competition among member states help explain – along with the interdependence between the EU and third countries – the way in which external governance architectures emerge and some of their main features.

The different forms of external governance can be framed starting from three ideal types: *hierarchical governance, network governance* and *market governance* (Lavenex and Schimmelfennig 2009). Hierarchical governance is characterised by asymmetric and hierarchic relationships between the EU and third countries and by a high level of institutionalisation, i.e. formalisation and precision of the rules (which are tailored to EU preferences and are non-negotiable and legally binding) and centralised organisational settings which ensure the monitoring and implementation of these rules. In hierarchical governance, the presence of clear rules and formal procedures to monitor and, if necessary, sanction actors' behaviour implies that the main mechanisms for the spread of the EU principles and rules are based on a progressive harmonisation in third countries, led by a logic of conditionality. Conditionality enables top-down transfer of EU standards beyond EU borders according to a scheme of external incentives (Schimmelfennig and Sedelmeier 2004). In network governance, the relationships between actors are not asymmetrical and hierarchical but formally equal and horizontal. Although power asymmetries among actors exist, they are not formalised into binding agreements. While hierarchical governance is highly institutionalised, with formal and legally binding rules controlled by centralised organisational structures, network governance is based on less institutionalised organisational structures, non-binding provisions, mutual agreement and common procedures for monitoring. Network governance can be promoted by transnational networks of experts and civil servants with less scope for the participation of political actors. Owing to the non-binding features of these forms of external governance, the main mechanisms for rule transfer involve coordination, learning and socialisation. In market governance, interactions among actors are basically horizontal, as in network governance, but the degree of institutionalisation is lower. Rules are not formal or codified, and there are no organisational structures to monitor and manage institutional activities. In market governance, mechanisms for the expansion of norms are mainly based on competitive dynamics, which can push third countries to deliberately adopt EU rules. Market governance describes the EU's indirect impact, which results mainly from its presence and the interdependent relationships that the EU develops in specific sectors with third countries, rather than from explicit coordination or rule promotion. That is to say, in market governance, third countries are encouraged to align with EU rules because ignoring them would incur an important cost (for example increasing the difficulty of attracting investments and funds from abroad), or because third countries choose to emulate the EU's example in domestic reforms.

To sum up, external governance varies from more asymmetric and institutionalised forms, in which third countries have less scope to negotiate or avoid EU rules and prescriptions (hierarchical modes of external governance), to forms in

Table 2.1 Modes of EU external governance.

Modes of EU external governance	Actors' constellation and pattern of interactions	Degree of institutionalisation	Mechanisms of rule expansion
Hierarchical governance	Vertical constellations, pattern of domination/ subordination	High institutionalisation, formal rules, legally binding, and centralised organisational structures	Harmonisation
Network governance	Horizontal constellation, formal equality among actors	Medium institutionalisation, formal and informal rules, less centralised organisational structures	Coordination
Market governance	Horizontal constellation, formal equality among actors	Low institutionalisation, informal rules, loose organisational structures	Competition

Source: Adapted from Lavenex and Schimmelfennig (2009, 800).

which relations among actors are more equal and horizontal, with less binding rules and tight organisational structures (network modes of external governance), and, finally, towards barely institutionalised and binding forms, in which interactions among actors are even more decentralised and symmetric (market modes of external governance) (Table 2.1).

Finally, the effectiveness of EU external governance can be assessed at three different levels: *rule selection*, related to the selection of rules in international negotiations and agreements; *rule adoption*, related to the adoption of rules in third countries and *rule application*, related to the concrete implementation of the rules into the political and administrative systems of third countries. The first level – rule selection – is important in the context of negotiations and agreements at the international level. In this case, to assess the effectiveness of external governance, it is necessary to analyse if and to what degree EU principles and rules are the focal point for the relationships between the EU and third states. Rule selection is only the starting point for assessing the effectiveness of external governance, but this level is important. When EU influence is not supported by the 'golden carrot' of membership, there is no guarantee that EU rules lead the process of negotiation or that they are able to work as focal points in agreements between the EU and third states. To assess the adoption of EU rules, it is necessary to look at third countries and analyse whether the rules have been transposed into domestic legislation. Non-EU countries can accept EU principles and rules as focal points in international agreements without transposing those principles and rules into domestic legislation. The second level of impact of external governance refers to the actual incorporation of the rules at the domestic level. This impact can be traced empirically by looking at the ratification of the agreements reached with the EU or at the adoption of laws or other legislative instruments that transpose EU rules, or the rules negotiated with the EU, into domestic legal systems. Rules adoption, however, does not necessarily imply their actual application, the level that corresponds to a deeper impact of EU external governance. Rules application is not the simple incorporation of EU rules into the domestic legal system; it implies the actual implementation of those rules.

The three levels of the effectiveness of external governance – *rules selection, rules application* and *rules adoption* – are strictly interconnected, but the sequence of effectiveness can be interrupted at any level, so it is useful to assess each of them separately. Moreover, it is also useful to take into account possible alternative outcomes, which can undermine the effectiveness of the institutional structures promoted by the EU. The behaviour of third countries can ignore or violate EU or the joint rules, preferring domestic rules or principles, norms and rules supported by other international organisations or states. Thus, any analysis of the politics of EU external energy governance should also focus on the possible interactions and/ or competition between EU initiatives and the ones carried out by other international actors or domestically originated preferences in third countries.

EU Energy Security beyond EU Borders

Until the beginning of the 2000s, EU measures in the area of energy security were mainly focused on creating an internal energy market. The expectation was that a more competitive and efficient internal market for energy would result in a more effective framework for security of supply as well. Externally, the most important EU initiative was the establishment of the Energy Charter Treaty (ECT), which was directed mainly at the former Soviet Union. Another initiative launched towards the former Soviet Union at the end of the 1990s was the Inogate programme (Interstate Oil and Gas Transport to Europe), which aimed to provide technical and financial assistance in the area of network infrastructures. Unlike the ECT, however, Inogate was not intended to develop a comprehensive set of rules for all energy infrastructure projects but advocated a project-by-project approach (Yafimava 2011). Moreover, this programme, which did not involve Russia, came to be perceived as potentially harmful to Moscow ratification of the ECT and was put aside in the early 2000s (Yafimava 2011).

The main idea of the ECT was to create a common European-Asian energy market and encourage European companies to develop untapped hydrocarbon resources in the post-Soviet space (Wälde 1996). Many former Soviet Union countries were particularly rich in energy resources but lacked the necessary economic capabilities to bring those resources to the markets. Furthermore, those countries were outside the system of international rules provided by the Gatt/WTO. The ECT appealed to those countries because they were searching for a new position in the post-Cold War order and wanted to increase their legitimacy and credibility in the eyes of Western energy companies (Andrews-Speed 1999; Wälde and Konoplyanik 2006). For the countries of Eastern Europe, in particular, the ECT was seen as a first step towards EU membership. In a relatively short time, this EU project, initially limited to the space around the EU, spread towards the Caspian region and Central Asia, and more than fifty countries joined the ECT. Unfortunately, things went differently with Russia, which was one of the main targets of the initiative. Russia signed the ECT, but after having provisionally applied it, the Russian government decided not to ratify the treaty in August 2009. So the EU was not able to promote its regulatory framework in Russia, despite Russia's heavy dependence on energy exports to European markets. In particular, although there were already some problems surrounding the ECT – especially with regard to different views on transit governance between the EU and Russia – its inability to play a role in the 2009 Russian-Ukrainian gas disputes (although Ukraine had signed and ratified the treaty) contributed to increasing disaffection with this initiative in Moscow[2] (Yafimava 2011).

At the end of the 1990s, the EU included energy issues in two regional initiatives: the Euro-Mediterranean Energy Forum, which was established in 1997 and was attached to the Barcelona process, and the Baltic Sea-Region Energy Cooperation, established in 1998. These initiatives can be considered the first efforts to specifically promote EU external energy governance, although they had important limitations, due in part to the poor development of the EU's internal energy policy.

At the beginning of the new millennium, the need to increase common efforts to improve EU energy security was clearly articulated in the 2000 Green Paper *Towards a European Strategy for the Security of Energy Supply*. Now the European Commission recognised that the measures already in place were not sufficient and started to explore other strategies to increase its external influence. The first steps were taken in 2002 with the Athens Memorandum of Understanding, which paved the way for the process of negotiation that concluded in 2006 with the entry of the treaty establishing the Energy Community into force. This treaty was signed by the EU, Serbia, Albania, Bosnia-Herzegovina, Bulgaria, Croatia, Romania, Kosovo, Montenegro and the Former Yugoslavian Republic of Macedonia (FYROM). The Energy Community Treaty (EnC) is a legally binding instrument that promotes the adoption of the *acquis communautaire* in third countries and widens and extends the sphere of the internal energy market at the EU's periphery. Originally, its targets were the candidate and potential candidate countries in Southeastern Europe and the Balkans. But, in 2010, Ukraine and Moldova joined the club and, in 2014, negotiations were launched with Georgia.

In the meantime the European Commission was promoting the process of building the Energy Community, with the 2006 Second Green Paper on energy, *A European Strategy for Sustainable, Competitive and Secure Energy*, the EU began to lay the foundations of an approach that would go beyond the simple expansion of its internal energy market to potential EU candidates. In the following years, hand in hand with the progressive strengthening of EU competences in the area of external energy relations – a process that culminated with the entry of the Lisbon Treaty into force – different political and diplomatic instruments were deployed to enhance the EU's relationships with important energy producer and transit countries.

First and foremost, the EU initiated bilateral dialogues through initiatives such as the Energy Dialogues or the Memorandum of Understanding (MoU). The first of this type of initiative was launched in 2000 to institutionalise the relationship between the EU and Russia. It was followed by the EC-Norway Energy Dialogue in 2002. Later, the EU continued to develop these forms of bilateral energy relationships, addressing other countries that are important for the diversification of EU energy supplies and routes (such as Turkey, Ukraine, Azerbaijan, Kazakhstan and Turkmenistan) or for their role in global energy markets, such as India, China and Brazil. In a decade (from 2002 to 2013), the number of countries involved in this type of bilateral energy relationship grew from two to 18.[3]

The EU also further developed its wider institutional architectures. In 2004, with the launch of the European Neighbourhood Policy (ENP), aimed at the countries in the southern Mediterranean and Eastern Europe, energy issues began to be included in such general policy frameworks. At first glance, the ENP seemed to apply the logic of conditionality adopted for the enlargement countries. But although it was based on the establishment of institutional structures and formal bilateral commitments to improve and monitor cooperation between the EU and third countries (in the form of Action Plans, Association Agendas and Association Agreements), the ENP lacked the promise of EU membership. It was based on more horizontal (rather than vertical) relations and incorporated only a soft version of conditionality aimed at a progressive 'approximation' of the third countries' rules and structures towards EU guidelines rather than full harmonisation (Lavenex 2008). Other regional initiatives – with an even lower degree of institutionalisation and less binding commitments – were then launched to improve the EU's cooperation and dialogue with the countries not included in the ENP, especially in the Caspian Sea Basin and Central Asia. In 2004, the Baku Initiative (BI) was established as an evolution and upgrade of the Inogate programme with Ukraine, Moldova, Turkey, Azerbaijan, Armenia, Georgia, Belarus, Kazakhstan, Tajikistan, Turkmenistan, Kyrgyzstan and Uzbekistan. In 2007, in the wake of the first Russian-Ukrainian gas dispute, two additional initiatives, in which energy security played an important role, were launched: the Black Sea Synergy (BSS, with Ukraine, Moldova, Turkey, Azerbaijan, Armenia, Georgia and Russia) and the Central Asia Strategy (CAS, with Kazakhstan, Tajikistan, Turkmenistan, Kyrgyzstan and Uzbekistan). Then, in 2009, the EU's interest in energy security in Eastern Europe and Caucasus was reaffirmed with the establishment of the Eastern Partnership (EaP, with Ukraine, Moldova, Azerbaijan, Armenia, Georgia and Belarus), which included a multilateral Platform on Energy Security. Regional energy cooperation was also enhanced in the Mediterranean through the Mediterranean Solar Plan and other initiatives formulated in the context of the Union for the Mediterranean (e.g. the Union for the Mediterranean Energy Platform).[4]

After the war in eastern Ukraine and the deterioration of the EU-Russia relations, energy security issues were more firmly anchored in the European Neighbourhood Policy (European Commission 2015). Similarly, strengthening energy security and competitiveness in the energy markets and enhancing the diversification of supply (including support for the EU Southern Gas Corridor) were reaffirmed as important objectives during the Eastern Partnership summits, held in

Vilnius and Riga in November 2013 and May 2015, respectively (Council of the European Union 2013, 2015).

To sum up, in order to extend its sphere of influence beyond its borders, the EU has supported the establishment of multilateral treaties, bilateral relations and regional governance structures, all of which aim to promote EU energy principles and rules in third countries. With this strategy, the EU seeks to not only design the 'rules of the game' according to its internal standards and preferences, but also to create institutional structures that allow the monitoring and enforcement of these rules. However, the final outcome of this strategy is far from a comprehensive and unitary system of governance. The EU strategy has emerged from an incremental process shaped by external events and the different interests of member states and third countries, and it has resulted in a complex and fragmented layer of initiatives, bilateral and multilateral, with political and/or legal elements, which combine and overlap in different ways for different groups of countries, many of which are involved in more than one institutional setting and participate in different forms of cooperation with the EU (Table 2.2).

Table 2.2 EU energy cooperation with neighbourhood countries and the countries of Caspian Basin and Central Asia.

Countries	Energy Charter Treaty	Energy Community	Bilateral energy dialogues	Regional initiatives
Enlargement countries				
Albania	X	X		
Bosnia-Herzegovina	X	X		
Macedonia (FRYOM)	X	X		
Iceland	X			
Montenegro	X	X		
Serbia				
Turkey	X	O	X	X
Kosovo		X		
ENP (Eastern Europe)				
Armenia	X	O		X
Azerbaijan	X		X	X
Georgia	X	C		X
Moldova	X	X	X	X
Ukraine	X	X	X	X
ENP (Mediterranean)				
Algeria			X	X
Egypt			X	X
Israel				X
Jordan				X
Lebanon				X
Morocco				X
Palestine				X
Tunisia				X

Countries	Energy Charter Treaty	Energy Community	Bilateral energy dialogues	Regional initiatives
Producer/transit countries in Central Asia				
Iraq			X	
Kazakhstan	X		X	X
Russia	(*)		X	X
Turkmenistan	X		X	X
Uzbekistan	X		X	X
Kyrgyzstan	X			X
Tajikistan	X			X

Note: X = Member; O = Observer; C = Candidate. (*) = Provisional application of the ECT until 18 October 2009; on August 2009 Russia has officially informed that it did not intend to become a Contracting Party to the Energy Charter Treaty. Among the 16 countries included in the ENP, the table considers only the 13 countries (12 plus Algeria that is negotiating an Action Plan with the EU) that by mid-2016 have formalised their cooperation with the EU through Action Plans (or Association Agendas for Eastern European countries). Some countries, such as Belarus, Iran, Libya and Syria, initiated a dialogue on energy issues with the EU, but the process has been halted by sanctions or internal turmoil. Belarus, Libya and Syria remain outside most of the structures of the ENP.

EU Energy Security Governance in the Caspian Sea Basin and Central Asia

Political and Energy Context of the Region

As anticipated, a true understanding of the politics of EU external energy governance requires that the domestic political- and energy-related situations of the countries targeted by EU initiatives and the international political and economic context in which they are embedded be included in the analysis. Although the countries of the Caspian Basin and Central Asia have different political systems, many of them are characterised by strict authoritarian regimes. Only Georgia, Armenia and Kyrgyzstan have the status of 'partly-free' countries according to the Freedom House ranking (Georgia has the highest score of the three in the areas of civil liberties and political rights), while Kazakhstan, Tajikistan, Azerbaijan, Uzbekistan and Turkmenistan are considered 'not free', with very poor performances in these areas (Freedom House 2015).

The countries in this region with major oil and gas resources are Azerbaijan, Kazakhstan, Turkmenistan and Uzbekistan, and the region as a whole is especially important for gas reserves, which account for about 12 percent of the worldwide total (Table 2.3). Azerbaijan and Kazakhstan both have significant oil and gas reserves and production. Uzbekistan has mainly gas reserves and is an important gas producer, and Turkmenistan has the highest gas reserves and production in the region. The other countries, Georgia and Armenia to the west and Tajikistan and Kyrgyzstan to the east, do not have relevant hydrocarbon resources, but they could play a role as transit countries for exporting the region's energy resources to Europe, bypassing the Russian territory and East and South Asia.

Table 2.3 Caspian and Central Asia proved oil and gas reserves, share of world total, and production.

	Oil			Natural gas		
	Reserves (Tmb)	% of world total	Production (Tbd)	Reserves (Tfc)	% of world total	Production (Bcm)
Azerbaijan	7	0,4	848	41,2	0,6	16,9
Kazakhstan	30	1,8	1701	53,2	0,8	19,3
Uzbekistan	0,6	–	67	38,3	1,1	57,3
Turkmenistan	0,6	–	239	617,3	9,3	69,3
Total	38,2	2,2	2855	750	11,8	162,8

Sources: BP Statistical review of World energy 2015.

Note: Tmb = thousand million barrels; Tfc = trillion cubic feet; Tbd = thousand barrels daily; Bcm = Billion cubic metres.

The Caspian Sea basin and Central Asia have emerged as an important area for energy security since the collapse of Soviet Union and the formation of independent states that struggled to affirm their political and economic autonomy after the Soviet era. Hydrocarbons helped the post-Soviet elite gain economic rent and reposition themselves into the post-Cold War international system. For the consumer countries in the West, the Caspian and Central Asian resources represented important potential additional sources for diversifying their supplies, while Western companies saw the opportunity to access relatively new and unexplored hydrocarbon provinces. For European countries and the US, helping these states exploit their energy potential also served the wider geopolitical goal of reducing Russian influence in the region. At the end of the 1990s, China became involved in this new game of energy and politics as well. Beijing wanted to secure new oil and gas for its growing energy demand and to expand its influence on a region that, after the collapse of the Soviet Union, was suddenly contestable. However, to develop the resources of these countries, the external players – governments and market actors – had to create new export routes. The main resource holders of the region are landlocked countries and, as a result of the Soviet era, the main export oil and gas pipelines channelled their energy to the Russian infrastructure system, granting Russian state-owned companies, such as Gazprom, a privileged monopsony position.

The efforts to bring Caspian and Central Asian hydrocarbons into international markets were strengthened at the very beginning of the 2000s, when energy markets were tightening and oil prices rising. Mainly as a combination of US diplomatic support, interregional cooperation and the involvement of major Western energy companies, two important new pipeline routes were opened. The first route – the Baku-Tbilisi-Ceyhan (BTC) oil pipeline – was built by a consortium led by British Petroleum (BP) and the Azerbaijani state-owned company, Socar, and was opened in 2006. This pipeline was designed to carry about 1 million barrels per day from the Azerbaijani and Kazakhstani oil fields to the international market, passing through Georgia and Turkey. The BTC was the first energy infrastructure of the region that bypassed Russia and allowed Azerbaijan and Kazakhstan to pursue their energy strategy of opening the national hydrocarbon sector to foreign companies and investors. On the other hand, Uzbekistan and Turkmenistan essentially retained the ownership structure inherited from the Soviet Union, with strong state control and discouragement of foreign involvement.

The second route – a gas pipeline parallel to the BTC, the Baku-Tbilisi-Erzurum pipeline (BTE) or South Caucasus Pipeline (SCP) – was built in 2007 by a consortium made up of BP, Socar and other energy companies to export the Azerbaijani gas westwards. This route, with an initial capacity of 7 bcm/y, was significant because it represented the first move to open up the Southern Gas Corridor, later strongly supported by the EU.[5] In theory, Turkmenistan could also have been involved in this route, but building a pipeline across the Caspian Sea has always represented a very difficult challenge. The legal status of the Caspian area is complicated due to a lack of agreement among its coastal states, and Russia and Iran have traditionally opposed similar energy projects (Russia also opposed a project to build a pipeline between Kazakhstan and Azerbaijan).

During this period, Central Asian resources also became the target of China's energy security strategy. Chinese energy companies and financial institutions became involved, especially in the Kazakhstani and Turkmenistani energy sectors. At the end of the 1990s, the China National Petroleum Corporation (CNPC) and the Kazakh oil company (KazMunayGas) began construction of an oil pipeline from Kazakhstan to China – the Kazakhstan-China Pipeline, with a capacity of 240,000 barrels of oil per day – which was completed in 2006. In 2009, a gas pipeline from Turkmenistan to China – the Turkmenistan-China Pipeline (also known as the Central Asia-China Gas Pipeline) – was built. It passed through Uzbekistan and Kazakhstan and later reached its capacity of 55 bcm/y. These new energy infrastructures, along with routes like the CAC pipeline system and the Caspian pipeline consortium, which channel the region's resources to their traditional destinations in Russian territory, completed the map of the export routes leading out of the Caspian region and Central Asia (Figure 2.1). (Another important new route is currently under consideration, the Turkmenistan – Afghanistan – Pakistan – India Pipeline, TAPI, intended to export Turkmenistani gas into South Asian markets.)

The new infrastructures and the opening to foreign investment favoured the growth of exports and a reorganisation of previous patterns of energy trade. Azerbaijan now exports the majority of its oil and gas to the European and Turkish markets, and Kazakhstan also exports the majority of its oil towards Europe. Turkmenistan's biggest gas market is China, followed by Russia, while Uzbekistan's gas exports are equally distributed between Russia and China. Turkmenistan also exports gas to Iran, which is its third export market after China and Russia. Exports to Iran started in 1997 with the construction of the Korpdezhe-Kurt-Kui pipeline which marked the first success of Turkmenistan's policy of diversifying exports away from Moscow (Pirani 2012). In 2010, another pipeline was built, the

Figure 2.1 Major Caspian and Central Asian oil and natural gas exports routes.

Note: Author's elaboration for illustration. Grey lines = oil pipeline; black lines = gas pipeline; dotted line = proposed gas pipelines.

so-called Dauletabad-Salyp Yar pipeline, to serve the northern region of Iran. However, Turkmenistan-Iran gas relations have been complicated by disputes over gas prices. Besides, the prospects of the development of the Iranians' own gas production reduce the expectations of increasing or maintaining this export route in the near future.

This geographical, infrastructural and market context forms the backdrop for the main EU external energy governance initiatives developed by the mid-2000s in the Caspian Basin and Central Asia. In particular, it is important to bear this situation in mind in order to understand the limits on the exportation of EU rules to the region, an issue that will be addressed further in the last section of this chapter.

Origins and Development of the EU Institutional Architecture in the Region

The combination of initiatives promoted by the EU and the different interests of non-EU countries has resulted in different models of institutional cooperation (Padgett 2011). The first model is similar to the ideal type of hierarchical governance and was initially adopted for the enlargement countries in southeastern Europe and the Balkans and was then extended to Ukraine and Moldova. These countries – mainly consumer or transit countries – are part of a legally binding and centralised institutional framework centred on the Energy Community. For countries outside the scope of the Energy Community, the EU has built a more flexible mix of instruments and regional political dialogues – similar to the ideal types of network governance or market governance – to promote transparency, legal standards and energy governance principles and practices in line with EU rules. This broad and heterogeneous group of countries includes some important producer countries, especially in the southern Mediterranean (such as Algeria) or Central Asia (such as Kazakhstan and Turkmenistan), that are unwilling to take part in binding forms of cooperation that could limit their energy sovereignty. Without the perspective of the membership and without conditionality, the EU has less room to influence domestic policy choices in these countries. However, many of them have agreed to participate in less institutionalised forms of cooperation. In the Caspian Sea Basin and Central Asia in particular, interactions among EU initiatives and third countries' interests and strategies have resulted in a fragmented institutional architecture that combines elements of network governance and market governance. This architecture is characterised by fairly stable and structured forms of cooperation, such as those based on the ENP and the Eastern Partnership (which also includes Ukraine and Moldova, which are also members of the Energy Community).[6] However, these forms of cooperation coexist and overlap with ad hoc and less institutionalised regional initiatives created for specific groups of countries or to address specific issues (such as the Baku Initiative, the Black Sea Synergy and the Central Asia Strategy) and with forms of bilateral diplomatic engagement formalised by instruments such the Energy Dialogue or the Memorandum of Understanding (Figure 2.2).

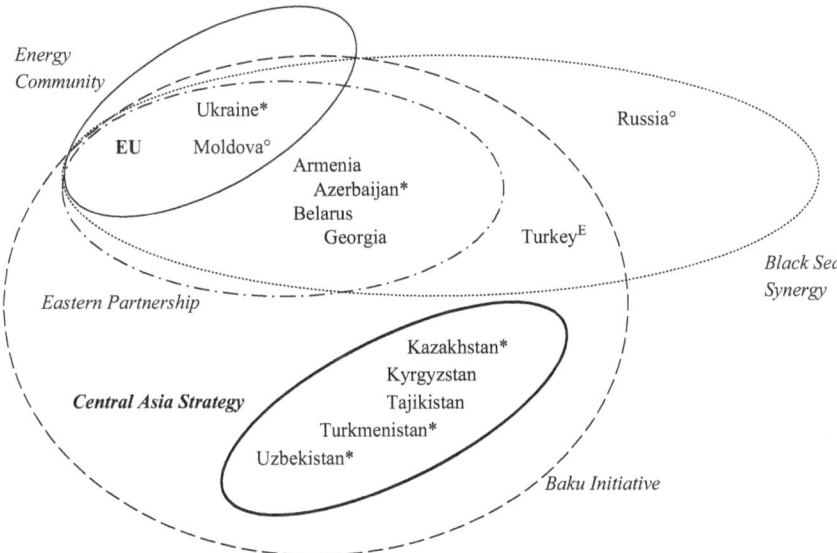

Figure 2.2 The EU institutional architecture for energy security in the Caspian Basin and Central Asia.

Note: (*) = Memorandum of Understanding; (°) = Energy Dialogue; (E) = Enlargement country.

The origins of a similar fragmented and complex governance architecture can be traced from 2004, when the Inogate programme was relaunched and transformed into a more ambitious regional framework with the establishment of the Baku Initiative. The Baku Initiative was announced during an intergovernmental conference that gathered the European Commission, the countries bordering the Caspian Sea (Azerbaijan, Iran, Kazakhstan and Russia), and their neighbourhoods in Eastern Europe and Central Asia (Armenia, Georgia, Kyrgyzstan, Moldova, Turkey, Ukraine and Uzbekistan). The conference aimed at creating an institutional framework to enhance cooperation on different aspects of energy governance: the harmonisation of legal and technical standards, the integration of energy markets, the modernisation of the existing energy infrastructures and the development of new infrastructures through new financial mechanisms. This initiative demonstrated the EU's capacity to promote new institutional structures far beyond its traditional sphere of influence and delinked from the perspective of future EU membership.

However, the first results were quite disappointing. The issue of security of supply, the EU's main concern, was framed essentially from a technical perspective – the issue was defined in terms of development, modernisation and monitoring of energy infrastructures and interconnections (Baku Initiative 2004), but divergences among the countries of the region, such as between Azerbaijan and Armenia, and the Russian position against a too-close cooperation with the EU, did not allow the definition of common objectives and strategies (Herranz-Surrallés and Natorski 2012). Notwithstanding these divergences, four Working Groups were established to institutionalise cooperation on: harmonising legal, regulatory and institutional frameworks for market liberalisation; enhancing the safety and security of the energy transportation network; developing sustainable energy; and attracting investments and facilitating projects.

The second intergovernmental conference of the Baku Initiative was held in Astana at the end of 2006. In the wake of the first Russian-Ukrainian gas crisis, the context was different from that of the 2004 conference. The number of participant countries shrank: Iran did not take part in the conference; Russia participated only as an observer; and Turkey, which joined the EU Enlargement policy in 2005, formally took part in the conference but limited its involvement in the initiative. With Moscow's withdrawal from the initiative, the entire process increased in political importance and shifted towards EU priorities. A specific Road Map was elaborated. The Road Map was based on the Working Groups established in 2004, but it indicated more precise objectives and provided for a monitoring process (Baku Initiative 2006). First of all, it was determined that market convergence in the region would be pursued on the basis of the principles and rules of the EU's internal energy market. Second, the Road Map explicitly stressed the importance of energy security, including not only the more technical aspects related to infrastructure modernisation, but also embracing 'the issues of energy exports/imports, supply diversification, energy transit and demand' (Baku Initiative 2006).

Although the Baku Initiative did not create a stable political structure – the last multilateral conference was the one held in Astana in 2006 – since then, the Baku

Initiative has been able to rely on the organisational and financial resources of the Inogate programme, funded by the EU (mainly through the European Neighbourhood and Partnership Instrument) and managed by the European Commission and the EU External Action Service (prior to 2007, Inogate was funded by the EU through the Technical Assistance to the Commonwealth of Independent States, or TACIS, programme). After the Astana conference, Inogate progressively shifted its focus towards the energy security objectives of the EU (Herranz-Surrallés and Natorski 2012).

The years 2005–07 were important because of the strengthening of the Baku Initiative, but also because of the launch of the Central Asia Strategy and the Black Sea Synergy. Those two initiatives grew out of a combination of two major dynamics. On one hand, after the Eastern Enlargement, the new member states and Germany were trying to orient the EU's geopolitical centre of gravity towards the East. On the other hand, these regional initiatives responded to the growing awareness of the need for better EU energy security that emerged in the European capitals in the wake of the Russian-Ukrainian gas crisis. The Central Asia Strategy should have supported the efforts of the European Commission in promoting the Nabucco pipeline project and accessing Turkmenistan's gas. However, the launch of the Central Asia Strategy also reflected the increased willingness of European countries to continue their military involvement in the International Security Assistance Force mission in Afghanistan. As a result, the Central Asia Strategy mainly emerged as a framework for enhancing bilateral relationships on traditional security issues (Boonstra 2011). This strategy was not accompanied by the establishment of a stable organisational, political or administrative structure (Table 2.4). Along with energy security, it also addressed other issues already comprised in other EU programmes. No new policy instruments were provided by this initiative. In the field of energy security, the strategy explicitly recalled other instruments, such as the Baku Initiative – the objectives of the Baku Initiative were also embraced by the Central Asia Strategy – and the Memorandum of Understanding signed by the EU and the countries of the region (CAS 2009).

The Black Sea Synergy was also launched in 2007, although, in practice, the process behind this regional initiative began some years before when, after the enlargement and the launch of the European Neighbourhood Policy, a possible convergence between the spheres of action of the EU and the Organisation of the Black Sea Economic Cooperation (Bsec) emerged (Japaridze et al. 2011). Bsec was created in 1992 to promote cooperation among the countries of the Black Sea region, and it includes twelve states: Russia, Greece, Romania, Albania, Armenia, Azerbaijan, Bulgaria, Georgia, Moldova, Serbia, Turkey and Ukraine. In the wake of the Eastern Enlargement, some EU members and some candidate countries involved in the Bsec – in particular Greece, Bulgaria and Romania – promoted the creation of an EU initiative focused on the Black Sea Basin. This project was presented during the German presidency of the EU, when the European Commission issued the Communication on the Black Sea Synergy (European Commission 2007). The initiative was then officially launched in 2008 during a meeting in Kiev. Energy issues were included in the Black Sea Synergy only in a very general way – some

Table 2.4 EU regional initiatives in the Caspian Basin and Central Asia: objectives, structures and policy instruments.

Initiative	Baku Initiative	Black Sea Synergy	Eastern Partnership	Central Asia Strategy
Energy objectives	Energy import/export, energy transit, diversification of supply, demand management, promotion of energy infrastructures, convergence towards EU energy markets	Consumer/ producer/ transit countries dialogue, transparent access to energy sources and markets, energy security and environmental sustainability	Energy infrastructures and interconnections development, diversification of supply, energy efficiency and renewables, convergence towards EU energy policy and markets	References to the energy objectives included in the Baku Initiative
Organisational structure (political level)	Meeting among heads of state or governments/ ministries (no clear stipulations regarding the frequency of meetings)	Meeting among heads of state or governments/ ministries (no clear stipulations regarding the frequency of meetings)	Biannual meeting among heads of state or governments. Annual meetings among foreign affairs ministries	Meeting among heads of state or governments/ ministries (no clear stipulations regarding the frequency of meetings)
Organisational structure (administrative level)	Inogate Secretariat Thematic Working Groups	No organisational structure provided	Four thematic platforms (Platform on Energy Security): meeting of civil servants twice a year. Panels and working group to support the thematic platform	No organisational structure provided
Policy instruments	Inogate programme (*)	No specific policy instruments provided	Inogate Programme, MoU Association Agreements	No specific policy instruments provided (references to Inogate Programme and MoU)

Note: (*) In April 2016, the Inogate Programme was replaced by the EU4Energy instrument.

references were made to dialogues between consumer/producer/transit countries, transparent access to energy sources and markets, energy security and environmental sustainability – and no new policy instruments were provided (Table 2.4). However, problems arose regarding the role and position of Russia, which decided not to sign the final Black Sea Synergy declaration. Furthermore, a few months after the launch of this initiative, the 2008 war in Georgia and the second Russian-Ukrainian gas crisis of 2009 dramatically changed the context. The Black Sea Synergy was partially overturned, and a new and more focused initiative was created: the Eastern Partnership (EaP). On one hand, the war in Georgia and the second gas crisis testified to the need for the EU to extend its external energy actions towards its new peripheries in the Caucasus and the Caspian Basin, but, on the other hand, it pointed out the difficulties of including Russia and the other countries of the region in the same process of cooperation.

The EaP, initially supported by Sweden and Poland in particular, was established in 2009 to strengthen EU external action towards Eastern Europe and beyond in the context of the European Neighbourhood Policy. It was also a reaction of the Eastern EU members to the project of the Union for the Mediterranean, which was supported by France. The EaP is based on bilateral and multilateral mechanisms. The multilateral dimension is the main difference between the EaP and the European Neighbourhood Policy (Delcour 2011). Since the first EaP summit held in Prague, in 2009, energy issues were included both in the bilateral and multilateral dimensions. In the first case, energy was one of the five key areas for cooperation identified by the European Commission, with the aims of strengthening energy security and promoting approximation and convergence towards EU principles and norms (Council of the European Union 2009). On the multilateral level, the EaP established biannual summits among the heads of state or government, annual summits among the ministries of foreign affairs, and biannual summits for the so-called thematic platforms. Thematic platforms also provided various meetings and working groups among experts and civil servants. The multilateral dimension of the EaP additionally included some flagship initiatives to raise the visibility of EU cooperation and actions and increase their effectiveness. One of the four thematic platforms was devoted to energy security – the Platform on Energy Security – and energy issues (diversification of energy supply and the Southern Gas Corridor, and regional energy markets and energy efficiency) represented two of the six flagship initiatives (Table 2.4). Energy security issues and market reforms in line with the EU principles and rules were recalled in all the subsequent Eastern Partnership summits, held in Warsaw (2011), Vilnius (2013) and Riga (2015). Hand in hand with development of the EU energy security strategy, attention has been also focused on energy infrastructures, with the aim to promote a 'conductive, transparent, regulatory and financial environment' for the implementation of the major energy projects (Council of the European Union 2013, 5). The same concerns have also been progressively institutionalised in the works of the Platform on Energy Security, including the issue of energy infrastructures.[7]

In the context of the ENP, EaP's objectives were supported by EU financial assistance under the 2007–13 European Neighbourhood and Partner Instruments,

ENPI (and later for the 2014–20 by its successor European Neighbourhood Instrument, ENI). However, no new specific policy instruments were provided for energy sector, although reference was made to the Inogate programme and the Memorandum of Understating already in place with some countries of the EaP (Table 2.4). In particular, under the Platform on Energy Security, cooperation with the Inogate programme has been established. This pattern of cooperation has been improved until April 2016, when Inogate has been replaced by another EU policy instrument, the 'EU4Energy' programme, which is a continuation of the previous regional energy initiative (see next section). Energy issues were also included in more general bilateral instruments, such as the Association Agreements (AAs), although as of 2016, only Georgia, Moldova and Ukraine had signed deals with the EU[8] (Table 2.4). Finally, an important objective of the bilateral and multilateral cooperation since the launch of the EaP has been the accession of the EaP partners in the Energy Community. Ukraine and Moldova joined the Energy Community in 2010, Georgia has been a candidate country since 2007 and began the negotiation process to access the Energy Community in 2014, and Armenia became an observer in 2011.

Output Level Effectiveness, Coherence and Clustering in the EU Governance Architecture

The divisions among member states and the ambiguous, or overtly adverse, position of Russia towards some EU initiatives have resulted in a complex and fragmented governance architecture for energy security, with partially overlapping membership, objectives and policy instruments. However, over time, this complex institutional system has been able to adapt and evolve to allow the countries interested in enhancing their cooperation with the EU to better pursue this goal. Robustness – the capacity to adapt to and resist external challenges – is a dynamic measure of an international institution. Robustness is a very important element, since it is closely related to effectiveness, which is a static measure of an institution's significance (Underdal 2004). Effectiveness requires a certain degree of robustness, especially if time is needed to resolve a specific set of problems. That is to say, effectiveness can be improved by the capacity of an international institution to rapidly adapt to new challenges and a changing environment. From this perspective, as illustrated by the institutional system promoted by the EU in the Caspian Sea Basin and Central Asia, complex governance architectures have some advantages over more comprehensive and integrated structures (Keohane and Victor 2011). In the former case, since principles and rules are not attached to a single institution, it is possible to adapt them to specific situations, different issues or coalitions of actors. In other words, complex governance architectures allow policy coordination to occur at different speeds and allow selective engagement by those actors interested in addressing only specific problems and issues.

Institutional fragmentation and complexity, however, might also have dysfunctional effects if there is poor coherence and poor coordination, or even conflict, among the different parts that constitute the wider governance architecture. This is not the case in the institutional system promoted by the EU in the Caspian Sea Basin and Central Asia. This system is a good example of a *cooperative governance architecture* (Biermann et al. 2009). Cooperative governance architectures are defined by two main elements. First, in cooperative architectures, the core principles of the different institutions that compose the wider complex system are compatible and not in conflict, i.e. they have a high degree of coherence. Second, although the system is fragmented, the coordination among the different institutions is improved by the establishment of various inter-institutional linkages (Oberthür and Gehring 2006). Inter-institutional linkages can be traced empirically at different levels and intensities: starting from an institution simply taking the work of the others into account, to more explicit linkages and references between the normative bases of different institutions or the elaboration and implementation of common projects.

In particular, if some actors recognise the legitimacy of a set of norms and principles in a specific institution, they can try to expand these principles and norms to other institutions with which they are involved. The expansion of the normative bases in complex governance architectures is important because similar norms at work in different institutions can help orient their development and functioning towards common goals (Rosendal 2001). This process can in turn enhance the legitimacy of those norms and principles that now are accepted by a larger number of actors. Overlapping membership can also facilitate the design and implementation of common projects, which enable the diffusion of information, know-how and best practices among different institutions. An important role in these processes can be played out by non-state actors, such as the experts and civil servants attached to the secretariats of international institutions (Oberthür and Gehring 2006). All these mechanisms of inter-institutional interplay management can improve the effectiveness of governance architectures by enhancing the compatibility of various elements of the system. This process of interconnection – or *clustering* (Oberthür 2002; Von Moltke 2005) – allows a complex governance architecture to benefit from its inherent functional specialisation and adaptability without sacrificing coherence or compatibility among individual pieces of the larger system. Thanks to clustering, some core structures that catalyse cooperation and provide the system's main functions can emerge.

From an institutional perspective, the main functions of an international regime for energy security are related to its capacity to provide a stable framework for negotiations, its oversight of compliance and, where appropriate, its sanction of behaviours that contradict established agreements (Sander 2013). The institutional system promoted by the EU in the Caspian Sea Basin and Central Asia is not based on legally binding agreements and centralised organisational structures – no country in the region is a member of the Energy Community – and it is far from the ideal type of the hierarchical mode of external governance. This system lacks well-defined and structured negotiating venues, defined decision-making procedures and specific provisions for oversight and control of compliance. Moreover, no specific sanctions are provided for cases of poor compliance or unwillingness of the third states to conform with the objectives agreed in the international negotiations with the EU. However, in these cases – closer to the ideal types of network or market governance – control of the fulfilment of the agreed objectives can be assigned to soft mechanisms, like the activities of monitoring and reporting. Venues for negotiations can be offered by less institutionalised structures, like intergovernmental summits, fora or meetings. Both these functions are important and constitute the first dimension for assessing the effectiveness of the institutional system, in particular its effectiveness at the output level (Underdal 2004). At this level, the institutional system is effective if it is able to create stable platforms for dialogue and negotiations among actors and if, through monitoring, reporting and similar activities, it is able to provide information on the achievement of the agreed objectives and targets.

Regarding the compatibility and coherence of the different elements of this governance architecture, it is worth noting that the EU pursues different specific objectives through its various initiatives, but these objectives are all informed by five key principles: transparency and competition in energy markets, protection of investments, convergence towards the EU regulatory standards and multilateralism (Stoddard 2012). These key principles reflect the broader EU goal to expand the same guiding principles and preferences behind European energy integration beyond its borders (Padgett 2011; Goldthau and Sitter 2014). These elements can be traced in almost all of the EU-sponsored initiatives in the Caspian Sea Basin and Central Asia and also in the Energy Community. Although no country of the region is yet a member of the Energy Community, this initiative is an important reference for the work of the Eastern Partnership and must be included in an analysis of the regional governance architecture. Moreover, many of these principles are also attached to the ECT, which already covered the countries of the region.[9] The only exception to the inclusion of these EU principles is the Black Sea Synergy. The Black Sea Synergy lacks explicit references to the approximation with the EU policy and regulatory standards, and it neglects important EU principles such as competition in energy markets and investment protection. Russia's involvement in this initiative prevented the inclusion of these goals among its guiding principles.

Over the years, some specific structures of the EU complex governance system have also emerged as more appropriate for pursuing EU objectives. Moreover, the linkages and inter-institutional interactions among the various elements composing the system have grown as a result of the diffusion of the normative bases from the core institutions towards more peripheral ones and the implementation of common projects. These processes have, in turn, increased the coherence of the overall system of governance, and some institutions have emerged to play more important roles and to carry political and administrative functions, while others have been gradually overshadowed.

Since its establishment, the Central Asia Strategy has not represented a real platform for multilateral energy cooperation. In the main documents it issued in the first years, specific references were made to the normative bases already adopted by the Central Asian countries in the context of the Baku Initiative. However, these themes later disappeared from the agenda of the Central Asia Strategy, which became mainly a platform for bilateral discussions of traditional security issues. In addition, no specific energy objectives were established, and, in the absence of appropriate organisational structures and mandates, monitoring activities were lacking.

Especially after the 2008 Russian military intervention in Georgia, the Black Sea Synergy was no longer an appropriate framework for addressing issues of high political content, such as those attached to energy security. No additional summits of the Black Sea Synergy were realised after the inaugural meeting in February 2008. The first document formulated to assess, in very general terms, the activities and results of the Black Sea Synergy was issued by the European Commission in 2008 (European Commission 2008). And a second document, again formulated in very general terms, was not issued until 2015. This last document merely describes the various energy initiatives already planned by the EU in the region (such as the Energy Community, Inogate etc.) and concludes by admitting that: 'in view of the above existing regional frameworks and initiatives on energy cooperation, the energy cooperation under the Black Sea Synergy has taken up a lesser priority in recent years' (European Commission 2015, 3).

The Eastern Partnership has proven to be more flexible than the Black Sea Synergy, because it includes a more homogenous set of non-EU countries, that is to say, countries that can be easily managed as a group. It is significant that neither Turkey nor Russia is in the Eastern Partnership. Each of these two countries holds a unique status with and posture towards the EU, and they differ significantly from the other countries of the region in their roles, capacities, resources and ambitions. Without their influence, the Eastern Partnership has developed towards a more structured and stable framework for cooperation and negotiation, thanks to summits involving high-level politicians, the meeting for the Ministries of Foreign Affairs and the work of the thematic platforms (Delcour 2011). As a result, the Eastern Partnership has promoted closer channels of communications at both the political and administrative levels and triggered a socialisation process among the actors involved (Korosteleva 2012). Moreover, since the Eastern Partnership is managed by the European Commission and the European External Action Service, it has been possible to more precisely define the objectives of energy cooperation and promote the monitoring of the results achieved.[10] Finally, since some countries included in the Eastern Partnership were already in the process of entering the Energy Community, EU institutions have tried to extend the normative base of the Energy Community to this regional initiative. The fact that the Eastern Partnership was managed by the European Commission has also favoured the practical implementation of common projects by these two institutions.[11]

A similar dynamic also characterised the relationships between these institutions and the Baku Initiative, which has progressively embraced the themes and normative elements of the Energy Community. The Energy Community, the most advanced and institutionalised form of EU external energy governance, has become the focal point around which orientate the development of energy cooperation between the EU and many other countries of the region. Also, in the case of the Baku Initiative, the existence of adequate administrative structures – the

Secretariat of the Inogate program – has facilitated the formulation and implementation of joint projects for monitoring the progress of cooperation and exchanging best practices among the Baku Initiative, the Energy Community and the Eastern Partnership.[12] On the other hand, inter-institutional relationships are much weaker in the Black Sea Synergy and the Central Asia Strategy. Some limited references to the activities of the other EU initiatives, and in particular to the Energy Community and the Baku Initiative, can be found in the documents on the implementation of the Black Sea Synergy issued, in 2008 and 2015, by the European Commission. However, this initiative is not included in the works carried out by the other institutions and, as mentioned above, in 2015, the European Commission recognised that energy issues were poorly addressed by this framework.

Some references to the Baku Initiative and the Eastern Partnership can also be found in the main documents of the Central Asia Strategy, in which the key energy objectives of the Baku Initiative, as determined by the Astana summit, are included. But the Central Asia Strategy is not provided with an organisational structure, and the implementation of its objectives has been delegated to the policy instruments already in place for the Baku Initiative, which cover all the countries of Central Asia. Table 2.5 illustrates the various inter-institutional linkages that have developed among the EU initiatives in the Caspian Basin and Central Asia (Table 2.5).

The main functions of the EU's governance architecture have progressively 'clustered' around those core institutions – the Eastern Partnership and the Baku Initiative – which have proved to be the most effective in providing frameworks for political cooperation among actors and which also have the most consistent administrative and organisational resources for monitoring actors' activities (Figure 2.3). These institutions – which are based on a coherent ensemble of guiding principles – have focused their work towards an increasingly more specific set of objectives, thanks to convergence on their normative bases. Sharing a common normative basis has additionally facilitated the implementation of joint projects, which in turn have strengthened the inter-institutional linkages and the possibilities for actors' socialisation and exchange of best practices.

Table 2.5 Inter-institutional linkages among the EU initiatives in the Caspian Basin and Central Asia.

	EnC	EaP	BI	BSS	CAS
EnC		JP	JP		
EaP	JP, NB, r		JP, NB, r	r	
BI	JP, NB, r	JP, NB			
BSS	r		r		
CAS		r	NB, r		

Note: JP = implementation of joint projects; NB = explicit references to the normative bases of the other institutions; r = generic references to the work of the other institutions.

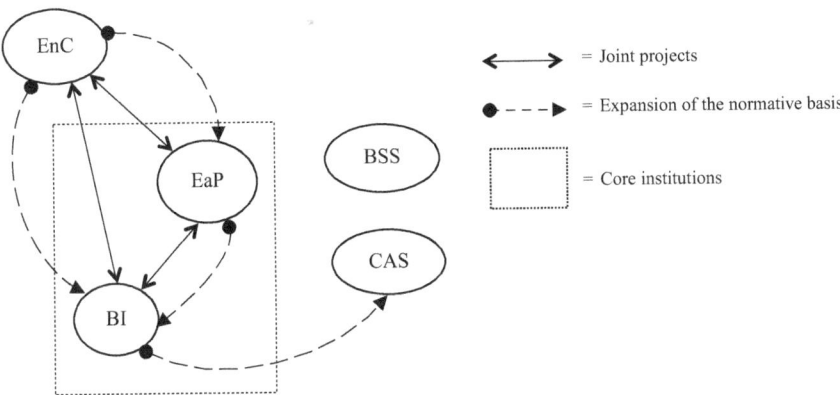

Figure 2.3 Clustering processes in the EU energy security governance architecture of the Caspian Basin and Central Asia.

Recent developments have confirmed the significance of the Eastern Partnership and its cooperation with the Energy Community and the inter-institutional linkages in the region, although with some important innovations. As anticipated, the Inogate programme was replaced by another EU instrument in April 2016: the so-called EU4Energy. The European Commission has asked the Energy Community to provide technical assistance to the EaP countries in the framework of this new initiative, which will last four years and focus on improving energy legislative and regulatory frameworks, implementing policy recommendations, and promoting investment in key, strategic energy infrastructure projects.[13] On the other hand, for the other countries previously included in the Inogate cooperation, the EU4Energy programme will be implemented with the assistance of the Energy Charter Secretariat and the International Energy Agency.

Assessing the Outcome Level Effectiveness of EU External Energy Security Governance

As explained in the previous sections, three levels of analysis must be considered in order to assess the outcome level effectiveness of EU external governance, i.e. *rule selection, rule adoption* and *rule application*. With regard to rule selection, we have already illustrated how, especially after the Astana summit and the agreement on the Road Map in the context of the Baku Initiative, EU rules became the focal points of cooperation between the EU and the countries of the Caspian basin and Central Asia. This was possible partially because of the inter-institutional linkages developed among the EU initiatives. The last initiative, the Eastern Partnership, confirmed this process of convergence, since it embraced the normative bases of the Energy Community and also included facilitating the accession of the ENP countries of the region (Armenia, Azerbaijan and Georgia) into this treaty-based framework as an important objective.

It is more problematic to assess the actual adoption and application of EU rules and standards at the domestic level. To perform this analysis, we focus on three important dimensions of the EU's external governance in the field of energy security: i) the convergence of third states' domestic energy governance towards the EU model; ii) the modernisation and development of energy infrastructures; and iii) the protection and attraction of investments in and to the energy sector.[14] For each dimension, the main indicators will be specified, and, using these indicators, we will assess the impact of EU external governance at the domestic level. In other words, we will ask if the EU rules and standards have been adopted and/ or applied in each country of the region.

With regard to market convergence, four main indicators are considered for the electricity and gas sectors: the implementation of the Third Party Access (TPA) rule; the implementation of the unbundling rule; the existence and functioning of independent regulatory authorities (IRAs); and the actions or plans for regional market integration, i.e. for the integration of national energy markets with those of neighbouring countries.[15] In the area of market convergence, the EU institutional system is highly effective in only one case (Georgia); in two other cases (Armenia and Kazakhstan) it is moderately effective and its effectiveness is low in all five of the other cases (Table 2.6).

Table 2.6 The effectiveness of the EU's external governance: energy market convergence.

	Energy market convergence						Effectiveness (*)
	TPA		Unbundling		IRA	Market integration	
	Elect.	Gas	Elect.	Gas			
Armenia	2	0	2	0	1	1	MEDIUM
Azerbaijan	0	0	0	0	0	1	LOW
Georgia	2	2	2	2	1	1	HIGH
Kazakhstan	2	1	2	2	0	0	MEDIUM
Kyrgyzstan	0	0	2	0	0	0	LOW
Tajikistan	0	0	0	1	0	0	LOW
Turkmenistan	0	0	0	0	0	0	LOW
Uzbekistan	0	0	1	1	0	1	LOW

Note: 0 = *no rule adoption* (rules are not transposed to the domestic level); 1 = *rule adoption* (rules transposed to the domestic level, but with no implementation); 2 = *rule application* (rules are in the process of being implemented, although they are not completely aligned with EU standards).

(*) To determine a total effectiveness score, 1 point was assigned for each case of rule application, 0.5 points for each case of rule adoption, and 0 points for each case of no rule adoption. If the total score for a country (C) falls in the range $0 \leq C \leq 2$, the effectiveness is LOW; a score of $2 < C \leq 4$ indicates MEDIUM effectiveness; and a score of $4 < p \leq 6$ indicates HIGH effectiveness.

With regard to energy infrastructure, three indicators are considered: the national programmes for the maintenance of the existing infrastructure; the adoption and implementation of long- and medium-term programmes for energy infrastructure rehabilitation/upgrades; and the national programmes and legislative framework for the development of new energy infrastructures (Table 2.7).

As shown in Table 2.7, EU external governance is, on average, more effective in the area of energy infrastructure than in the area of market convergence, with six countries receiving medium scores and only two receiving a low score. This could be because energy infrastructure issues are, by their nature, more technical than market governance, where important political and administrative reforms to

Table 2.7 The effectiveness of the EU's external governance: energy infrastructure and investment protection and attraction.

Energy infrastructure

	Maintenance	Rehabilitation/ upgrading	Infrastructure development	Effectiveness (*)
Armenia	2	1	1	MEDIUM
Azerbaijan	1	1	1	MEDIUM
Georgia	1	1	2	MEDIUM
Kazakhstan	1	1	1	MEDIUM
Kyrgyzstan	0	0	0	LOW
Tajikistan	0	0	0	LOW
Turkmenistan	1	1	1	MEDIUM
Uzbekistan	1	1	1	MEDIUM

Investment protection and attraction

	Investment framework	Investment climate	Investment planning	Effectiveness (*)
Armenia	1	1	1	MEDIUM
Azerbaijan	1	1	1	MEDIUM
Georgia	1	1	1	MEDIUM
Kazakhstan	0	1	1	LOW
Kyrgyzstan	1	0	0	LOW
Tajikistan	1	1	1	MEDIUM
Turkmenistan	0	0	1	LOW
Uzbekistan	1	1	1	MEDIUM

Note: 0 = *no rule adoption* (rules are not transposed to the domestic level); 1 = *rule adoption* (rules transposed to the domestic level, but with no implementation); 2 = *rule application* (rules are in the process of being implemented, although they are not completely aligned with EU standards).

(*) To determine a total effectiveness score, 1 point was assigned for each case of rule application, 0.5 points for each case of rule adoption, and 0 points for each case of no rule adoption. If the total score for a country (C) falls in the range $0 \leq C \leq 1$, the effectiveness is LOW; a score of $1 < C \leq 2$ indicates MEDIUM effectiveness; and a score of $2 < p \leq 3$ indicates HIGH effectiveness.

unbundle the network or create independent regulatory authorities are required. However, no country in this region has yet completely implemented all EU standards at the domestic level (the only exceptions are Armenia in the area of infrastructure maintenance and Georgia for infrastructure development).

Finally, with regard to investment protection and attraction, three indicators are considered: the investment legislative framework; the investment climate, i.e. the general conditions that can be more or less supportive for investment (rule of law with regard to the enforcement of contracts, property rights, transparency of the banking and financial system and appropriate standards of transparency in public administration); and the investment planning strategy for projects of common interest, i.e. for those projects of regional interest aimed at interconnecting the energy markets of two or more neighbourhood countries.[16] In the area of investment protection and attraction, the situation is similar to that recorded in the area of energy infrastructure: there is no country that has fully implemented the EU standards, and five countries score with a medium level of effectiveness (Table 2.7).

All in all, although the EU has been able to promote some convergence towards its preferred rules and standards in the process of international cooperation, the effectiveness of EU governance architecture at the outcome level has been very poor, especially in terms of rule adoption and rule application. However, there are some signs suggesting that the governance structures promoted by the EU can also have some impact on those countries that are traditionally well outside its sphere of influence. The countries involved in the more structured process of cooperation, i.e. the Eastern Partnership, are those in which EU external governance has generally been more effective, while for the countries outside the scope of this initiative, the score is in general very low (Table 2.8). But there are also important exceptions to this general rule. Azerbaijan holds the lowest position of the countries included

Table 2.8 The overall effectiveness of the EU's external governance architecture.

	Sector of energy cooperation			Total country score (TS)	Effectiveness (*)
	Market convergence	*Infrastructure*	*Investment*		
Georgia	5	2	1.5	8.5	HIGH
Armenia	3	2	1.5	6.5	MEDIUM
Kazakhstan	3.5	1.5	1	6	MEDIUM
Uzbekistan	1.5	1.5	1.5	4.5	MEDIUM
Azerbaijan	0.5	1.5	1.5	3.5	LOW
Tajikistan	0.5	0	1.5	2	LOW
Turkmenistan	0	1.5	0.5	2	LOW
Kyrgyzstan	1	0	0.5	1.5	LOW

Note: (*) The overall effectiveness score was assigned by adding the scores assigned to each country for each of the twelve indicators in the three dimensions of energy cooperation: market convergence, infrastructure, and investment protection and attraction. If the total score for a country (TS) falls in the range $0 \leq TS \leq 4$, the effectiveness is LOW; a score of $4 < TS \leq 8$ indicates MEDIUM effectiveness; and a score of $8 < TS \leq 12$ indicates HIGH effectiveness.

in the Eastern Partnership (Georgia and Armenia) and also scores lower than some countries outside the Eastern Partnership – such as Kazakhstan and Uzbekistan, which have intermediate scores – highlighting that less institutionalised and structured forms of cooperation might have some positive effect in broadening the scope of the EU's external action. This situation can be explained by the fact that, unlike Georgia and Armenia, Azerbaijan is a producer state, so the ruling elite have a strong interest in maintaining strict control over its domestic energy sector. For Kazakhstan, in contrast, it is worth remembering that this country was among the first post-Soviet Union republics to open up its energy sector to Western investment and companies. In this case, in other words, some 'liberal' domestic energy reforms were already on the government agenda before the EU external governance architecture was put in place.

These empirical findings are consistent with those of other research and demonstrate that, on one hand, there is a process of mutual reinforcement between participation in the more institutionalised EU external governance structures and convergence towards EU rules; and, on the other hand, without the actual perspective of membership and conditionality, it is very difficult to export EU rules and principles, especially in the most economically and politically sensitive sectors, such as the energy sector (e.g. EPI 2014). Without conditionality, rules transfer is driven mainly by processes of socialisation and voluntary coordination, and the domestic context and preferences is critical to understanding the actual impact of EU initiatives. In particular, as anticipated, Georgia – the only country with a high score on our scale – confirmed its intention to strengthen its ties with Europe, in 2014, by signing the EU Association Agreement and starting negotiations with the European Commission to join the Energy Community (the Association Agreement, however, only fully entered into force on July 2016). Georgia also has the highest score, according to Freedom House, of any country in the region and is considered, along with Armenia, 'partly-free' (Freedom House 2015). However, in 2015, Armenia decided to join the Russian-led Eurasian Economic Union, and since 2014, its gas sector has been controlled and run by a vertically integrated operator fully owned by Russia's Gazprom. Armenia is also heavily dependent on Russia for its oil and gas needs; thus, it is not yet clear if Armenia will follow its path of cooperation with the EU in the future or will strengthen its economic and energy ties with Moscow. Influences from other external powers are, indeed, another important element to consider in order to fully understand the potential and limitations of EU external governance.

Potential and Limitations of EU External Energy Governance

Much research on EU external action in the area of energy security has applied a geopolitical perspective and highlighted the shortcomings of the EU's approach. These shortcomings are caused by the EU's limited powers and resources in this policy field and the strategic incoherence produced by divisions among the member states. However, as illustrated above, the main yardstick for assessing the EU's performance in terms of external governance is not the state-centric model – often implicitly used as reference point for the study of the EU's external action in foreign energy matters – but the processes developed by the EU to promote institutional structures and policy transfer. In the Caspian Sea basin and Central Asia, divisions among member states, Russia's ambiguous or adverse position towards some EU energy initiatives, and the interests and preferences of third states have resulted in a complex and fragmented governance structure with partially overlapping membership, objectives and policy instruments. However, over time, this complex institutional system has been able to adapt and allow some countries to strengthen their energy cooperation with the EU.

To be sure, the EU institutional system in the region – i.e. the manifestation of the provider state model's external face – developed mainly in the form of network governance, especially for the countries included in the Eastern Partnership, and market governance. In these cases, the main mechanisms for expanding the EU regulatory space beyond its borders are socialisation, voluntary patterns of cooperation and competition. Moreover, agreed-on objectives are tracked through soft mechanisms, such as monitoring activities and reports on the implementation of programmes. This EU system has proved to be quite effective at the level of rule selection. The processes of international cooperation have focused on EU rules, norms and standards, thanks in part to the inter-institutional linkages established among the various energy initiatives created by the EU in different periods and in response to different inputs. But this system has also proven to be poorly effective at promoting actual transposition and implementation of EU rules and standards in third countries, i.e. at rule adoption and rule application. It is worth recalling, however, that in this region, the processes of EU rule transfer cannot rely on the logic of conditionality. Furthermore, EU rules frequently have to compete with the rules and principles supported by other important external players, such as Russia and China, or those supported by national governments, in line with their preferred domestic energy policy agendas.

Thus, the limitations of EU external energy governance in the region are linked to a combination of both external and internal factors. First of all, the EU is not the only actor that, after the collapse of the Soviet Union, tried to extend its influence on regional energy and political dynamics. Russia has continued to play a very crucial role, especially with regard to the main producer countries, relying on its geographical proximity, the infrastructural system inherited from the past period and its ties with the post-Soviet ruling elite (Dellecker and Gomart 2011). Russia has also developed multilateral international initiatives to promote energy cooperation, or has included an energy dimension in other types of initiatives (Stoddard 2012, 9–11). After the collapse of the Soviet Union, Moscow sought to organise energy cooperation in Central Asia, first within the framework of the Commonwealth of Independent States and, later, in the 2000s, through the Eurasian Economic Community (Eurasec). (In 2015, Eurasec was replaced by the Eurasian Economic Union as a continuation and upgrading of the previous initiative.) The members of Eurasec – Belarus, Kazakhstan, Kyrgyzstan, Russia, Tajikistan and Uzbekistan (Uzbekistan was a member of Eurasec until 2008) – agreed on a framework for energy cooperation in 2003, and the idea of a unified energy market was launched in 2008. However, this initiative was not very effective, making progress only in the field of electricity rather than in the more strategic hydrocarbon sector. It has also proven difficult for Russia to achieve bilateral cooperation with its neighbours in the oil and gas sectors. The major producer countries, especially Uzbekistan, Turkmenistan and Kazakhstan, have preferred to pursue a multivector foreign policy and to use their energy resources to build interdependence with various external actors in order to maximise their autonomy and sovereignty (Ipek 2007; Hanks 2009; Anceschi 2010).

A similar situation has also characterised another regional initiative with potential effects on regional energy governance and cooperation: the Shanghai Cooperation Organisation (SCO). The SCO was established in 2001 by China, Kazakhstan, Kyrgyzstan, Russia, Tajikistan and Uzbekistan. Its aim was to support economic and military cooperation in Central Asia (in 2016, India and Pakistan joined the SCO as well). This initiative was driven mainly by China, but, in 2006, Russia proposed the inclusion of an energy component with the creation of the 'SCO Energy Club'. Although the idea of an Energy Club was endorsed by the other SCO members, the initiative did not really develop into a framework for energy cooperation (Kazantsev 2008; Stoddard 2012). Divergences of interests between China and Russia and among Central Asian countries prevented the development of effective multilateralism or the establishment of a common rule-based system for energy cooperation (e.g. Matusov 2007). This outcome is in line with the general logic and functioning of the SCO initiative, which was mainly intended to promote Chinese economic interests without provoking conflicts with Russia. For the other countries of the region, however, the SCO represents a practical way of implementing their multi-vector foreign policies by cultivating relationships both with China and Russia.

Eurasec (now the Eurasian Economic Union) and the energy initiatives linked to the SCO are very different from the EU's initiatives. They do not embrace and promote market-based principles and rules, instead allowing the countries of the region to maintain their preferred domestic institutional structures for energy governance. This means that these initiatives are neutral towards many factors that can challenge energy politics in producer states. These characteristics also reflect the general views of Beijing and Moscow on international governance. China and Russia are committed to non-interference in third countries and aim at promoting cooperation through intergovernmental relationships rather than multilateral and legally binding frameworks, which, in contrast, characterise much of the EU's approach to external governance.

The preferences for a strong sovereignty perspective in international governance and foreign affairs are also widely diffuse in the major countries of the region. These preferences are even stronger in the case of energy policy, which, in the main producer states, is strictly intertwined with national security and regime survival. Azerbaijan, Turkmenistan, Kazakhstan and Uzbekistan are strongly dependent on revenues from oil and gas, and the stability of their political systems and their autonomy in economic affairs are based on this dependence[17] (e.g. Franke, Gawrich and Alakbarov 2009; Overland, Kjaernet and Kendall-Taylor 2010; Ostrowski 2011). The EU's efforts to promote a market-based energy governance contrast with the producer states' preferences for maintaining tight control over energy business. Moreover, because of the growing interest of China and Chinese energy companies in the resources of the region, these countries can attract important investments without being forced to embrace domestic reforms. If Azerbaijan is committing an increasing part of its resources to European markets – as witnessed by its participation in the opening of the EU Southern Gas Corridor – Turkmenistan and Uzbekistan are strengthening their energy relations with China. Having different sources of investment and access to different export markets also reduce the potential effect of any mechanism of competition triggered by the EU, i.e. the requirement of complying with EU rules and standards in order to gain financial or political resources. In addition, it is worth noting that the strengthening of Azerbaijan's energy ties with Europe does not seem to have led to the transformation of Azerbaijan's domestic energy governance to comply with the EU model, or to have had much effect on the country's broader political structure. As already highlighted by Youngs (2009), the EU approach to energy security is quite inconsistent with governance reforms or democracy in producer states.

To sum up, for the Caspian and Central Asian producers, energy is a very important component of their multi-vectored foreign policy, as it is the main tool they can use to bandwagon with and balance against the major external powers (Overland, Kjaernet and Kendall-Taylor 2010; Stoddard 2012). These countries have little interest in accepting international binding commitments that can undermine the mechanisms that allow the survival of domestic regimes. But they are interested in taking part in less institutionalised and demanding governance structures that offer incumbent state leaders the opportunity to strengthen their political legitimacy at the domestic and international levels.

Notwithstanding these important structural limits of the EU's external energy security governance, the complex institutional architectures created by the EU, and their origins, evolution and achievements, must be factored into any assessment of the EU energy security politics. In other words, the approach of the external governance – which can help clarify the processes of network building and norms and policy transfer promoted by the EU – sheds some light on some of the less visible mechanisms and elements of the EU's external energy actions, which complement the other pillars of the EU's energy security strategy.

Notes

1 The overall assessment of the effectiveness of an international regime is a very complex subject matter; for a review of the main issues, see Young (2011). For example an important method for assessing the effectiveness of a regime is the use of counterfactual reasoning, i.e. what would have happened without the establishment and functioning of the regime under scrutiny? In this chapter, the analysis is based on the two dimensions of output level effectiveness and outcome level effectiveness (see, in particular, Underdal 2004), and only limited counterfactual reasoning is provided.

2 Initially, Russia also proposed replacing the ECT with a new international legal frame-work (the so-called 'Conceptual Approach to the New Legal Framework for Energy Cooperation'), but this project has not been developed further (Belyi 2015).

3 These data consider both types of bilateral energy initiatives, the Memorandum of Understanding and the Energy Dialogue. See the data available at: https://ec.europa.eu/energy/en/topics/international-cooperation [accessed 28 June 2016].

4 The Union for the Mediterranean includes Algeria, Egypt, Israel, Jordan, Lebanon, Monaco, Morocco, Palestine, Tunisia, Mauritania, Albania, Bosnia and Herzegovina, Montenegro, Turkey and Syria.

5 The development of the Southern Gas Corridor will be further explored in Chapter 3.

6 After the war in Eastern Ukraine and the Russian annexation of Crimea, the EU-Ukraine energy cooperation has been upgraded. The recent developments in the EU-Ukraine bilateral relations will be further discussed in Chapter 3.

7 See the various reports on the activities of the Platform on Energy Security available at: https://ec.europa.eu/energy/en/events/eastern-partnership-platform-energy-security [accessed 2–6 September 2016].

8 Georgia and Moldova signed an Association Agreement and also a Deep and Compre-hensive Free Trade Area agreement with EU in 2014 (these agreements fully entered into forced only in July 2016). Ukraine also signed its Association Agreement with the EU on June 2014, and since January 2016 a Deep and Comprehensive Free Trade Area has been provisionally applied.

9 Another international initiative that aims at improving transparency in upstream hydro-carbon governance in the region is the Extractive Industries Transparency Initiative, EITI (see Stoddard 2012). Azerbaijan, Kazakhstan, Kyrgyzstan and Tajikistan partici-pate in the EITI, but this initiative is not an EU-led project and is not considered in this chapter.

10 A process for monitoring bilateral cooperation (in the framework of the ENP Associa-tion Agenda and ENP Progress Reports) and multilateral cooperation has been in place since the establishment of the Eastern Partnership. Moreover, the rules and procedures for the functioning of the thematic platforms have been progressively formalised, and in this case, monitoring and assessment processes have also been launched (see the documents available at: http://eeas.europa.eu/eastern/index_en.htm [accessed 22 Sep-tember 2016]).

11 Specific references to the objectives and norms of the Energy Community have been included in the works of the Energy Security Platform of the Eastern Partnership since the first meeting held in 2009 (see the documents at: https://ec.europa.eu/energy/en/events/eastern-partnership-platform-energy-security [accessed 20 September 2016]). Later, the Eastern Partnership and the Secretariat of the Energy Community began to cooperate to implement Joint Projects in different fields (see the reports on the meetings and workshops organised by the Energy Security Platform, available at: https://ec.europa.eu/energy/en/events/eastern-partnership-platform-energy-security [accessed 20–24 September 2016]).

12 See the reports on the activities of the Inogate programme; available at: www.inogate.org/ [accessed 18–22 September 2016]. An important project is the so-called 'Inogate Technical Secretariat Project'. This project aims to simultaneously support the works of the Eastern Partnership and the Baku Initiative and to achieve the various objectives included in the MoU, signed by the EU with Central Asian states.

13 See 'Platform 3 Energy security core objectives and revised work programme 2014–2017', 30 April 2016, available at: https://ec.europa.eu/energy/sites/ener/files/docu-ments/Revised%20Work%20Programme%20Platform%203%202014–2017%20final.pdf [accessed 28 September 2016].

14 These objectives are included in the Road Map of the Baku Initiative and the Eastern Partnership. The empirical analysis is mainly based on the data provided by the Inogate programme (Inogate 2012) and by the International Energy Agency (IEA 2015).

In 2015, the International Energy Agency published a report in collaboration with Ino-gate assessing the countries of the region according to the objectives stated in the Road Map of the Baku Initiative. For this evaluation of the convergence of energy markets and of investment protection and promotion, these data were integrated with the data provided by the Global Competitiveness Report of the World Economic Forum (WEF 2015) and the European Integration Index for Eastern Partnership Countries (EPI 2014).

15 To assign the scores for these indicators, the data from Inogate (2012) and International Energy Agency (IEA 2015) have been integrated with those provided for the countries of the Eastern Partnership by the Integration Index for Eastern Partnership Countries (EPI 2014) (see, in particular, 'Energy: legislation convergence and energy policy' in the section 'Sectorial approximation' of the EPI Report). The data included in the EPI Report are based on documents and legislation issued by EU institutions and the coun-tries of the Eastern Partnership and on assessments by independent experts.

16 To assign the scores for the indicators 'legislative framework' and 'investment climate', the data from Inogate (2012) and the International Energy Agency (IEA 2015) have been integrated with the data provided in the Global Competitiveness Report 2014–15 (WEF 2015) (see, in particular, the scores assigned for the pillar 'Institutions' in the WEF Report).

17 In 2012, total hydrocarbon rents (oil and gas rents) accounted for about 21 percent of the GDP in Uzbekistan, 25 percent in Kazakhstan, 43 percent in Turkmenistan and 46 percent in Azerbaijan (Pirani 2012).

References

Anceschi, L. 2010. Integrating Domestic Politics and Foreign Policy Making: The Cases of Turkmenistan and Uzbekistan. *Central Asian Survey* 29(2): 143–158.

Andrews-Speed, P. 1999. The Politics of Petroleum and the Energy Charter Treaty as an Effective Investment Regime. *Journal of Energy Finance and Development* 4(1): 117–135.

Baku Initiative, 2004. *Conclusions and Annex of the Ministerial Conference on Energy Co-Operation between the EU, the Caspian Littoral States and Their Neighbouring Countries*. Baku, 13 November.

Baku Initiative, 2006. *Ministerial Declaration on Enhanced Energy Co-Operation between the EU, the Littoral States of the Black and Caspian Seas and Their Neighbouring Countries: Annex 1, Road Map*. Astana, 30 November.

Belyi, A. V. 2015. *Transnational Gas Markets and Euro-Russian Energy Relations*. Basing-stoke: Palgrave Macmillan.

Biermann, F., Pattberg, P., Van Asselt, H., Zelli, F. 2009. The Fragmentation of Global Governance Architectures: A Framework for Analysis. *Global Environmental Politics* 9(4): 14–40.

Boonstra, J. 2011. *The EU's Interests in Central Asia: Integrating Energy, Security and Values into Coherent Policy*. EDC Working Paper No. 9, January 2011.

CAS, 2009. *The European Union and Central Asia: The New Partnership in Action*. Brussels, 3 December.

Council of the European Union, 2009. *Joint Declaration of the Prague Eastern Partnership Summit*. Prague, 7 May 2009.

Council of the European Union, 2013. *Joint Declaration of the Eastern Partnership Summit*. Vilnius, 28–29 November 2013.

Council of the European Union, 2015. *Joint Declaration of the Eastern Partnership Summit*. Riga, 21–22 May 2015.

Delcour, L. 2011. *The Institutional Functioning of the Eastern Partnership: An Early Assessment.* Eastern Partnership Review, Estonian Center of Eastern Partnership, WP n. 23.

Dellecker, A., Gomart, T. (eds.) 2011. *Russian Energy Security and Foreign Policy.* London: Routledge.

EPI, 2014. *European Integration Index for Eastern Partnership Countries.* Available at: www.eap-index.eu [accessed 15 May 2016].

European Commission, 2007. *Black Sea Synergy: A New Regional Cooperation Initiative.* Brussels, 11 April 2007, COM(2007) 160 final.

European Commission, 2008. *Report on the First Year of Implementation of the Black Sea Synergy.* Brussels, 16 June 2008, COM(2008) 391 final.

European Commission, 2015. *Black Sea Synergy: Review of a Regional Cooperation Initiative.* Brussels, 20 January 2015, SWD (2015) 6 final.

Franke, A., Gawrich, A., Alakbarov, G. 2009. Kazakhstan and Azerbaijan as Post-Soviet Rentier States: Resource Incomes and Autocracy as a Double 'Curse' in Post-Soviet Regimes. *Europe-Asia Studies* 61(1): 109–140.

Freedom House, 2015. *Freedom in the World 2015.* Available at: https://freedomhouse.org/report/freedom-world/freedom-world-2015#.V5pZKvkrK70 [accessed 3 December 2015].

Goldthau, A., Sitter, N. 2014. A Liberal Actor in a Realist World? The Commission and the External Dimension of the Single Market for Energy. *Journal of European Public Policy* 21(10): 1452–1472.

Goldthau, A., Sitter, N. 2015. *A Liberal Actor in a Realist World: The European Union Regulatory State and the Global Political Economy of Energy.* Oxford: Oxford University Press.

Hanks, R. R. 2009. 'Multi-Vector Politics' and Kazakhstan's Emerging Role as a Geo-Strategic Player in Central Asia. *Journal of Balkan and Near Eastern Studies* 11(3): 257–267.

Herranz-Surrallés, A., Natorski, M. 2012. The European Energy Policy towards Eastern Neighbors: Rebalancing Priorities or Changing Paradigms?, in Morata, F., Sandoval, I. S. (eds.), *European Energy Policy: An Environmental Approach*, pp. 132–155. Cheltenham: Edward Elgar.

IEA, 2015. *Eastern Europe, Caucasus and Central Asia.* Paris: International Energy Agency.

Inogate, 2012. *Status Report 2011: An Energy Review of the Partners Countries.* Brussels. October 2012.

Ipek, P. 2007. The Role of Oil and Gas in Kazakhstan's Foreign Policy: Looking East or West? *Europe-Asia Studies* 59(7): 1179–1199.

Japaridze, T., Manoli, P., Triantaphyllou, D., Tsantoulis, Y. 2011. *The EU's Ambivalent Relationship with the BSEC: Reflecting on the Past, Mapping out the Future.* ICBSS, Policy Brief, n. 20, January 2010.

Kazantsev, A. 2008. Russian Policy in Central Asia and the Caspian Sea Region. *Europe-Asia Studies* 60(6): 1073–1088.

Keohane, R., Victor, D. G. 2011. The Regime Complex for Climate Change. *Perspectives on Politics* 9(1): 7–23.

Korosteleva, E. A. 2012. *Eastern Partnership: A New Opportunity for the Neighbours?* London: Routledge.

Lavenex, S. 2004. EU External Governance in 'Wider Europe'. *Journal of European Public Policy* 11(4): 680–700.

Lavenex, S. 2008. A Governance Perspective on the European Neighbourhood Policy: Integration beyond Conditionality? *Journal of European Public Policy* 15(6): 938–955.

Lavenex, S. 2011. Concentric Circles of Flexible 'EUropean' Integration: A Typology of EU External Governance Relations. *Comparative European Politics* 9(4): 372–393.

Lavenex, S., Lehmkuhl, D., Wichmann, N. 2009. Modes of External Governance: A Cross-National and Cross-Sectoral Comparison. *Journal of European Public Policy* 16(6): 813–833.

Lavenex, S., Schimmelfennig, F. 2009. EU Rules beyond EU Borders: Theorizing External Governance in European Politics. *Journal of European Public Policy* 16(6): 791–812.

Matusov, A. 2007. Energy Cooperation in the SCO: Club or Gathering. *China and Eurasia Forum Quarterly* 5(3): 83–99.

Oberthür, S. 2002. Clustering of Multilateral Environmental Agreements: Potentials and Limitations. *International Environmental Agreements: Politics, Law and Economics* 2(4): 317–340.

Oberthür, S., Gehring, T. 2006. *Institutional Interaction in Global Environmental Governance: Synergy and Conflict among International and EU Policies*. Cambridge: MIT Press.

Ostrowski, W. 2011. Rentierism, Dependency and Sovereignty in Central Asia, in Cummings, S., Hinnebusch, R. (eds.), *Sovereignty after Empire: Comparing the Middle East and Central Asia*, pp. 282–303. Edinburgh: Edinburgh University Press.

Overland, I., Kjaernet, H., Kendall-Taylor, A. (eds.) 2010. *Caspian Energy Politics: Azerbaijan, Kazakhstan and Turkmenistan*. London: Routledge.

Padgett, S. 2011. Energy Co-Operation in the Wider Europe: Institutionalizing Interdependence. *Journal of Common Market Studies* 49(5): 1065–1087.

Pirani, S. 2012. *Central Asian and Caspian Gas Production and the Constraints on Export*. Oxford Institute for Energy Studies, NG-69, December 2012.

Rosendal, G. K. 2001. Impacts of Overlapping International Regimes: The Case of Biodiversity. *Global Governance* 7(1): 95–117.

Sander, M. 2013. Conceptual Proposals for Measuring the Impact of International Regimes on Energy Security. *Energy Policy* 63: 449–457.

Schimmelfennig, F., Sedelmeier, U. 2004. Governance by Conditionality: EU Rule Transfer to the Candidate Countries of Central and Eastern Europe. *Journal of European Public Policy* 11(4): 661–679.

Stoddard, E. 2012. Capturing Contestation in Caspian Energy: Regime Complexity and Eurasian Energy Governance. *Political Perspectives* 6(1): 3–25.

Underdal, A. 2004. Methodological Challenges in the Study of Regime Effectiveness, in Underdal, A., Young, O. R. (eds.), *Regime Consequences: Methodological Challenges and Research Strategies*, pp. 27–49. Dordrecht: Kluwer Academic Publisher.

Von Moltke, K. 2005. Clustering International Environmental Agreements as an Alternative to a World Environment Organization, in Biermann, F., (eds.), *A World Environment Organization: Solution or Threat for Effective International Environmental Governance?*, pp. 175–204. London: Routledge.

Wälde, T. (ed.) 1996. *The Energy Charter Treaty: An East-West Gateway for Investment and Trade*. London: Kluwer Academic Publisher.

Wälde, T., Konoplyanik, A. 2006. Energy Charter Treaty and Its Role in International Energy. *Journal of Energy and Natural Resources Law* 24(4): 523–558.

WEF, 2015. *The Global Competitiveness Report 2015–2016*. Geneva: World Economic Forum.

Yafimava, K. 2011. *The Transit Dimension of EU Energy Security: Russian Gas Transit across Ukraine, Belarus, and Moldova*. Oxford: Oxford University Press.

Young, O. R. 2011. Effectiveness of International Environmental Regimes: Existing Knowledge, Cutting-Edge Themes, and Research Strategies. *Proceedings of the National Academy of Sciences* 108(50): 19853–19860.

Youngs, R. 2009. *Energy Security: Europe's New Foreign Policy Challenge*. London: Routledge.

3 The New Politics of Pipeline

From the Nord Stream to the
Southern Gas Corridor

As we saw in Chapter 2, the EU's efforts to extend its energy regulatory space beyond its borders have not been very effective outside the context of the Energy Community, especially with producer countries, with the exception of Norway (see below). In Central Asia, which the EU has targeted, especially with regard to the development of the Southern Gas Corridor, the complex institutional system created by the European Commission has had a very limited impact. The EU's approach to external governance, in particular, has failed to address important issues related to security of gas supply, so much so that the European Commission has taken a more proactive approach to supporting the Nabucco pipeline and promoting the Southern Gas Corridor.

The EU's approach to external governance represents a manifestation of the EU as a provider state, a model that is based on a peculiar reconfiguration of the state-market nexus according to the market approach to energy policy. However, in matters of pipeline infrastructure development and diversification of supply, this model seems poorly equipped to illustrate the current political dynamics and the roles played by the main state and non-state actors.

Europe's pipeline infrastructure system is characterised by the geographic locations of the gas reserves to which it connects (Schubert, Pollak and Kreutler 2016, 226–230). These include the North Sea gas fields, various Russian fields, the Central Asian fields and the reserves of North Africa. These regions are linked to the markets of member states by three main corridors: the first runs southward from the Norwegian and North Seas to the UK and the European continent (the North-South corridor) and has a capacity of about 130 bcm/y; the second runs northward from Algeria and Libya to Spain and Italy (the South-North corridor) and has a capacity of about 65 bcm/y; and the third runs eastward from, or through, Russia and the former Soviet Union to the Baltic States and Eastern and Central Europe, channelling natural gas to the larger Western European markets (the East-West corridor). This last corridor is the most complex in terms of the transit countries involved and the length of the pipeline system, and it is further divided into two main routes: one passes through the former Soviet Union countries (mainly Ukraine and to a lesser extent Belarus) with a capacity of about 162 bcm/y; the other one, which was recently established, connects Russia directly to Germany through the Baltic Sea with the Nord Stream (composed of two parallel pipelines

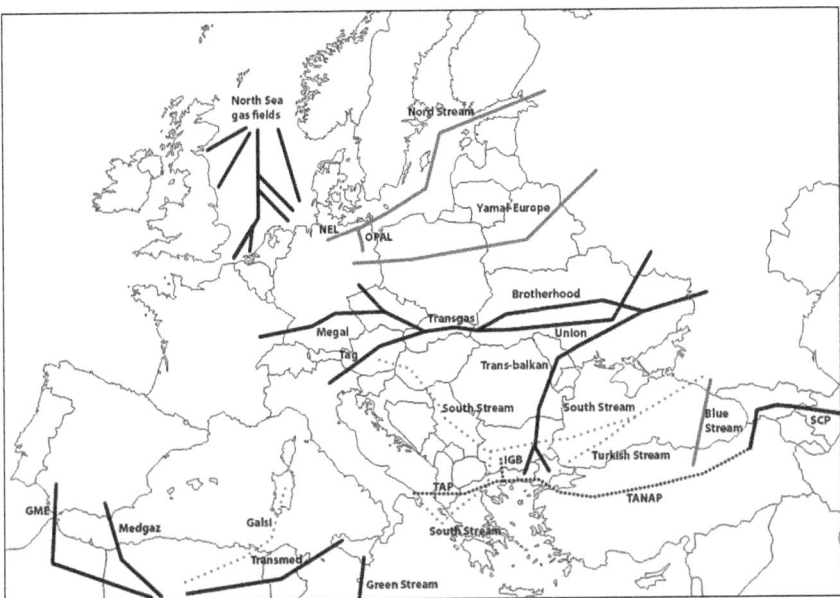

Figure 3.1 The main pipeline routes serving the EU market along the North-South, East-West, South-East-West and South-North corridors.

Note: Author's elaboration for illustration. Grey line = pipelines on the East-West corridors built after the end of the Cold War; dotted grey lines = proposed pipelines; black dotted lines = pipelines currently under construction.

with a combined capacity of 55 bcm/y) (Figure 3.1). Finally, a fourth South-East-West corridor (the so-called Southern Gas Corridor) is currently under development to connect Caspian gas fields (in Azerbaijan) and possibly Central Asian resources to EU markets, avoiding Russian territory. The most developed project in this corridor is the Trans-Adriatic-Pipeline (TAP), with an initial capacity of 10 bcm/y. It will be connected to the Trans-Anatolian Natural Gas Pipeline (TANAP) and will carry Azerbaijani gas through Greece, Albania and then Italy after crossing the Ionian Sea (Figure 3.1). TANAP is a pipeline that connects with the South Caucasus Pipeline (SCP) and carries natural gas from Azerbaijan to Greece over Turkish territory. Its construction started in 2015, and it is expected to be completed by 2018, whereas TAP's construction started in May 2016 and is expected to be completed by 2020.[1] TAP's capacity is not impressive in terms of total EU gas demand, but the initial capacity could double to 20 bcm/y in the future if additional supplies come on stream. TAP will also have a 'physical reverse flow' feature, which would allow gas from Italy to be diverted to Southeastern Europe. There are also plans to connect TAP with the Ionian-Adriatic-Pipeline (IAP), which serves the Balkans, and the IGB Pipeline (Gas Interconnector Greece-Bulgaria), which is currently under development and will link Greece and

Bulgaria. These connections could possibly improve the diversification of gas supply in this vulnerable region (Figure 3.1).

Many of the pipelines composing the first three corridors – like the Brotherhood, Union and Trans-Balkan along the East-West axis – were built during the Cold War era, hand in hand with the development of the European gas market, and they reflect the political and economic situation of that period (Figure 3.1). More importantly, looking at these corridors, it is clear that these energy axes are well outside the scope of the EU's external energy governance and regulatory approach. The only exception to this rule is Norway, which is very different to other non-EU producers. Gas trade between European countries and Norway began in the 1970s, and since then, the North-South corridor has never been a matter of concern for European energy security. Coming from a member of NATO, a democratic country committed to a market economy, Norwegian supplies are largely perceived as domestic resources within the EU. Furthermore, since 1994, EU-Norway relations have been governed under the framework of the European Economic Area agreement (EEA). The EEA covers areas such as the single market legislation (including the internal energy market legislation that Norway must implement), competition law, state aid and free movement of goods, and in these areas, Norway functions in many ways much like an EU member state (Talus 2013, 232).

In contrast, when discussing the East-West axis from Russia, the South-North axis from Algeria and Libya, and the South-East axis designed to connect the Caspian region and possibly Central Asia, the politics of pipeline and diversification of supply must be framed differently; in these cases, the reconfiguration in the state-market nexus cannot be described by the provider state model. In addition to efforts made with the ECT, the EU has established several bilateral agreements to institutionalise its energy relations with Russia. The first was the EU-Russian Energy Dialogue, which was established in 2000, during the Romano Prodi's presidency of the European Commission. Then, after the second Russian-Ukrainian gas crisis, two new bodies were launched: the Early Warning Mechanism, in 2009, to facilitate early evaluation of potential risks to energy supply and promote a rapid reaction in case of an emergency; and the Gas Advisory Council, in 2011, to provide recommendations on gas issues in the context of the Energy Dialogue. In 2013, the *EU-Russia Energy Cooperation Roadmap until 2050* was signed by the European Commission and the Russian Ministry of Energy. However, although these new forums have facilitated dialogues on some energy-related issues, like previous forums, they have not provided international agreements or other legally binding documents and have only touched 'the surface of EU-Russia energy relations' (Waloszyk 2014, 85). The deterioration of EU-Russia relations after the Russian annexation of the Crimea has further limited the usefulness of these frameworks for addressing important issues related to diversification of gas supply and energy security.[2] Moreover, member states' governments have largely refused to renounce their foreign and commercial energy relationships with Moscow and rely on these EU-level mechanisms for dialogue and exchange of information.

Similarly, EU-level bilateral and multilateral efforts have been mostly ineffective with Algeria and Libya. Algerian policymakers have showed no interest in accepting the export of EU principles and rules or in entering binding forms of cooperation with Brussels (Darbouche 2010). In 2013, Algeria signed a Memorandum of Understanding on Energy Cooperation with the EU and, in 2015, a Political Dialogue on Energy Matters. However, the practical effects of these non-binding and very general dialogues on international energy politics are not yet clear. During the Gaddafi regime, Libya also had little interest in enhancing its cooperation with the EU or in accepting EU market rules and principles. And, obviously, the turmoil initiated by the 2011 Western military intervention and the fall of the Gaddafi regime has not been conductive to any renewal of or improvements in institutionalised cooperation in the energy sector. Finally, the EU's external governance framework has had a very limited effect on the main countries involved in the Southern Gas Corridor, and so, as mentioned above, the European Commission decided to adopt a more proactive and strategic approach in this case.

Against this backdrop, this chapter focuses on the transformation of the European politics of pipelines by analysing the main developments occurring along the East-West, South-North and South-East corridors. The chapter is organised as follows. In the first section, the parallel origins and development of the European gas market and external import infrastructure system will be illustrated through the lens of the partner state model. Second, the first breaches into this original model and the main factors of transformation affecting its ideational, institutional and market fundamentals will be highlighted, placing particular attention on the development of the IEM and EU energy security policies. The emerging institutional framework of European security of gas supply will then be described, as well as the model of the catalytic state that is growing out of the reconfiguration of the state-market nexus in the new EU environment. Finally, the gradual transformation into this model will be further illustrated through the examples of the East-West corridor and Southern Gas Corridor. For the East-West corridor, the division between 'old' and 'new' member states and the recent events and political dynamics triggered by the War in Eastern Ukraine and the Russian annexation of the Crimea will be also considered. The chapter demonstrates the emergence of a new state-market nexus in European politics of security of gas supply. This new nexus is in line with the catalytic state model but also includes specific dynamics embedded in the different characteristics of the various corridors that supply the EU market.

Origins and Development of the European Security of Gas Supply Infrastructure System

Structuring Markets, Politics and Corridors in the European Gas Sector

The gas market in Europe is of relatively recent origin. It emerged on a significant scale between the late 1960s and 1970s, after the large Dutch Groningen gas field went into production and gas from Algeria, Norway and the Soviet Union started to flow into Western countries in growing quantities (Radetzki 1999). Since this initial period, the (Western) European gas market – with the exception of the UK, which has long differed from continental Europe – has developed on two separate levels, national and European, creating a two-level market structure (Stern 1990; Estrada et al. 1995). The national level was characterised by the establishment of national or regional transport and wholesale monopolies, which developed existing transport networks, expanded national production and later, along with the producers, contributed to the establishment of the major gas importation infrastructures. The European level was characterised by a two-sided oligopoly, balanced between the major producers and the major national companies. The oligopoly of sellers consisted mainly of national companies handling exports from countries outside Western Europe (Sonatrach in Algeria, Gazprom in Russia, and Statoil and GFU, the public export consortium, in Norway) and from the Netherlands (Gasunie), each of which had an export monopoly.[3] The oligopoly of purchasers, which included the national gas companies of Western Europe that had monopolies (or quasi-monopolies) on wholesale supply in their country, included Ruhrgas in Germany, GDF in France, ENI-Snam in Italy, Distrigaz in Belgium and OMV in Austria, later joined in the 1980s by the Spanish Enagas. A high level of state involvement in the national transportation system, whether direct (France and Italy) or indirect (Germany), allows states to control their gas dependency relationships with foreign states, as is the case in Germany, France, Belgium, Italy and Austria, and to control their national resources management policies, as in the Netherlands.

The two-level market structure dominated by monopsony buyers and monopoly sellers of gas allowed for a balance of market power between producers and purchasers (Radetzki 1999). On one hand, importers' governments considered the strength of the national transmission companies essential for ensuring sufficient bargaining power to obtain favourable import prices. On the other hand, exporters regarded the power of national transmission companies as a guarantee that the purchase obligations under long-term contracts – usually indexed to the price of the oil that the natural gas was replacing – would be fulfilled. Long-term oil-linked contracts also included take-or-pay clauses ensuring that the buyers would take a minimum annual volume of gas (usually 85 percent). These contractual obligations were important since they favoured the sharing of risks – suppliers took the price risks and buyers the volume risks – and allowed the commercial development of energy resources and infrastructures.[4]

The interactions between political, economic and technological factors, along with the geographical distribution of gas resources, explain the two-level structuration of the Western European market and the contractual and pricing mechanisms for gas trade (Radetzki 1999; Finon 2004). Among the political factors, the idea that the state should be strongly involved in the management of the energy sector and that market forces alone could not deliver the level of supply security required by governments is crucial. This guiding principle has been at work in many Western European countries since the end of World War II, reinforced by the oil shocks of the 1970s. It was embedded in the general institutional and ideational structure of state economic policymaking, although its practical implementation was very country-specific (Kohl 1982; Prontera 2008). However, the politics of energy security and international pipeline development followed some common patterns, especially with regard to the interactions between Western countries and non-Western producers (i.e. the Soviet Union and North African countries), which were (and are) the most problematic from a political point of view. Although commercial considerations were important in these relationships, foreign policy and security concerns were at the top of the agenda.

With regard to relationships with the Soviet Union, political considerations related to the *détente* during the Cold War were crucial to establishing strong interdependence in the gas sector. On one hand, Western countries followed a political (albeit informal) restriction, limiting the share of Soviet gas in their imports to about 30 percent. On the other hand, Western governments provided strong diplomatic, financial and political support to their companies and in many cases cooperated to develop the huge infrastructural system needed to channel Soviet resources into European markets (Stern 1990; Mabro and Wybrew-Bond 1999; Victor and Victor 2006; Högselius 2013; Verda 2016). Western governments also provided diplomatic and financial support to national companies seeking to establish relationships with North African countries, and the same interactions between political goals (such as economic penetration in these regions), energy needs and commercial considerations were at work there (e.g. Hayes 2006). But with each other, Western countries acted more competitively. Foreign policies with North African countries were less constrained by the security structure of the Cold War than East-West relationships. Moreover, the geographical collocation of gas resources in Algeria and Libya allowed European consumer countries to develop infrastructure connecting them to those countries in isolation, i.e. without acting together with other Western allies. This infrastructure involved the construction of pipelines across the Mediterranean Sea or the use of LNG technology. Although different projects stemming from the Algerian gas fields were discussed, the only pipeline that materialised during the Cold War, in 1983, was the so-called Transmed (also known as the 'Enrico Mattei pipeline'), connecting Algeria and Southern Italy (by crossing Tunisia and the Mediterranean Sea), developed by the Italian ENI and Sonatrach (Figure 3.1).

As discussed in Chapter 1, despite the differences between the East-West and South-North gas corridors, the international politics of pipeline and energy security was easily captured by the traditional 'triangular diplomacy' framework (Stopford and Strange 1991), as the most important energy agreements were the outcomes of government-to-government, government-to-company and company-to-company negotiations (see Figure 1.1 in Chapter 1). In particular, governments were at the centre of all key decisions in gas infrastructure projects, as they guaranteed contracts with state-backed financing and created 'gas demand at national level to match the rigid structure of supply from abroad' (Hayes and Victor 2006, 325). The model of the partner state, in which governments have direct (such as in Italy and France) or indirect (such as in Germany) control of the national gas market and are actively involved in supporting the 'national champions' abroad in negotiations with producers' governments and their national companies, suitably captures the basic dynamics of the period. This outcome was possible because national gas markets in Western Europe were in the first stages of development, with significant growth potential, and because, after the oil shocks, gas (along with nuclear energy) was seen as an important means for reducing dependence on Middle Eastern oil. Governments could also ensure rapid implementation of infrastructure projects through the centralisation of the decision-making processes. In the general ideological and political climate of the period, opposition from local communities to such projects was minimal, and social movements and party politics were mainly concerned with nuclear programmes. Finally, competences over foreign energy relations, the national energy market and infrastructure development were firmly in the hands of national governments, while European Community regulatory structures and powers were lacking in the gas sector.

The First Breaches into the Original Model

The traditional institutional, ideational and market structure and the related politics of energy security outlined by the partner state model and triangular diplomacy framework began to change in the late 1980s. Although some technological and economic developments, such as the maturation of the European gas markets, began to undermine this system, the most important attack came from the construction of the IEM and its commitments to the new market paradigm of energy policy. The transformation was incremental. Initially, Western European countries promoted limited liberalisation and privatisation of their energy sectors. The latter was not a requirement of the IEM project, but it was in line with its market approach logic. Security of gas supply and pipeline politics, however, continued to play out essentially according to the same patterns of triangular diplomacy and the partner state. These patterns were reinforced by the continuous increase of gas demand in Europe, where the construction of combined-cycle gas power plants in the 1990s and early 2000s created what became known as the 'dash for gas' in a number of countries (Honoré 2010). Despite these continuities, some breaches did appear in the original model, especially along the East-West corridor, as new actors entered in the game, new commercial strategies were pursued by energy companies and new routes were built in the wake of the enormous geopolitical changes triggered by the end of the Cold War and the collapse of the Soviet Union. Resistance to some old logics and political dynamics and the simultaneous development of new ones can be seen at work in the South-North corridor as well. Along that corridor, new pipelines were built as well, and the transformation of domestic energy markets interacted with the international politics of pipeline, although more continuity with the previous dynamics can be traced.

The East-West Corridor

East-West energy relations grew stronger after the end of the Cold War and the collapse of Soviet Union: Russian exports to Western and Eastern Europe rose from 100 bcm at the beginning of the 1990s to 160 bcm in 2005 (Henderson and

Mitrova 2015). As in the past, this development was supported by both economic and political rationales. For Russia, increasing gas exports to Europe was an important financial priority. In many European capitals, gas trade was considered an important tool for integrating Moscow into the Western international economic order. Natural gas was also cheaper and considered much more environmentally friendly than oil, and it was again regarded as an important alternative to energy dependence on the unstable Middle East (Mabro and Wybrew-Bond 1999). Besides, after the end of the Cold War, Western European countries no longer viewed Moscow as a threat, and dependency on Russian gas ceased to be a preoccupation for decision makers in Washington. Energy resources enabled the Russian Federation to increase its trade surplus, allowing European goods to be exported to the opening and large Russian domestic market. All in all, Russian gas helped major European consumers tap their growing energy demand and supported the replacement of oil and coal in the power sector while strengthening Moscow's economic ties with the West.

Given this context, the simplest and least expensive way to reinforce this new East-West interdependence was to upgrade the infrastructure system built during the Soviet era. However, new export routes began to represent an important alternative for Gazprom, the Russian gas export monopoly that emerged from restructuring of the Soviet state-controlled gas system. In particular, the deepening of the gas trade offered Gazprom and Western consumers the opportunity to diversify Russian export routes away from Ukraine, now a crucial transit state in the political economy of East-West energy interdependence.

The end of the Cold War, the fragmentation of the Soviet bloc and the emergence of new, independent countries between Russia and its lucrative Western markets resulted in an entirely 'new geography' for the Eurasian gas network (Yafimava 2011, 29–31). Transit issues and political and commercial relationships that were previously handled in the framework of vertical and largely hierarchical relations between Moscow and its satellite states became more complex, and these issues became important factors in the political and economic calculations of governments and companies. At the time of the Soviet Union's collapse, about 80 percent of Russian gas exports to Europe ran through Ukrainian infrastructures. After the collapse of the Soviet Union, Ukraine, like the other Soviet Union republics, gained control over the branch of the former Soviet gas system in its territory; the Soviet gas industry assets were transferred to a new national company, Naftogaz, in 1998. Moreover, the Ukraine route proved to be problematic, with disputes arising in the 1990s over gas prices, payments and accumulated debts (e.g. Balmaceda 2008; Yafimava 2011; Pirani 2012).

In this environment, it made sense for Gazprom and its major Western partners to explore the possibility of alternative routes in order to diversify transit risks and reduce the bargaining power of the main gateway for Russian exports into European markets. The practical realisation of this strategy began in 1994 with the construction of the Yamal-Europe pipeline, which would export Russian gas to north-eastern Germany through Belarus and Poland; it was completed in 1997 (Figure 3.1). The implementation of this new route was facilitated by a combination of political and economic factors (Victor and Victor 2006). Commercially, the new route would serve the growing northern and eastern German gas market, and it was backed by long-term contracts between Gazprom and its clients. Politically, Poland's convergence with Europe guaranteed its reliability as a transit country. Poland was also expected to become an important final market for Russian gas, and although the Polish government was wary of excessive energy dependence on Moscow, the new gas supplies enabled Poland to expand gas consumption in the electricity sector, which was still strongly dependent on coal. Furthermore, the project would connect the Polish grid with the German gas market, strengthening the ties between the two countries.

The new route across Belarus and Poland represented an innovation, not only because it involved new transit countries, but also in terms of the companies involved in the project and their strategies. Instead of its traditional partner, Ruhrgas, this time Gazprom cooperated with Wintershall, a subsidiary of the Basf group, and through the creation of a joint venture, Wingas, the Russian company gained direct access to the downstream German gas sector. With this move, Gazprom was pursuing a strategy of vertical integration into the liberalising European market to gain a larger share of the final price paid by consumers for Russian gas.

During the 1990s, the German energy market saw the introduction of some competition. The Yamal-Europe pipeline received an important boost when the largest user of gas in Germany, Basf, decided to take direct action to find alternative supplies, cheaper and more convenient than those offered by Ruhrgas. The new pipeline project and the joint venture with Gazprom were in line with the commercial strategies of both companies. The German government welcomed limited competition, although it also took care that the new entrants did not excessively penalise the traditional incumbent, Ruhrgas. Externally, the project took advantage of the long-standing relations Berlin and Moscow had established in the energy sector, and Russia welcomed a project that would diversify export routes away from the problematic Ukraine.

South-North Corridor

During the 1990s, the international politics of pipeline was conducted according to the traditional framework of the partner state and triangular diplomacy along the South-North corridor as well, despite some important changes in the energy markets of Southern European consumers. In Italy, the most important player in the development of new pipeline projects was, as previously, ENI, supported by the diplomatic and political efforts of the government. At the national level, there were significant opportunities to expand gas consumption, especially in the electricity sector, as a result of the abandonment of nuclear power in 1987, the development of combined-cycle technology and the phasing out of fuel oil power plants (Honoré 2013). Domestic reforms had begun to liberalise the national energy markets, and the previous state-owned monopolies, Enel and ENI, were partly privatised (with state ownership still predominant). However, competition was still underdeveloped, and there were no players that could effectively contend with

ENI's leading position in the domestic gas sector. Thus, the main issue for the incumbent was to turn abroad to ensure an adequate supply for the growing national consumption. This strategy was also consistent with the traditional expectations of the government, which delegated responsibility for the security of the country's gas supply to ENI.

At the international level, ENI relied on its previous relationships to develop new pipeline projects and pursued a gas agreement with Libya. ENI began its negotiations with the Libyan government and its energy arm, the National Oil Corporation (NOC), in the early 1990s, with the aim of constructing a subsea pipeline (the Green Stream) from Libya to Sicily, in southern Italy (Figure 3.1). However, in 1992–93, Libya became the target of multilateral sanctions by the United Nations (UN) following the Lockerbie incident, reinforcing the unilateral sanctions that had been applied by the US since 1986. The UN sanctions confirmed the international isolation of the Gaddafi regime and its blacklisting as a 'rogue state', putting the entire project at risk. Without formally violating the sanctions, Italy continued to maintain its relationship with the Libyan government, which rested on its colonial legacy, geographical proximity and oil and commercial interests. ENI and the NOC reached a preliminary agreement in 1996, but the practical implementation of the project was very complicated because of the UN and the US sanctions still in place. In the same year, the Italian government of Romano Prodi decided to increase dialogues with Libya in order to reintegrate it into the international community (Coralluzzo 2008, 120–122). In April 1999, Gaddafi handed over the two suspected Lockerbie terrorists to international justice, partly thanks to the mediation of the Italian government, and in exchange, the UN sanctions were immediately suspended. With Libya reintegrated into the international community, the construction of the pipeline project was accelerated. And, as in the previous period, Italian energy security and foreign policy in the Mediterranean Sea reinforced each other. The Libyan and Italian governments actively supported the project, while the operational details and practical implementation were handled by the NOC and ENI, which established a joint company to build and manage the pipeline system, which finally came into operation in 2004.[5]

During the 1990s, the Spanish gas and electricity markets were also opened to competition. This new environment encouraged investment, especially in the new gas-fired power generation, and stimulated growing gas demand. The liberalisation of the Spanish market paved the way for the emergence of an important new market player, Gas Natural. This company was created in 1992 by the merging of various regional companies and different gas pipeline shares from the Spanish oil company Repsol. Gas Natural, seeking to expand its business in the liberalised domestic market, pushed through an agreement with Sonatrach for a pipeline leading from the Algerian Hassi R'Mel gas fields to Morocco and then under the sea at the Straits of Gibraltar to connect with Spain and Portugal – a route that had already been discussed but abandoned in the previous decade (Hayes 2006). The new pipeline – the Gazoduc Maghreb Europe pipeline, or GME, also known as the 'Pedro Duran Farell pipeline' – was completed in few years, and it began to supply Algerian gas to Spain and Portugal in 1996 and 1997, respectively (Figure 3.1).

Commercially, the project was backed by long-term contracts between Sonatrach, the Spanish company Enagas and the Portuguese company Transgas. Politically, the pipeline received several forms of support from the Spanish government. First, Madrid acted at the international level to support the negotiations between Gas Natural (which purchased 90 percent of Enagas from the Spanish state in 1994) and Sonatrach, and also facilitated the negotiations over the pipeline sections in Algeria and Morocco. Second, the Spanish government played an important role in 'creating' gas demand at the national level. In this period, the government enacted a National Energy Plan that incentivised the conversion of part of the existing power generation capacity to gas. This plan helped increase natural gas consumption in Spain from about 6 bcm in 1992 to 15 bcm at the beginning of the 2000s (Esmap 2003). Finally, the government took direct action to finance the pipeline section in Morocco through a company, Sagane, which was created by the Spanish public sector for this purpose. The GME pipeline received also the support of the EU, which funded its feasibility study under the TEN-E programme. In addition, the European Investment Bank (EIB) provided more than 1.1 billion Euros for various sections of the pipeline, including some located outside Europe. The EIB financing provided a significant part of the project's capital requirements and facilitated the mobilisation of funds from other sources (Esmap 2003).

The Emerging Institutional Framework of EU Security of Gas Supply

Challenging the Original Model: The European Commission vs. National Champions

Due to the strong resistance of many member states and gas industries – which regarded the introduction of liberalisation 'as the equivalent of the end of civilisation' (Stern 1998, 91) – the move towards the IEM and the market paradigm of energy policy could only gradually challenge the institutional and power structures of the European gas market. However, the liberalisation of the gas sector – promoted by the gas directives of the 1990s and the 2000s, which focussed on unbundling and Third Party Access (TPA) – along with the European Commission's involvement in energy diplomacy and infrastructure development (including oversight of IGAs and the TEN-E framework) increasingly began to put pressure on the main building blocks of the original partner state model, specifically: the monopolistic (or quasi-monopolistic) features of national gas markets and their vertically integrated industrial structures; the practice of direct government intervention in the regulation of gas industries; the national bilateral energy diplomacy and foreign policy support for the national champions; and the close linkage between the commercial interest of national champions and a country's long-term energy security strategy. Other factors contributed to challenging the original model, such as economic dynamics (e.g. the maturation of European gas markets and declining demand for gas), the decentralisation of energy governance and the spread of principles and practices related to environmental protection

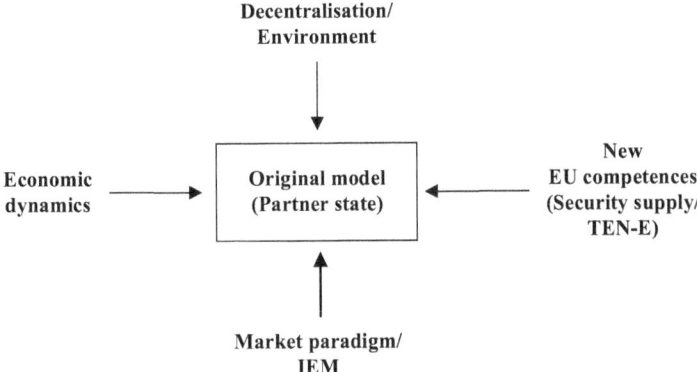

Figure 3.2 The main challenges to the partner-state model in the European gas sector.

(Figure 3.2). But the European Commission's willingness to complete the IEM represented a major attack on the existing equilibrium between states and markets.

As we saw, during the second part of the 1990s and the first part of the 2000s, the model of the partner state resisted: despite some limited changes in the market environment of EU member states, the partner state model continued to characterise the politics of pipeline development. The larger Western consumers, such as Italy, Germany and France, accepted limited liberalisation of their gas sectors but continued to support their national champions domestically and internationally. Similarly, member states that were more supportive of liberalisation, such as Spain and the Netherlands, did not hesitate to defend their own domestic energy companies from external takeover (as witnessed by the Spanish government's opposition to the German E.On bid for Endesa) or their bilateral energy policies (Youngs 2009). From the perspective of the member states, the establishment of the internal energy market was not seen in terms of rules-based development, as the European Commission believed, but as an opportunity for national champions to build Europe-wide 'corporate energy empires', supported by their home governments (Grätz 2009).

By the mid-2000s, many member states still rejected the European Commission's proposal to unbundle the gas industry because they anticipated that it would weaken the position of European gas companies vis-a-vis the producers' national companies. At the same time, many European governments – and again, especially the major importing countries in the continental European market, i.e. Germany, Italy and France – continued to regard bilateral deals as the best way to secure their gas supply. They also favoured asset swaps with non-European suppliers in order to guarantee their national companies access to the energy resources of producer countries. Commercially, European companies still regarded long-term contracts as the main tool for promoting new infrastructure and the stability and predictability of gas flows and prices. Between 2004 and 2006, in anticipation of further development in the IEM, the major Gazprom clients in Western Europe (ENI, GDF, OMV, E.On and Ruhrgas) – which were also the dominant players in their respective national markets – extended their long-term contracts (or signed new ones) to 2020–35 and established joint ventures with the Russian monopolist (Locatelli 2008).

Against this background, the European Commission decided to push the liberalisation agenda in order to overcome the limits of the First and Second Energy Packages, challenge the power of national champions and promote a more common approach to energy security. In the eyes of the Commission, the problems of energy security and market integration were strictly interconnected: member states would only embrace a more common approach towards external energy relations if the EU internal market was completely integrated. To this end, the European Commission took a two-fold approach, incorporating antitrust pressure and legislative proposals (Buchan 2011, 364–368). In 2005, it launched a competition inquiry into the energy sector. Then, between 2006 and 2007, the European Commission's DG Competition initiated formal antitrust investigations against several national incumbents for anticompetitive practices in their home markets. This pressure was accompanied by a legislative proposal for a Third Energy Package in 2007. The new proposal focused on enhancing ownership unbundling, the powers of national energy regulators and the European Commission's role in the oversight of the internal energy market.

There was an important contrast between the approach of the European Commission and traditional European gas consumers regarding the opening of the market as a possible tool to enhance security of gas supply. In September 2007, the European Commission proposed the inclusion of a reciprocity clause – the so-called 'Gazprom clause' – in the Third Energy Package. Initially, the European Commission's proposal – supported mainly by Poland and Lithuania (Raszewski 2012) – suggested a clause that would completely prevent any third-country companies from acquiring control over transmission assets in the EU unless this was permitted by an agreement between the EU and the third state on mutual market access to transmission assets. A similar provision would practically stop asset swaps between non-EU companies – such as Gazprom – and European companies. France, Italy and Germany argued against this provision by pointing out the need for any internal market liberalisation to be matched by 'negotiated reciprocity in producers' states' (Young 2009, 38). For these countries, bilateral deals remained the preferred strategy for securing such reciprocity; if the 'carrot' of downstream access was removed from their toolboxes, their ability to enter the producer's upstream sector, and their overall security of supply, would have been weakened. Due to this resistance, the original Commission's proposal was reviewed, but companies from third countries were now obliged to comply with the same unbundling requirements and limitations as the EU companies. That is to say, third-country companies, like Gazprom, now would have to prove their subsidiaries' compliance with effective unbundling regulations to the national regulatory authorities (NRAs) in order to be involved in the gas transmission systems of EU member states. NRAs can prevent this involvement by refusing to 'certify' the Transmission System Operators (TSOs) – according to Third Energy Package 'each undertaking which owns a transmission system acts as a transmission system operator' (Directive 2009/73/EC, Art. 9) – when a company does not comply with EU unbundling rules or when 'the security of energy supply of the member state and the Community' is 'put at risk' (Directive 2009/73/EC, Art. 11). NRAs, however, have to consult the European Commission prior to granting or rejecting an applicant TSO's 'certification'. At the end, in 2009, thanks to this and other changes in the original proposal and despite the initial opposition, the Third Energy Package was approved, and it entered into force in 2011.[6]

This new legislation provides for TPA to the networks regulated by NRAs – whose powers and independence were strengthened – and for three different models for unbundling vertically integrated companies. These three models resulted from a compromise negotiated by EU institutions and member states. They are the ownership unbundling (OU) model, the Independent System Operator (ISO) model and the Independent Transmission Operator (ITO) model.[7] NRAs can grant exemptions from TPA rules and other provisions of the Third Energy Package (on unbundling, for example) for a defined period of time for particularly risky investment projects, such as cross-border gas pipelines or LNG terminals, which could not be implemented if the usual rules were applied. However, these temporary exemptions must be approved by the European Commission and must fulfil a specific set of criteria, including improving security of supply and enhancing competition in the gas market (Directive 2009/73/EC, Art. 36). Other important elements introduced with the Third Energy Package, which have enhanced the role of the European Commission in oversight matters previously delegated to member states and national regulatory authorities, are the Agency for the Cooperation of Energy Regulators (ACER) and the European Network of Transmission System Operators for Gas (ENTSO-G).[8]

To sum up, the Third Energy Package devoted particular attention to infrastructure development and strengthened the regulatory powers of the European Commission. These powers now include oversight of the application of EU rules and antitrust and competition policy but also other important tasks. The European Commission can decide on temporary exemptions from certain provisions of the Third Energy Package (in this case the European Commission prevails over national regulators, while national regulators can grant certification for TSO status); on the award of the 'Project of Common Interest' (PCI) status under the TEN-E scheme (where the European Commission adopts PCI lists); and, finally, the European Commission can oversee the IGAs signed by member states and third countries (in this case the European Commission has the power to request amendments or cancellations)[9] (Pirani and Yafimava 2016). However, these regulatory powers, which allow the European Commission to promote as well as block or delay new pipeline projects, apply only within EU borders. By the beginning of the 2010s, the EU had intensified its efforts to 'speak with one voice' and to develop an EU-level energy diplomacy. Despite these efforts, beyond EU borders, diversification of supply and pipeline politics has continued to be strongly influenced by the decisions of member states and the strategies of companies and third countries.

It is worth noting that during this power struggle between the European Commission and member states, other important transformations were occurring in the EU gas markets. The 2008 economic crisis, coupled with other developments such as the diffusion of renewables in electricity generation and the arrival of cheap imported coal, paved the way for the emergence of a new market environment characterised by declining gas demand – especially in the major EU markets (i.e. Germany, Italy, France, Spain and the UK) (2010) – and, post-2014, by declining energy prices. This context prompted many European companies to renegotiate their long-term contracts and add more flexibility to gas trade. This trend was reinforced in the following years, challenging the previous oil-linked pricing regime in favour of hub prices and gas-to-gas competition, especially in the markets of Northwestern Europe (Stern and Rogers 2011, 2014). In 2013, oil-indexation accounted for less than half of total EU gas consumption, although it still dominated Central Europe, the Mediterranean region and Southeastern Europe and was the preferred solution for important traditional suppliers, such as Russia and Algeria, and new ones, such as Qatar (DG Energy 2014). In 2015, the move towards gas-to-gas competition was going on in all the EU markets, although still with a faster pace in Northwestern Europe (IGU 2015).

Diversification of Supply, Pipeline Politics and the Catalytic State

The innovations of the Third Energy Package and the enhanced regulatory powers of the European Commission consolidated the overarching EU institutional framework for security of gas supply. This framework particularly seeks to encourage cross-border pipeline development through the regulatory incentives in the Third Energy Package – such as exemptions from the TPA rule – and financial and other forms of regulatory support in the TEN-E scheme managed by the European Commission. However, the EU's direct financial support is far from the past practices of the partner state and is still in line with the logic of the market approach. First of all, EU financial support for infrastructure development is intended to promote security of supply but also competition in the internal market, and it provides very limited contributions (mainly for feasibility studies) to the projects.[10] In addition, this contribution is intended only for those projects that demonstrates 'clearly market failures' which would prevent private investment to be undertaken (European Commission 2010). This principle, stated in the 2006 TEN-E guidelines (Decision 1364/2006/EC, which repealed the previous 96/391/EC and 1229/2003/EC decisions), was confirmed in the new 2013 TEN-E guidelines by Regulation 347/2013. Indeed, Regulation 347/2013 clearly states that the 'market should have the priority to invest', then 'if investments are not made by the market, regulatory solutions should be explored', and only if these two steps are not sufficient, 'Union financial assistance could be granted'.[11] Regulation 347/2013 also addresses the problems of local opposition and delays for major energy infrastructure by providing common rules and standard procedures for authorisation and permitting processes to be implemented by member states (along with new rules to foster cost allocation across borders). Basically, according to the market approach, with regard to pipeline development, the EU should create a common regulatory environment with clear and transparent criteria, and the primary role of the member states is to provide an effective regulatory framework and enforce procedures that guarantee the certainty of investment returns to companies involved in the projects. As pointed out by the European Commission, 'permitting procedures have proved to be complex and time-consuming', while the 'volatile regulatory and legal environment in several member states has been having negative consequences on the certainty of the investment return', and these elements have contributed to freezes on the implementation of the major European trans-boundary pipeline projects (European Commission 2014).

The aforementioned developments challenged the instruments and strategies previously used by European governments even more. The model of partner state had already been undermined by the transformations occurring in European gas markets and, politically, confronted by increasing local opposition to energy infrastructure and the decentralisation of energy decision-making in several member states. However, despite the member states' acceptance of the further move towards the market approach with the Third Energy Package, they were very far from disengaging with energy diplomacy and pipeline politics. In other words, the breakdown of the partner state model did not pave the way for the emergence of the provider state in matters of diversification of supply: the reconfiguration in the state-market equilibrium and in the actors' constellation resulted in a set of interactions better represented by the catalytic state model.

Chapter 1 described the main features of this model and stressed that the catalytic state and the related (hexagonal) network diplomacy framework provide an alternative to the market approach and to the traditional practice of the partner state for understanding the new politics of energy security in Europe (see Figure 1.2 and Table 1.1 in Chapter 1). The next sections will present empirical evidence that illustrates the merits of this model in the areas of pipeline politics and diversification of supply. Four political dynamics revealing the 'rise of the catalytic-state' and the emergence of new patterns of interactions in line with the hexagonal diplomacy framework will be highlighted: i) governments' creation of coalitions to promote or defend their preferred energy security options in the EU multi-layered political-diplomatic environment; ii) the new 'indirectly supportive' relationships between governments and energy companies; iii) companies' activation to gain support at the EU level; and iv) the new local dimension of pipeline politics and the work of governments at this level, mediating between energy companies and local actors to enable the realisation of projects. Those dynamics coexist with the traditional government-to-government and company-to-company negotiations and illustrate how national governments act as facilitators in the implementation of their preferred energy projects.

In what follows, the emergence of the catalytic state and new patterns of interactions in line with the hexagonal diplomacy framework will be illustrated, first in the case of the South-North gas corridor, then in the case of the East-West corridors – where, however, the new dynamics interact with crucial political events such as the Russian-Ukrainian gas crisis, the war in Eastern Ukraine and the Russian annexation of the Crimea – and finally, in the case of the Southern Gas Corridor. In this latter case, the rise of the catalytic state seems particularly evident. This can be explained by the fact that, unlike the other corridors, this one represents an entirely new route for European gas supplies, so path dependence and policy legacies play a minor role in this case.

The South-North Corridor and the First Move towards the Catalytic State

As noted above, the EU multilateral framework has not been effective in energy relations with Algeria and Libya, and these countries have resisted the exportation of EU rules and principles. During the 2000s, the larger southern European consumers, France, Italy and Spain, developed their energy relations with Algiers and Tripoli on a bilateral and often competitive basis. Each of them has tried to strengthen its energy ties with these producers and win advantageous deals for its own energy companies. However, in this case – which, at least in these aspects, was not so different from the competitive, bilateral energy approach to Northern Africa in the Cold War period – pipeline politics developed with some new peculiarities that stemmed mainly from the changing domestic market environment in the EU countries.

At the beginning of the 2000s, the further liberalisation of the Italian and Spanish energy markets gave the possibilities to new entrants, mainly electricity companies, to challenge the predominant position of the traditional incumbents (ENI and Enagas-Gas Natural) and secure their own gas needs by creating new pipeline infrastructures to directly access North African resources. In particular, two projects appeared on the agenda and were discussed by governments and energy companies. The first, the so-called Medgaz, was a subsea pipeline connecting the Algerian Hassi R'Mel gas fields with Spain near Almeria with a capacity of 8 bcm/y (a project that, as the GME pipeline, had already been considered in the previous decades) (Figure 3.1). The second, the so-called Galsi, was a new pipeline route to connect the same Algerian fields with the Italian market (Figure 3.1). It ended in the Sardinian Region and also had an 8 bcm/y capacity. Both projects were initially formulated without the involvement of the traditional incumbents and attracted the interest of different national and European companies. Both projects were also supported by their respective national governments, which were interested in promoting competition in the now-liberalised domestic market and ensuring additional supply for tapping the expected increases in gas consumption. At the EU level, Rome and Madrid promoted the inclusion of these gas infrastructures as a project of 'European interest' under the TEN framework recently established by Decision No. 1364/2006/EC. Internationally, the Italian and Spanish governments negotiated bilaterally with Algeria to support the companies' efforts and facilitate the completion of the pipelines. Although, eventually, only Medgaz was realised (Galsi encountered some problems and was suspended), these two pipelines illustrate the emergence of some new political dynamics in line with the catalytic state model. In both cases, national governments took action to facilitate the realisation of the project, with diplomatic support at the EU and the international level. National governments also indirectly supported a coalition of energy companies that were not the traditional incumbents (although in Spain, Gas Natural eventually took part in the Medgaz project). Moreover, especially in Italy, local politics was an issue in pipeline development, and the intervention of public authorities (in this case, the regional government) was important to enable the implementation of the project.

The (Uncompleted) Galsi Pipeline

The Galsi pipeline project dates back to 2003, when the Galsi company was established with the participation of the Algerian company Sonatrach (36 percent); the German company Wintershall (13.5 percent); the Italian company Edison (18 percent), Enel (13.5 percent); Hera (9 percent); and the Italian Sardinian regional government, through its financial company, Sfirs (10 percent). This project was opposed by ENI, which until 2005 consistently claimed that the growth of the Italian gas market did not warrant new import pipelines, warning of an impending 'gas bubble'.[12] On this basis, the company refused to participate and lobbied against Galsi (Luciani and Mazzanti 2006). In 2006, after company-to-company negotiations, Sonatrach signed some important long-term supply contracts with the Italian firms involved in the project. On 16 November 2007, the Italian and Algerian governments signed an intergovernmental agreement recognising the 'strategic importance' of the pipeline – both for 'improving the Italian energy security of supply and to commercialise Algerian gas' – and committing themselves to facilitate all the necessary authorisations for the project.[13] The first gas was expected to arrive in Sardinia by the end of 2014, and the authorisation process, which involved the regional and national government, was completed in 2012.

Sardinia is the only Italian region that is not served by natural gas, and the participation of the regional government in the project was important to accelerate the authorisation processes and to overcome local opposition. The Italian Constitutional Reform of 2001 included energy as a subject of competing legislation between central and regional governments. It challenged the centralised institutional structure that had previously presided over the functioning of energy markets and redistributed decision-making power to sub-state actors.[14] This development, coupled with the growing public awareness about the environmental impact of localised energy infrastructures, resulted in a new pattern of energy politics in which regional governments and local communities could, potentially, veto the implementation of projects. During the second half of the 2000s, institutional conflicts over energy issues between the Italian state and regional governments increased dramatically, as did demonstrations against large energy infrastructural projects by citizens, citizen committees, civil society organisations and local governments (Prontera 2015). A 2009 policy paper written for the Italian Ministry of Foreign Affairs by a group of experts identified authorisation processes as the major 'risk factor' for country's energy security strategy.[15]

In the case of Galsi, however, local issues were effectively addressed. But at the end of the 2000s, new developments began to undermine the strategies of companies and the Italian government and eventually halted the project. After the 2008 global financial crisis, it became clear that the evolution of Italian gas consumption would not proceed as expected at the beginning of the 2000s. The Italian economic downturn, along with increases in renewable electricity generation, resulted in stagnant gas demand. For the first time since the origin of the Italian gas market, the prospect of a 'structural excess of supply' was contemplated by analysts and regulators (AEEG 2009; Scarpa 2012). On the other hand, also Algeria was encountering many internal problems to implement its export strategy owing to a stagnant gas production and an increasing domestic gas consumption (Aissaoui 2016). In this new market environment, the Galsi pipeline was first postponed in 2010 and then suspended in 2014 (in May 2014, the Sardinian region decided to leave the Galsi consortium). On May 2015, the idea of the Galsi project was relaunched again during a meeting between the Italian Prime Minister Matteo Renzi and the Algeria's Prime Minister Abdelmalek Sellal.[16] However, the structural problems that led to its suspension have not yet been resolved and no concrete steps for its realisation have been taken afterwards.

The (Completed) Medgaz Pipeline

Medgaz was originally proposed in 2001 by a joint venture between the Spanish oil company Cepsa, which was already involved in upstream Algerian oil, and Sonatrach. The project was then joined by other companies – the Spanish Iberdrola (20 percent) and Endesa (12 percent) and the French GDF (12 percent) (as a result, Sonatrach's share was reduced to 36 percent and Cepsa's to 20 percent) – and long-term contracts for a total volume of 8 bcm/y were signed, paving the way for the realisation of the pipeline. However, in the following years, the project encountered various problems. The shareholder composition changed, and in 2007, Gas Natural, with the support of the Spanish government, decided to participate in the project, taking a 10 percent share from Sonatrach.[17] It is worth noting here that in the mid-2000s, with the ongoing liberalisation of the EU market, the Algerian Sonatrach aspired to enter the European downstream sector. This strategy, however, met with resistance from several member states, such as Spain, France and Italy, and contributed to the tensions between Algeria and the EU (Proedrou 2012). In Spain's case, these tensions were additionally reinforced by the Zapatero government's foreign policy regarding the Western Sahara question. Algeria's President Bouteflika considered Spain's position on the Sahara question too markedly pro-Moroccan, and that has been interpreted as a factor contributing to Algeria's energy price increases (by about 20 percent) to Spain (Darbouche 2007). To address these problems, the Spanish government engaged in complex negotiations with Algeria around the ownership structure of Medgaz (to avoid Sonatrach gaining the majority share of the pipeline) and Sonatrach's expansion in the Spanish market. These bilateral negotiations allowed Spain and Algeria to reach a compromise, paving the way for the realisation of Medgaz. Pipeline construction started in 2008 and the first gas was transported to the Spanish market in 2011 (Medgaz is the last infrastructure built along the South-North corridor).

Nord Stream, South Stream and EU-Russia Energy Interdependence

The collapse of Soviet Union brought the issue of transit countries into East-West energy interdependence. This development was already evident in the 1990s, when Gazprom and Germany, the major European consumer of Russian gas, decided to create the first route that bypassed Ukraine. However, in the aftermath of the 2004 and 2007 EU Eastern Enlargements, the issue of gas transit and diversification of pipeline routes acquired a more important political status. With the Eastern Enlargements, the EU's security of supply strategy had to consider the needs and concerns of the new member states in Eastern Europe and the Baltic. These states were strongly dependent on Russian supplies and had a different perspective on EU-Russia interdependence than the major Western consumers. In particular, Germany and Italy, by far the larger importers of Russian gas, have a long tradition in managing their relationships with Russian companies and tend to consider Moscow a reliable supplier. They also learnt, during the Cold War period, to manage their energy interdependence with Russia in periods of high political tension, and to generally consider energy – and commercial – relations with Moscow a way of easing those tensions, as well as an important opportunity for their own economic development. For obvious historical reasons, the new EU members have a very different perspective on EU-Russian energy and political relations. Furthermore, their gas markets are smaller than those of Western consumers, and their political, economic and international weight results in a very different perception of the risks of excessive dependence on Russian supplies. While the Western Europe-Russian interdependence is a more balanced and symmetrical relation, the asymmetries are striking in Eastern Europe and the Baltic region. Traditionally, Russia and Russian energy companies have been very careful to be reliable commercial partners for their large, lucrative Western markets. But with countries of the former Soviet Union and Soviet bloc, Russia has adopted a more assertive strategy, in some cases using energy trade to exert political pressure or oppose unwelcome commercial strategies (Aalto 2008; Balmaceda 2012, 2013).

Moreover, since the 2005 Orange Revolution, relations between Russia and Ukraine have deteriorated, with important effects on gas trade to and through Ukraine and on Eastern countries' perception of the Russian approach to energy and international politics in its former sphere of influence. A first gas dispute took place in 2006. As we saw, the practical impact of this event on European consumers was limited but, following the dispute, when the European Commission adopted, in 2008, the *Second Strategic Review – An EU Energy Security and Solidarity Action Plan,* it made plain its desire to diversify EU sources of gas through a 'Southern Corridor' (European Commission 2008). In this context, the Nabucco pipeline – which had already been proposed in 2002 by a consortium composed of the Turkish company Botas, the Bulgarian Energy Holding, Transgaz (Romania), MOL (Hungary), OMV (Austria) and RWE (Germany) and was intended to bring gas from South Caucasus, Turkmenistan and possibly Iran to Europe – officially emerged as a priority in Brussels (De Micco 2015). Since then, the development of the Southern gas corridor and the Nabucco project have interacted with events on the East-West energy corridor and EU-Russia gas relations. In this section, however, I will focus mainly on the latter corridor, and the politics of pipeline along the Southern Corridor will be analysed in the next section.

After 2006, the dispute between Moscow and Kiev continued, and a second and more important crisis took place in 2009, when Russia cut off all gas flows to Ukraine. Shortfalls were felt especially in certain Eastern EU member states (Bulgaria, Romania, Austria and the Czech Republic) and in the Balkans.[18] When, eventually, the war broke up in Eastern Ukraine and Russia annexed the Crimea in March 2014 – triggering the application of EU (and US) economic sanctions to Moscow – the deterioration of Ukrainian-Russia relations had already manifested its effects on pipeline routes and regional energy politics.

Russia's annexation of the Crimea has only further aggravated the clash, already latent, which divides 'old' and 'new' member states and is grounded in different perceptions about the risks of gas dependency on Moscow. This new political context interacts with the broader changes occurring in the EU gas market. Two main phases can be identified to illustrate the transformation of the politics of pipeline along the East-West corridor that started with the beginning of the new millennium, after the short window of opportunity to integrate the Russian market into a common set of rules and principles closed with Moscow's withdrawal from the ECT and the renationalisation of energy assets under Putin's presidency. The first phase – from the beginning of the 2000s to the beginning of the 2010s – is marked by efforts to realise a new kind of 'strategic partnership' between Gazprom and its traditional Western clients, in a market environment in which European demand was expected to grow steadily and in which Russian supplies would need to match that growth.[19] Commercially, this approach is characterised by asset swaps between Gazprom and its main European clients who had signed long-term gas contracts.[20] These agreements potentially allowed Gazprom to penetrate the liberalised EU downstream sector in exchange for Moscow's permission for the major European energy companies to access the protected Russian upstream energy sector. Pipeline development in this approach is based on company-to-company negotiation, backed by government-to-government deals and long-term contracts, and it is well represented by the Nord Stream project (launched in 2005) and South Stream, which was launched in 2007 and was a competitor of the Nabucco. At first glance, the political dynamics behind these projects – largely based on bilateral relations between Germany and Russia and Italy and Russia and their respective energy companies – seem to mirror the traditional practices of the partner state. However, both projects have to be understood in relation to the new EU market, regulatory and political-diplomatic environment, characterised, especially as demonstrated by the case of the South Stream, by the growing activism of the European Commission in energy diplomacy and pipeline politics.

The second phase begins with the entry of the Third Energy Package into force in 2011, continues with the European Commission's challenge of Gazprom's position in the EU market, and then takes off with the 2014 crisis in Ukraine, the annexation of the Crimea and the cancellation of the South Stream. This period is also marked by a new market environment. Indeed, the slump in EU gas demand after the 2008 economic crisis and the completion of Nord Stream changed the outlook of the EU gas market to the point that there were few doubts that the total pipeline capacity for Russian export to Europe was far greater than required for the foreseeable future, and that the real issue was whether or not it was necessary to partially diversify away from Ukraine[21] (Pirani and Yafimava 2016). These events have challenged the previous 'strategic partnership' approach, opening a period with more fluid and uncertain political dynamics. On one hand, Russia has pushed its export diversification strategy in order to avoid the Ukrainian route. First, Moscow proposed the Turkish Stream, a pipeline that would have been based on commercial rather than strategic relations between Gazprom and its clients (in this plan, Gazprom would only have focused on bringing gas to EU borders without necessarily entering the liberalised EU market). When, however, this project encountered problems due to the deterioration of Moscow-Ankara relations after Turkey shot down a Russian military jet over the Syrian border, Russia turned to its traditional partner, Germany, proposing the Nord Stream 2.[22] The Nord Stream 2 was confirmed also when the Turkish Stream was relaunched in August 2016, in the wake of the rapprochement between Putin and the Turkish President Erdogan after the failed coup in Turkey. Meanwhile, Gazprom had also begun to implement asset swaps with its main Western clients – in late 2015 with the German Wintershall and at the beginning of 2016 with the Austrian OMV – although, in the new EU market context, its long-term contractual strategy began to change as competition from hub gas prices was increasing. On the other hand, the European Commission, in the wake of the general deterioration in EU-Russia relations, has begun to use its regulatory power and competition policy more assertively, targeting Gazprom's strategy. After the approval of the Energy Union in 2015, the European Commission has also assumed a more negative position towards any Russia diversification projects intended to reduce gas transit through Ukraine, including Nord Stream 2.

To sum up, the two phases are marked by some differences with regard to the political, economic and regulatory environment underpinning gas trade relations between the EU and Russia, but what they have in common are the efforts made by Gazprom and some of its traditional Western European clients to diversify export routes away from the 'problematic' Ukraine. Figure 3.3 below offers a simplified timeline of the main events that have affected the politics of pipeline along the East-West corridor between 2005 and 2016. An indepth analysis of the different phases mentioned here follows in the next sections.

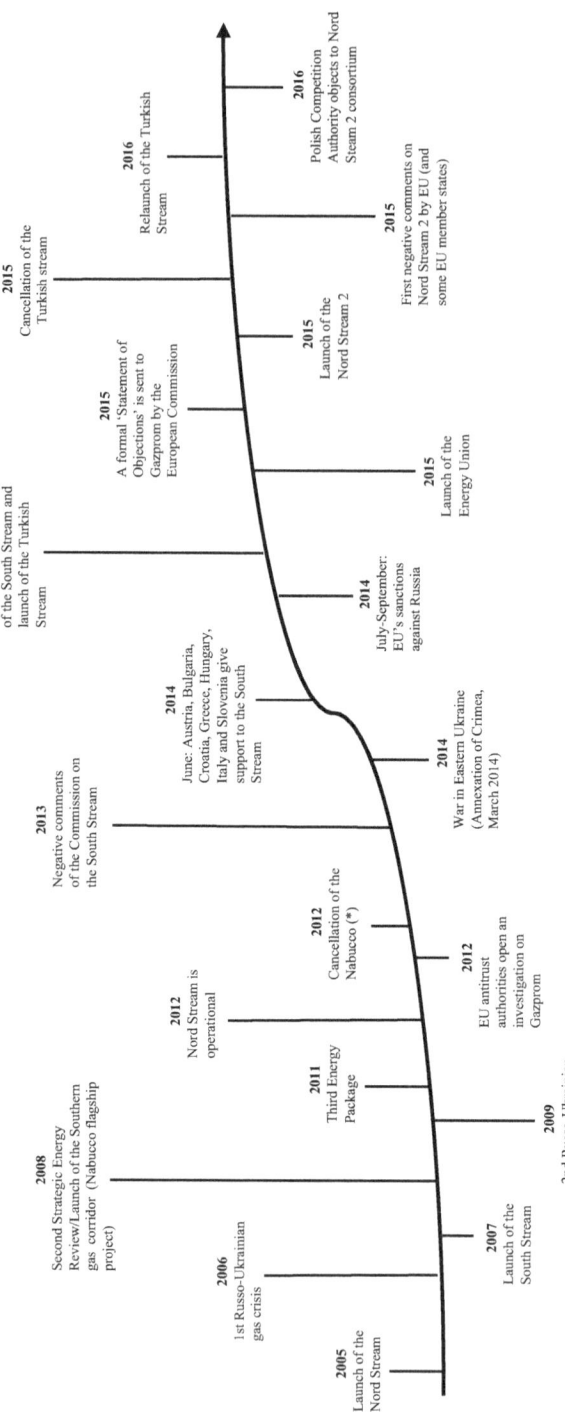

Figure 3.3 East-West gas corridor: timeline of the major events (2005–16).

Sources: De Micco (2015) and author's own elaboration.

Note: (*) = In 2012 Nabucco was reshaped into the Nabucco West project; Nabucco West was cancelled in 2013.

Strategic Partnership and Transit Diversification Away From Ukraine

In 2003, Gazprom's diversification strategy had already targeted the Turkish market with the construction of the Blue Stream, which ran from Russian territory under the Black Sea to export gas directly to Turkey (see Figure 3.1). This solution proved effective for tapping the growing Turkish demand for gas: in the following years, the pipeline reached its maximum capacity of 16 bcm/y, and Ankara became the third largest consumer of Russian gas in terms of volume (after Germany and Italy). The next logical targets from Gazprom's point of view were then its first and second clients: Germany and Italy.

German-Russian Relations and the Nord Stream

By the end of the 1990s, the German market had been liberalised in accordance with EU policy, but the government did not give up its close relations with the major energy companies (Sander 2007; Westphal 2008, 99–102; Grätz 2009). Domestically, the government supported the restructuration of the electricity and gas sectors – such as in the case of the merger between E.On and Ruhrgas in 2003 – creating an oligopolistic structure with few major private companies that were able to compete in the European and international markets. Especially during the Schröder Government (1998–2005), the main guiding principle was still that managing external energy dependency required powerful companies and that security of supply could not be left exclusively in the hands of market dynamics (Westphal 2008). In Germany's relations with Russia, this approach was coherent with the strategies of the major German companies, E.On-Ruhrgas and Wintershall. These companies were interested in having the political and diplomatic support of their government, signing new gas deals with Gazprom and accessing the protected Russian upstream sector. These factors combined help explain the strengthening of the German-Russian energy partnership and the unwillingness of the German government to pursue a more multilateral approach to EU-Russia energy relations.

In 2005, Putin and Schröder signed an agreement for the realisation of the Nord Stream that clearly represents these dynamics, which seem to reproduce previous patterns of East-West energy relations in the new, liberalised, EU market. However, the development of the Nord Stream also illustrates the emergence of new dynamics interacting with the old ones. First of all, it is reductive to frame the Nord Stream as only a bilateral project based on German-Russian relations (Bendik 2008; Smith 2012; Svyatets 2016). Originally, the idea of building a pipeline under the Baltic Sea connecting Russia and Germany was proposed, in 1997, by Gazprom and the Finnish company Neste (which later became Fortum). A feasibility study for a route passing through the Exclusive Economic Zones (EEZs) of Finland, Sweden and Denmark was carried out in 1998. In 2001, Gazprom, Fortum and the German companies Ruhrgas and Wintershall reached an agreement for the construction of the pipeline. In 2005, after the Finnish company Fortum withdrew from the project, Gazprom signed an agreement with E.On and Wintershall, and in 2006, these three companies created Nord Stream AG, a joint company to manage and operate the two parallel lines composing the infrastructure. In the wake of the 2006 and 2009 Russian-Ukrainian gas crises, the consortium was enlarged: between 2007 and 2010, the Dutch company Gasunie and the French GDF-Suez acquired stakes in the project.[23] (Gazprom is the major shareholder of the Nord Stream AG consortium with 51 percent, followed by Wintershall and E.On with 15.5 percent each and Gasunie and GDF-Suez with 9 percent each.) As with the first route bypassing Ukraine, Yamal-Europe, Gazprom involved Wintershall but also another major German company, E.On, and two additional companies from other EU countries, in this case the Netherlands and France. Furthermore, before the pipelines were built, Gazprom had already signed long-term contracts with customers in several member states, including Germany, Denmark, the Netherlands, Belgium, France and the UK. The enlargement of the Nord Stream consortium had both an economic rationale, as it helped to assure a final market for the incoming Russian gas, and a political logic. Broadening the coalition involved in the pipelines, and especially including other European companies, was important to increase support at the European level and minimise the risks of opposition from the European Commission.

In 2000, the Nord Stream had already been included by the European Commission in the TEN-E framework as a project of 'European interest', and the project's feasibility study was co-financed by the EU in 2003 and 2006. Although the project's status as one of European interest was confirmed again after the 2004 Eastern Enlargement, the Baltic States and Poland criticised it vigorously, stating that it was a major risk to their own energy security. In a report prepared in 2008 for the European Parliament, experts claimed that 'without the German involvement there would be likely to be problems with the TEN status, but with the active involvement of such a Member State, as evidenced by the bi-lateral agreement of 2005, the present status of the project would seem secure' (Lee et al. 2008, 11). Indeed, notwithstanding the continued opposition from Poland and the Baltic states (many concerns were also expressed by Ukraine and the US), the European Commission confirmed that the EU 'strongly' supported the Nord Stream 'as an additional source of gas supplies from Russia'.[24]

Another point of possible disagreement and tension was related to the environmental impact of the Nord Stream and the complex process of obtaining all the permissions necessary for laying down the pipeline in the Baltic Sea (Smith 2012, 124–126). The Nord Stream would pass through the EEZs of Finland, Sweden and Denmark (along with Germany and Russia), and a vocal campaign of protest was organised by several environmental NGOs (Greenpeace, WWF, the Baltic Fund for Nature etc.) (Svyatets 2016). However, in the end, despite some modifications to the original plan and the involvement of NGOs and local authorities in the environmental assessment process, in 2009, Denmark, Sweden and Finland granted their permission for the construction of the pipeline. Only Estonia, in 2007, rejected a request by the Nord Stream developers to carry out a seabed survey in its EEZ. But with the approval of the other countries, the construction of the pipeline began in 2010. The first line was completed in September 2011, and a second line was completed in 2012, when the Nord Stream reached its full capacity of 55 bcm/y.

The Nord Stream was officially inaugurated in November 2011, in a ceremony attended by the German Chancellor Angela Merkel, the French Prime Minister François Fillon and the Russian President Dimitry Medvedev. The ceremony was held in the German city of Lubmin, where the pipeline ends. The offshore section of the Nord Stream was connected to two onshore sections in the German territory, the OPAL and NEL pipelines, participated by German operators and by Gazprom (Figure 3.1). The Merkel government's support for the Nord Stream and for the increase of Gazprom's participation in the German gas sector demonstrate that the continuation of the Russian-Germany energy partnership was not an idiosyncratic result of the close relations between Schröder and Putin, but a long-term, broad strategy pursued by German political and economic actors. This strategy seems to have been confirmed again after the Russian annexation of the Crimea by the proposal of the Nord Stream 2 project in late 2015 and by the completion of Gazprom's total acquisition of Wingas (this operation also included an asset swap allowing the Basf group to obtain access to some Western Siberian oil and gas fields and Gazprom to access offshore fields developed by Wintershall in the Netherlands, Denmark and the UK).[25]

With the completion of this new route, Russian gas to Northwest and Central Europe was now mainly supplied through the Nord Stream and the Yamal-Europe pipeline, while much of the gas transiting through Ukraine was directed to Italy (25 bcm), with supplies also going to Austria (5 bcm), Hungary (6 bcm), Bulgaria (2.7 bcm), Greece (2.6 bcm), the Balkans and Turkey (13 bcm) (Pirani et al. 2014, 8). It is therefore not surprising that Italy, along with other countries in Southeast Europe, was the main supporter of another route to diversify Russian export away from Ukraine, i.e. the South Stream.

Italian-Russian Relations and the South Stream

While the Nord Stream was under development in 2006–07, the South Stream pipeline appeared on the agenda as another way to diversify Russian export routes away from Ukraine. This time Gazprom targeted the Southeastern European gas market and its second largest EU client: Italy. During the 2000s, the Italian energy sector had also been liberalised and restructured according to EU policy. But the former incumbent, ENI, continued to play an important role in energy security politics by exploiting its traditional position in the upstream and midstream supply chains and its influence in domestic politics (despite a partial privatisation, the Italian state still owned 30 percent of the company). In 2006, ENI and Gazprom signed a 'strategic partnership agreement', which gave Gazprom the opportunity to launch direct deliveries of Russian gas to the Italian market, and which contemplated extending existing contracts for gas supply to Italy to 2035. The agreement also opened the possibility that the two companies would work together on gas exploration and production projects in Russia and develop new gas transmission routes.[26]

ENI had already cooperated with Gazprom on the construction and operation of the Blue Stream, and in 2007, an agreement was reached regarding the construction of the South Stream. This pipeline, with the impetus provided by the Russia-Ukraine gas dispute of 2006, was intended to export Russian gas to Eastern and Southern Europe, bypassing Ukraine and passing through the Black Sea (with an offshore pipeline). The gas would reach Bulgaria and then other EU countries via an onshore route to be decided later; it would either travel southwards towards Greece and Italy or northwards towards Serbia, Hungary, Slovenia and Austria (Figure 3.1). The strong support of both governments in the negotiations signalled that Italy and Russia considered the project of strategic importance (Frappi and Varvelli 2010). Italian political support was first granted by the centre-left government of Romani Prodi and then reinforced in May 2009 by the new centre-right government when an agreement between the Italian Prime Minister Silvio Berlusconi and Vladimir Putin upgraded the original programmed capacity of the South Stream from 31 bcm/y to 63 bcm/y.

The upgrade of the project was partially in response to the second Russia-Ukraine gas crisis of January 2009, but it was also due to the very important role attributed to the South Stream in supplying not only the Italian market but the European one. Although the European Commission's approach to EU energy security was still focused on the Nabucco project and the Southern Gas Corridor, between 2009 and 2010, the governments of Austria, Bulgaria and Hungary signed bilateral transit IGAs with Russia. The South Stream was not included among the TEN-E projects of 'European interest' – a status that was instead accorded to Nabucco and other projects of the Southern Gas Corridor – but in 2011, the French EDF and the German Wintershall (already a partner with Gazprom in the North Stream) joined the South Stream AG consortium with a 15 percent share each, paving the way, in theory, for the pipeline's completion[27] (Sartori 2012). In the following years, the Nabucco project was first rescaled into Nabucco West in 2012, and then definitively abandoned in 2013. However, in the wake of the European Commission's opposition, the South Stream encountered many problems, and at the end of 2014, it was abandoned as well in favour of a new project, the so-called Turkish Stream.

From Strategic Partnerships towards a New Approach to European-Russian Gas Relations?

The strategic partnership approach, based on Gazprom's penetration into the EU gas markets, was undermined at the beginning of the 2010s by several developments. First of all, in 2011, with the entry of the Third Energy Package into force, the EU's regulatory environment worsened dramatically for Gazprom (Pirani et al. 2014; Stern, Pirani and Yafimava 2015). Gazprom's business model, based on vertical integration, was challenged by the new unbundling provisions, and its strategy for penetrating the EU's liberalised market was now much more complicated. Furthermore, in 2012, the European Commission's DG Competition initiated an investigation on Gazprom's practices in the EU market for allegedly failing to adhere to the EU's competition rules and abusing its dominant position in Central and Eastern Europe. Finally, in December 2013, the European Commission directly targeted the South Stream, stating that the IGAs concluded between Russia and the EU countries involved in the onshore section of the pipeline were not in line with the Third Energy Package. The concomitant outbreak of the Ukrainian crisis at the end of 2013 further aggravated the prospect for South Stream completion. Although some member states, especially Italy, still supported the project – in June 2014, Italy, Austria, Bulgaria, Croatia, Greece, Hungary and Slovenia sent a joint letter to the Commission's President Barroso to defend the South Stream[28] – the European Commission maintained its position. Two infringement procedures were opened against Bulgaria for its onshore section of the South Stream: one for the incompatibility of the project with the Third Energy Package and the other for violation of the EU rules for pipeline procurement. These procedures, along with pressure from the European Commission – and from the US – resulted in the suspension of the construction of the South Stream's Bulgarian section by the end of the summer of 2014.

It is worth noting that, in April 2014, in response to the EU actions targeting the South Stream, Moscow challenged the Third Energy Package to the Dispute Settlement Body of the WTO (on 7 March 2016, a panel was composed to address the issue).[29] On the other hand, in 2013, before the Ukrainian crisis, the European Commission had encouraged the South Stream to apply for an exemption from the Third Energy Package. However, as pointed out by Stern, Pirani and Yafimava (2015, 4), the Third Energy Package's (in)compatibility argument, which was the main reason for the South Stream's suspension, was somewhat flawed. In 2014, the Third Energy Package did not contain any rules for construction and utilisation of new pipeline capacity, but only rules for existing pipeline capacity (thus the former would fall under the rules for existing capacity). The set of rules for new capacity was still under development (these rules should be formalised as an additional chapter in the Capacity Allocation Mechanisms Network Code expected to become applicable in 2017–18). Owing to this regulatory void, it was 'somewhat disingenuous' of the EU to continue to insist that South Stream had to conform to EU legislation and regulation, given that the detail of the latter in relation to large, new gas transportation infrastructure was several years away from clarification (Stern, Pirani and Yafimava 2015, 4). Moreover, Gazprom had already rejected this solution because of the problems the company had experienced in the new regulatory environment with the OPAL pipeline in German territory, which Gazprom was unable to use at full capacity (Stern, Pirani and Yafimava 2015). The case of the OPAL pipeline enhanced Gazprom's distrust of the exemption model and its implementation by the European Commission (Belyi and Goldthau 2015; Pirani and Yafimava 2016). Indeed, although the German regulator granted Gazprom an exemption to use the 100 percent of OPAL's capacity, DG Competition reduced it to 50 percent. It was only after long negotiations between the European Commission and the Russian energy minister that a temporary solution was reached, in

2013, allowing Gazprom to utilise 100 percent of pipeline capacity if no access requests from third parties were advanced. However, in September 2015, after the Ukrainian crisis, the remaining 50 percent of OPAL's capacity was auctioned by Gazprom – as requested by the Commission – and no third-party interest was manifested, but the EU's competition authority did not change its position on the 50 percent capacity limit for the Russian company.[30] At the same time, the European Commission, Russia and Gazprom were also in the middle of negotiations regarding the antitrust investigation initiated in 2012. These negotiations were also unfruitful, and on 22 April 2015, the European Commission sent Gazprom a formal 'Statement of Objection', alleging that some of its business practices in Central and Eastern Europe constituted an abuse of its dominant market position, in breach of EU antitrust rules.[31] Gazprom denied the charges and, in September 2015, responded to these allegations with a proposal to the European Commission requesting an out-of-court settlement[32] (as of November 2016, negotiations were still pending).

These challenges – the deterioration of EU-Russia relations in the wake of the Ukrainian war and the Russian annexation of the Crimea, and Gazprom's problems in the post-Third Energy Package EU regulatory environment – prompted Moscow to explore a new approach for its gas exports to Europe. This approach was manifested when, during a joint conference in Ankara on 1 December 2014, Putin and the Turkish President Erdogan announced the cancellation of the South Stream and its replacement with the so-called Turkish Stream. The new pipeline's capacity of 63 bcm/y was similar to that of the South Stream. Its route was also similar for about two-thirds of its offshore section. But then the new project would lead to western Turkey rather than Bulgaria (Figure 3.1). Furthermore, the original South Stream involved major Western European companies, while Gazprom planned to develop the Turkish Stream singlehandedly. More importantly, with the Turkish Stream, Gazprom changed to a new strategy for penetrating the EU market. The idea now was to bring gas only as far as the Turkish-Greek border and then leave the responsibility for its transportation and commercialisation in the EU to European companies. This approach, however, would require new infrastructures in the EU as well as renegotiations and changes in the gas 'delivery points' agreed on by Gazprom and many of its European clients, which received gas through Ukraine under long-term supply contracts (many of which would not expire until the 2020s or even the 2030s) (Franza 2015; Stern, Pirani and Yafimava 2015). These contracts state specific delivery points (mostly on the Slovak-Austrian border), and it would be difficult for Gazprom to change them unilaterally, i.e. without new agreements with the European importers (Franza 2015). Despite these important commercial obstacles, several countries that had been involved in the South Stream onshore route, such as Romania, Greece and Hungary, expressed interest in the new project, which was in line with their energy security agendas. However, as mentioned above, the development of the Turkish Stream was halted when the Kremlin suspended this new route in response to a Turkish attack on a Russian bomber on the Syrian-Turkish border in November 2015.[33] These events contributed to the return to a more traditional path for Russian gas export policy: the strengthening of Russian-German energy ties with the proposal of the Nord Stream 2. But this time, after the Ukrainian War, this traditional path was also far from easy to follow. On the other hand, after the Moscow-Ankara rapprochement, the Turkish Stream project was relaunched in August 2016: the idea now was to build a reduced version of the original project with a capacity of 32 bcm/y, of which 14 bcm/y would be intended for the Turkish domestic market and the rest for the European one.[34] As a result, although it is too soon to assess whether and/or when these two new projects will be effectively completed, different approaches seem to now coexist in the Russian strategy of diversification away from the Ukrainian gas route.

Post-2014 Developments and the Politics of the East-West Energy Corridor after the Ukrainian War

The war in Eastern Ukraine, Moscow's support for the separatist forces and the annexation of the Crimea drove relations between Russia and the EU to their lowest level since the end of the Cold War.[35] There were several important consequences for East-West gas interdependence. First, the Kremlin and Gazprom decided to accelerate their gas export strategy based on diversification away from the Ukrainian route. In June 2015, Gazprom declared that after 2019 – when its main transit contracts with the Ukrainian company Naftogaz would expire – no more gas would be channelled to Europe via this route.[36] In the following weeks, however, Putin directly reversed this decision, ordering Gazprom to negotiate new transit contracts with Naftogaz and the Ukrainian authorities.[37] Indeed, as we saw, although additional diversification away from Ukraine remained a priority for the Kremlin and Gazprom, a complete transit diversification away from this route would have been very difficult to realise by 2019, both from a commercial point of view and because of the political opposition from the EU (Pirani and Yafimava 2016).

The second consequence was that the EU took a more direct role in mediating negotiations and agreements between Moscow and Kiev on transit issues and supplies to Ukraine and strengthened its bilateral cooperation with Kiev. The European Commission brokered trilateral agreements regarding transit issues and supplies – backed by EU financial assistance – with Russia and Ukraine to ensure the continuation of gas transit to Europe and gas imports to Ukraine. These trilateral agreements (the so-called 'winter packages' of 2014–15 and 2015–16) allowed the continuation of transit through Ukraine and guaranteed a minimum level of Russian gas imports to the country. The European Commission also promoted the establishment of reverse flows, mainly on the Slovakia-Ukraine gas interconnector, to supply Ukraine: between July 2014 and June 2015, Ukraine imported about 10 bcm of gas from the EU, which accounted for more than 70 percent of total Ukrainian gas imports during that period (European Commission 2015a). The EU and Ukraine also improved bilateral cooperation during this time. In June of 2014, they signed the Association Agreement, and in the Energy Union package of February 2015, the EU proposed an upgrade to its Strategic Partnership with Kiev

(European Commission 2015b). A Memorandum of Understanding, backed by 1.8 billion euros of financial assistance, including energy as well as other sectors, was then signed by the EU and Ukraine in May 2015.[38] Then, at the beginning of September 2016, the European Commission reasserted its proposal for relaunching trilateral talks with Kiev and Moscow to mediate a third gas deal for the winter of 2016–17.

Finally, the third consequence was that the EU assumed a more assertive political position towards the Russian strategy of building pipeline routes outside Ukraine. This position also aimed to preserve the economic benefits Ukraine enjoys as transit country. However, this position – supported by EU institutions – was not equally supported by all member states and European energy companies, as demonstrated by the plans for the Nord Stream 2 project.

Gazprom proposed the Nord Stream 2 in summer 2015, when the problems with the Turkish Stream were becoming evident. The project proposed to double the capacity of the Nord Stream (from 55 bcm/y to 110 bcm/y) by adding two new pipelines along the existing route, to be completed by 2019–20. To realise it, Gazprom involved several major European energy companies, concluding shareholder agreements with the German companies Wintershall and Uniper (formerly E.On) France's Engie (formerly Gdf-Suez), Austria's OMV and the Anglo-Dutch Shell.

The appearance of this project on the European energy agenda has prompted lively debate. Unlike with the Nord Stream, the European Commission's attitude was clearly negative, as Nord Stream 2 would undermine its intention to maintain Ukraine's important transit role. The Commission's Vice President, Maroš Šefčovič, who is also responsible for the Energy Union, made several declarations against the Nord Stream 2, pointing that the project was not in line with the goals of the Energy Union and could undermine the energy security of Central and Eastern EU members.[39] Similar concerns were raised by the European Commissioner for Climate Action and Energy, Miguel Arias Cañete. On one hand, he pointed out that the Nord Stream 2 was a commercial project and that the Commission should mainly assess whether it would comply with EU law, but on the other hand, he stated that Nord Stream 2 did not follow a core policy objective of European energy security, i.e. diversification. In his words, if constructed, the Nord Stream 2 'would not only increase Europe's dependence on one supplier, but it would also increase Europe's dependence on one route'.[40]

In the Communication *On the State of the Energy Union* issued in November 2015, the European Commission formalised its negative position on the Nord Stream 2. The Commission also reasserted that the project had 'to comply fully with EU law' and added that 'the EU will only support infrastructure projects that are *in line with the core principles* of the Energy Union, including the EU Energy Security Strategy' (European Commission 2015a, italics added). Later, the European Council held on December 2015 stated, 'any new infrastructure should entirely comply with the Third Energy Package and other applicable EU legislation *as well as with the objectives of the Energy Union*' (European Council 2015, italics added). As has been correctly pointed out by Jonathan Stern, the additional requirement of compliance not only with EU law but also with the Energy Union's objectives – which are more vague and open to different interpretations – introduced an additional degree of 'politicisation' in the decision-making process.[41]

This development was the result of the very strong opposition that the Nord Stream 2 was encountering from several member states in Eastern and Central Europe and the Baltics (as well as Ukraine and the US). Many EU countries raised economic concerns (the potential loss of transit fees) and political concerns (related to energy security). In March 2016, eight EU members, headed by Poland and Slovakia (Poland, Romania, Hungary, Slovakia, the Czech Republic, Lithuania, Latvia and Estonia), sent a letter to the President of the European Commission Jean-Claude Junker to express their firm opposition to the new pipeline, warning of the 'potentially destabilising geopolitical consequences' of the project and the 'risks for energy security in the region of central and eastern Europe'.[42]

This coalition of member states was not able to halt the project. However, soon after that, in April 2016, during a speech in front of the European Parliament, the Commission's Vice President, Maroš Šefčovič, reiterated that the European Commission would observe Nord Stream 2 carefully to make sure that the project was in line 'both with the European law and security of supply objectives', adding that Nord Stream 2's implications go 'clearly beyond the legal discussion'.[43] In the same speech, Maroš Šefčovič also stressed that 'EU law applies in principle also to offshore infrastructure under the jurisdiction of member states including their Exclusive Economic Zones'.[44] On one hand, this interpretation of the EU law requirements is quite problematic, because many historical precedents – all the existing and planned offshore pipelines bringing gas from North Africa to Europe (i.e. Green Stream, GME, Medgaz, Transmed and Galsi) – were not made subject to a Commission ruling or asked to fulfil unbundling or TPA requirements (Goldthau 2016; Pirani and Yafimava 2016). On the other hand, it clearly illustrates the problems with the current EU legal environment for new pipeline development. As effectively pointed out by Goldthau (2016, 25) this legal environment 'leaves ample room for a more strategic political reading of relevant EU regulation' and as such political consideration rather than 'the regulatory framework in the strict sense' will be crucial to determining Nord Stream 2's realisation.

If political elements will be crucial, it is worth noting the positions of the larger Western European consumers involved in the project. As mentioned above, the Nord Stream 2 has been endorsed by important energy companies from Germany, France, Austria and the Netherlands. Furthermore, 'old' EU members, which are major markets for Russian gas, have not opposed the project (with the partial exception of Italy, described in more detail below). Obviously, Germany's position is particularly important. The German Chancellor, Angela Merkel, has underlined that the project is a 'commercial project' led by private investors, not opposing Nord Stream 2, but at the same time asserting German willingness to keep Ukraine as a transit state.[45] While similarly defending Ukraine's transit role, a more active diplomatic role in supporting the pipeline has been played by the German Vice Chancellor and Economic Affairs and Energy Minister Sigmar Gabriel (Gabriel is also the chairman of the Social Democratic Party of Germany, SPD). Gabriel has actively promoted the Nord Stream 2: negotiating with Moscow, asserting German competences on its development and stressing that its realisation is in Germany's interests and that Germany won't allow 'external interference' on decision-making.[46] But he also tried to alleviate the concerns of other countries, especially Poland, by highlighting the benefits of the Nord Stream 2 beyond Germany for European gas supply security.[47]

Germany's position on the Nord Stream 2 might seem peculiar in light of the project's strong opposition from several member states and the European Commission. However, Germany's strategy on energy security was clearly illustrated in 2012, in a policy document issued by the Ministry of Economy: *Germany's New Energy Policy*. This document stated that with regard to energy policy, 'the Commission should play an important role in the early coordination of member states. At the same time, however, the Federal Government *must pursue its own foreign energy policy to accommodate Germany's specific interests* and circumstances at the international level', adding that 'ultimately, German foreign energy policy seeks *to better promote the interests of the German energy industry abroad* by engaging in energy dialogues with key non-EU countries' (German Federal Ministry of Economics and Technology 2012, 50–52, italics added).

As anticipated, the only old EU member to overtly criticise Nord Stream 2 was Italy. Prime Minister Renzi demanded a debate on this project in the run-up to the meeting of the European Council in December 2015. Italy's position, however, more than targeting the Nord Stream 2, was aimed at reaffirming Italian discontent regarding the role played by the Commission in the cancellation of the South Stream. The Italian government played this card in part in the hope of obtaining a role for Italian companies in the project and to ensure that, if built, the new pipeline would bring gas to Italy as well.[48] As a further confirmation of Rome-Moscow energy ties, on February 2016, following a meeting between Gazprom's CEO and the Italian Minister of Economic Development, a Memorandum of Understanding was signed by Gazprom, Edison and Greece's DEPA to develop a gas pipeline project between Greece and Italy, possibly enabling the realisation of a southern route for the supply of Russian gas to Europe.[49]

In addition to the attitude of Western consumers, among the eastern EU countries, Poland's position is especially important, as we saw earlier. After having voiced its opposition to Nord Stream 2 several times, Poland has also taken more direct measures to oppose the project. In July 2016, the Polish Office of Competition and Consumer Protection (UOKiK) issued a statement of objections to the Nord Stream 2 consortium's prospective members (although the pipeline is not set to cross Poland territory, the Western companies that plan to join the venture have assets in Poland).[50] According to the statement, UOKiK found that the agreement and resulting consortium would strengthen Gazprom's advantage in the Polish natural gas market and limit competition in the sector. As a result, in August 2016, the Western companies – Uniper, Engie, OMV, Shell and Wintershall – decided to pull out from the Nord Stream 2 consortium. At the same time these companies reasserted their support for the project. In a statement issued on 12 August, they emphasised that each of them will 'individually contemplate alternative ways' to contribute to the pipeline.[51] However, this development – leaving Gazprom singlehandedly in charge of the project – further complicates the financial prospects of the pipeline's realisation.

To sum up, the opposition of the European Commission and of several member states represents a serious challenge to Nord Stream 2. But this opposition does not necessarily imply an abandonment of the project – although, in theory, the Commission can use its leeway in the application of its regulatory powers to delay or further complicate Nord Stream 2's realisation – especially if support from Germany and other Western European countries continues. The situation in Eastern Ukraine is an important element. If all the parties involved in the conflicts respect the Minsk 2 agreements and if EU-Russian relations ease, the political prospect for the realisation of the Nord Stream 2 will improve. On the other hand, if the situation in Eastern Ukraine degenerates (and with it EU-Russia relations), it is possible that the political prospect for the Nord Stream 2 could become much more complicated.

In this regard, some signs of a 'rapprochement' between the European Commission and Gazprom, as of the end of 2016, are worth noting. On 28 October 2016, the European Commission eventually decided to allow Gazprom to use 30–40 percent more of OPAL pipeline's capacity (the capacity will be auctioned, and Gazprom will be allowed to bid).[52] This decision caused a protest by the Ukrainian Naftogaz, which warned of the potential loss of transit revenues for the country, but it was defended by the European Commission.[53] Meanwhile, negotiations between the European Commission and Gazprom were also relaunched to settle the EU antitrust charges.[54]

The 'New' Politics of Pipeline and the Southern Gas Corridor

Recent developments along the South-North and East-West gas corridors have highlighted the transformations occurring in the traditional politics of European security of supply. The model of the partner state, with its triangular diplomacy framework, cannot effectively illustrate the political dynamics embedded in the new EU regulatory and institutional environment. Neither can these new political dynamics be encompassed by the provider state model, which envisages only a limited role for public authorities in setting the stage for market actors' activities. Rule-making and enforcing are becoming important features of the current European politics of pipeline and security of supply, and the European Commission in particular has gained important powers in this regard. The European Commission can block or delay international pipeline projects, as demonstrated in the case of the South Stream. Its regulatory powers, however, apply only within the borders of the EU and seem to work mainly in a negative way (i.e. to block or delay planned international projects) rather than in a positive way (i.e. to promote new external importing infrastructures). Besides, externally, especially in the case of the Southern Gas Corridor, the European Commission has pursued a highly proactive approach, departing from the ex ante diplomacy of the provider state model, while member states have continued to develop their national foreign energy policies.

In sum, the main elements of the catalytic state and the emergence of interaction patterns in line with the hexagonal diplomacy framework are particularly evident in the case of the Southern Gas Corridor. Figure 3.4 briefly summarises, in

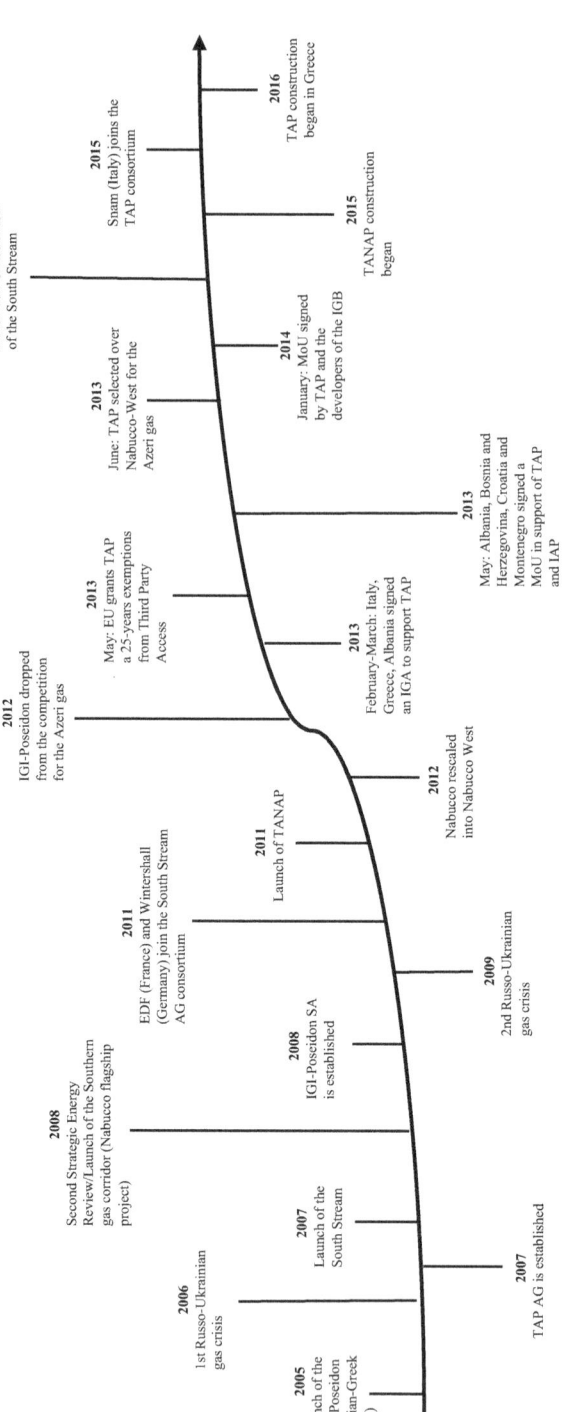

Figure 3.4 Southern Gas Corridor: timeline of the major events (2005–16).

chronological order, the recent key events that have affected the development of this corridor. In what follows, the European Commission's activism will first be illustrated. Then, the new politics of pipeline will be described, focusing on the efforts of member states to create coalitions to support their preferred projects, on the 'indirectly supportive' relationships between governments and energy companies and on the governments' activation at the subnational level to enable the realisation of energy infrastructures. Taken together, these dynamics reveal the overall role of government as facilitator in the realisation of international pipeline projects and confirm the pattern of transformation already identified in the cases of the other corridors.

Departing From Ex Ante Diplomacy

As illustrated in Chapters 1 and 2, signs of developments compatible with the second step towards the provider state model can be found in the various efforts made by the European Commission to expand the rules of the internal energy market beyond EU borders. However, the development of the Southern Gas Corridor reveals a clear departure from this approach. The concept of the Southern Gas Corridor emerged in 2007–08 with the EU Second Strategic Energy Review issued after the first Russo-Ukrainian gas dispute. Initially, this concept referred to the Nabucco project, the Trans-Adriatic-Pipeline (TAP), the Interconnector Turkey-Greece-Italy (ITGI) and later the Trans-Caspian-Pipeline (TCP) as well (Figure 3.5). However, as anticipated, Nabucco, which was expected to deliver gas

Figure 3.5 Competing projects in Southeast Europe and Southern Gas Corridor competitors for the Azerbaijani gas supply.

Note: Author's elaboration for illustration.

from the Caspian Sea and Middle Eastern regions to Europe with a throughput capacity of 31 bcm/y, emerged as the main EU flagship initiative for diversification of gas supply. The European Commission not only funded the Nabucco consortium (with a grant covering 50 percent of the cost of the feasibility study), included Nabucco into the TEN-E framework as a project of 'European interest', and decided to grant the project a 25-year long 50 percent exemption from TPA requirements, but it also ensured continuous political and diplomatic support to this pipeline (Baev and Øverland 2010; Sartori 2012, 2013). First, the European Commission repeatedly expressed its preference for Nabucco over competing Southern Gas Corridor pipeline projects and other competitors such as the South Stream. Second, it intensified – although without success – its bilateral political and diplomatic efforts to ensure that the pipeline had the necessary gas resources, engaging several countries in Central Asia and the Caspian, such as Kazakhstan, Turkmenistan, Uzbekistan and Azerbaijan. The European Commission also appointed a 'European Coordinator', Jozias Van Aarsten, to find solutions to possible problems in the project's realisation and to promote dialogue among member states, energy companies and financial institutions. Furthermore, in 2011, it obtained – for the first time – a mandate from the European Council to negotiate an international agreement with Azerbaijan and Turkmenistan in order to establish a legal framework for the Trans-Caspian-Pipeline. Finally, the European Commission proposed the establishment of the Caspian Development Corporation as a mechanism to aggregate European gas demand, assist European gas companies to purchase gas from Central Asia and convince Caspian producers to commit gas volumes to the Southern Corridor.

Despite this strong political and diplomatic support from the European Commission, however, the ambitious Nabucco project failed and was abandoned in late 2011, when Azerbaijan and Turkey announced the construction of TANAP. TANAP, which would connect with the South Caucasus Pipeline (SCP), overlapped with the Nabucco's eastern section in Turkey (Figure 3.5). This project – with a capacity of 16 bcm/y – was intended to serve fewer countries than Nabucco and was expected to be less expensive than the EU project (5 billion euros versus 8 billion euros) (De Micco 2015). This pipeline was based on an agreement between Turkey and Azerbaijan and their respective national companies: the Turkish companies TPAO and Botas, which hold a 20 percent share of TANAP and would retain the right to negotiate discounted supplies for the Turkish market, and the Azerbaijani Socar, which obtained the shareholding majority (80 percent).[55] The selection of TANAP over Nabucco exposed one of the main limits of the EU-sponsored pipeline: its lack of sound commercial feasibility – especially because it would be difficult for Nabucco to access additional resources other than Azerbaijani gas. In 2012, this resulted in the rescaling of the original concept into Nabucco West (Figure 3.5). The European Commission granted its diplomatic and political support to this project as well. The new project was intended to compete for the development of the Azerbaijani Shah Deniz II gas field; it would be supplied by TANAP and would connect the Greek-Turkish border to Austria.

In the cases of Nabucco and Nabucco West, however, the European Commission's activism collided with the preferences and actions of many member states, which were proactively supporting different energy companies and pipeline routes to supply the markets of Southeast Europe or to access Azerbaijani resources during the same period (circa 2006–12) (Table 3.1).

In the case of the Southern Gas Corridor, the EU approach is not compatible with the provider state model and its ex ante diplomacy, but this does not mean that the European Commission 'has assumed the traditional role of the state' (Talus 2015, 211), at least not the traditional role that the European states had in the previous system under the partner state model. First of all, as correctly pointed out by Herranz-Surrallés (2015, 12–13), the implementation of EU-level energy diplomacy has been constrained by the market-approach logic still embedded in the European Commission's strategy and policy instruments. Although some tools, like the Caspian Development Corporation to 'create gas demand' or the bilateral negotiation of the intergovernmental agreements for the Trans-Caspian-Pipeline, seem to resemble past practices associated with the partner state tradition, the actions of the European Commission are not designed to support national companies; they are inspired by different guiding principles. These actions are intended to promote a different set of rules, such as the third-party access, de-monopolisation and gas company diversification. Therefore, also in the case of Nabucco, the EU followed a different model than that of the traditional practices: the so-called 'merchant pipeline' model (Finon 2011).

Table 3.1 Main pipeline projects in Southeast Europe and Southern Gas Corridor competitors for the Azerbaijani gas supply (2006–12).

Pipeline	Origin of gas/ Capacity (Bcm/y)	Transit countries	Shareholders/ Proponents (*)
Competitor to the Southern Gas Corridor			
South Stream	Russia (63 Bcm/y)	Black Sea (subsea pipeline), Bulgaria; north route (Serbia, Hungary and Slovenia); south route (Greece, Italy)	Gazprom, ENI, EDF, Wintershall
Competitors for the Azerbaijani gas supply			
IGI-Poseidon	Azerbaijan (10 Bcm/y)	Greece, Italy	Edison, Depa
TAP	Azerbaijan (10–20 Bcm/y)	Greece, Albania, Italy	Axpo, E.On, Statoil
Nabucco West	Azerbaijan (16 Bcm/y)	Bulgaria, Romania, Hungary, Austria	OMW, MOL, Transgaz, Bulgargaz, Botas, RWE

Note: (*) = Shareholders/Proponents in 2012.

According to this model, pipelines are built without contracts with gas producers and on the basis of unregulated prices. This is different from the traditional 'ship-or-pay' model followed for example by the South Stream project, where companies from producer and consumer countries hold a majority stake in the new infrastructure, which is backed by long-term gas supply contracts. In the case of Nabucco, the Commission supported the idea of a pipeline independent from the Turkish network, fully dedicated to European supplies and with a legal regime guaranteeing Third Party Access. However, this approach was not in line with the preferences of many actors involved in the Nabucco route. Ankara, for example was reluctant to accept the proposed transit model, which implied that the Turkish state-owned company Botas would lose control of transmission pipelines on Turkish territory (Winrow 2009).

Furthermore, externally, although member states have delegated some competences to EU institutions, they have not pooled their sovereignty in the area of foreign energy relations; they continue to support specific energy projects and companies according to national interests, and they are reluctant to cede their power to the EU (Aalto and Korkmaz Temel 2014).

A closer look at the recent history of the development of the Southern Gas Corridor reveals that EU institutions are becoming an important 'node' in multi-actor natural gas network diplomacy, but also that member states' governments and energy companies are still key players, although their strategies and roles are moving away from the partner state tradition.

Creating Coalitions to Promote and Defend Member States' Preferred Energy Security Options

Nabucco and Nabucco West were only the EU-sponsored pipelines competing for development of the Southern Gas Corridor. Other projects, promoted by different coalitions of governments and energy companies, were also competing both to access Azerbaijani resources and to serve the gas market of Southeastern Europe (Table 3.1; Figure 3.5). The first was IGI-Poseidon, proposed in 2005 by the French-Italian company Edison and the Greek state-owned company DEPA. This pipeline was intended to supply the Italian market through the Interconnector Turkey-Greece (which was completed in 2007) and the Interconnector Greece-Italy (IGI-Poseidon) with about 10 bcm/y of gas from Azerbaijan. IGI-Poseidon was strongly supported by the Italian and Greek governments, which signed an intergovernmental agreement to facilitate its implementation in 2005. They also promoted the inclusion of this infrastructure as a project of 'European interest' in the TEN-E scheme (EU financial aid was granted for the feasibility study for IGI-Poseidon). In 2007, the Italian government also signed a Memorandum of Understanding with the Azerbaijani government to facilitate negotiations between Edison and the state-owned Azerbaijani gas company Socar, which was involved in the development of the Shah Deniz II gas field. And, in 2008, the company IGI-Poseidon SA was established as 50–50 percent joint venture between DEPA and Edison.

The second project was the South Stream. As seen previously, this pipeline, which would export Russian gas to Eastern and Southeastern Europe, bypassing Ukraine, was initially supported mainly by Rome and Moscow. But later, in the wake of the second Russian-Ukrainian gas crisis, the governments of Austria, Bulgaria, Hungary, Greece and Slovenia also signed bilateral transit agreements with Russia supporting this route, and the French company EDF and German Wintershall joined the South Stream consortium.

Austria, Bulgaria, Hungary and their respective energy companies (OMV, Bulgargaz and MOL) were already involved in the Nabucco/Nabucco West project – which Romania and Germany also supported (and Romania's Transgaz and Germany's RWE) – but they had strong incentives to participate in the South Stream as well in order to pursue their specific energy security agendas (Schmidt-Felzmann 2011). Austria and Hungary wanted to benefit from participation in the South Stream by increasing their roles in gas transit to Western European states. Moreover, by participating in both projects, both countries could diversify their supplies and bolster their bargaining power vis-à-vis producer states. For Bulgaria, participating in the South Stream promised to increase its role as a transit country and reduce its vulnerability to disruption from gas deliveries from Ukraine, which was an important domestic issue after the 2009 crisis.

Different and partially overlapping coalitions among member states and energy companies were created in this period to promote the realisation of specific pipeline projects, in some cases obtaining support from EU institutions to different degrees (Figure 3.6). Inter-state coalitions were also created to defend particular projects. Specifically, the Italian government sought to create coalitions with Germany and France (Paris had stakes in IGI-Poseidon through EDF participation in Edison), in order to strengthen its position vis-à-vis the European Commission and defend its preferred energy routes – the South Stream and IGI-Poseidon projects – over the competing Nabucco and Nabucco West projects (Sartori 2012). Moreover, as further development of the Southern Gas Corridor has shown,

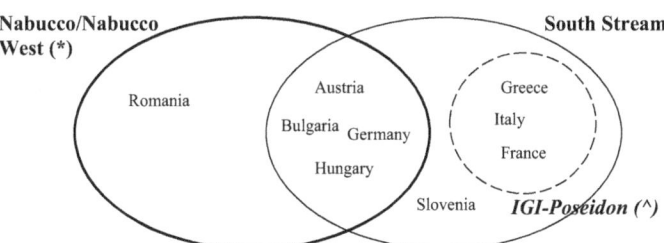

Figure 3.6 Overview of member state coalitions participating in Nabucco/Nabucco West, South Stream and IGI-Poseidon.

Note: (*) Specific EU support=identification of the project as having a 'European interest', EU financial support and active diplomatic support from the European Commission; (^) General EU support=identification of the project as having a 'European interest' and EU financial support.

inter-state coalitions were also created ex-post, i.e. to support projects not originally backed by member states or their energy companies (see below).

'Indirectly' Supporting Energy Companies

At first glance, the strategy of member states, especially the larger Western consumers such as Italy, France and Germany, seems to resemble the practice of the partner state. On the other hand, for the smaller countries of Southern and Eastern Europe, creating coalitions, searching for the support of EU institutions, and taking part in different (competing) projects seems a rational strategy to limit risks to their gas supply security, since they are unable to influence major pipeline projects to any substantial degree (Giamouridis and Paleoyannis 2011). However, first, in the new context, national governments have to complement their traditional diplomatic activities with actions intended to create coalitions to promote/defend their preferred strategy at the European level. Second, their relationships with energy companies are becoming more complex than the previous 'mutually supportive' approach of the partner state. German companies took part in the competing Nabucco and South Stream projects and later in the competing Trans-Adriatic-Pipeline and Nabucco West projects. The Italian government supported ENI-Gazprom South Stream as well as Edison and the IGI-Poseidon pipeline (although ENI refused to participate and lobbied against this project) (Luciani and Mazzanti 2006). During the same period, the Italian government also enacted several measures to reduce ENI's market power in the national market, such as antitrust ceilings, compulsory gas release programmes and mandatory pipeline upgrades (Honoré 2013). Finally, the Italian government continued to support IGI-Poseidon when, in 2012, Edison became part of the French group EDF.

The new 'indirectly supportive' relationship between government and energy companies, and their roles in the emerging European security of gas supply institutional structure, is illustrated by the final competition among the projects of the Southern Gas Corridor for development of the Azerbaijani gas resources. In theory, the pipelines with, initially, a larger probability of success in the bidding organised by the Shah Deniz II consortium were the EU-backed Nabucco West and the Italian- and Greek-supported IGI-Poseidon. The other main contender was the Trans-Adriatic-Pipeline (TAP). This project, initially proposed in 2003, was relaunched in 2007 when a joint venture (TAP AG) was established between two non-EU companies, the Swiss company EGL (now Axpo) and the national Norwegian company Statoil (Statoil was one of the companies operating the Shah Deniz II consortium, with a 25.5 percent share). Later, in 2010, those two were joined by the German company E.On. In regard to transit routes and capacity, the TAP, which would link Albania to Italy through a subsea pipeline after passing through Greek territory, was very similar to the IGI-Poseidon, although it was not backed by the governments of Greece or Italy (Figure 3.5). Indeed, in 2012, when the IGI-Poseidon was dropped from the bidding organised by the Shah Deniz II consortium in favour of the TAP, the Italian and Greek governments tried to defend their preferred solution (i.e. IGI-Poseidon). Consequently, observers expected that this project, which was not yet backed by any intergovernmental agreement, would be very difficult to realise.[56] However, Italy and Greece reviewed their position in the following months. During this period, the TAP company worked intensively to obtain the political support of the main actors interested in the pipeline route, including the European Commission, many Western Balkan states, Italy and Greece.[57]

In 2013, the European Commission granted the TAP the status of 'Project of Common Interest'. Moreover, the Italian and Greek governments changed their position once they realised that, after the IGI-Poseidon was dropped from the competition, the TAP was the only remaining project that would bring Azerbaijani gas into their domestic markets – the other competitor was Nabucco West. That was consistent with their national strategies of diversification of supply and economic development based on strengthening their countries as gas hubs for the wider European market.[58] It is worth noting that in this period, in the wake of the so-called 'Arab spring' and the war in Libya, supplies to Italy from the Green Stream were experiencing several problems. There were also concerns about possible difficulties with Algeria, which, at that time, was the second largest supplier of gas to Italy (after Russia). In fact, after their initial hesitation, both Rome and Athens worked to create a coalition to facilitate the realisation of the TAP. Between February and March 2013, Italy, Greece and Albania signed a trilateral intergovernmental agreement to establish the international framework for the implementation of this project. They also created a Trilateral Ministerial Committee to coordinate their actions in support of the TAP. Furthermore, in order to expand the coalition of actors supporting the pipeline, the Italian government worked with the Croatian government to connect the TAP project and the Ionian-Adriatic-Pipeline (IAP) project, which would bring Azerbaijani gas to the Balkans. On 23 May 2013, Albania, Bosnia and Herzegovina, Croatia and Montenegro signed a MoU promising support and cooperation in the realisation of both the TAP and IAP pipelines. Meanwhile, the European Commission – following approval from the regulatory authorities in Italy, Greece and Albania – had granted (on 17 May 2013) TAP a 25-year exemption from Third Party Access and from regulated tariffs for all of its 10 bcm/y capacity (as well as exemption from ownership unbundling for 25 years).

The Italian and Greek governments continued to demonstrate their political support for the TAP after this project was selected over Nabucco West by the Shah Deniz II consortium on 28 June 2013, and both governments strengthened their bilateral diplomatic engagement with Azerbaijan to facilitate its completion. In September 2013, after company-to-company negotiations several European buyers (Axpo, Bulgargaz, DEPA, Enel, E.On, Gas Natural, GDF-Suez, Hera, and Shell Energy Europe) signed 25-year sales agreement for the 10 bcm/y TAP capacity. According to these agreements, around 1 bcm/y 'will go to buyers intending to supply to each of Bulgaria and Greece and the rest will go to buyers intending to supply Italy and adjacent market hubs'.[59] In January 2014, TAP also signed a MoU with ICGB, the company held by the Bulgarian Energy Holding, the Greek DEPA and Edison. This MoU promised to develop the Interconnector Greece-Bulgaria

(IGB) and establish technical cooperation to connect the two systems. Finally, at the beginning of 2015, the Italian company Snam (Snam, previously part of the ENI group, became the Italian Independent Transmission System Operator, 30 percent owned by the Italian state, in 2012) joined the TAP consortium, acquiring a 20 percent share from Statoil. As a result of this and other purchases, at the end of 2016, TAP's shareholders were the English company BP (20 percent), the Azeri Socar (20 percent), the Italian Snam (20 percent), the Belgium Fluxys (19 percent), the Spanish Enagas (16 percent) and the Swiss Axpo (5 percent). Snam, Fluxys and Enagas are Transmission System Operators, and the fact that some of the nine companies that signed agreements to purchase Azeri gas are active in Central and Northwestern Europe means that part of the TAP's volume could reach Austria (and the Baumgarten gas hub), Germany, France, Switzerland and even the UK.[60]

Mediating Between Energy Companies and Local Actors

The political dynamics triggered by the development of the Southern Gas Corridor highlight the new relationships between governments and energy companies and also the new subnational dimension of pipeline politics and governmental efforts to mediate between energy companies and local actors. In Greece, the IGI-Poseidon project experienced several problems related to opposition from local governments and communities along the planned route, which touched tourist areas on the country's Ionian coast (Giamouridis and Paleoyannis 2011, 78). In 2007, the local council of Perdika and Syvota voted against the passing of the pipeline through their territories, causing delays in the original plan and prompting DEPA to propose a new route close to the adjacent town of Parga. In 2008, however, the local council of Parga also refused to allow the construction of a compressor station within its borders. The conflicts between local communities, DEPA and central governments intensified in the following years. In 2011, the Greek government was finally able to resolve the disputes and mediate a compromise for a new route passing through the city of Florovouni. Similarly, when the TAP announced its plan for construction across Greek territory, several municipalities and local communities demanded changes to the planned route. This prompted the TAP consortium to carefully assess these requests so as not to delay the realisation of the project and to implement a 'social investment programme', together with local communities, in an attempt to win additional support.[61] However, the concerns of local communities were not completely appeased, and, in 2015, the Greek government proposed the creation of a joint committee between the Ministry of the Environment and Energy and TAP to address the issue.[62]

In Italy, the TAP project was particularly contested in the Puglia region. In 2014, the Regional Committee on Environmental Impact Assessment rejected the TAP proposal, questioning the environmental compatibility of the project in relation to its intended landing place on the Puglia mainland. The regional government only has consultative power in the decision-making process, and the final decision lies in the hands of the national government and the Minister of the Environment. Nonetheless, the negative judgement from the regional committee, along with the opposition of many municipalities and local communities affected by the project, complicated efforts to realise the plans for the TAP. The TAP company started a local campaign to 'win friends' by offering sponsorships to local events in the municipalities affected by the pipeline route.[63] The national government also took action, mediating negotiations between the company and local administrators to facilitate a compromise. However, these strategies have not appeased local protests. On the contrary, they have prompted stronger debate at the local and national levels. This debate has not lessened, even since the Italian Ministry of the Environment finally gave its opinion in favour of the realisation of the TAP at the end of August 2014. Although the plan for the realisation of the TAP has proceeded since then (in April 2016, TAP engaged the Italian company Saipem to construct the offshore section of the pipeline), conflicts still persist, especially between the central government and the regional government of Puglia.

Concluding Remarks

Signs of transformations towards the catalytic state model can be found along all the main corridors of European gas supply. However, the rise of this model seems to be most evident in the Southern Gas Corridor. A historical perspective on this topic, describing the beginning of the politics of pipeline and security of gas supply in Europe and tracing its development through the concept of the partner state, avoids two major risks. The first of these is representing the current approach of the main European consumers as a simple continuation of the previous system (which was rather embedded in the specific institutional, ideational and market structure of the formative and consolidative phases of the European gas sector). The second is assuming that the EU's departure from a pure market-based approach and the provider state model implies the transfer of the former role of the state to the European Commission. Indeed, the internal and external activism of the European Commission, rather than indicating that the EU itself is becoming similar to the original European partner state, seems to indicate the development of an important component of the new 'multilayered political-diplomatic environment' of the European gas sector, in which the practice of networked (hexagonal) diplomacy attached to the catalytic state model is emerging. The model of the catalytic state seems particularly appropriate for describing both the move towards a liberalised and de-monopolised market structure, and the establishment of new methods of energy governance, as well as the continuous and active role of national governments in the current institutional, ideational and market environment.

The strategic importance of pipeline routes for national governments is not limited to the goals of reducing the risks of disruptions, improving security of supply or minimising the leverage of external actors. Pipelines are also important with regard to national economic development, both for traditional transit countries, which can extract revenues from their geographically favourable position between producers and consumers, and for the countries that want to play the role of energy hubs in the new, liberalised EU market. That is to say, since the mid-2000s, rising concerns about security of gas supply have favoured the emergence of 'solidarity' – recognised in the Lisbon treaty – as a principle for enhancing EU energy security and increasing the EU's role in international energy politics. But, at the same time, the process of the liberalisation and integration of the EU gas market – which in theory should also contribute to implement the 'solidarity' principle – has also paved the way for the emergence of new competitive dynamics. Member states compete, not only to assert their own views of energy security at the EU level and/or promote their national energy security agendas, but also to promote their economic objectives – such as becoming 'energy hubs' or supporting national energy companies – through energy policy and diplomacy.

Finally, it is worth noting that in the case of the Southern Gas Corridor, the European Commission tried to act strategically, like a governmental agent, to facilitate the development of its preferred pipeline project. It negotiated with producer countries, coordinated member states and sought to coordinate market actors through the Caspian Development Corporation. In theory, these dynamics seem to show a first effort at moving towards a catalytic state model at the EU level. But the European Commission's strategy has been ineffective because EU-level governmental agents lack many instruments available to member states' governments. At the same time, some very recent developments seem to point in this direction, opening the question of whether the EU, as an international state, could, in the near future, mirror the catalytic state model currently at work on the national level. At the beginning of 2015, the European Commission launched the 'Southern Gas Corridor Advisory Council' gathering Azerbaijan, Albania, Bulgaria, Georgia, Greece, Italy, Turkey, the UK and also the US to support the development of the TAP and IAP pipelines. Then, at the beginning of 2016, the EU High Representative for Foreign Policy, Federica Mogherini, took part in the second meeting of the Advisory Council in Baku, reiterating the European Commission's support for the planned pipeline and its intention to better integrate energy relations in the EU's overall foreign policy with Azerbaijan. Despite these recent moves, an evolution of the EU into a catalytic state is very far from certain. The EU's strategy and development in energy security matters will probably also be affected by other important political events affecting the wider integration process and undermining EU solidarity and cooperation, such as the refugee crisis, the spread of Eurosceptic movements all over Europe and the effects of 'Brexit'. Moreover, as illustrated by the case of Nabucco, the EU political and diplomatic initiatives have few chances to achieve their goals in the area of pipeline politics if they are not equally supported by credible commercial and financial commitments and energy companies' strategies.

Notes

1 The plans for the opening of the Southern Gas Corridor were not halted by the failed military coup in Turkey of 15–16 July 2016. After the events, the Turkish government and the companies involved in the project confirmed that TANAP would proceed according to schedule. See 'Turkey's coup and its gas supply plans', 21 July 2016, available at: www.naturalgaseurope.com/turkeys-coup-and-energy-plans-30711 [accessed 3 August 2016].

2 Formally, these bodies are still in place, but they are currently dormant. For example, according to the European Commission's website, the last meeting of the EU-Russia Gas Advisory Council was held in Moscow on November 2013. available at: https://ec.europa. eu/energy/en/topics/international-cooperation/russia [accessed 25 September 2016].

3 Gazprom was created in 1989, when the Soviet Union Gas Industry Ministry was restructured into a corporation.

4 For a discussion of the long-term oil-linked contracts in the European gas market and their development, see Stern (2007, 2009).

5 During this period, ENI, in partnership with Sonatrach, managed also to expand Transmed's capacity, which in 1995 reached 24 bcm/y (Transmed's capacity was additionally increased in 2009).

6 The Third Energy Package consists of two directives, one concerning common rules for the internal market in gas (2009/73/EC) and one concerning common rules for the internal market in electricity (2009/72/EC). It also includes three regulations, one on the conditions for access to the natural gas transmission networks (No 715/2009), one on the conditions for access to the network for cross-border exchange of electricity (No 714/2009) and one on the establishment of the Agency for the Cooperation of Energy Regulators, ACER (No 713/2009).

7 Under the OU model, all integrated energy companies must sell off their gas and electricity grids. Under the ISO model, the supply company can still own the physical network, but it has to delegate all operation, maintenance and investment to an independent company. Under the ITO model, the supply company can own and operate the network, but the network must be managed by a subsidiary of the parent company, which can make all financial, technical and other decisions independently from the parent company, and a supervisory body is in charge of preserving the financial interest of the mother company without being involved in the day-to-day business.

8 ACER has the task of advising the Commission on internal energy market issues, coordinating and complementing the work of national regulatory authorities, developing EU-wide market rules and guidelines, and improving regulation of cross-border energy infrastructures. The main task of ENTSO-G is to draft network codes aligned with the principles that ACER sets out in its guidelines, which address aspects of network security, interconnection and access.

9 As described in Chapter 1, the new proposal of the European Commission on the IGAs decision provides for ex ante compatibility assessments of intergovernmental agreements. This is partly because renegotiation and cancellation can be difficult and costly after IGAs have been signed by member states and third states. This proposal was included in the 'energy security package' presented by the European Commission on 16 February 2016 and is still under discussion at the time of this writing.

10 The co-financing rate for TEN-E projects rarely amounts to more than 0.01–1 percent of the total investment cost of the project (European Commission 2010).

11 Since 2014, Projects of Common Interest have been able to access new funds and financial instruments through the Connecting Europe Facility (Regulation 1316/2013).

12 See the declarations of the former CEO of ENI, Vittorio Mincato, 'Mincato: troppa offerta di gas, il mercato è a rischio', in *Corriere della Sera*, 27 March 2003, p. 27.

13 See 'Accordo intergovernativo tra la Repubblica Italiana e la Repubblica democratica e popolare di Algeria relativo al gasdotto tra l'Algeria e l'Italia attraverso la Sardegna Galsi', Rome, 16 November 2007.

14 The role of regional and local governments in the Italian energy policy will be also discussed in Chapter 4 and Chapter 5. On April 2016, the Italian Parliament passed a new law to reform the Italian Constitution. The new law also provides for a recentralisation of decision-making power on energy issues (reforming Title V of the Italian Constitution). The reform proposal was subject to a referendum that was held on 4 December 2016. However, this constitutional reform was rejected by voters (59.1 percent of Italians voted 'No' against the proposed reforms in the referendum).

15 See 'Rapporto 2020. Le scelte di politica estera', Italian Ministry of Foreign Affairs, Rome.

16 See 'Algeria to increase exploration efforts, confirms Galsi pipeline project', 18 May 2015, available at: www.naturalgaseurope.com/algeria-to-increase-exploration-efforts-confirms-galsi-pipeline-project-23936 [accessed 28 August 2016].

17 Later, the shareholding composition changed again: currently the Medgaz consortium includes Sonatrach (43 percent), Cepsa (42 percent) and Gas Natural (15 percent).

18 The 2006 and 2009 Russian-Ukrainian gas crises have been widely covered by the literature, see, e.g. Stern (2006), Pirani, Stern and Yafimava (2009) and Pirani (2012).

19 For this characterisation of the strategic partnership approach to European-Russian gas relations and for its transformation after the cancellation of the South Stream, see, in particular, Stern, Pirani and Yafimava (2015). This approach was also characterised by efforts to sign a new EU-Russia Partnership and Cooperation agreement (negotiations were launched in 2008) and relaunch the EU-Russia energy dialogue (the joint 'EU-Russia Energy Roadmap 2050' was established in March 2013). See also Henderson and Pirani (2014).

20 For a review of the main deals reached between Gazprom and the major European energy companies in this period, see Locatelli (2008).

21 Another effect of this new market environment was to open an important differential between the oil-linked prices of the Russian long-term contracts and the prices paid by consumers at the European gas hubs. This evolution towards market-based pricing in the European market challenged Gazprom's traditional commercial strategy, but the company has been able to adapt to this new context and has made concessions to its clients to reduce the gap between its prices and hub prices (see Stern 2014).

22 The Nord Stream 2 consists of two pipelines, each with a design capacity of 27.5 bcm/y, to be constructed along the same route through the Baltic Sea as the original Nord Stream.

23 In April 2015, GdF-Suez changed its name to Engie, but the French state still holds about a 33 percent share of the company.

24 See 'Putin threatens to scrap gas pipeline as talks with EU leaders approach', in *The Wall Street Journal*, 13 November 2008, available at: www.wsj.com/articles/SB122653533902022571 [accessed 5 March 2016].

25 See 'BASF, Gazprom complete asset swap', 1 October 2015, available at: www.naturalgaseurope.com/basf-gazprom-complete-asset-swap-25688 [accessed 25 February 2016].

26 See 'Gazprom and ENI ink agreement on strategic partnership', 14 November 2006, available at: www.gazprom.com/press/news/2006/november/article63661/ [accessed 1 March 2016].

27 The competition between Nabucco and the South Stream and the development of the Southern Gas Corridor will be further investigated in the next section.

28 See 'Renzi leads belated effort in support of South Stream', in *Euractiv*, 10 June 2014, available at: www.euractiv.com/section/global-europe/news/renzi-leads-belated-effort-in-support-of-south-stream/ [accessed 26 February 2016].

29 See, 'WTO, Dispute DS476', available at: www.wto.org/english/tratop_e/dispu_e/cases_e/ds476_e.htm [accessed 20 September 2016]. As of November 2016, the dispute is still pending.

30 Pirani and Yafimava (2016, 30) consider this decision 'increasingly illogical' from the perspective of competition, suggesting that it may have been supported by a political rather than a regulatory rationale.

31 According to the European Commission, Gazprom was 'breaking EU antitrust rules by pursuing an overall strategy to partition Central and Eastern European gas markets with the aim of maintaining an unfair pricing policy in several of those Member States' (See 'Antitrust: Commission sends statement of objections to Gazprom', Press Release available at: http://europa.eu/rapid/press-release_MEMO-15-4829_en.htm [accessed 19 February 2016]). In the view of the Commission, Gazprom was implementing this strategy by hindering cross-border gas sales, charging unfair prices (in Bulgaria,

Estonia, Latvia, Lithuania and Poland), and making gas supplies conditional on obtaining unrelated commitments from wholesalers concerning gas transport infrastructure.

32 See 'Gazprom responds to EU charges of hindering competition, unfair pricing', in *The Wall Street Journal*, 28 September 2015, available at: www.wsj.com/articles/gazprom-responds-to-eu-charges-of-hindering-competition-unfair-pricing-1443462289 [accessed 5 April 2016]; and 'Gazprom seeks EU deal with no admission of antitrust breach', 29 September 2015, available at: www.bloomberg.com/news/articles/2015–09–29/gazprom-pushes-for-eu-deal-with-no-admission-of-antitrust-breach [accessed 6 September 2016]. At this writing (November 2016), a final solution is still pending.

33 In June 2016, Turkish President Erdogan apologised for downing of the Russian jet and Moscow and Ankara began to normalise their relations; see 'Russia and Turkey seek to repair ties after Putin and Erdogan phone call', 29 June 2016, available at: www.ft.com/cms/s/0/210057f2–3df6–11e6–8716-a4a71e8140b0.html#axzz4FL5Jdw5K [accessed 22 July 2016].

34 See 'Turkey to transit Russian natural gas to Europe via Turkish Stream pipeline – Erdogan', 9 August 2016, available at: www.rt.com/business/355245-turkey-restart-tukish-stream/ [accessed 2 September 2016].

35 An analysis of the war in Eastern Ukraine and of the security and international consequences triggered by this event is well beyond the scope of this section. In what follows, only the major implications of this crisis for the European politics of pipeline along the East-West gas corridor will be addressed.

36 See, 'Gazprom reaffirms plans to bypass Ukraine in 2019', 10 June 2015, available at: www.euractiv.com/section/europe-s-east/news/gazprom-reaffirms-plans-to-bypass-ukraine-in-2019/ [accessed 6 April 2016].

37 See 'Russia backs down from abandoning gas transit through Ukraine', 26 June 2015, available at: www.reuters.com/article/russia-gazprom-ukraine-idUSL8N0ZC3AG20150626 [accessed 6 April 2016].

38 Since the outbreak of the crisis in early 2014 and then in 2015, the European Commission has already provided 1.61 billion euros under two similar Macro Financial Assistance programmes (http://europa.eu/rapid/press-release_IP-15–5024_it.htm).

39 See, for example 'Šefčovič warns energy firms over Nord Stream II participation', 7 September 2015, available at: www.politico.eu/article/sefcovic-warns-energy-firms-over-nord-stream-ii-participation/ [accessed 8 April 2016] and 'Šefčovič: Nord Stream is not in conformity with the Energy Union's goals', 11 February 2016, available at: www.euractiv.com/section/europe-s-east/interview/sefcovic-nord-stream-is-not-in-conformity-with-the-energy-union-s-goals/ [accessed 9 April 2016].

40 See 'Commissioner Arias Cañete at the European Parliament Plenary: Opening and concluding remarks', Strasbourg, 7 October 2015, available at: http://europa.eu/rapid/press-release_SPEECH-15–5797_en.htm [accessed 8 April 2016].

41 See 'We need transparency over Nord Stream 2', available at: www.ft.com/cms/s/0/0028981c-ae56–11e5-b955–1a1d298b6250.html#axzz46AmvtlCA [accessed 18 April 2016].

42 See 'EU leaders sign letter objecting to Nord Stream-2 gas link', 16 March 2016, available at: http://uk.reuters.com/article/uk-eu-energy-nordstream-idUKKCN0WI1YV [accessed 8 April 2016].

43 See 'Speech by Vice-President Maroš Šefčovič on Nord Stream 2-Energy Union at the crossroads', European Parliament, Brussels, 6 April 2016, available at: http://europa.eu/rapid/press-release_SPEECH-16–1283_en.htm [accessed 1 September 2016].

44 Ibid.

45 See 'Merkel defends Nord Stream-2 pipeline', 18 December 2015, available at: www.rt.com/business/326440-merkel-gas-nord-stream2/ [accessed 22 April 2016].

46 See 'Faithful friend: German Vice Chancellor stands up for Nord Stream 2 project', 20 December 2015, available at: http://sputniknews.com/business/20151220/1032052337/faithful-friend-german-vice-chancellor-nord-stream.html [accessed 20 April 2016];

and 'Mounting political risks threaten Russia's new European gas pipeline', 27 March 2016, available at: www.forbes.com/sites/jeremymaxie/2016/03/27/mounting-political-risks-threaten-russias-new-european-gas-pipeline/#5dcbe5955d85 [accessed 26 April 2016].

47 Ibid.

48 See 'Putin and Renzi discuss potential energy projects', 8 January 2016, available at: www.euractiv.com/section/europe-s-east/news/putin-and-renzi-discuss-potential-energy-projects/ [accessed 28 May 2016]; and 'Nord Stream, Matteo Renzi chiama Vladimir Putin. L'Italia vuole partecipare alla creazione del gasdotto', 10 January 2016, available at: www.huffingtonpost.it/2016/01/10/nord-stream-renzi_n_8949454.html [accessed 29 May 2016].

49 See 'Gazprom revives "Poseidon" Adriatic link', 26 February 2016, available at: www.euractiv.com/section/energy/news/gazprom-revives-poseidon-adriatic-link/ [accessed 18 April 2016].

50 See 'UOKiK issues objections to a concentration: – Nord Stream 2', 22 July 2016, available at: www.uokik.gov.pl/news.php?news_id=12477&print=1 [accessed 20 September 2016].

51 See 'Russia to build Nord Stream 2 despite Polish objection', 22 August 2016, available at: https://euobserver.com/economic/134694 [accessed 21 September 2016].

52 See 'EU approves increased Gazprom use of Opal pipeline', 25 October 2016, available at: www.wsj.com/articles/eu-approves-increased-gazprom-use-of-opal-pipeline-1477416799 [accessed 2 November 2016]; and 'Gazprom gets improved Opal terms', 31 October 2016, available at: www.naturalgasworld.com/european-commission-sets-new-opal-terms-34209 [accessed 2 November 2016].

53 See 'Naftogaz warns of loss of transit revenue', 27 October 2016, available at: www.naturalgasworld.com/naftogaz-warns-of-loss-of-transit-revenue-34165 [accessed 1 November 2016].

54 See 'Gazprom to propose EU antitrust settlement', 27 October 2016, available at: www.naturalgasworld.com/gazprom-to-propose-eu-antitrust-settlement-34141 [accessed 4 November 2016].

55 In the following years, the TANAP's shareholding composition has changed. In 2016, TANAP was owned by Socar (58 percent), Botas (30 percent) and BP (12 percent).

56 See the joint press release by the Italian and the Greek government in *Il Sole 24 Ore*, 21 February, 2012, and the press accounts available at: www.reuters.com/article/2012/02/20/shah-deniz-idUSL5E8DK31320120220 [accessed 22 June 2016].

57 See the interview of the External Affairs Director of the TAP available at: www.naturalgaseurope.com/michael-hoffmann-tap-europe-energy-security [accessed 25 July 2016].

58 There are different definitions and categories for the concept of 'gas hubs'. In this chapter, the term mainly refers to the idea of 'transit hubs', the primary role of which is to facilitate the transit of large quantities of gas for onward transportation. On gas hubs and on transit hubs, see Heather (2012).

59 See 'Shah Deniz major sales agreements with European gas purchasers concluded', 19 September 2013, available at: www.bp.com/en_az/caspian/press/pressreleases/Shah-Deniz-sales-agreements-European-purchasers.html [accessed 10 September 2016].

60 See 'The Southern Gas Corridor and the EU gas security of supply: What's next?', 28 March 2015, available at: www.naturalgaseurope.com/southern-gas-corridor-and-eu-gas-security-of-supply-22688 [accessed 3 September 2016].

61 See, for example 'TAP pipeline offers Europe new gas supply', available at: www.dw.de/tap-pipeline-offers-europe-new-gas-supply/a-17974204 [accessed 26 August 2016].

62 See 'TAP route changes not ruled out, Greek minister says', available at: http://en.trend.az/business/energy/2375439.html [accessed 25 September 2016].

63 See 'Ue chiede a Italia di accelerare su Tap', ansa.it, 13 June 2014, and 'Cos'è il gasdotto Tap, al centro dell'incontro Renzi-Aliyev', available at: www.europaquotidiano.it/2014/07/13/trans-adriatic-pipeline/ [accessed 26 September 2016].

References

Aalto, P. (ed.) 2008. *The EU-Russian Energy Dialogue: Europe's Future Energy Security.* Farnham: Ashgate Publishing.

Aalto, P., Korkmaz Temel, D. 2014. European Energy Security: Natural Gas and the Integration Process. *Journal of Common Market Studies* 52(4): 758–774.

AEEG, 2009. *Annual Report to the European Commission on Regulatory Activities and the State of Services in the Electricity and Gas Sectors.* Rome, 31 July.

Aissaoui, A. 2016. *Algerian Gas: Troubling Trends, Troubled Policies.* Oxford Institute for Energy Studies, NG-108, May 2016.

Baev, P. K., Øverland, I. 2010. The South Stream versus Nabucco Pipeline Race: Geopolitical and Economic (Ir)rationales and Political Stakes in Mega-Projects. *International Affairs* 86(5): 1075–1090.

Balmaceda, M. M. 2008. *Energy Dependency, Politics and Corruption in the Former Soviet Union: Russia's Power, Oligarch's Profits and Ukraine's Missing Energy Policy, 1995–2006.* London: Routledge.

Balmaceda, M. M. 2012. Russia's Central and Eastern European Energy Transit Corridor: Ukraine and Belarus, in Aalto, P. (ed.), *Russia's Energy Policies: National, Interregional and Global Levels*, pp. 136–156. Cheltenham: Edward Elgar Publishing.

Balmaceda, M. M. 2013. *The Politics of Energy Dependency: Ukraine, Belarus, and Lithuania between Domestic Oligarchs and Russian Pressure.* Toronto: University of Toronto Press.

Belyi, A. V., Goldthau, A. 2015. *Between a Rock and a Hard Place: International Market Dynamics, Domestic Politics and Gazprom's Strategy.* EUI Working Papers, RSCAS 2015/22.

Bendik, S. W. 2008. *Nord Stream: Not Just a Pipeline: An Analysis of the Political Debates in the Baltic Sea Region Regarding the Planned Gas Pipeline from Russia to Germany.* FNI Report 15/2008.

Buchan, D. 2011. Energy Policy: Sharp Challenges and Rising Ambitions, in Wallace, H., Pollack, A., Young, A. R. (eds.), *Policy-Making in the European Union*, pp. 357–381. Oxford: Oxford University Press.

Coralluzzo, W. 2008. Italy and the Mediterranean: Relations with Maghreb Countries. *Modern Italy* 13(2): 115–133.

Darbouche, H. 2007. *Russian-Algerian Cooperation and the 'Gas OPEC': What's in the Pipeline?* Ceps Policy Brief, No. 123, March 2007.

Darbouche, H. 2010. 'Energising' EU-Algerian Relations. *The International Spectator* 45(3): 71–83.

De Micco, P. 2015. *Changing Pipelines, Shifting Strategies: Gas in South-Eastern Europe, and the Implications for Ukraine.* European Parliament, Policy Department, DG EXPO, July 2015.

DG Energy, 2014. *Quarterly Report on European Gas Markets.* European Commission, DG Energy, Vol. 7, issue 3.

Esmap, 2003. *Cross-Border Oil and Gas Pipelines: Problems and Prospects.* Joint UNDP/World Bank Energy Sector Management Assistance Programme, June 2003. Available at: www.esmap.org/node/383 [accessed 8 March 2016].

Estrada, J., Arild, M., Kare, D. M. (eds.) 1995. *The Development of European Gas Markets: Environmental, Economic and Political Perspectives.* Chichester: John Wiley Publisher.

European Commission, 2008. Second Strategic Energy Review. An EU Energy Security and Solidarity Action Plan. COM(2008) 781 final.

European Commission, 2010. *On the Implementation of Trans-European Energy Networks in the Period 2007–2009*. Brussels, COM(2010) 203 final.

European Commission, 2014. *Implementation of TEN-E, EEPR and PCI Projects*. Brussels, SWD(2014) 314 final.

European Commission, 2015a. *State of the Energy Union 2015*. Brussels, SWD(2015) 404 final.

European Commission, 2015b. *Energy Union Package: A Framework Strategy for a Resilient Energy Union with a Forward-Looking Climate Change Policy*. Brussels, COM(2015) 80 final.

European Council, 2015. *European Council Meeting 17 and 18 December 2015*. Conclusions, 18 December 2015, Brussels.

Finon, D. 2004. European Gas Markets: Nascent Competition and Integration in a Diversity of Models, in Finon, D., Midttun, A. (eds.), *Reshaping European Gas and Electricity Industries Regulation, Markets and Business Strategies*, pp. 183–237. Oxford: Elsevier.

Finon, D. 2011. The EU Foreign Gas Policy of Transit Corridors: Autopsy of the Stillborn Nabucco Project. *OPEC Energy Review* 35(1): 47–69.

Franza, L. 2015. *From South Stream to the Turk Stream: Prospects for Rerouting Options and Flows of Russian Gas to Parts of Europe and Turkey*. CIEP Paper, 2015/5.

Frappi, C., Varvelli, A. 2010. Le strategie di politica energetica dell'Italia. Criticità interne e opportunità internazionali. *Quaderni di Relazioni Internazionali* 13: 98–114.

German Federal Ministry of Economics and Technology, 2012. *German's New Energy Policy*. Berlin.

Giamouridis, A., Paleoyannis, S. 2011. *Security of Gas Supply in South Eastern Europe: Potential Contribution of Planned Pipelines, LNG, and Storage*. Oxford Institute for Energy Studies, NG-52, July 2011.

Goldthau, A. 2016. *Assessing Nord Stream 2: Regulation, Geopolitics, Energy Security in the EU, Central Eastern Europe and the UK*. EUCERS, Strategy Paper n. 10, July 2016.

Grätz, J. 2009. Energy Relations with Russia and Gas Market Liberalization. *Internationale Politik und Gesellschaft* 3(2009): 66–80.

Hayes, M. H. 2006. The Transmed and Maghreb Projects: Gas to Europe from North Africa, in Victor, D. G., Jaffe, A. M., Hayes, M. H. (eds.), *Natural Gas and Geopolitics: From 1970 to 2040*, pp. 49–90. Cambridge: Cambridge University Press.

Hayes, M. H., Victor, D. G. 2006. Politics, Markets, and the Shift to Gas: Insights from the Seven Historical Case Studies, in Victor, D. G., Jaffe, A. M., Hayes, M. H. (eds.), *Natural Gas and Geopolitics: From 1970 to 2040*, pp. 319–353. Cambridge: Cambridge University Press.

Heather, P. 2012. *Continental European Gas Hubs: Are They Fit for Purpose?* Oxford Institute for Energy Studies, NG-63, June 2012.

Henderson, J., Mitrova, T. 2015. *The Political and Commercial Dynamics of Russia's Gas Export Strategy*. Oxford Institute for Energy Studies, NG-102, September 2015.

Henderson, J., Pirani, S. (eds.) 2014. *The Russian Gas Matrix: How Markets Are Driving Change*. Oxford: Oxford University Press.

Herranz-Surrallés, A. 2015. An Emerging EU Energy Diplomacy? Discursive Shifts, Enduring Practices. *Journal of European Public Policy*: 1–21, doi: 10.1080/13501763.2015.1083044. 23 September 2015.

Högselius, P. 2013. *Red Gas: Russia and the Origins of European Energy Dependence.* London: Palgrave Macmillan.

Honoré, A. 2010. *European Natural Gas Demand, Supply, and Pricing: Cycles, Seasons, and the Impact of LNG Price Arbitrage.* Oxford: Oxford University Press.

Honoré, A. 2013. *The Italian Gas Market: Challenges and Opportunities.* Oxford Institute for Energy Studies, NG-76, June 2013.

IGU, 2015. *Wholesale Gas Price Survey.* 2015 Edition, International Gas Union.

Kohl, W. L. (ed.) 1982. *After the Second Oil Crisis: Energy Policies in Europe, American and Japan.* Lexington: Lexington Books.

Lee, R., Egede, T., Frater, L., Vaughan, S. 2008. *Legal Implications of the Nord Stream Project.* Policy Department External Policies, European Parliament, Briefing Paper, April 2008.

Locatelli, C. 2008. Gazprom's Export Strategies under the Institutional Constraint of the Russian Gas Market. *OPEC Energy Review* 32(3): 246–264.

Luciani, G., Mazzanti, M. R. 2006. Italian Energy Policy: The Quest for More Competition and Supply Security. *International Spectator* 41(3): 75–89.

Mabro, R., Wybrew-Bond, I. (eds.) 1999. *Gas to Europe: The Strategies of Four Major Suppliers.* Oxford: Oxford University Press.

Pirani, S. 2012. Russo-Ukrainian Gas Wars and the Call on Transit Governance, in Kuzemko, C., Belyi, A. V., Goldthau, A., Keating, M. F. (eds.), *Dynamics of Energy Governance in Europe and Russia*, pp. 169–186. London: Palgrave Macmillan.

Pirani, S., Henderson, J., Honoré, A., Rogers, H., Yafimava, K. 2014. *What the Ukraine Crisis Means for Gas Markets.* Oxford Energy Comment, Oxford Institute for Energy Studies, March 2014.

Pirani, S., Stern, J., Yafimava, K. 2009. *The Russo-Ukrainian Gas Dispute of January 2009: A Comprehensive Assessment.* Oxford Institute for Energy Studies, NG-27, February 2009.

Pirani, S., Yafimava, K. 2016. *Russian Gas Transit across Ukraine Post-2019: Pipeline Scenarios, Gas Flow Consequences, and Regulatory Constraints.* Oxford Institute for Energy Studies, NG-105, February 2016.

Proedrou, F. 2012. *EU Energy Security in the Gas Sector: Evolving Dynamics, Policy Dilemmas and Prospects.* Farnham: Ashgate Publishing.

Prontera, A. 2008. *L'Europeizzazione della politica energetica in Italia e Francia.* Macerata: EUM.

Prontera, A. 2015. Italian Energy Security, the Southern Gas Corridor and the New Pipeline Politics in Western Europe: From the Partner State to the Catalytic State. *Journal of International Relations and Development*, doi: 10.1057/jird.2015.31. 14 August 2015.

Radetzki, M. 1999. European Natural Gas: Market Forces Will Bring about Competition in Any Case. *Energy Policy* 27(1): 17–24.

Raszewski, S. 2012. Security and Economics of Energy in North East Europe, in Kuzemko, C., Belyi, A. V., Goldthau, A., Keating, M. F. (eds.), *Dynamics of Energy Governance in Europe and Russia*, pp. 130–148. Basingstoke: Palgrave Macmillan.

Sander, M. 2007. A 'Strategic Relationship'? The German Policy of Energy Security within the EU and the Importance of Russia, in Overhaus, M., Maull, H., Harnish, S. (eds.), *Dealing with Dependency: The European Union's Quest for a Common Energy Policy.* Foreign Policy in Dialogue, vol. 8, issue 20, pp. 16–24.

Sartori, N. 2012. *The European Commission's Policy towards the Southern Gas Corridor: Between National Interests and Economic Fundamentals.* IAI WP 12/1, January 2012, Rome.

Sartori, N. 2013. *Energy and Politics: Behind the Scenes of the Nabucco-TAP Competition.* IAI WP 13/27, July 2013, Rome.

Scarpa, C. 2012. *Italy between Excess Supply and Shortage.* Presentation in Berlin, 22 November 2012.

Schmidt-Felzmann, A. 2011. EU Member States' Energy Relations with Russia: Conflicting Approaches to Securing Natural Gas Supplies. *Geopolitics* 16(3): 574–599.

Schubert, S. R., Pollak, J., Kreutler, M. 2016. *Energy Policy of the European Union.* London: Palgrave.

Smith, H. 2012. Russian Foreign Policy and Energy: The Case of the Nord Stream Gas Pipeline, in Aalto, P. (ed.), *Russia's Energy Policies: National, Interregional and Global Levels*, pp. 117–136. Cheltenham: Edward Elgar Publishing.

Stern, J. 1990. *European Gas Markets: Challenge and Opportunity in the 1990s.* London: Dartmouth Publishing Company.

Stern, J. 1998. *Competition and Liberalization in European Gas Markets: A Diversity of Models.* London: Royal Institute of International Affairs.

Stern, J. 2006. *The Russian-Ukrainian Gas Crisis of 2006.* Oxford Institute for Energy Studies, January 2006.

Stern, J. 2007. *Is There a Rationale for the Continuing Link to Oil Product Prices in Continental European Long Term Gas Contracts?* Oxford Institute for Energy Studies, NG-19, April 2007.

Stern, J. 2009. *Continental European Long-Term Gas Contracts: Is a Transition away from Oil Product-Linked Pricing Inevitable and Imminent?* Oxford Institute for Energy Studies, NG-21, September 2009.

Stern, J. 2014. Russian Responses to Commercial Change in European Gas Markets, in Henderson, J., Pirani, S. (ed.), *The Russian Gas Matrix: How Markets Are Driving Change*, pp. 50–81. Oxford: Oxford University Press.

Stern, J., Pirani, S., Yafimava, K. 2015. *Does the Cancellation of South Stream Signal a Fundamental Reorientation of Russian Gas Export Policy?* Oxford Energy Comment, Oxford Institute for Energy Studies, January 2015.

Stern, J., Rogers, H. 2011. *The Transition to Hub-Based Gas Pricing in Continental Europe.* Oxford Institute for Energy Studies, NG-49, March 2011.

Stern, J., Rogers, H. 2014. *The Dynamics of a Liberalised European Gas Market: Key Determinants of Hub Prices, and Roles and Risks of Major Players.* Oxford Institute for Energy Studies, NG-94, December 2014.

Stopford, J., Strange, S. 1991. *Rival States, Rival Firms: Competition for World Market Shares.* Cambridge: Cambridge University Press.

Svyatets, E. 2016. *Energy Security and Cooperation in Eurasia: Power, Profits and Politics.* London: Routledge.

Talus, K. 2013. *EU Energy Law and Policy: A Critical Account.* Oxford: Oxford University Press.

Talus, K. 2015. European Union Energy: New Role for States and Markets, in Belyi, A., Talus, K. (eds.), *States and Markets in Hydrocarbon Sectors*, pp. 198–213. London: Palgrave-Macmillan.

Verda, M. 2016. A Link of Steel: The Western Europe-Russia Gas Pipeline Network in the Post-Soviet Era, in Bardazzi, R., Pazienza, M. G., Tonini, A. (eds.), *European Energy and Climate Security: Public Policies, Energy Sources, and Eastern Partnership*, pp. 37–65. Cham, Heidelberg, New York, Dordrecht, London: Springer.

Victor, N. M., Victor, D. G. 2006. Bypassing Ukraine: Exporting Russian Gas to Poland and Germany, in Victor, D. G., Jaffe, A. M., Hayes, M. H. (eds.), *Natural Gas and Geopolitics: From 1970 to 2040*, pp. 122–168. Cambridge: Cambridge University Press.

Waloszyk, M. 2014. *Law and Policy of the European Gas Market*. Cheltenham: Edward Elgar Publishing.

Westphal, K. 2008. Germany and EU-Russia Energy Dialogue, in Aalto, P. (ed.), *The EU-Russian Energy Dialogue: Europe's Future Energy Security*, pp. 93–119. Aldershor: Ashgate.

Winrow, G. M. 2009. *Problems and Prospects for the 'Fourth Corridor': The Positions and Role of Turkey on Gas Transit to Europe*. Oxford Institute for Energy Studies, NG-30, June 2009.

Yafimava, K. 2011. *The Transit Dimension of EU Energy Security: Russian Gas Transit across Ukraine, Belarus, and Moldova*. Oxford: Oxford University Press.

Youngs, R. 2009. *Energy Security: Europe's New Foreign Policy Challenge*. London: Routledge.

4 The Politics of LNG Development in Western and Eastern Europe

Liquefied natural gas or LNG is a form of natural gas that can be stored and transported by LNG tankers over long distances. This technology has been a crucial component of energy security for countries not easily connected by pipeline, such as Japan or Taiwan. Recently, however, LNG has also become a way for countries traditionally served by pipelines, such as those on the European continent, to diversify gas suppliers.

Although the LNG industry is capital-intensive, in the last decades LNG trade has steadily grown. Because regasification terminals are the least expensive component of the LNG chain, global regasification capacity has especially grown, and this has more than doubled global liquefaction capacity (IGU 2016). These developments have been paralleled by a growing flexibility in LNG trade and increasing interconnections among the main regional markets: Asia Pacific, Europe and North America. Technological advances, such as the emergence of Floating and Storage Regasification Units (FSRU), have added further flexibility to the LNG business and enhanced the potential contribution of LNG to consumers' energy security strategies worldwide. Different from pipelines, which tightly connect producers and consumers and often involve transit countries, LNG allows non-landlocked importers to design relatively more autonomous energy security policies to diversify their supplies – although the construction of regasification facilities can be a costly option, especially for small or isolated markets. On the other hand, the flexibility of LNG also means that producers can more easily redirect their gas to where prices are higher (usually in the Pacific Basin). Additionally, the more global the LNG market becomes, the less capacity and hard power tools European countries and the EU as whole have to secure the routes of international LNG trade. In this respect, unless important changes are made to European foreign and security policies, the EU could possibly become only a 'consumer' of security provided by the US, as is the case with the global oil market.

In the EU, LNG has been mainly concentrated in Western and Southern Europe, while in Eastern Europe only recently have governments taken action to promote regasification facilities as a broader strategy to diversify gas supplies and improve competition in their less mature markets. LNG has become an important political issue, especially as a means for the Baltic States to ease their complete dependence on Russian gas. However, despite the Baltic States' shared interest in diversifying their gas supplies, cooperation between them has been problematic due to the different situations of their energy markets, a lack of trust and their different foreign policy approaches towards Moscow.

In Western Europe as well, governments have supported LNG for improving diversification of gas supplies and increasing competition in their domestic markets according to their national agendas. But in this case LNG has not had the same political meaning of increasing national independence and security vis-à-vis the former hegemon. On the contrary, in many Western countries, especially in Southern Europe, LNG penetration has facilitated the ability of newcomers to challenge the predominant position of former state-owned incumbents in national gas markets. Moreover, while EU institutions have been more directly involved in LNG development in the Baltics, in Western European countries the main effect of the EU on the politics of LNG has been indirect and related to the wider process of constructing the internal energy market already analysed in Chapter 3.

Notwithstanding these important differences grounded in the specific political, institutional and market contexts in which the politics of LNG development has taken place, some similarities can be highlighted in both cases. In particular, in both Western and Eastern Europe national governments have played a crucial role in promoting LNG and interacted with a wider set of market and non-market actors to pursue their goals, although with different degrees of involvement and effectiveness.

In the first section of this Chapter the basic features of the emerging, global LNG market are briefly illustrated. Then, the main historical steps of the LNG industry and EU policies are presented, including recent events that have brought new players and new rules of the game that have challenged the traditional approach, especially among Western consumers. In the third section, the focus moves to the Baltic region. The politics of LNG in Lithuania, Estonia and Latvia is in particular analysed, considering both the domestic dynamics and the role of important external players such as the EU and Russia. Finally, the fourth section focuses on the three main Western Mediterranean consumers (France, Italy and Spain) that were among the firsts 'old' member states to build LNG receiving terminals in the 1970s and the 1980s. In this section the analysis provides a historical perspective on the gradual shift from the traditional politics of LNG – the partner state model – to the current situation in which a broader set of public and private actors are involved in LNG development and market dynamics interact with government strategies – although with peculiarities related to the specific political and institutional contexts of each country. In particular, the 'rise' of the catalytic state in France, Italy and Spain will be illustrated by focusing on two main periods: i) the 1990s, when the first breaches appeared into the original partner state model, and ii) the 2000s when the main elements of the catalytic state begun more clearly to emerge.

The Emerging Global Market of LNG

The LNG business took off in the1960s, with the first LNG shipments going from Algeria to the UK and France, and from Libya to Italy and Spain. In the late 1960s LNG also arrived in the Pacific Basin, with the first cargos going from Alaska to

Japan. Initially, the Atlantic Basin and especially Europe was the main market for LNG. In the following decade this situation changed dramatically (Stern and Koyama 2016). Different developments halted the LNG expansion in the Atlantic Basin, such as price disputes between importers and Algeria and Libya, the liberalisation of the US gas sector with the 1978 Natural Gas Policy Act, which created a surplus of supply over demand, and the increase in domestic production and the arrival of relative cheaper pipeline gas from abroad in Europe. On the other hand, after the oil shocks the major Asian industrial economies – Japan, South Korea and Taiwan – witnessed a steady growth of LNG consumption, and since the early 1980s the Pacific Basin has become the main area for LNG trade.

In the 1990s, worldwide investment in LNG infrastructure grew. Economies of scale throughout the value chain and technical advances facilitated cost reductions making LNG more competitive (Ruester 2010; Jacobs 2011). At the beginning of the 2000s, the rise in gas prices and the fast development of many Asian economies further incentivised investments in liquefaction facilities (de Jong, van der Linde and Smeenk 2010). Along with traditional LNG suppliers (Algeria, Australia, Indonesia and Malesia), new players entered the market, such as Trinidad and Tobago, Nigeria, Egypt, Equatorial Guinea and Qatar, which in 2006 became the world's largest LNG exporter. In turn, the volume of LNG offered to international markets and LNG trade increased. In 2000 LNG trade accounted for about 20 percent of global gas trade, in 2007 it accounted for about 25 percent and at the beginning of the 2010s it surpassed 30 percent (ENI 2015a). LNG trade has not only grown in volume, but also in geographic reach. Although the Pacific Basin remains the main region of LNG consumption – also due to the growing role of newcomers such as China and India – many countries around the world are now involved in LNG trade with growing interconnections among the main regional markets (Europe, North America and the Asia Pacific) (Table 4.1).

The 2000s were also a period of important transformations in the institutional structures and industrial organisation of LNG business (Jensen 2003, 2004; Ruester 2010). Originally, the LNG business model was similar to the traditional scheme for piped gas. Bilateral long-term contracts, with a duration of 20 years or more, indexed to oil and committed to a substantial buyer in a specific market were the rule. However, from the beginning of the 2000s, driven by arbitrage opportunities, high market prices, market liberalisation and the opening of the liquid US market, new business models emerged allowing greater market flexibility (i.e. contracts were more flexible, contract durations decreased and spot markets gained in liquidity) (CIEP 2008, 41–42; Hirschhausen et al. 2008). This development was paralleled by a transformation in the organisational structure of LNG trade (Jensen 2004; Ruester 2010). When LNG was an infant industry, sellers were typically either major oil companies or the national oil companies of producing countries (or joint ventures among them), whereas LNG buyers were either monopoly state-owned gas companies, especially in Western Europe, or regulated utilities, mainly in Asia. With the expansion and the new flexibility of LNG trade and the liberalisation of many Western gas markets, this structure has progressively been challenged

Table 4.1 Major LNG exporting and importing countries in 2010 and 2015.

	Ranking 2010 *(% of world's total)*		*Ranking 2015* *(% of world's total)*	
Main LNG	1	Qatar (26)	1	Qatar (31)
exporting countries	2	Indonesia (11)	2	Australia (12)
	3	Malaysia (10)	3	Malaysia (10)
	4	Australia (9)	4	Nigeria (8)
	5	Nigeria (8)	5	Indonesia (6)
	6	Trinidad (7)	6	Trinidad (5)
	7	Algeria (6)	7	Algeria (5)
	8	Russia (5)	8	Russia (4)
	9	Oman (5)	9	Oman (3)
	10	Egypt (3)	10	Papua New Guinea (3)
Main LNG	1	Japan (32)	1	Japan (34)
importing countries	2	South Korea (15)	2	South Korea (13)
	3	Spain (9)	3	China (8)
	4	UK (6)	4	India (6)
	5	Taiwan (5)	5	Taiwan (6)
	6	France (5)	6	UK (4)
	7	China (4)	7	Spain (3)
	8	India (4)	8	Turkey (2)
	9	US (4)	9	Brazil (2)
	10	Italy (3)	10	Mexico (1)

Sources: IGU (2011, 2016).

(Ruester 2010). Vertical integration and strategic partnerships have complicated the original picture. Today private oil majors and producers' national oil companies take part in the downstream sector in consumer countries, and gas or electricity utilities take increasing part in upstream activities as a means to secure their own gas supplies. Transformations have involved the business model of LNG regasification terminals as well (Le Fevre 2016, 186–191). The key feature of the original model – integrated or dedicated model – was that the terminal was built and financed on the basis of exclusive access for specific upstream development in producer countries (i.e. LNG regasification terminals formed part of an integrated LNG supply chain). However, in the last two decades different business models have emerged: the merchant/hybrid and the tolling terminals. In the first case, the terminal is not linked to a specific source of gas but is owned by companies seeking new sources of supply and choosing LNG as an attractive option. In other words, in the merchant/hybrid model different from the integrated model the terminal is developed independently of the supply source. The tolling terminals, instead, are developed and owned by companies that are not involved in upstream ventures or as LNG buyers, but that rent the terminal capacity to third parties (usually the LNG seller or the gas buyer).

Recently, especially in the Atlantic Basin, this trend towards greater flexibility has been reinforced by the US shale gas revolution, the further liberalisation of the European gas market and the expansion of Asian demand. These developments have created the context for more active and intercontinental LNG trade and further challenged the original business practices and the traditional long-term/oil-linked price regime in favour of short-term contracts, spot markets and gas-to-gas competition in gas hubs[1] (Stern and Rogers 2012; Belyi 2015; Corbeau and Ledesma 2016). It is worth noting, however, that short-term LNG trade represents only about the 30 percent of the total LNG trade and long-term contracts are still considered 'the pillar of the LNG industry' (Corbeau 2016, 575). But although the idea of a global LNG market as flexible as the oil market is far from the reality (as economic, institutional and political constraints continue to favour the regionalisation of LNG trade), interconnections between the various regional markets are growing both with regard to physical gas flows and price signals.

The US shale gas revolution – with the US expected to potentially become a major LNG supplier by 2020 – has also attracted wider interest in Europe. The European Commission has tried to include an energy chapter in negotiations on the Transatlantic Trade and Investment Partnership (TTIP). But to date negotiations remain difficult and pending and on both sides of the Atlantic oppositions to this agreement are growing. Moreover, internal political constraints remain high and the recent low price environment has added additional uncertainty to several US LNG projects (Corbeau 2016; De Micco 2016). In assessing the prospect of importing US LNG into the EU, global market dynamics are also important, such as the generally lower prices of Russian gas or the traditionally higher LNG prices paid by Asian consumers (although since 2014–15 also in this region gas prices have dropped). Obviously, political considerations are important as well, such as some European countries' 'willingness to pay' to reduce dependence on Moscow.

LNG in the EU Gas Market: The New Players and the New 'Rules of the Game'

As anticipated, although the LNG business first developed in Western Europe, in the 1960s, the penetration of this technology into the continent was halted in the following decades. Increasing domestic production and the pipeline gas that began to arrive from Russia, Norway and North Africa relegated LNG to a niche in the Southern European gas market (CIEP 2008). Regasification terminals were located in France, Italy and Spain due to their favourable geographic positions, and Algeria was their main supplier. Gradually, by the end of the 1990s this situation changed. In this period LNG started to be considered a good solution in terms of diversification of supply and costs (Corbeau and Flower 2016). LNG was available from a growing number of suppliers, via different routes and did not have to face the transit risks of pipeline gas. Besides, it was becoming cheaper, through substantial reductions in capital and shipping costs that enabled price competition with pipeline gas. In a market context characterised by an expected growing gas demand in many EU countries, notably in the power sector, new

LNG terminals were built in other member states: first in Belgium, Greece and Portugal and then in the mid-2000s in the UK, where LNG became an important element for compensating for declining North Sea production. In 2006, there were 12 LNG terminals in the EU: five in Spain, two in France and one each in Belgium, Greece, Italy, Portugal and the UK. The total receiving capacity of these terminals was about 78 bcm/y and was mainly concentrated in Spain (with 43 bcm/y) and France (15 bcm/y) (ENI 2015a).

In the second part of the 2000s new capacity was built, additional projects were planned and more countries became involved in LNG trade. LNG regasification terminals were incentivised in the context of the EU internal energy market (IEM) rules. Many national governments enacted additional measures to improve LNG development as a strategy both to increase competition in their domestic market and to diversify their gas suppliers. Member state strategies, however, were developed according to national agendas with no coordination at the European level. In 2008, the European Commission debated the opportunity to issue a comprehensive action plan for LNG. But, in the end, the existing framework of the IEM (e.g. the TPA exemption and the TEN-E scheme) was considered sufficient to support LNG penetration into the EU gas market (Hirschhausen et al. 2008).

The first LNG projects in Southern Europe were mainly based on bilateral long-term contracts, implemented according to the integrated business model and were promoted by the traditional national champions (i.e. Enagas in Spain, GDF in France and ENI in Italy). In the 1990s–2000s, however, LNG trade became more flexible and open to new market players and business strategies. In the wake of EU energy market liberalisation, the general trend towards more flexibility in global LNG trade and the European Commission's efforts to eliminate territorial restrictions for long-term contracts, LNG contributed to making the EU gas market more liquid and competitive, notably in Northwest Europe. Moreover, new companies – European electricity utilities, producers' national oil company, oil majors etc. – entered the LNG business, further contributing to enhanced competition in many national markets. In the EU liberalised market structure, LNG offered advantages, such as flexibility and smaller size compared to long-distance pipelines. But access to existing LNG terminals was often on a negotiated basis, so new entrants opted to build their own LNG terminals, notably in Italy and in the UK and Spain, where new projects were realised according to the merchant/hybrid or tolling models as well (Corbeau and Flower 2016; Le Fevre 2016). European utilities also began to take part in LNG upstream ventures to secure their supplies and to overcome national incumbents' dominant positions and a rigid supply structure that was in many cases still linked to pipelines built in the pre-liberalisation period.

LNG development not only favoured the entrance of new market players into the EU gas market and the move towards greater flexibility in gas trade, but it also widened the set of European suppliers beyond Algeria, Norway and Russia, the traditional partners. After an initial period dominated by Algeria, a variegated set of producers became involved in supplying the EU. In 2014, Qatar accounted for more than 40 percent of the total LNG supply to the EU. After Algeria, in second position with 25 percent, important suppliers were Nigeria (10 percent), Trinidad and Tobago (7 percent), Peru and Oman (Eurogas 2015). On the demand side, regasification capacity steadily grew in traditional importers, and new member states such as Lithuania (in 2014) and Poland (in 2016) joined the 'LNG club' (Figure 4.1). Counting only large-scale terminals, EU regasification capacity in 2016 reached 213.6 bcm/y (Table 4.2). Planned projects – projects that lack a final investment decision – could result in additional 146 bcm/y in the coming years (European Commission 2016a). These projects are spread among several regions and countries: in Northern and Central Europe (one project in Germany, Denmark and Ireland), in the Balkans (one project in Croatia and Albania) and in the Baltics and Eastern Europe (one project in Finland, Estonia, Latvia and Romania).

Current EU LNG regasification capacity is considered sufficient overall (European Commission 2016b). In many countries installed LNG capacity in theory might cover a significant portion of annual consumption, while in other countries such as Spain and Portugal LNG capacity largely exceeds annual consumption (Table 4.2). However, in recent years (2011–14), as a result of the Fukushima nuclear accident – which prompted a surge of Japanese LNG imports, higher demand and LNG prices in other Asian markets, combined with competition from pipeline gas and stagnant gas demand in Europe, utilisation rates for the EU LNG

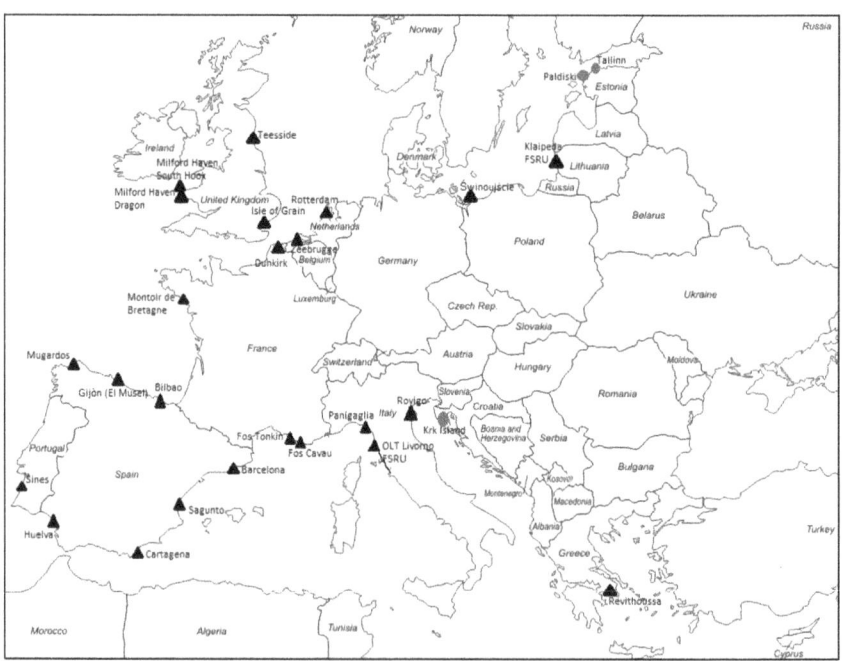

Figure 4.1 LNG importing terminals in the EU member states (existing and planned).

Note: Author's elaboration for illustration. Black triangle = existing LNG terminals; grey circles: planned LNG terminals included in the 2015 EU PCI list and recalled in the 2016 EU LNG Strategy (European Commission 2016a).

Table 4.2 LNG terminals and LNG installed capacity in the EU.

	LNG existing terminals	Installed annual capacity/bcm	Annual consumption/bcm (LNG installed capacity as % of annual consumption) (*)
Spain	7	68.9	27.6 (249)
UK	4	52.3	68.3 (76)
France	4	34.7	39.2 (88)
Italy	3	14.8	61.4 (24)
Netherlands	1	12	31.8 (37)
Belgium	1	9	15.1 (59)
Portugal	1	7.9	4.3 (183)
Greece	1	5	2.8 (178)
Lithuania	1	4	2.3 (173)
Poland	1	5	16.7 (29)
Total	22	213.6	—

Source: European Commission (2016a) and author's own elaboration.

(*) = total annual consumption in 2015 (BP 2015).

terminals have been relatively low. The average rate of LNG utilisation (of total installed capacity) has decreased from 53 percent in 2010 to 25 percent in 2013, compared with a global average of 33 percent (European Commission 2016a). On the other hand, as a result of the lack of coordination and cooperation among member states, EU regasification capacity is mainly concentrated in Northwest Europe and the Iberian Peninsula, whereas there is limited access to LNG in Central and Southeast Europe, the more vulnerable regions from a security of supply perspective. Against this background, in its 2016 communication on *An EU strategy for liquefied natural gas and gas storage*, the European Commission has reaffirmed that although, 'in principle, LNG terminals should be financed through tariffs (. . .) EU funds can help to make up for the weak commercial viability of terminals that are particularly important for security of supply' (European Commission 2016b, 4). In this regard the 2016 LNG strategy pointed to a subset of LNG projects already included in the 2015 PCI list, including an LNG terminal in Krk (Croatia) and an LNG terminal in the Baltic region (Paldiski or Tallinn in Estonia) (Figure 4.1). Moreover, in 2015 EU funds contributed to the construction of the first Polish LNG terminal at Świnoujście.

LNG Development in Eastern Europe

The Soviet Legacy and the Baltics as 'Energy Islands'

When Estonia, Latvia and Lithuania gained independence, their energy infrastructural systems were still integrated with the former Soviet one. In the gas sector, supplies were brought to the Baltics only from Russia via Gazprom-owned pipelines. Since the 1990s, policymakers in Vilnius, Tallinn and Riga have begun to consider their energy dependency on Moscow to be an important issue to address, as well as one imbued with significant political and symbolic elements and with ramifications into domestic politics (e.g. Sprūds and Rostoks 2009; Grigas 2012, 2013; Raszewski 2012).

In the first period after independence, the Baltics took control of their gas sectors and established state-owned vertically integrated companies. However, when these companies were privatised between the end of the 1990s and the beginning of the 2000s, Gazprom also became an important player in their domestic gas markets. Along with the German E.On-Ruhrgas and the other Russian company Itera, Gazprom acquired important stakes in all Baltic national companies. Gazprom acquired the 37 percent of the Estonian Eesti Gaas (Itera acquired a 10 percent share), 34 percent of the Latvian Latvijas Gāze (Itera acquired 16 percent) and 37 percent of the Lithuania Lietuvos Dujos (Grigas 2013). These companies were involved in the import, transmission and sales of natural gas and in the case of Latvia also the management of the Inčukalns storage facility, the only underground storage facility in the region. Gazprom's and Itera's acquisitions reinforced the commercial ties between the Baltics and Moscow and strengthened the constellation of domestic actors supporting the status quo with regard to energy diversification and market openings. The 1997 Latvian privatisation agreement also granted Latvijas Gaze exclusive rights to ensure transportation, storage, distribution and sales of natural gas until 2017, a deal that would later further complicate the liberalisation process of that country.

Once the Baltics joined the EU (and NATO) they became the most vulnerable member states. Not only did they rely on a single gas supplier (Russia), but also they were not connected with the EU energy networks. Moreover, different from other post-Soviet states, the Baltics were not transit states for Russian gas exports to the lucrative Western markets. This situation increased the perception of vulnerability in Vilnius, Riga and Tallinn: should there be a Russian gas cut off, no major EU members would be affected and there would be little incentive for a common EU response. Only Lithuania had a different position in this regard, as it is a transit state for the Russian enclave of Kaliningrad. This situation was used by Vilnius as a bargaining tool with Moscow in the 1990s and in more recent years (Drezner 1999; Grigas 2013; Mišík and Prachàrovà 2016).

Latvia also has a comparative advantage with the Inčukalns storage facility. Inčukalns, with a capacity of about 4 bcm, is the only significant gas storage facility in the region. Besides Latvia, it serves Lithuania, Estonia and northwest Russia in the winter period (Sprūds 2009). In theory this facility could ensure the gas supply if there were a disruption in Russian exports to the Baltics. Indeed, the Baltic States have very small markets. In 2015 gas demand was about 2.7 bcm in Lithuania, 1.6 bcm in Latvia and only 0.7 bcm in Estonia (Dudzińska 2015). But the fact that Gazprom is a partial owner of Inčukalns storage through its participation in Latvijas Gāze has increased the perception of insecurity among Baltic policymakers, especially in Estonia and Lithuania. Finally, although Estonia did not inherit the advantages of Lithuania and Latvia, of the three it has traditionally had the lowest level of gas among its energy mix. During and after the 2000s, the contribution of gas to Estonia's total energy consumption was constantly around 10 percent.[2] In the same period the contribution of gas to Latvia's energy consumption oscillated between 25 percent and 30 percent, whereas in Lithuania it increased from about 20 percent in the mid-2000s to over 35 percent at the end of the decade.[3] In particular, Lithuanian gas consumption increased after EU accession, which brought the complete closure of the Ignalina nuclear power plant in late 2000s. This nuclear power plant had accounted for the majority of Lithuanian national electricity production and its closure also affected Latvia, which imported electricity from Lithuania (Godzimirski, Vilpišauskas and Romas 2015).

With the closure of the Ignalina nuclear power plant in 2009, the Lithuanian government established a special task force to explore possible solutions to improve its national energy security. Several meetings took place with representatives of the other Baltic governments and the European Commission. Indeed, during this period concerns also arose in Brussels about the very peculiar situation of these new member states that, with a single Estonia–Finland electricity interconnector, were practically isolated from EU power and gas networks. In this context and in the wake of the Russian-Ukrainian gas crisis, the phrase 'energy islands' began to circulate, describing the Baltics' situation (Godzimirski, Vilpišauskas and Romas 2015, 60–61).

Initially, the Lithuanian government tried to negotiate with the EU to postpone the closure of the Ignalina nuclear power plant, but without success. However, the European Commission agreed to launch a new instrument to improve regional energy security. In 2008, the EU Baltic Energy Market Interconnection Plan (BEMIP) was established with the participation of the European Commission and the eight countries surrounding the Baltic Sea: Sweden, Denmark, Estonia, Finland, Germany, Latvia, Lithuania and Poland. (Norway, as a European Economic Area member, took part in the initiative as an observer.) A high-level group was established to elaborate a first action plan, which was endorsed in 2009 by the Baltic Sea region member states and the European Commission. The action plan aimed at developing regional electricity and gas markets, accelerating the adoption of the EU rules, enhancing physical interconnections, diversifying sources and routes of natural gas supplies and enhancing coordination in the oil sector. Financially, the European Economic Recovery Plan supported it. BEMIP projects could also be funded through the European Regional Development Fund, the EU's Cohesion Fund and, later, as PCI through the Connecting Europe Facility. Although the initiative involved all the EU members around the Baltic Sea, its main goal was to help end the isolation of Lithuania, Estonia, Latvia and Finland. With regard to gas interconnections, the main projects considered were the upgrading of the existing networks between Lithuania and Latvia and between Latvia and Estonia (including the upgrading of the Inčukalns gas storage facility), creating a pipeline connecting Poland and Lithuania (PolLit), creating an offshore pipeline connecting Estonia and Finland (the Balticconnector) and adding several LNG terminals proposed by the Baltic states (BEMIP 2009).

The Difficult Path towards LNG: Competing Projects, Market and Regulatory Constraints and Limited Cooperation

Since the end of the 1990s, the idea of building an LNG regasification facility to end the isolation of the Baltic States has been widely discussed among decision makers and experts. In coordinating the BEMIP initiative, the European Commission included all of the LNG terminals proposed by Lithuania, Estonia, Latvia and Finland, although at that time, many projects seemed to be in an embryonic state (lacking clear timescales and developers) and seemed to mainly reflect the political will of the Baltic governments rather than sound commercial feasibility (Table 4.3).

Nevertheless, the European Commission also clearly recommended that only 'one LNG terminal' be built in the east Baltic Sea area 'as the relative small gas markets in Finland, Estonia, Latvia and Lithuania do not generate scope for more than one' (BEMIP 2009, 20). Thus, only one 'regional' terminal would obtain EU financial support. This support is especially important due to the small Baltic markets and to the limited economic resources that these states can mobilise for such costly infrastructure. In 2009, the High Level Group of the BEMIP decided to create a task force to identify the project that would serve as the 'regional' LNG. All of the Baltic States tried to gain the support of the European Commission and, thus, obtain financial aid for their preferred projects. Lack of cooperation prevented these states from selecting one specific project and, in turn, prevented the European Commission from deciding which 'regional' project to support. By 2011, the stalemate had not been resolved. Latvia insisted that an LNG terminal near Riga was the most appropriate solution due to the proximity of the Inčukalns storage facility. The Latvian Prime Minister, Valdis

Table 4.3 LNG projects under consideration in the East Baltic region up to 2009.

Country/LNG project	Main features of the project (location/ capacity/costs)	Target timescales	Project's status	Responsible body
Finland/Finngulf LNG	Location: Inkoo or Skoldvik Capacity: 2–3 bcm/y Costs: –	—	Feasibility study ongoing	Gasum Oy
Lithuania/New LNG terminal	Capacity: 3 bcm/y Costs: €270–320m	2012–18	—	—
Estonia/New LNG terminal	Location: Paldiski or Tallinn Capacity: 2.5 bcm/y Costs: €480m	2015	—	Eesti Gaas, others
Latvia/LNG terminal	—	2012–18	—	—

Source: Author's compilation from BEMIP Action Plan (BEMIP 2009).

Dombrovskis, proposed to focus first on the construction of the – Poland-Lithuania pipeline. Lithuania and Estonia were still committed to realising an LNG terminal, but they would only agree to the Riga location if the European Commission recognised it as the most appropriate place for the regional project; the fact that the Inčukalns facility was under the control of Gazprom worried Vilnius and Tallinn.[4] Hence, the Baltics decided to ask the European Commission to take a position and resolve the dispute. In response, the European Commission commissioned a study to determine which state should receive financial support for the regional LNG terminal. The final report, by the consulting firm Booz & Co. (2012), confirmed that the Baltics market, including Finland, could support only one regional LNG facility and that the best location for this terminal – also according to the EU N-1 rule – would be on the shore of the Gulf of Finland in Estonia or Finland.

Meanwhile, the Lithuanian government had become convinced that a regional LNG terminal would not be built before 2020 and decided to push forward with its own energy security strategy. During this period, the Lithuanian government was the most active in reforming its national gas sector, reducing Gazprom's presence in its national market and enhancing energy diversification. This position was in line with Lithuania's more assertive foreign policy towards Moscow. In this respect, it was closer to the Polish position than to that of Estonia and Latvia, which had traditionally opted for more pragmatic engagement with the former hegemon (Leonard and Popescu 2007).

Lithuania's decisive move in this direction occurred from 2010 to 2012. In this period, the centre-right conservative government led by Andrius Kubilius, appointed in October 2008, issued its National Energy Independence Strategy (with the goal of making the country energy independent by 2020) and a new Law on Natural Gas. It also decided to fully implement the EU's Third Energy Package by adopting ownership unbundling, the most stringent of the unbundling options. In theory, Lithuania – like Estonia and Latvia – was exempted from the unbundling provisions of the Third Energy Package by virtue of its peculiar situation as an 'energy island'. Lithuania had foregone its right to this exemption in 2008. But the government's original intention, at least in the first years, was to apply the Independent Transmission Operator model – the least stringent unbundling option and the most favourable solution for a vertically integrated incumbent (and thus for Gazprom). However, the new conservative government renounced the exemption and opted for the ownership unbundling model that required the sale of pipelines managed by Lietuvos Dujos by the end of 2014, with the intention of limiting Gazprom's influence on the Lithuanian domestic gas sector (Dudzińska 2012; Pakalkaité 2016). The government's decision was accompanied by the announcement of plans to build a floating LNG facility, which was to become operational by December 2014 at the port of Klaipeda, the largest port of Lithuania (NEIS 2012). Klaipeda was also chosen for the location of a gas pipeline connecting this area with the Lithuanian gas network, which in turn is connected with the Latvian system and the Inčukalns gas storage facility. The government set the deadline of December 2014 for the LNG facility because it had decided that the new terminal would need to fulfil the EU N-1 rule attached to Regulation 994/2010 on the Security of Gas Supply, which would have to be implemented by 3 December 2014 (Pakalkaité 2016).

The Lithuanian government's decision on ownership unbundling triggered a strong reaction by the major shareholders of Lietuvos Dujos, Gazprom and E.On, and also by some opposition parties and domestic actors involved in the gas business (Grigas 2013, 86–87; Jankauskas 2015). In particular, the Russian company and Moscow tried to convince Lithuania to change its position through indirect threats of higher gas prices and international arbitration. The issue of gas prices was particularly important and politically sensitive for the Lithuanian government: in 2011, Lithuania was estimated to pay, on average, 20 percent more for Russian gas imports than Latvia and 15 percent more than Estonia (Pakalkaité 2016, 15–16).[5] In 2012, Vilnius initiated a legal action against Gazprom at the Stockholm Arbitration Tribunal for alleged distortion of gas prices in Lithuania between 2004 and 2012.[6] Lithuania also approached the European Commission and formally voiced its complaints to the Directorate-General for Competition (DG Competition). (In 2012, DG Competition launched its antitrust investigation against Gazprom [see Chapter 3].) The same year, Gazprom, in turn, decided to take Lithuania to an international arbitration according to UNCITRAL rules, claiming that the unbundling provision violated an existing bilateral investment protection treaty. However, the Gazprom move and Moscow's position did not reverse government policy and, after a year of tough negotiations, an agreement was reached to continue the unbundling process. It is worth noting that, by 2011, the European Commission and, in particular, the DG for Energy (DG ENER), was involved in these negotiations. This involvement followed upon a request from the Lithuanian government, which hoped to strengthen its bargaining position vis-à-vis the Russian company (Pakalkaité 2016). By the beginning of 2010, the Lithuanian government had already involved the European Commission, which provided comments and feedback on draft laws for the transposition of the Third Energy Package and the LNG terminal. But the EU's engagement in the bilateral negotiations between Lithuania and Gazprom and E.On – in which the European Commission participated until mid-2014 – represented a more proactive and direct involvement in support of the Lithuanian government's plans. (At the time, the only precedent for the Commission's close involvement in bilateral negotiations between a member state and its energy suppliers was the 2010 case of Poland's negotiations with Gazprom) (Pakalkaité 2016, 17–19).

Lithuania's approach did not change with the new government led by Algirdas Butkevičius of the Social Democratic Party, who was appointed in December 2012. Although the party had previously opposed the ownership unbundling, it now embraced the energy security agenda of Kubilius's cabinet, which was also supported by Lithuanian President Dalia Grybauskaite. According to the newly appointed government's plan, the gas pipelines and gas transmission network would be separated from Lietuvos Dujos, and the network would be taken over by a new state-owned company, Amber Grid, which was created in 2013. The following year, Gazprom and the German E.On decided to sell their shares in Lietuvos

Dujos to the state-owned energy company Lietuvos Energija.[7] Finally, in 2015, Gazprom pulled out of the international arbitration case against Lithuania, arguing that the case was no longer relevant since the company had sold its related assets.[8]

The other Baltic States have been more cautious in reforming their gas sectors. Both Estonia and Latvia sought exemptions from the Third Energy Package provisions until 2014 and opted for the Independent Transmission Operator model. Nonetheless, in 2012, Estonia, under the liberal – conservative coalition government led by Andrus Ansip, reviewed its position and decided not to apply the exemption. It also opted for the ownership unbundling model, requiring Eesti Gaas to sell its natural gas transportation network before the end of 2014.[9] In November 2013, EG Võrguteenus, the owner of the gas transmission network, was separated from Eesti Gaas. In 2015, the company was acquired by the state-owned electricity transmission system operator Elering, which also acquired the stakes of Gazprom and Itera. Latvia took a very different approach: In 2014, the coalition government led by the liberal – conservative Unity party postponed the implementation of the Third Energy Package provisions until 2017. This decision was influenced by the 1997 privatisation agreement that had granted Latvijas Gaze exclusive rights to gas supply and distribution until 2017, but it was also in line with Latvia's more pragmatic and less assertive foreign policy approach toward Moscow (Grigas 2013; Āboltiņš 2015).

All in all, the differing approaches towards domestic gas market liberalisation and the differing paces of implementation of the Third energy package created additional problems for securing a regional LNG solution. The position of Latvia was especially concerning for the other Baltics, creating an additional complication in a process of cooperation that was already problematic due to existing divisions between Vilnius, Tallinn and Riga. In this context, Lithuania was firmly committed to putting forward its diversification plan. The disputes with Gazprom, and later the – Russian-Ukrainian conflict, further strengthened the government's willingness to accelerate efforts toward a national LNG terminal.

Between 'Independence' and Regional Integration

From 2012 to 2013, despite intensive discussion, Estonia and Finland were not able to agree on the location of the regional LNG terminal. Meanwhile, in Lithuania, work on the Klaipeda terminal was moving ahead in parallel with the efforts to implement the Third Energy Package and the ownership unbundling. However, the Lithuanian LNG was not a candidate for EU financial support as it was not a regional project but a national initiative. Moreover, this project was not commercially viable without the involvement and financial support of the Lithuanian state. Against this background, the government first negotiated an agreement with the Norwegian company Höegh LNG for a 10-year lease of a floating LNG storage and regasification unit (with a maximum capacity of about 4 bcm/y) to be delivered by the end of 2014 (Dudzińska 2012). A state-owned company controlled by the Ministry of Energy, Klaipedos Nafta, was then directly involved in the project, and the Lithuanian government made a financial contribution to the terminal's construction and operation, imposing a fee on all users of the transportation system distributing gas for the terminal. These government decisions were opposed by some domestic actors. These included the Lithuanian Gas Association – the main members of which had ownership and/or long-term gas supply relations with Gazprom – and the fertiliser producer Achema, the largest single gas consumer in Lithuania (Pakalkaité 2016). In November 2012, the Lithuanian Gas Association also filed a complaint to the EU DG Competition, arguing that the planned LNG terminal would receive illegal and incompatible state aid. However, the government's state aid, totalling about 448 million euros, was approved in 2013 by the European Commission. The DG Competition also approved a 'purchase obligation' allowing the Lithuanian government to oblige certain electricity and heat producers to buy a certain amount of LNG cargo (Goldthau and Sitter 2015, 87). Although both measures gave rise to competition concerns, the EU Competition Commissioner, Joaquin Almunia, stressed that the aid would 'reduce Lithuania's dependence on a single source of gas supplies and enhance its security of supply' and added that, by diversifying gas supply sources, the terminal would also 'stimulate competition between gas suppliers' and eventually 'benefit consumers' (European Commission 2013a). The project also received support from the European Investment Bank, which lent 87 million euros to Klaipedos Nafta for the construction and operation of the LNG facility. Finally, in 2014, Litgas, part of the state-owned company Lietuvos Energija, contracted a volume of 540 million cubic metres of gas for five years from the Norwegian company Statoil.

With state-backed financial guarantees and a strong government commitment, the construction of the import facility at Klaipeda obtained all necessary permits and was completed in a short period of time. By December 2014, the terminal was operative. The government decided to operate the terminal under the TPA regime. Although its primary goal was to ease national energy security concerns with its capacity, which would be enough to cover all Lithuanian consumption and a significant part of Latvian and Estonian gas demands, the facility would allow its Baltic neighbours to diversify their gas supplies (Jankauskas 2015).

The opening of the Klaipeda LNG terminal had significant symbolic and political resonance for Lithuania's quest for energy and national security. This significance is obviously reflected by the name chosen for the floating LNG storage and regasification unit leased by Norway's Höegh and docked at the Klaipeda port: the *Independence*. The opening ceremony was a national event involving the participation of Lithuanian President Dalia Grybauskaite, Lithuania's prime minister and representatives from Latvia, Estonia, Norway, the US, Finland, Sweden and the European Council. During the ceremony, President Grybauskaite underlined that the new LNG terminal was an 'important strategic project' that meant 'not only energy independence, but also political freedom', and she emphasised that 'from now on, nobody will dictate us the price for gas or buy our political will'.[10] The Lithuanian government also stressed that the project would help to guarantee security for the entire region.

At the end of 2014, Lithuania renegotiated its import contracts with Gazprom and received a 20 percent discount for Russian pipeline gas – a deal that, according to the Lithuanian energy minister, was a result of the new bargaining position granted by the LNG terminal (Cedigaz 2014).[11] Moreover, Estonia began to import gas from Lithuania via the Latvian pipeline system. According to the Lithuanian Ministry of Energy, in the second part of 2015, these supplies accounted for about 20–25 percent of total Estonian gas imports.[12] In October 2015, Lithuania and Latvia also signed a Memorandum of Understanding, covering the period from 2015 to 2017, to enhance cooperation in the gas sector and 'encourage the entry of new gas suppliers in the market'.[13] Besides, with the Lithuanian LNG terminal in operation with infrastructure close to the Latvian border, at the end of 2015, the European Commission sent a letter to Latvia arguing that the new situation removed the country's status as an 'energy island' and its exemption from the Third Energy Package rules.[14] This development added additional pressure to the Latvia's plan to liberalise its gas market by 2017.

Since the beginning of its operations, the Klaipeda terminal has prompted some important new political and market dynamics in Lithuania and beyond. However, its role as a 'game changer' for the entire Baltic region is complicated by the competing projects under development in neighbourhood countries (Romanova 2015). On one hand, after the war in eastern Ukrainian, the European Commission relaunched the BEMIP initiative to promote regional cooperation, and Poland, Lithuania, Latvia and Estonia reached an agreement for the completion, by the end of 2019, of the – Poland-Lithuania gas interconnector (GIPL). GIPL, which has a starting capacity of 2.4 bcm/y from Poland to Lithuania and 1 bcm/y from Lithuania to Poland, also obtained EU funds under the Connecting Europe Facility in the form of a grant for studies (around 10 million euros) and a grant for completion (around 295 million euros).[15] On the other hand, the new BEMIP Action Plan and Memorandum of Understanding, issued in 2015, also reasserted the need to build the other PCIs, including the LNG regional terminal associated with the Estonia–Finland Balticconnector (BEMIP 2015a, 2015b).

With regard to the regional LNG in particular, after trying unsuccessfully to convince the EU to support two different terminals, and after long, bilateral negotiations, Finland and Estonia eventually reached a compromise (Purju 2015). According to the agreement, the regional terminal would be built in Finland, and a small-scale LNG terminal would be built in Estonia to provide bunkering services and for the security of supply stocks. Meanwhile, the Estonian LNG project would remain on the PCI list 'as an alternative solution, ready to be realized' if the other project were 'delayed' (Communique 2014). This safeguard clause was to be applied if the application for EU funding – necessary for the regional LNG terminal construction – was not submitted by Finland by the end of 2016. As of 2015, Latvia was also considering a 'moderate-size LNG' national terminal (a FSRU at Skulte near the municipality of Limbaži), but without direct state involvement, only on a commercial basis and only if Estonia and Finland were not successful in launching the regional project.[16] At the end of 2015, the Finish state-owned company Gasum, the developer of the Finland LNG terminal, opted out of the LNG regional project, asserting that it was not commercially viable and that there was not sufficient demand for it in the Finnish market.[17] Gasum also decided to opt out of the Balticconnector, but in this case, the Finnish government confirmed its support of the pipeline construction. The Estonian government also decided to establish a new state company for the completion of the Balticconnector but left the LNG regional projects on the ground for private investors.[18] Two options in particular were under consideration after the cancellation of the Finnish LNG; both were included in the 2015 PCI list and eligible for EU financial support. One, proposed by the Dutch company Vopak, was near Tallinn (at the port of Muuga), and the second, proposed by the Estonian holding company Alexela, was near Paldiski (Figure 4.1). However, by the end of 2016, it was not yet clear if or when one of these two competing projects could be actually completed, although both are counting on the EU Connecting Europe Facility for decisive financial support.

Concluding Remarks

The Baltic States have tried for several years to coordinate their actions and create a coalition to build 'regional' LNG infrastructure to help reduce their gas dependence on Russia. However, differing domestic preferences, constraints and policy legacies have made it difficult to find a compromise between their national positions. These states, whose markets are small and isolated, have tried to gain support from the European Commission for their preferred national LNG solutions, seeking much-needed financial assistance to facilitate these projects' realisation. The European Commission has tried, with little success, to mediate a compromise between the Baltic States. Meanwhile, Lithuania has taken direct action to operate its own terminal and 'create' domestic demand for LNG. In this regard, the Lithuanian state's involvement mirrors the traditional practice of partner states. However, this more traditional strategy must incorporate the new interaction patterns found within the EU's multi-layered political-diplomatic environment and liberalised market context. In this new institutional milieu, the Lithuanian government has been able to realise the project at Klaipeda by mobilising and attracting financial resources, negotiating supply contracts and obtaining the support of EU institutions for its energy security agenda. Lithuania, also, directly involved the European Commission in negotiations with foreign energy companies on the implementation of the Third Energy Package, which was developed in parallel with the LNG terminal.

The LNG project has obvious political significance for Lithuania's international relations with Moscow. However, the operation of the LNG terminal has also triggered a domestic debate about its overall costs. After the terminal started importing gas from Norway, Gazprom offered to reduce prices to its Lithuanian clients – a move in line with the Russian company's current strategy of adapting its commercial deals to new market situations (e.g. Henderson and Mitrova 2015). As a result, Norwegian gas from Klaipeda became more expensive than Russian gas, and at the end of 2015, Lithuania sought to renegotiate the LNG contract with Statoil.[19] Some important industrial clients and business organisations have questioned the mandatory 'purchase obligation' from the LNG facility and have asked the government for a different supporting scheme so that the terminal's costs may be distributed more widely among consumers or even among the population at large.[20] Despite these issues, the Lithuanian government has continued to support the LNG option and apply a 'supply security charge', i.e. an extra charge related to natural gas supply security and added to the natural gas transmission tariff, in order to collect funds to cover all installation and fixed operating costs of the LNG terminal.[21] At the beginning of 2016, a new agreement was also reached between Lithuania and Statoil. The LNG price was reduced by 15–20 percent, the original contract was extended from five to 10 years, and the volume that Lithuania will import from Norway increased from 2.7 to 3.7 bcm.[22] In the same period, the fertiliser producer Achema, which had previously opposed the LNG project, decided to buy Norwegian gas via the Klaipeda terminal instead of from Gazprom. Because of the Achema decision, in 2016, Norway is expected to supply more gas than Russia to the Lithuanian market.[23]

In addition, since 2015, the Lithuanian government has been negotiating with the Norwegian company Höegh to buy the *Independence* before its lease runs out in 2024, thus reasserting the government's 'willingness to pay' for its diversification strategy. (As of the end of 2016, negotiations were still pending.) The government has also continued to point to Russian and Gazprom efforts to manipulate the Lithuanian gas market and energy sector.[24] Finally, owing to uncertainties with the Estonian's PCI projects, Lithuania is promoting the idea of using the Klaipeda terminal as the 'regional' Baltic LNG terminal – the next PCI list update will take place in 2017 – and thus possibly receiving EU support for acquiring the *Independence* (Pakalkaité 2016).

LNG Development in Western Europe

The Traditional Politics of LNG: Between National Champions and Foreign Policy Goals

As we saw, LNG in Europe originally developed in the Mediterranean Basin with France, Italy and Spain as the main importing countries and Algeria and Libya as the main exporting countries. Spain opened its first LNG import terminal in 1969 near Barcelona; Italy opened its in 1971 at Panigaglia near La Spezia. France followed with two terminals: at Fos-sur-Mer (Fos Tonkin) near Marseille (1972) and Montoir-de-Bretagne near Nantes (1980). The main pattern of LNG development was basically similar in these countries. It resembled the traditional practice of the partner state and triangular diplomacy already at work in pipeline politics, and in particular the competitive partner state variant of this model. In France and Italy the main promoters and developers of the projects were the gas monopolists GDF and ENI-Snam. In Spain as well, after its establishment in 1972, the national gas company Enagas took control of the supply contracts and the Barcelona regasification plant previously owned by Catalana de Gas. These national champions negotiated with the national companies of producer states that had taken control of liquefaction exporting facilities originally built with the aid of major Western companies: the Algerian Sonatrach (GDF and Enagas) and the Libya National Oil Company (ENI and Enagas). Company-to-company negotiations aimed at signing long-term contracts were backed by state diplomacy according to the traditional 'mutually supportive' relations between Western governments and their national champions. Rome, Madrid and Paris regarded these gas deals not only as a means to improve their security of supply but also as instruments to pursue wider foreign policy goals in the Mediterranean region (e.g. Ghilès 1995; Naylor 2000).

Another common feature of early LNG politics was the centralisation of decision-making processes in the hands of national governments and the lack of opposition from local authorities and communities. LNG facilities, like pipelines and other large infrastructure, were generally regarded as important symbols of modernisation and opportunities for local industrial development. As recently recalled by a local Italian administrator of Panigaglia where the first Italian terminal was built, in the 1970s 'the city jumped with joy at the news that this terminal would be built, because it signified wealth and jobs'.[25]

Despite these similarities, there were differences among these countries, first of all with regard to the role of LNG in their security of gas supply. As we saw in Chapter 3, since the 1970s both Italy and France have been involved in negotiating gas agreements with Moscow, and Soviet gas would become an important component of their energy security. This was true especially in Italy, whereas France's nuclear programme was the main answer after the oil shocks. Italy was also engaged in developing subsea pipeline connections with Algeria because this technology was considered more secure and affordable than LNG for tapping the growing domestic gas demand. When in 1983 the Transmed pipeline came into operation, connecting Algeria and southern Italy, Libyan LNG supplies decreased and then were stopped at the end of the decade. On the other hand, Spain's peculiar geographic location made it difficult for this country to receive either Soviet gas or North Sea and Dutch resources. The Spanish gas market was still underdeveloped and did not warrant the construction of costly and long pipeline networks to channel gas resources from the eastern and northern gas corridors. Like Italy, Spain tried to build pipelines in the 1980s to secure Algerian supplies, but without success. The Spanish government hence further promoted LNG to support the penetration of natural gas into the Iberian Peninsula. At the end of the 1980s Enagas opened two new LNG terminals at Huelva (in 1988) and Cartagena (in 1989) and LNG imports grew throughout the 1990s along with domestic energy consumption.

From an institutional point of view, although France, Italy and Spain are traditionally grouped among the 'state-influenced market economies' (SMEs), they also have different features (Colli, Mariotti and Piscitello 2014). France is the ideal type of directive state acting in a positive enhancing manner in economic policymaking. Italy, on the other hand, is stylised as a capitalism 'state-led by misdirection' to stress the predominant hindering effects of state action (Schmidt 2012). Finally, in Spain – which originates from an authoritarian corporatist capitalism – the state has done more to hinder than to enhance the economy over the long term (although Spain has generally outperformed Italy). Italy and Spain are also characterised by a regionalised institutional structure ('compound polity'), while France is an example of 'simple polity', with highly centralised political power (Schmidt 2009). As we will see in the next sections, these specific features will affect the pace and timing of the move towards the catalytic state as well as the effectiveness of states' *faire-avec* policies. For example in Italy and Spain – compound polities – the subnational dimension of energy security has been more pronounced, both in a positive way (with enhancing effects on state's strategy) and in a negative way (with hindering effects). On the other hand, more resistance to the emerging trends can be seen in France, with its highly centralised structure and stronger tradition of state direction.

The 1990s and the First Breaches of the Original Model

The original model of LNG development – with its patterns of domestic politics, government-company relations and foreign policy focused on the Mediterranean – began to change at the very beginning of the 1990s. This transformation resulted from the combined effect of Italy's and Spain's first efforts to open up their national energy markets and improve the diversification of their supplies and the parallel worldwide expansion of the LNG business. In Italy, local politics and environmental issues were also new factors affecting LNG development.

In Spain, the growing role of natural gas in the national economy began creating concern for security of supply. At that time Algeria accounted for the vast majority of Spanish imports; in 1992–1994 Algerian LNG accounted for more than the 50 percent of Spain's total gas imports (Enagas 2011). In order to ease this situation, the socialist government of Felipe González let it be known that it would tolerate no more than 60 percent of total gas supply coming from one country; therefore, with only limited imports from Norway and exhausted domestic production, Enagas had little choice but to seek alternative LNG suppliers (Shepherd and Ball 2006, 208–209). The Spanish company targeted two new LNG exporting projects under development in Nigeria and Trinidad and Tobago. However, the Nigerian project suffered various problems that caused delays, prompting Enagas to focus on the second venture. In the mid-1990s a contract was negotiated and signed between Enagas and the developers of the Trinidadian liquefaction plant. Later, the Spanish oil major, Repsol (at that time the primary shareholder in Enagas), which was privatised in 1994, and the newly established distribution company Gas Natural took direct shares in the Trinidadian project. Repsol also created a joint venture with British Gas (another shareholder of the Trinidad project) in 1998 to build a new LNG terminal at Bilbao and an associated gas-fired power plant. As we saw in Chapter 3, in this period government's energy security agenda largely overlapped with Gas Natural's commercial strategy. Madrid acted at international level to support Gas Natural's negotiations with Sonatrach for the construction of the Gazoduc-Maghreb-Europe pipeline. However, the government was concerned for the low level of supply diversification and competition in the domestic market. At the end of the 1990s the market share of Gas Natural was about 70 percent and the company supplied about the 85 percent of Spanish gas imports (IEA 2009).

In this context, LNG became the favoured option both for the government's energy security strategy and for newcomers, especially electricity utilities, wishing to compete with Gas Natural and bypass the difficulties of accessing Enagas pipelines. At the beginning of the 2000s new market players decided to take part in the Bilbao project, which was completed in 2003 and was the first of more LNG terminals developed in the context of the liberalisation of the Spanish electricity and gas markets.

At the very beginning of the 1990s, also in Italy, a process of limited domestic market opening provided opportunities for new players to enter the LNG game. The Italian state-owned electricity company Enel, willing to secure direct gas supply for its gas power plants and supported by the government, sought LNG sources abroad. In 1992, Enel signed a 20-year contract for 3.5 bcm/y with the developer of the Nigerian LNG, NLNG. The company's intention was to start supplying the Italian market by the middle of the decade through a new regasification facility to be built in Montalto di Castro north of Rome. However, the authorisation process for the proposed LNG terminal encountered many problems rooted in its environmental compatibility and local discontent. The Italian government was not able to find a definitive solution and a second site was proposed at Monfalcone in the Gulf of Trieste. This site was also strongly opposed on environmental grounds, especially by local government and communities. In 1996, a local referendum was held in Monfalcone and its citizens voted against the LNG project. Although the referendum was only consultative, the project was definitively abandoned. Owing its inability to build a receiving terminal in Italy, Enel tried to avoid its contractual obligations with the Nigerian LNG and invoked the 'force majeure clause' to suspend the contract.[26] However, the Nigerian LNG brought Enel to international arbitration and the impasse was resolved only in 1997. Thanks to the mediation of ENI (which had a share in the consortium developing the Nigerian LNG), Enel signed a LNG – pipeline swap deal with GDF. According to this deal, the Nigerian LNG contracted by Enel would be sent to the Montoir-de-Bretagne terminal in France and then delivered to Enel at various delivery points across Europe.

The 2000s: Liberalisation, New Players and Policy Instruments

During the 2000s, national governments enacted new measures to promote LNG in a market environment characterised by an expected growing gas demand and the implementation of the IEM provisions. In France and Italy several projects were considered, but in the end only two new terminals in each country were built (at Fos Cavaou and Dunkirk in France and at Rovigo and Livorno in Italy) (Table 4.4). LNG hence remained a minor component of Italian security of gas supply, accounting for about 5–10 percent of total gas imports (Figure 4.2). In France pipeline imports were predominant as well, although during the 2000s LNG (mainly from Algeria) accounted for about 25–30 percent of total gas imports (Figure 4.2). On the other hand, in Spain four new terminals were completed at Bilbao, Sagunto, Mugardos and El Musel (Table 4.4), and LNG continued to be a

Table 4.4 LNG terminals in France, Italy and Spain.

	Site	Start-up date	Capacity (Bcm/y)*	Developers (**)	Owners (***)	Third Party Access (TPA)
France	Fos-sur-Mer (Fos Tonkin)	1972	3	GDF	Elengy (Engy group, former GDF)	Yes
	Montoir-de-Bretagne	1980	10	GDF	Elengy (Engy group, former GDF)	Yes
	Fos Cavaou	2010	8.3	GDF, Total	Elengy (Engy group, former GDF) (72.5%), Total (27.5%)	Yes (90% of capacity subscribed on long-term basis, 10% available for short-term contracts)
	Dunkirk	2015	13	EDF, Fluxys, Total	EDF (65%), Fluxys (25%), Total (10%)	TPA exemption granted for 20 years. EDF is not allowed to subscribe more than 8 bcm/y of long-term regasification capacity
Italy	Panigalia	1971	3.3	ENI-Snam	GNL Italia (Snam group)(^)	Yes
	Rovigo	2009	8	Edison, Exxon-Mobil, Qatar Petroleum	Qatar Petroleum (22%), Edison (7.3%), Exxon-Mobil (70.7%)	80% capacity used by Edison on a long-term basis for 25 years 20% capacity open for regulated TPA
	Livorno	2013	3.8	E.On, Iride, ASA, OLT Energy Toscana, Golar	Uniper (former E. On) (48.24%), Iren (^^) (49.07%), Golar (2.69%)	In 2014 developers renounced to TPA exemption

(Continued)

Table 4.4 (Continued)

	Site	Start-up date	Capacity (Bcm/y)*	Developers (**)	Owners (***)	Third Party Access (TPA)
Spain	Barcelona	1969	17.1	Enagas (+)	Enagas	Regulated TPA
	Huelva	1988	11.8	Enagas	Enagas	Regulated TPA
	Cartagena	1989	11.8	Enagas	Enagas	Regulated TPA
	Bilbao	2003	7	BP, Repsol, Iberdrola, EVE	Enagas (50%), EVE (50%)	Regulated TPA
	Sagunto	2006	8.8	Union Fenosa, Iberdrola, Endesa, Oman Oil	Infraestructuras de Gas (Unión Fenosa Gas and Oman Oil Company) (50%), Iniciativas de Gas (Enagás and Osaka Gas) (50%)	Regulated TPA
	Mugardos	2007	3.6	Union Fenosa, Endesa, Xunta Galicia, Sonatrach, Tojeiro Group, Galician Government, Caixa Galicia, Banco Pastor, Caixanova	Tojeiro Group (51%), Galicia Government (24%), First State Investment (15%), Sonatrach (10%)	Regulated TPA
	El Musel	2013	7.1	Enagas	Enagas	Construction completed in 2013 but mothballed

Notes:

(*) = Send out nominal capacity in 2015 (GIIGNL 2016).

(**) = Companies involved in the early stages of the terminal's development (GIIGNL Reports, various years).

(***) Ownership in 2015 (GIIGNL 2016).

(^) = In 2012 Snam, previously owned by ENI, became the Italian Independent Transmission System Operator (30 percent owned by the Italian state).

(^^) Iren was established, in 2010, after a fusion between Iride and Enia (Iren is controlled by Italian municipal companies).

(+) = In 2012 Enagas became the Spanish Independent Transmission System Operator (5 percent owned by the Spanish state).

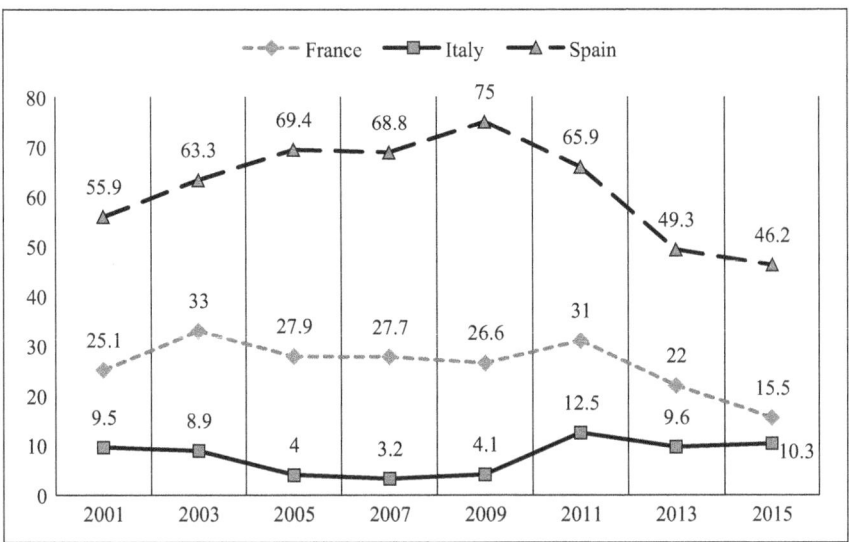

Figure 4.2 LNG import in France, Italy and Spain (percent of total gas imports).

Sources: Author's elaboration from BP Statistical Review of World Energy (various issues)

major component of the country's gas supply. (This situation changed slightly after 2011, when the Medgaz pipeline connecting Spain with Algeria started operation.) (Figure 4.2).

In many cases the new terminals were developed by a different set of companies than the traditional gas incumbents (Table 4.4). In this period, new LNG supplies also arrived, supported by the international activism of old and new players involved in the French, Italian and Spanish markets that signed medium- and long-term contracts with different exporters and, in some cases, took part in liquefaction facilities abroad while pursuing integrated business strategies along the entire LNG value chain (Table 4.5). Only Spain, however, achieved a wider diversification of LNG suppliers (Table 4.6). In French and Italy diversification was more limited: in Italy, at the beginning of the 2010s Qatar became the prominent supplier while Algeria remained the main LNG exporter to France (Table 4.6).

The main dynamics behind LNG development in each country will be examined below, paying particular attention to the interactions between government policy and market forces, state and non-state actors and domestic and foreign policies. The subsequent section will extend the analysis and summarise the main events occurring in France, Italy and Spain after 2010 amid a very different market context characterised by lower gas demand. The analysis aims to illustrate the move toward the catalytic state in the politics of LNG by highlighting the following: i) how governments have tried to combine market-based and more direct policy tools; ii) the emergence of new modes of public involvement in ownership,

Table 4.5 Long- and medium-term contracts (above four years) signed by companies operating in Spain, France and Italy and companies' shares in liquefaction facilities abroad (only extra European Economic Area).

| | Contracts | | | Companies' shares (%) in |
	Exporter	Import terminal	Buyer (Start–end/duration)	liquefaction facilities
Spain	Algeria/Sonatrach	Barcelona, Huelva, Cartagena, Sagunto	Endesa (2002–2017) Cepsa (2002–2022) Iberdrola (2002–2022)	
	Egypt/Egas	Barcelona, Huelav, Cartagena, Sagunto	BPGM (2005–2025) Union Fenosa Gas (2005–2029)	Damietta (Union Fenosa Gas 80%)
	Nigeria/NLNG	Barcelona, Huelva, Cartagena, Bilbao, Sagunto	Gas Natural Fenosa (1999–2021; 2002–2014) Endesa (2005–2025) Iberdola (2005–2025) ENI (2006–2028) Galp Energia (2005–2016)	
	Trinidad Tobago/ Atlantic LNG	Cartagean, Barcelona, Huelva, Bilbao	Gas Natural Fenosa (1999–2018; 2002–2023) Repsol (2006–2023)	Atlantic LNG T1 (Repsol 20%) Atlantic LNG T2&3 (Repsol 25%) Atlantic LNG T4 (Repsol 22.2%)
	Qatar/QatarGas, RasGas	Barcelona, Huelva, Cartagena, Sagunto	Gas Natural Fenosa (2001–2009; 2002–2007; 2005–2025) ENI (2004–2023) Endesa (2005–2025)	
	Oman/Qalhat LNG	Spain terminals	BPGM (2004–2009) Union Fenosa Gas (2006–2025)	Qalhat (Union Fenosa Gas 7.4%)
	Peru/Peru LNG	—	Repsol (2010–2018) (*)	Pampa Melchorita (Repsol 20%)

Country	Supply source	Terminal	Buyer (contract period)	Liquefaction stake
France	Algeria/Sonatrach	Fos-Montoir, Fos Cavou	GDF-Suez (1992–2013; 1972–2013; 1976–2013) (all extended until 2019)	
	Egypt/ELNG	Montoir, Fos Cavou	GDF-Suez (2005–2025)	Idku (GDF-Suez 5%)
	Nigeria/NLNG	Montoir	GDF-Suez (1999–2022)	NLNG (Total 15%)
	Qatar/Qatargas	Fos Cavou	Total (2009–2034)	Qatargas 1 T1&2 (Total 10%) (^)
				Qatargas 1 T3 (Total 10%)
				Qatargas 2 T2 (Total 16.7%)
	Qatar/RasGas	Dunkirk	EDF (2017–2021)	
	Yemen/Balhaf	–	GDF-Suez (2009–2029)	Yemen LNG (Total 36.9%)
Italy	Algeria/Sonatrach	Panigaglia	ENI (1997–2014)	
	Nigeria/NLNG	(**)	Enel (1999–2022)	NLNG (ENI 10.4%) (^^)
	Qatar/RasGas	Rovigo	Edison (2009–2034)	

Sources: GIIGNL (2011, 2012) and author's own elaboration.

Notes:

(*) = In 2013, Repsol sold its stake in Peru LNG as well as its LNG sale contracts to Shell;

(**) = Swap deal between Enel and GDF (LNG sent to Montoir-de-Bretagne);

(^) = Total has a 5 percent share in Abu Dhabi LNG at Das Island.

(^^) = Through its participation in Union Fenosa Gas (ENI has the 50 percent share of the company) ENI is involved in Egypt and Oman. ENI has also other important shares in liquefaction facilities in Africa (70 percent of the Area 4 LNG in Mozambique and 13.6 percent in Angola LNG), Australia and Indonesia (ENI 2015b).

Table 4.6 French, Italian and Spanish main LNG suppliers (percent of total LNG supply).

	2001	2003	2005	2007	2009	2011	2013	2015
France	Algeria 93%	Algeria 93%	Algeria 53% Egypt 16% Nigeria 30%	Algeria 60% Nigeria 29% Egypt 9%	Algeria 56% Nigeria 18% Egypt 12%	Algeria 39% Nigeria 25% Qatar 22%	Algeria 60% Qatar 21% Nigeria 14 %	Algeria 66% Nigeria 15% Qatar 6%
Italy	Nigeria 57% Algeria 43%	Nigeria 63% Algeria 37%	Algeria 96 % Egypt 4%	Algeria 100%	Qatar 53% Algeria 43%	Qatar 70% Algeria 18 %	Qatar 95%	Qatar 97%
Spain	Algeria 52 % Nigeria 17 %	Algeria 49% Nigeria 28%	Algeria 23% Nigeria 22% Qatar 20 % Egypt 16% Trinidad and Tobago 2 %	Nigeria 34% Qatar 18% Algeria 18% Egypt 16% Trinidad and Tobago 8.6%	Algeria 19% Nigeria 18% Qatar 18% Egypt 15% Trinidad and Tobago 15% Norway 5% Oman 4%	Nigeria 27% Qatar 19% Algeria 16% Trinidad and Tobago 10% Peru 8%	Qatar 23% Algeria 21% Nigeria 20% Trinidad and Tobago 13% Peru 10%	Algeria 28% Nigeria 27% Qatar 22% Trinidad and Tobago 8% Peru 7%

Sources: Author's elaboration from BP Statistical Review of World Energy (various issues).

including public-private partnership; and ii) how governments took part in a networked pattern of energy diplomacy.

Spain

The diversification of Spanish LNG supplies was favoured by ongoing reforms in the domestic energy market and by the steady growth in energy demand, that was driven by the construction of new gas-fired power plants, the expansion of the gas network and the growth in per-capita consumption (Honoré 2011). In particular, liberalisation and privatisation of the Spanish electricity and gas sectors anticipated EU reforms and received a boost with the appointment of the centre-right government of José María Aznar in 1996. The Aznar government completed the privatisations of the main Spanish energy companies initiated under the socialist government of Felipe González. The privatisation of Enagas, initiated in 1994, was completed in 1998. The same year also saw the completion of the privatisation of the electricity company Endesa (which began in 1988) while the oil company Repsol's privatisation was completed in 1997 (it began in 1989). With Royal Decrees 1377/1996 and 2033/1996 the Spanish gas market was also opened to competition and LNG importing terminals were subject to regulated TPA in order to encourage the access of new players into the domestic market. Then, in 1998 the Spanish government issued Law 34/1998, the so-called Hydrocarbon Law, which further liberalised the gas sector but also set a 60 percent limit on natural gas imports from any one supply country. The Hydrocarbon Law also limited individual company ownership of Enagas to a maximum of 5 percent (voting rights were limited to 3 percent), with an exclusion for the state-owned holding company Sociedad Estatal de Participaciones Industriales (SEPI, which currently holds a 5 percent share).

At the beginning of the 2000s, other measures were enacted to support investments in gas infrastructure: measures to guarantee a reasonable profitability for new LNG terminals; a national mandatory plan for infrastructure development based on projections of energy consumption and prepared by the government in consultation with the gas transmission system operator (Enagas), the energy regulator and the regional autonomous communities; and measures to facilitate the localisation procedures of LNG facilities (García 2006; Honoré 2011). Support for LNG as a means to reduce Spanish strong dependence on Algerian gas – up to 50 percent in 2004 – also continued under the socialist government of José Luis Zapatero (2004–11) in a context still characterised by an expected growing demand for gas.

As a result of this new institutional framework and market environment, the capacity of existing terminals was increased and three new importing terminals – envisaged in the 2002–11 national mandatory plan (Mityc 2002) – were rapidly built at Bilbao (2003), Sagunto (2006) and Mugardos (2007). However, unlike in past projects, the main developers and operators in these cases were not Enagas but wider consortia (Bahia de Bizkaia Gas, BBG, at Bilbao and Reganosa at Mugardos) and joint venture (Saggas at Sagunto) involving Spanish (Enagas,

Repsol, Iberdrola, Endesa and Union Fenosa) and non-Spanish companies[27] (Table 4.4). Among the latter, there were both major international oil companies, such as BP, and the national oil companies of producer states (Sonatrach and Oman Oil). Regional governments (Xunta Galicia and Galician governments), banks (Caixa Galicia, Banco Pastor and Caixanova) and utilities (Ente Vasco de la Energia, EVE) were also involved in the projects. The LNG terminals were developed through (local) public-private partnership with the participation of regional governments, particularly in the cases of Mugardos and Bilbao. On the other hand, in the case of Sagunto, direct public involvement was realised only later when, at the beginning of the 2010s, Enagas took shares in the Saggas joint venture. The participation of the regional governments was conducive to the rapid implementation of the projects and to the avoidance of local opposition or delays in infrastructure development.[28] Regional governments were also involved in the mandatory national planning process, another element that sped up the subsequent implementation of the LNG infrastructure. The crucial role of this measure is also demonstrated by the fact that while it was possible to develop LNG infrastructure outside the planning based system, nobody has chosen to do so because of the higher risks in developing these facilities without the guaranteed cost recovery (IEA 2009).

While favouring the access of new market players to the domestic market, in this period the Spanish government also reasserted its commitment to improve supplier diversification. Royal Decree 1766/2007 renewed the provisions in the Hydrocarbon Law by requiring direct suppliers and consumers carrying supplies for more than 7 percent of national consumption to diversify their portfolios so that their supplies from the main supplying country stood below 50 percent (should supplies exceed this percentage the government has the final say on how to resolve the issue). Finally, in 2006, Enagas was awarded the construction of another regasification terminal located in the north of Spain, in Asturias at El Musel (Port of Gijon). This project was included in the new national mandatory plan for infrastructure development issued in 2006 to renew the previous plan, and it was expected to start operation in 2010 (Mityc 2006).

All in all, the Spanish strategy – for a country that still remained poorly connected with the European network – was effective in ensuring adequate gas supplies and infrastructure for the growing domestic demand. In 2009 national regasification capacity was 58 bcm/y, compared with a natural gas demand of about 35 bcm (IEA 2009). The Spanish strategy was also effective in promoting the diversification of suppliers beyond the traditional Mediterranean focus, due to the international activities of a variegated set of companies operating in the domestic market that had negotiated and signed medium- and long-term contracts with producer companies (Table 4.5). The new geography of supply prompted the Spanish government to strengthen bilateral engagements, especially with Nigeria, Latin American and new Mediterranean LNG players such as Egypt.[29] In Egypt (2005), Oman (2006) and Peru (2010) Spanish companies also took shares in liquefactions facilities (Table 4.5). Internationally, the Spanish government took also action at the EU level to shift the sole focus of EU external energy policy from Russia to the neglect of Mediterranean and African producers, notably Algeria (Pérez and Vaquer I Fanés 2008).

Italy

In Italy as in Spain, LNG development interacted with reforms enacted in the 2000s aimed at liberalising national energy markets and improving the diversification of supply. (In this period the former gas and electricity monopolists ENI and Enel were also partially privatised, although the Italian state still owned about 30 percent of these companies.) At the beginning of the new millennium the centre-left government of Giuliano Amato issued Legislative Decree n. 164/2000 to implement Directive 98/30/EC and provided a system of incentives to guarantee investment returns in the construction of new LNG terminals. Then, in 2000 the government authorised the construction of two new LNG terminals. First, an offshore terminal was to be built in the North Adriatic Sea off the coast of Ravenna. This project, based on an offshore gravity-based structure located 14 kilometres from the coast, was proposed in 1998 by the Italian Edison in a joint venture with Exxon-Mobil. (The terminal received its environmental impact assessment [EIA] in 2000 with the consent of local authorities.) Second, an onshore terminal was to be built by British Gas in the Puglia region near Brindisi. The centre-right government of Silvio Berlusconi, appointed in 2001, embraced this strategy. The new government enacted Law n. 273/2002 that allowed exemption for 20 years from TPA for new gas-importing infrastructure, including LNG receiving terminals. Law n. 273/2002 also granted a special financial contribution of 70 million euros to the Ravenna offshore terminal, as it was regarded as a strategic project intended to improve both the security of supply and competition.

The reforms ongoing at the national level to implement the internal energy market and the new regulatory framework incentivised LNG projects. Especially new entrants to the Italian market were interested in LNG to secure gas supplies and avoid the existing pipeline importing system still controlled by the former monopolist ENI. On the other hand, during this period ENI was interested in expanding its LNG business abroad by acquiring a stake in liquefaction ventures (e.g. in Nigeria) and regasification activities to serve international (mainly European) clients. (In 2003 ENI also acquired 50 percent of the Spanish company Union Fenosa Gas, which was involved in the Sagunto and Mugardos terminals and in liquefaction activities in Egypt.)

Between 2001 and 2004, in a market environment characterised by an expected growing gas demand, various additional projects were presented by the Italian Edison (Rosignano); Enel (Taranto, Vado Ligure and Muggia); LNG Terminal, owned by the Italian group Falck (Lamezia Terme, Corigliano Calabro and San Ferdinando near Reggio Calabria); Petrolifera Gioa Tauro, owned by the Italian company Italpetroli (also near Reggio Calabria); and Offshore LNG Toscana (OLT, owned by E.On 46.7 percent, Iride 41.7 percent, ASA 5 percent, OLT Energy Toscana 3.7 percent and Golar LNG 2.6 percent) for an FSRU off the coast of Livorno (Table 4.7). Many of these projects were still in an initial phase, but

Table 4.7 Projects for LNG terminal in Italy (2001–9): main features and localisation issues.

LNG site (Region)	Proponents/shareholders (*)	bcm/y	Date of operations (prevision in 2009)	Notes/localisation issues
Porto Levante, Rovigo, offshore (Veneto)	Terminale GNL Adriatico (Edison 10%, Exxon-Mobil 45%, Qatar Terminal 45%)	8	2009	TPA exemption for 25 years and 80% of total capacity Financial contribution received from the Italian government (70 million euro) Opposition from local communities and NGOs
Brindisi (Puglia)	Brindisi LNG (100% British Gas)	6	(in 2003 it was expected to enter in operation in 2007)	TPA exemption for 20 years and 80% of total capacity Regional government opposition (Puglia gave its negative opinion in the EIA procedure) Local government opposition (the Brindisi municipality opposed the authorisation procedure in front of domestic administrative courts) Opposition from local communities and NGOs
Rosignano, Livorno (Tuscany)	Edison, BP, Solvey	8	—	Regional government opposition (Tuscany gave its negative opinion in the EIA procedure) Regional government available to support only one project (see below, Livorno FSRU) Opposition from local communities and NGOs
Taranto (Puglia)	Enel	5–8	—	Abandoned in 2004 after Enel acquired a 50% share of Brindisi LNG. In 2005 Enel withdrew from the Brindisi LNG project.
Vado Ligure (Liguria)	Enel	5–9	—	
Muggia (Friuli)	Enel	5–9	—	

Location	Operator	Capacity	Year	Status/Opinion
Lamezia Terme (Calabria)	LNG Terminal (Falck Group)	6–10	—	Negative opinion from the regional government. Projects cancelled in 2004.
Corigliano Calabro, (Calabria)	LNG Terminal (Falck Group)	8	—	
San Ferdinando, Reggio Calabria (Calabria)	LNG Terminal (Falck Group)	6–12	—	In 2005 the two projects were merged and a new project was presented by the LNG MedGas (see below).
Gioa Tauro, Reggio Calabria (Calabria)	Petrolifera Gioa Tauro (Italpetroli)	4–8	—	
Gioa Tauro, Reggio (Calabria)	LNG MedGas (Sorgenia 35%, Iride 35%, Belelli 30%)	12	2014	Positive opinion from regional government Opposition from local governments and NGOs
Livorno, FSRU (Tuscany)	OLT (E.On 46 %, Iride 41%, ASA 5%, OLT Energy Toscana 3.7%, Golar LNG 2.6%)	3–6	2010	TPA exemption for 20 years and for total capacity Support from local governments (ASA is a local multi-utility controlled by the Municipality of Livorno and others Tuscany's municipalities) Opposition from local governments (negative opinion from the Municipality of Pisa) Opposition from local communities and NGOs
Taranto (Puglia)	Gas Natural	8	—	Regional government opposition (Puglia gave its negative opinion in the EIA procedure) Opposition from local governments, communities and NGOs
Zaule, Trieste (Friuli)	Gas Natural	8	2013	Regional government available to support only one project in the Gulf of Trieste (see below) (**) (***)

(Continued)

Table 4.7 (Continued)

LNG site (Region)	Proponents/shareholders (*)	bcm/y	Date of operations (prevision in 2009)	Notes/localisation issues
Trieste, offshore (Friuli)	Terminale Alpi Adriatico (Endesa 100%)	8	—	Regional government available to support only one project in the Gulf of Trieste (**) (***)
Porto Empedocle, Agrigento (Sicily)	Nuove Energie (Enel 90%)	8	2014	TPA exemption for 25 years for the total capacity Opposition from local governments, communities and NGOs
Rada di Augusta, Siracusa (Sicily)	Ionio Gas (ERG 50%, Shell 50%)	8	2014	Opposition from local governments, communities and NGOs
Porto Recanati, Anona (Marche)	GDF-Suez	5	—	Regional government opposition (Marche gave its negative opinion in the EIA procedure) Opposition from local governments, communities and NGOs
Falconara Marittima, Ancona (Marche)	API Energia	4	2018	—
Panigaglia, La Spezia (Liguria)	GNL Italia (ENI 100%)	8	—	Upgrading of the existing LNG facility Regional government opposition (Liguria gave its negative opinion in the EIA procedure) Opposition from local governments

Sources: AEEG (2004, 2005, 2006, 2007, 2008, 2009) and author's own elaboration.

Notes:
(*) Proponents/shareholders as March 2009 (AEEG 2009).
(**) Slovenian government has also opposed these projects. In 2008, Italy and Slovenia created a joint working group to discuss the two LNG terminals planned in the Gulf of Trieste.
(***) The first 2013 PCI list included an 'onshore LNG terminal in the Northern Adriatic' adding that 'the precise location of the LNG terminal in the Northern Adriatic will be decided by Italy in agreement with Slovenia' (European Commission 2013b). No Northern Adriatic LNG terminals have been included in the second PCI list, issued in 2015 (European Commission 2015).

several problems related to local opposition appeared on the agenda and would later become even more evident. These problems in particular involved the British Gas terminal near Brindisi and the two terminals proposed by LNG Terminal in Calabria, which were opposed especially by the regional government and were eventually abandoned in 2003–04. Enel likewise decided to abandon the three projects it presented and join the British Gas project at Brindisi (Table 4.7).

In 2004 a new law was enacted by the government (the so-called 'Marzano Decree', Law No. 239 of 23 August, 2004), which provided for a simplification of the authorisation procedure for the terminal's construction and increased investor incentives. The new law established that whoever invested directly or indirectly in LNG facilities could request an exemption from TPA for at least 20 years and a minimum of 80 percent of the new capacity (previously exemptions were up to 20 years and a maximum of 80 percent of capacity).

In 2006 the new centre-left government of Romani Prodi confirmed its support for LNG expansion. LNG development was now framed not only as an answer to security of supply concerns – which had increased in the wake of the first Russian-Ukrainian gas crisis – but also as a wider industrial strategy for the country. This position was especially promoted by the new Ministry of Infrastructure, which highlighted that the goal of the government was to transform Italy into an 'energy hub' in the Mediterranean, an energy exporter and a global player in LNG industry. According to the Ministry, in Italy at least 11 LNG terminals were needed, of which four were to be given higher priority by accelerating their authorisation and localisation procedures.[30] Externally, the Italian government was working to include an energy policy dimension into the Union for the Mediterranean in parallel to its traditional bilateral energy relations with North African producers, including new LNG producers like Egypt where ENI had a stake in regasification facilities through Union Fenosa (Frappi and Vervelli 2010; Coticchia, Giacomello and Sartori 2011).

In the second part of the 2000s the number of the LNG projects presented increased (Table 4.7). Projects were presented by different categories of companies: Italian utilities (e.g. Enel, Edison and Sorgenia), European utilities (e.g. Endesa, British Gas, E.On, Gas Natural and GDF), oil majors (e.g. Exxon-Mobil, Shell and BP) and producers' national companies pursuing an integrated business model, as in the case of the Rovigo LNG offshore terminal that had Qatari participation. In the case of the Livorno FSRU terminal, regional and local governments also took part in the project through the utilities they controlled: Iride (a multi-utility mainly owned by Italian municipalities) and ASA (a local multi-utility controlled by the municipality of Livorno and other Tuscan municipalities). Iride also took part in the LNG MedGas project at Gioa Tauro. Especially the Livorno project was similar to the (local) – public-private partnership established in Spain for the Mugardos and Bilbao LNG terminals. Exemption from TPA was allowed for the most advanced projects; however, problems continued to arise with the localisation processes, with many LNG terminals being strongly opposed by regional and local governments, local communities and NGOs on environmental grounds (Table 4.7).

The decision-making power of subnational actors had been enhanced with the Italian Constitutional reform of 2001.[31] According to the Italian environmental law, regional and local governments have only a consultative role the in EIA procedure, but they have other important tasks related to LNG terminal localisation (e.g. deciding on economic and/or environmental compensation for local communities where LNG terminal and facilities are to be built) and their opposition can halt or create delays in investment plans. Against this background, the national government took action to mediate compromises between regional and local actors and energy companies – often in the context of the so-called 'conference of services' – but on many occasions its active involvement was not able to resolve the problems or speed up the localisation procedures. At the end of the decade (in 2009) only the offshore project presented in 1998 by Edison and Exxon-Mobil was completed. Edison – at that time controlled by the French EDF and some Italian municipal utilities (EDF will acquire the 99.4 percent of Edison's share in 2012) – also negotiated and signed a long-term contract with RasGas to import Qatari gas (Table 4.5). However, the other terminals were still lacking the necessary permits and encountering several hurdles.

France

Different from the Spanish and Italian cases, in France – where the opening of domestic energy markets was slower – at the beginning of 2000s only one proposal for a new LNG terminal had been advanced as a joint venture between the traditional incumbent GDF and the French oil major Total. This project involved the construction of a terminal at Fos Cavaou to be operational by 2009 and to be reserved for GDF and Total (later EDF was allowed use 10 percent of the terminal's capacity). This situation changed somewhat after the mid-2000s. In 2005, the centre-right French government led by Dominique de Villepin issued a new national energy strategy (Law n. 2005–781, 13 July 2005) that focused on LNG to diversify gas supplies and improve energy security (as increasing gas demand was expected, especially in the electricity sector). In 2006 the government also promoted the merger of GDF with Suez in order to create a global energy player, but the French state remained in control of the new company, acquiring a 35 percent share of GDF-Suez.

After the government called for new LNG development and the clarification of the regulatory framework for investors (with Law 9 August 2004 the government implemented directive 2003/55/EC and granted TPA exemption for new LNG facilities) between 2006 and 2009 four new projects were presented at Dunkirk (located about 10 kilometres from the Belgian border), Anfiter, Le Verdon and Fos Faster. Proponents were the former electricity monopolist EDF (still 85 percent owned by the French state), private French utilities (Poweo), European utilities (E.On, Austrian Verbund, 4Gas) and international oil majors (Shell) (Table 4.8).

During the 2000s, new long-term contracts were signed with Egypt and Qatar by GDF-Suez and Total (another contract had been signed by GDF in 1999 to

Table 4.8 Projects for LNG terminals in France (2006–9): main features and localisation issues.

LNG site (Region)	Proponents/ shareholders	Bcm/y	Date of operations (prevision in 2008)	Notes/ localisation issues
Dunkirk (Nord-Pas-de-Calais-Picardie)	EDF	6–13	2012	Public debate (September-December 2007)
Anfiter (Normandie)	Gaz de Normadie (Poweo 34%, E.ON 24.5%, Verbund 24.5%, Cim)	9	2012	Public debate (September-December 2007)
Le Verdon (Aquitaine)	4Gas	6–9	2012	Public debate (September-December 2007) Suspended by the French government in 2009
Fos Faster (Provence-Alpes-Côte d'Azur)	Shell	8	2015	Public debate (– September-December 2010)

Sources: CRE (2007, 2008a, 2009); and www.debatpublic.fr/.

import LNG from Nigeria) (Table 4.5). French companies, especially Total, also took part in liquefaction ventures mainly in Nigeria and Qatar (Table 4.5). The internationalisation of French companies in the LNG business was supported by government diplomacy and foreign policy. In this period the French President Sarkozy tried to reorient the focus of EU foreign policy towards the Mediterranean region – notably with the launch of the Union for the Mediterranean – but he also further strengthened France's relations with Qatar and Nigeria (e.g. OBG 2009; Alao 2011; Melly and Darracq 2013).

With regard to the new domestic infrastructure under discussion, in 2008, it was already clear that not all the projects presented would be completed because the forecasted demand did not support all the planned investment (CRE 2008b). However, according to French law a public debate procedure was launched for the localisation process of these new terminals. In particular, public debates regarding the Antifer, Dunkirk and Le Verdon projects took place between September and December 2007. It was the first time in the history of public debates that similar procedures were launched for projects also sponsored by private investors. This situation created problems since it was generally difficult for local communities 'to agree on the development of LNG terminals sponsored by private operators, sometimes from other countries' (CRE 2008b, 33). Indeed, in general the projects encountered widespread local opposition.[32] Energy companies proposed changes to the original plans to respond to local concerns and negotiated environmental and social compensation schemes with local actors. However, the project at Le Verdon especially faced significant opposition on environmental grounds. In August 2009 the French government suspended it.[33] On the other hand, the GDF-Total project at Fos Cavaou moved ahead; it received final approval from local authorities and began operations in 2010 under the TPA regime, which was also applied to the other existing terminals operated by GDF.

Post-2010 Developments and the Changing Context of LNG Politics

At the beginning of the 2010s the market context was very different from the one expected in the previous decade when many regasification projects were planned. From 2008 to 2014 gas demand in Spain fell 33 percent mainly due to the decrease in gas consumption for electricity generation (CNMC 2015). And as a result of the LNG terminals built in previous years, a large surplus of capacity now existed. In order to prevent any further expansion of importing facilities, through Royal Decree-Law 13/2012 the Spanish government established a moratorium on new regasification plants. Due to insufficient gas demand the government also decided to mothball the new terminal completed in 2013 by Enagas at El Musel, with the aim of saving up to 67 million euros in regulated costs on annual basis.[34]

This new market context also prompted Spain to change its agenda to cope with its surplus of LNG infrastructure. Since 2014–15 the centre-right government led by Mariano Rajoy has taken action to promote a more liquid and competitive gas hub market and to review the framework for regulates activities. In 2014 with Royal Decree-Law 8/2014 and Law 18/2014, changes were enacted to ensure the economic sustainability of LNG storage, transport and distribution activities. In 2015, Law 8/2015 amended the Hydrocarbons Law and established an organised gas market managed by Mibgas. Actions were also taken to facilitate the recovery of gas demand by supporting new uses of LNG for ships and road trucks, and in this way the Spanish government also supported the EU's clean fuel strategy launched in 2013. Finally, in the wake of the war in eastern Ukraine, the Spanish government has increased its efforts to gain EU support for the construction of the MidCat gas pipeline – a project already proposed in 2007 and intended to link northeast Spain with France along the Mediterranean coast – as a way to export its gas surplus towards France and other European markets. This project was included in the 2015 PCI list. In March 2015, the Spanish government also promoted a deal with France, Portugal and the European Commission – the so-called 'Madrid declaration' – to support its realisation. In 2016, MidCat received a 5.6 million euro grant from the European Commission under the Connecting European Facility for the studies necessary to launch construction. However, its completion, expected in 2021 or 2022, is far from certain (see the following discussion). Spain also continued to try to balance the EU external energy policy focus toward Russia with a more important attention for North Africa. In May 2015, the new Spanish European Commissioner for Climate Action and Energy, Miguel Arias Cañete, launched an EU-Algeria bilateral political dialogue on energy matters. On the other hand, Spain has reasserted its commitment to improve its security of supply through 'bilateral actions' and by strengthening trade relations with producers (NES 2015).

In Italy, many projects that had been presented in previous years have continued to struggle to overcome regional and local opposition. In 2011, the Italian government enacted another law (Legislative Decree no. 93/2011) to speed up the authorisation procedures for strategic national infrastructure, including LNG terminals. However, in 2012, British Gas eventually decided to abandon the project in Brindisi due to the difficulties it encountered in the authorisation process.[35] Moreover, the perspective of an increasing gas demand in Italy had disappeared and many companies decided to postpone investment plans. Only one project was successfully completed: the offshore terminal off the coast of Livorno in 2013. The same year, Monti's technocrat government issued a National Energy Strategy (Interministerial Decree, 8 March 2013) – formulated under the previous centre-right government of Silvio Berlusconi – in a context of growing concern for the country's security of supply owing increasing instability in Libya and Northern Africa. In the National Energy Strategy the Italian government on one hand reasserted the need to develop 'strategic' LNG terminals to improve security of supply; on the other hand, it specified that the country needed additional LNG capacity (above the existing terminals at Panigaglia, Rovigo and Livorno) for no more than 8–16 bcm/y (eight in case of realisation of the Trans Adriatic Pipeline and 16 without this infrastructure) (SEN 2013). For this additional capacity, the government would have applied regulatory conditions guaranteeing the recovery of investment costs to be borne by the system through energy tariffs. Above this threshold, the projects could have applied for a TPA exemption but no public financial support would have been granted.

In 2014–15, although eventually some projects obtained all the necessary authorisations (Falconara Marittima, Gioa Tauro, Porto Empedocle and Zaule), many plans were postponed, and it is not yet clear whether the new terminals will be completed.[36] The Italian government, like Spain's, is looking to use LNG for fuel trucks and ships hoping to catch with the EU's clean fuel strategy. However, problems have arisen with the recent Livorno offshore terminal, which was struggling to market its gas. In 2014, the project developers renounced their previously obtained TPA exemption and the new government of Matteo Renzi enacted a Law (Decree of 28 August 2014 of the Ministry of Economic Development) assigning the terminal the status of 'strategic' and 'essential' infrastructure for the Italian energy system. With this law the government granted developers a return on their investments – the so called 'guarantee factor' that is charged to end customers as a component of the distribution tariff – even in case of no or low utilisation.[37] This decision prompted a lively debate, especially with the prominent opposition party – the Five Stars Movement – which submitted parliamentary questions at the national and EU levels.

Externally, the Italian government – along with Spain – took action at the EU level to include a reference to the Mediterranean dimension of the EU energy security in the framework of the Energy Union. This renewed attention by the

Italian government, especially to the concept of a 'Mediterranean hub', was also affected by the important natural gas field (the Zohr field) discovered by ENI off the cost of Egypt in 2015 (see Chapter 5). Moreover, the Renzi government has tried to relaunch the Italian foreign policy towards Africa in parallel with and in support of the internalisation activities of ENI, which was conducting important energy and LNG business, especially in Mozambique, Nigeria and Angola.[38] The government, however, has been pursuing other foreign policy goals at the same time, such as in the area of immigration policy – a particular concern for Italy in the context of the so-called EU refugee crisis.

In France, the developer of the Dunkirk terminal, EDF, asked the government for the full exemption from TPA as a way to favour the planned investment. The French government agreed with this request and supported it in front of the European Commission. The European Commission demanded some changes to the original proposal but decided in March 2010 to grant the TPA exemption to the project (EDF and its subsidiaries, however, were not allowed to subscribe more than 8 bcm/y of long-term regasification capacity).[39] In 2011, the Belgian Fluxys and the French Total joined EDF in the construction of the Dunkirk terminal and a joint company, Dunkerque LNG, owned by EDF (65 percent), Fluxys (25 percent) and Total (10 percent) was established. For the Dunkirk facility, the plan was now to build a 13-bcm/y terminal to be connected by two different pipelines with the French and Belgium markets, while the expectation was for the Fos Faster project to become operational by 2017[40] (the public debate for this project took place between September and December 2010). Total's participation in the Dunkirk terminal was supported by the French government. Indeed, this project was also intended to alleviate concerns and protests by workers regarding the recent closure of Total's oil refinery located near Dunkirk. In 2011, President Sarkozy reiterated the state's commitment to the terminal's construction. It was completed in 2015 with the first LNG cargo arriving in summer 2016. A new contract was also signed by EDF in June 2016 to import gas from Qatar, and French-Qatari relations were also strengthened under the new French President François Hollande.[41] On the other hand, in 2015, the Shell project at Fos Faster was abandoned due to the uncertain prospect of domestic gas demand.[42] The uncertain prospect of gas demand also prompted the French energy regulator to raise doubts about the MidCat pipeline, questioning its advantages for European security of supply and pointing to the considerable costs of this infrastructure for French consumers.[43]

Concluding Remarks

Starting in the 1990s, the traditional model of LNG development in Southern Europe began to change. Whereas national champions developed the first LNG terminals, and imports were focused on the Mediterranean Basin, in this period new market players – electricity utilities, oil majors etc. – entered the LNG business. They took part in regasification activities at home and/or liquefaction ventures abroad and signed medium- and long-term contracts with a wider set of producers. In the 2000s, this trend was reinforced hand-in-hand with liberalisation of the domestic market and the parallel transformation of LNG trade and business worldwide. Previously 'mutually supportive' relations between national governments and gas monopolists have changed. National government are still interested in promoting LNG and supply diversification; however, in line with the model of the catalytic state, they have applied a different set of policy instruments combining market-oriented tools with more direct *ad hoc* measures and new modes of public involvement in ownership (e.g. public-private partnership). Governments have also 'indirectly' supported different categories of companies in order to pursue their energy security agenda (and industrial policy objectives). This does not mean that governments in France, Italy and Spain have stopped backing national companies abroad. They continue to support their internationalisation and to mesh bilateral energy relations with industrial and foreign policy objectives. As a result, in the current context old and more traditional patterns of interaction coexist with new diplomatic practices – including those actions oriented to refocus EU attention on national agendas – and more complex – public-private partnerships have been established to promote LNG infrastructure. Moreover, the fragmentation of the state and decision-making has also been a factor in the new politics of LNG. Different from other regions (e.g. the Baltics) or policy sectors (e.g. pipelines), however, in this case the EU supranational level has not played a direct role in LNG politics – although the construction of the IEM has obviously widely affected the context of LNG development. On the other hand, the subnational level has been important, particularly in the 'compound' polities. In Spain, the involvement of regional and local actors has facilitated the development of LNG, while, especially in Italy, regional and local opposition has in many cases halted the plans of the government and energy companies (but the only projects that have been realised are those developed with the contribution of local governments through their companies, i.e. Ravenna and Livorno). As illustrated, the three cases also differ in other aspects. In Spain, the less mature market, planning and mandatory infrastructure development have been important drivers for LNG expansion. And France seems to be the country in which elements of the traditional approach have remained more persistent, including decision-making centralisation and the state's role in implementing the national energy-security agenda. This result is in line with the country's long practice of highly centralised and state-driven energy and industrial policy. National government decided which projects to support (e.g. Dunkirk) and which to halt (e.g. Le Verdon). Several projects have been proposed, but in the end the only ones completed have been those proposed by the state-owned companies GDF-Suez (now Engie) and EDF. Finally, it is worth noting that in the post-2010 market context, declining demand has created new problems. On one hand, especially Spain and Italy are trying to expand demand for their LNG; on the other hand, the costs of operating and maintaining receiving terminals are becoming important new issues in political debates at the national level, triggering a 'domestication' of energy security politics.

Notes

1 Short-term contracts are generally considered those contracts with duration below four years (see for example the classification of the GIIGNL 2011, 2012).
2 'Data from Eurostat statistics', available at: http://ec.europa.eu/eurostat/web/energy/data/database [accessed 4–5 May 2016].
3 Ibid.
4 See 'Baltic countries ask EU to solve LNG terminal row', 15 November 2011, available at: www.euractiv.com/section/energy/news/baltic-countries-ask-eu-to-solve-lng-terminal-row/ [accessed 3 June 2016].
5 For a brief discussion of the Gazprom 'political' pricing of gas in Lithuania, see Stern (2014, particularly pp. 92–97). For a discussion of Gazprom's pricing of gas during Lithuania's transposition of the Third Energy Package, see also Grigas (2013) and Pakalkaité (2016).
6 Eventually, in June 2016, the Stockholm arbitration court ruled against Lithuania's request of 1.6 billion dollars in compensation from Gazprom for overcharging on gas supplies to the country between 2004 and 2012. See 'Lithuania loses case against Gazprom at Stockholm arbitration court', 22 June 2016, available at: http://af.reuters.com/article/commoditiesNews/idAFL8N19E2I3 [accessed 25 June 2016].
7 In the years since, the Lithuanian energy sector has been additionally transformed. For a review of the situation at the end of the 2016, see Pakalkaité (2016).
8 See 'Gazprom drops one arbitration case against Lithuania', available at: www.natural gaseurope.com/gazprom-lithuania-arbitration-case-23046 [accessed 30 May 2016].
9 See 'Russia, Estonia: New energy law strains relations', 18 June 2012, available at: www.naturalgaseurope.com/russia-baltics-energy-relations [accessed 4 June 2016].
10 See 'Lithuania welcomes "game changing" LNG vessel', 27 October 2014, available at: www.lngindustry.com/liquid-natural-gas/27102014/Lithuania-welcomes-FSRU-Independence-1675/ [accessed 27 June 2016].
11 As a result of this new deal, Lithuania would pay at least 10 percent more for LNG imported from Norway than for Russian pipeline gas in 2015 (Cedigaz 2014).
12 See 'Lithuanian energy minister reflects on the year in Lithuanian LNG', 8 December 2015, available at: www.naturalgaseurope.com/lithuanian-energy-minister-klaipeda-lng-terminal-baltic-gas-facility-26897 [accessed 30 June 2016]; and 'Imports from Lithuania account for 22% of Estonia's total gas imports', 22 December 2015, available at: www.baltic-course.com/eng/energy/?doc=114656 [accessed 30 June 2016].
13 See 'Latvia and Lithuania to work on developing a gas market', 16 October 2015, available at: www.reuters.com/article/baltic-gas-idUSL8N12G3F020151016 [accessed 3 October 2016].
14 See 'Latvia under pressure on EU unbundling rules', 10 December 2015, available at: http://interfaxenergy.com/gasdaily/article/18627/latvia-under-pressure-on-eu-unbundling-rules [accessed 1 October 2016].
15 See 'End of energy isolation in the Baltics: How the Gas Interconnector Poland-Lithuania (GIPL) works', available at: http://europa.eu/rapid/press-release_MEMO-15–5845_en.htm [accessed 2 July 2016].
16 See 'Latvia looks to Norway for LGNT construction', 2 February 2015, available at: www.naturalgaseurope.com/latvia-lng-terminal [accessed 3 July 2016].
17 See 'Estonia's LNG plans hit reality check', 8 February 2016, available at: www.natural gaseurope.com/estonia-tallinn-lng-terminal-prospects-dampened-revised-lithuania-statoil-contract-28030 [accessed 1 July 2016].
18 Ibid.; and 'Estonia's Alexela awaits EU decision on LNG funding', 10 February 2016, available at: www.naturalgaseurope.com/estonias-alexela-awaits-eus-decision-on-paldiski-lngt-financing-28078 [accessed 2 July 2016].
19 See 'Lithuania looking to alter LNG supply deal with Statoil', 27 November 2015, available at: www.lngworldnews.com/lithuania-looking-to-alter-lng-supply-deal-with-statoil/ [accessed 12 July 2016].

20 See, for example 'Lithuania "extorts" money for LNG terminal maintenance', 9 April 2015, available at: www.naturalgaseurope.com/lithuania-achema-lng-terminal-maintenance-23073 [accessed 25 July 2016]; and 'Lithuania mulls all-affecting LNG terminal security tax', 5 May 2015, available at: www.naturalgaseurope.com/lithuania-lng-terminal-security-tax-23433 [accessed 26 July 2016].

21 Since 2015, Lithuanian transmission system users have been paying a 'supply security charge' for supporting the LNG terminal. The charge is set by the National Commission for Energy Control and Prices (NCC). From 1 July 2016, the charge, exclusive of VAT, amounts to EUR 354.61 per MWh/day/year. Data available at: www.ambergrid.lt/en/transportation-services/tariffs-prices/tarrifsefectivefrom [accessed 4 October 2016].

22 See 'Lithuania negotiates LNG price cut with Statoil', 25 January 2016, available at: www.lngworldnews.com/lithuania-negotiates-lng-price-cut-with-statoil/ [accessed 5 October 2016].

23 See 'Norway to surpass Russia as Lithuania's top gas supplier in 2016', 8 February 2016, available at: http://af.reuters.com/article/commoditiesNews/idAFL8N15N1UF?pageNumber=2&virtualBrandChannel=0 [accessed 6 October 2016].

24 See 'Gazprom "up to shady games in Lithuania" – Vilnius', 7 April 2016, available at: www.naturalgaseurope.com/lithuanian-intelligence-gazprom-continues-shady-games-in-lithuanian-gas-market-28959 [accessed 27 July 2016].

25 Interview with Massimo Federici, mayor of La Spezia, in 'Italy seeks gas relief: Ships and trucks could help save Italy's underused LNG terminals', available at: www.politico.eu/article/italy-lng-gas-ports-fuel-greenhouse-emissions-eu/ [accessed 21 June 2016].

26 See 'La Nigeria tira dritto contro l'Enel arbitrato sui danni del contratto gas', 20 February 1997, available at: http://ricerca.repubblica.it/repubblica/archivio/repubblica/1997/02/20/la-nigeria-tira-dritto-contro-enel.html [accessed 15 June 2016].

27 In 2009, the Italian Enel acquired about 90 percent of Endesa. In 2015, Enel reduced its share in Endesa to 70 percent.

28 In this regard, Spain was an exception. In many other EU member states, national governments struggled to overcome local opposition to LNG localisation (see Cameron 2008).

29 Since the beginning of the 2010s Egyptian gas exports have decreased. In 2015 Egypt began importing LNG to satisfy its natural gas consumption. Further details on the recent developments of the Egyptian gas sector will be discussed in Chapter 5.

30 See 'Gas: Di Pietro, a Italia servono subito 4 rigassificatori e 11 in tutto. Al lavoro con Bersani per accelerare procedure', Press release, Adnkronos, 19 August 2006, available at: www1.adnkronos.com/Archivio/AdnAgenzia/2006/08/19/Economia/Energia/GAS-DI-PIETRO-A-ITALIA-SERVONO-SUBITO-4-RIGASSIFICATORI-E-11-IN-TUTTO_093209.php [accessed 16 June 2016].

31 On April 2016, the Italian Parliament passed a new law to reform the Italian Constitution. The new law also provides for a recentralisation of decision-making power on energy issues (reforming Title V of the Italian Constitution). However, Italian voters rejected these constitutional changes in a referendum that was held on 4 December 2016 (see also Chapter 5).

32 See the reports of the public debates available at: http://cpdp.debatpublic.fr/cpdp-leverdon/; http://cpdp.debatpublic.fr/cpdp-dunkerque-gaz/; http://cpdp.debatpublic.fr/cpdp-antifer/ [accessed 9–18 June 2016].

33 See 'L'Etat s'oppose à un terminal méthanier en Gironde', 19 August 2009, available at: www.lemonde.fr/planete/article/2009/08/19/l-etat-s-oppose-a-un-terminal-methanier-en-gironde_1229822_3244.html [accessed 2 July 2016]. See also 'Pegaz LNG project suspended', 5 August 2009, available at: www.icis.com/resources/news/2009/08/05/9313202/pegaz-lng-project-suspended/ [accessed 2 July 2016].

34 See 'Enagas: Musel LNG terminal to be mothballed after completion', 24 April 2012, available at: www.lngworldnews.com/enagas-musel-lng-terminal-to-be-mothballed-after-completion-spain/ [accessed 6 July 2016].

35 See 'Italy pledges investigation after BG gives up on Puglia project tied up in red tape for 11 years', 7 March 2012, available at: www.telegraph.co.uk/finance/newsbysector/energy/9129214/Italy-pledges-investigation-after-BG-gives-up-on-Puglia-project-tied-up-in-red-tape-for-11-years.html [accessed 6 July 2016].
36 In March 2015, Enel decided to exit from the LNG project at Porto Empedocle. See 'Enel cede Porto Empedocle', 25 March 2015, available at: www.ilsole24ore.com/art/impresa-e-territori/2015–03–25/enel-cede-porto-empedocle-063737.shtml?uuid=ABqdemED [accessed 12 July 2016].
37 See 'Olt decision: The administrative court states enough is enough', 10 July 2015, available at: www.ispionline.it/it/energy-watch/olt-decision-administrative-court-states-enough-enough-13654 [accessed 7 July 2016].
38 See, for example 'Italy Renzi's pivots to Africa for alternatives to Russian gas', 5 December 2014, available at: https://www.ft.com/content/ed33efb6-7bcc-11e4-b6ab-00144feabdc0 [accessed 19 June 2016]; and 'Renzi: Dal Mozambico gas per i prossimi 30 anni. Descalzi (Eni): La nostra scoperta più importante', 20 July 2014, available at: www.ilsole24ore.com/art/notizie/2014–07–20/renzi-dal-mozambico-gas-i-prossimi-30-anni-descalzi-eni-nostra-scoperta-piu-importante – -153210.shtml?uuid=ABVNricB [accessed 20 June 2016].
39 See 'EDF wins TPA exemption for Dunkirk LNG terminal', 10 March 2010, available at: www.icis.com/resources/news/2010/03/10/9341670/edf-wins-tpa-exemption-for-dunkirk-lng-terminal/ [accessed 22 June 2016].
40 See 'Fos Faster LNG terminal given go-ahead', 25 May 2011, available at: www.ogj.com/articles/2011/05/fos-faster-lng-terminal.html [accessed 5 July 2016].
41 In May 2015, France and Qatar signed an important 6.3 billion euro deal for the sale of 24 Rafale fighter jets. See 'France, Qatar sign Rafale deal, Hollande hails Gulf ties', 4 May 2015, available at: www.reuters.com/article/us-france-qatar-rafale-idUSKBN0NP0OE20150504 [accessed 27 July 2016].
42 See 'Fos: le projet de terminal méthanier Fos Faster abandonné', 12 January 2015, available at: www.lemarin.fr/secteurs-activites/shipping/20614-fos-le-projet-de-terminal-methanier-fos-faster-abandonne [accessed 5 July 2016]; and 'Fos Faster renonce à son terminal gazier', 22 January 2015, available at: www.usinenouvelle.com/editorial/fos-faster-renonce-a-son-terminal-gazier.N308312 [accessed 7 July 2016].
43 See 'French regulator snubs Midcat', 16 June 2016, available at: www.naturalgaseurope.com/french-regulator-snubs-midcat-30137 [accessed 23 June 2016].

References

Āboltiņš, R. 2015. Natural Gas in the Baltic States: The Dividing Factor, in Liuhto, K. (ed.), *Natural Gas Revolution and the Baltic Sea Region*, pp. 148–160. Turku: Centrum Balticum, BSR Policy Briefing, 1/2015.

AEEG, 2004. *Rapporto annuale 2004*. Autorità per l'Energia Elettrica e il Gas, Milan, 2004.

AEEG, 2005. *Rapporto annuale 2005*. Autorità per l'Energia Elettrica e il Gas, Milan, 2005.

AEEG, 2006. *Rapporto annuale 2006*. Autorità per l'Energia Elettrica e il Gas, Milan, 2006.

AEEG, 2007. *Rapporto annuale 2007*. Autorità per l'Energia Elettrica e il Gas, Milan, 2007.

AEEG, 2008. *Rapporto annuale 2008*. Autorità per l'Energia Elettrica e il Gas, Milan, 2008.

AEEG, 2009. *Rapporto annuale 2009*. Autorità per l'Energia Elettrica e il Gas, Milan, 2009.

Alao, A. 2011. *Nigeria and the Global Powers: Continuity and Change in Policy and Perceptions*. South African Foreign Policy and African Drivers Programme, Occasional Paper n. 96, October 2011.

Belyi, A. V. 2015. *Transnational Gas Markets and Euro-Russian Energy Relations*. Basingstoke: Palgrave Macmillan.

BEMIP, 2009. *Baltic Energy Market Interconnection Action Plan, Final Report*. Baltic Energy Market Interconnection Plan. Available at: https://ec.europa.eu/energy/sites/ener/files/documents/2009_11_25_hlg_report_170609_0.pdf [accessed 23 June 2016].

BEMIP, 2015a. *BEMIP 2015 Action Plan (For Competitive, Secure and Sustainable Energy)*. Available at: https://ec.europa.eu/energy/sites/ener/files/documents/BEMIP_Action_Plan_2015.pdf.

BEMIP, 2015b. *Memorandum of Understanding on the Reinforced Baltic Energy Market Interconnection Plan*. Luxemburg, 8 June 2015.

Booz&Co, 2012. *Analysis of Costs and Benefits of Regional Liquefied Natural Gas Solution in the East Baltic Area, Including Proposal for Location and Technical Options under the Baltic Energy Market Interconnection Plan*. Available at: https://ec.europa.eu/energy/sites/ener/files/documents/20121123_lng_baltic_area_report.pdf [accessed 22 September 2016].

BP, 2015. *BP Statistical Review of World Energy*. British Petroleum. Available at: www.bp.com/en/global/corporate/energy.../statistical-review-of-world-energy.html.

Cameron, P. 2008. *LNG: Study on Interoperability of LNG Facilities and Interchangeability of Gas and Advice on the Opportunity to set up an Action Plan for the Promotion of LNG Chain Investments*. Study for the European Commission DG, Final Report, May 2008.

Cedigaz, 2014. *Cedigaz News Report*. Vol. 53, issue 19, November 14. Cedigaz, The International Association for Natural Gas.

CIEP, 2008. *The Geopolitics of EU Gas Supply The Role of LNG in the EU Gas Market*. Clingendael International Energy Programme, 1 May 2008.

CNMC, 2015. *Spanish Energy Regulator's National Report to the European Commission*. 23 July 2015. Comisión Nacional de los Mercados y la Competencia.

Colli, A., Mariotti, S., Piscitello, L. 2014. Governments as Strategists in Designing Global Players: The Case of European Utilities. *Journal of European Public Policy* 21(4): 487–508.

Corbeau, A.-S. 2016. Conclusion: LNG Markets – the Great Reconfiguration, in Corbeau, A.-S., Ledesma, D. (eds.), *LNG Markets in Transition: The Great Reconfiguration*, pp. 554–577. Oxford: Oxford University Press.

Corbeau, A.-S., Flower, A. 2016. The Maturing of the LNG Business, in Corbeau, A.-S., Ledesma, D. (eds.), *LNG Markets in Transition: The Great Reconfiguration*, pp. 44–95. Oxford: Oxford University Press.

Corbeau, A-S., Ledesma, D. (eds) 2016. *LNG Markets in Transition: the Great Reconfiguration*. Oxford: Oxford University Press.

Coticchia, F., Giacomello, G., Sartori, N. 2011. Securing Italy's Energy Supply and Private Oil Companies. In Giacomello, G., Verbeek, B. (eds.), *Italy's Foreign Policy in the 21st Century: The New Assertiveness of an Aspiring Middle Power?* pp. 175–195. New York: Lexington Books.

CRE, 2007. *Activity Report 2007*. Commission de Régulation de l'énergie.

CRE, 2008a. *Activity Report 2008*. Commission de Régulation de l'énergie.

CRE, 2008b. *Report by the Working Group on the Regulation of LNG Terminals in France*. Commission de Régulation de l'énergie, April 2008. Available at: http://gttm.cre.fr/ [accessed 24 June 2016].

CRE, 2009. *Activity Report 2009*. Commission de Régulation de l'énergie.

De Jong, D., Van der Linde, C., Smeenk, T. 2010. The Evolving Role of LNG in the Gas Market, in Goldthau, A., Witte, J. M. (eds.), *Global Energy Governance: The New Rules of the Game*, pp. 221–246. Washington, DC: Brookings Institution Press.

De Micco, P. 2016. *Could US Oil and Gas Exports Be a Game Changer for EU Energy Security?* European Parliament, Directorate-General for External Policies, Policy Department, February 2016.

Drezner, D. W. 1999. *The Sanctions Paradox: Economic Statecraft and International Relations*. Cambridge: Cambridge University Press.

Dudzińska, K. 2012. *Energy Policy in the Baltic States: United or Separate?* PISM Policy Paper 37/2012.

Dudzińska, K. 2015. *A System of Unconnected Vessels: The Gas Market in the Baltic States*. PISM Bulletin, n. 56/788, 2 June 2015.

Enagas, 2011. *El Sistema Gasista Español*. Informe 2011.

ENI, 2015a. *World Oil and Gas Review 2015*.

ENI, 2015b. *ENI in LNG*, May 2015.

Eurogas, 2015. *Eurogas Statistical Report 2015*.

European Commission, 2013a. *State Aid: Commission Authorises €448 Million Aid for Construction of Lithuanian LNG Terminal*. Press release, Brussels, 20 November 2013. Available at: http://europa.eu/rapid/press-release_IP-13–1124_en.htm [accessed 16 June 2016].

European Commission, 2013b. *Commission Delegated Regulation n. 1391/2013 of 14 October 2013 Amending Regulation n. 347/2013 of the European Parliament and of the Council on Guidelines for Trans-European Energy Infrastructure as Regards the Union List of Projects of Common Interest*. Official Journal of the European Union, 21.12.2013.

European Commission, 2015. *Commission Delegated Regulation n. 2016/89 of 18 November 2015 Amending Regulation n. 347/2013 of the European Parliament and of the Council as Regards the Union List of Projects of Common Interest*. Official Journal of the European Union, 27.01.2016.

European Commission, 2016a. *Commission Staff Working Document Accompanying the Document on an EU Strategy for Liquefied Natural Gas and Gas Storage*. Brussels, SWD(2016) 23 final.

European Commission, 2016b. *An EU Strategy for Liquefied Natural Gas and Gas Storage*. Brussels, COM(2016) 49 final.

Frappi, C., Varvelli, A. 2010. Le strategie di politica energetica dell'Italia. Criticità interne e opportunità internazionali. *Quaderni di Relazioni Internazionali* 13: 98–114.

García, L. A. R. 2006. The Liberalisation of the Spanish Gas Market. *Energy Policy* 34(13): 1630–1644.

Ghilès, F. 1995. España Y El Gas Argelino. *Política Exterior* 9(44): 169–176.

GIIGNL, 2011. *The LNG Industry, Annual Report*. The International Group of Liquefied Natural Gas Importers.

GIIGNL, 2012. *The LNG Industry, Annual Report*. The International Group of Liquefied Natural Gas Importers.

GIIGNL, 2016. *The LNG Industry, Annual Report*. The International Group of Liquefied Natural Gas Importers.

Godzimirski, J. M., Vilpišauskas, R., Romas, S. 2015. *Energy Security in the Baltic Sea Region: Regional Coordination and Management of Interdependencies*. Vilnius: Vilnius University Press.

Goldthau, A., Sitter, N. 2015. *A Liberal Actor in a Realist World: The European Union Regulatory State and the Global Political Economy of Energy*. Oxford: Oxford University Press.

Grigas, A. 2012. *The Gas Relationship between the Baltic States and Russia: Politics and Commercial Realities*. Oxford Institute for Energy Studies, NG-67, October 2012.

Grigas, A. 2013. *The Politics of Energy and Memory between the Baltic States and Russia.* London: Routledge.

Henderson, J., Mitrova, T. 2015. *The Political and Commercial Dynamics of Russia's Gas Export Strategy.* Oxford Institute for Energy Studies, NG-102, September 2015.

Hirschhausen, C. von, Neumann, A., Ruester, S., Auerswald, D. 2008. *Advice on the Opportunity to Set up an Action Plan for the Promotion of LNG Chain Investments.* Study for the European Commission, DG-TREN, Dresden, May 2008.

Honoré, A. 2011. *The Spanish Gas Market: Demand Trends Post Recession and Consequences for the Industry.* Oxford Institute for Energy Studies, NG-55, July 2011.

IEA, 2009. *Energy Policies of IEA Countries, Spain 2009 Review.* Paris: International Energy Agency.

IGU, 2011. *2011 World LNG Report.* International Gas Union.

IGU, 2016. *2016 World LNG Report.* International Gas Union.

Jacobs, D. 2011. *The Global Market for Liquefied Natural Gas.* Bulletin of the Reserve Bank of Australia, September, pp. 17–25.

Jankauskas, V. 2015. The Recent Developments in the Lithuanian Gas Market, in Liuhto, K. (ed.), *Natural Gas Revolution and the Baltic Sea Region*, pp. 171–188. Turku: Centrum Balticum, BSR Policy Briefing, 1/2015.

Jensen, J. T. 2003. The LNG Revolution. *The Energy Journal* 24(2): 1–45.

Jensen, J. T. 2004. *The Development of a Global LNG Market: Is It Likely? If so, When?* Oxford Institute for Energy Studies, NG-5.

Le Fevre, C. 2016. Regasification Terminals: Adapting to a New Environment, in Corbeau, A.-S., Ledesma, D. (eds.), *LNG Markets in Transition: The Great Reconfiguration*, pp. 181–208. Oxford: Oxford University Press.

Leonard, M., Popescu, N. 2007. *A Power Audit of EU-Russia Relations.* Policy Paper of the European Council on Foreign Relations.

Melly, P., Darracq, V. 2013. *A New Way to Engage? French Policy in Africa from Sarkozy to Hollande.* Chatham House. May 2013. Available at: www.chathamhouse.org/sites/files/chathamhouse/public/Research/Africa/0513pp_franceafrica.pdf [accessed 5 October 2016].

Mišík, M., Prachàrovà, V. 2016. Before 'Independence' Arrived: Interdependence in Energy Relations between Lithuania and Russia. *Geopolitics* 21(3): 579–604.

Mityc, 2002. *Secretaría General de Energía, Planificatión de los sectores de electricidad y gas 2002–2011.* Ministerio de Industria, Turismo y Comercio.

Mityc, 2006. *Secretaría General de Energía, Planificatión de los sectores de electricidad y gas 2002–2011, Revisión 2005–2011.* Ministerio de Industria, Turismo y Comercio.

Naylor, P. C. 2000. *France and Algeria: A History of Decolonization and Transformation.* Gainesville: University Press of Florida.

NEIS, 2012. *National Energy Independence Strategy of the Republic of Lithuania.* Vilnius: Ministry of Energy.

NES, 2015. *National Energy Security Strategy.* Departamento de Seguridad National, Presidencia del Gobierno, Madrid, July 20, 2015.

OBG, 2009. *The Report: Qatar 2009.* London: Oxford Business Group.

Pakalkaité, V. 2016. *Lithuania's Strategic Use of EU Energy Policy Tools: A Transformation of Gas Dynamics.* Oxford Institute for Energy Studies, NG-111, September 2016.

Pérez, F. A., Vaquer I Fanés, J. 2008. Spain in the Genesis of Europe's New Energy Policy, in Barbé, E. (ed.), *Spain in Europe 2004–2008*, Monograph of the Observatory of European Foreign Policy, n. 4, February 2008, Bellaterra, Barcelona: Institut Universitari d'Estudis Europeus.

Purju, A. 2015. Impact of LNG on the Energy Market of Estonia, in Liuhto, K. (ed.), *Natural Gas Revolution and the Baltic Sea Region*, pp. 161–171. Turku: Centrum Balticum, BSR Policy Briefing, 1/2015.

Raszewski, S. 2012. Security and Economics of Energy in North East Europe, in Kuzemko, C., Belyi A. V., Goldthau, A., Keating, M. F., (eds), Dynamics of energy governance in Europe and Russia, pp. 130-148. Basingstoke: Palgrave Macmillan.

Romanova, T. 2015. LNG in the Baltic Sea Region in the Context of EU-Russian Relations, in Liuhto, K. (ed.), *Natural Gas Revolution and the Baltic Sea Region*, pp. 24–38. Turku: Centrum Balticum, BSR Policy Briefing, 1/2015.

Ruester, S. 2010. *Recent Dynamics in the Global Liquefied Natural Gas Industry*. Resource Markets, Working Paper RM-19, January 2010.

Schmidt, V. A. 2009. Putting the Political Back into Political Economy by Bringing the State Back in Yet again. *World Politics* 61(3): 516–546.

Schmidt, V. A. 2012. What Happened to the State-Influenced Market Economies? France, Italy, and Spain Confront the Crisis as the Good, the Bad, and the Ugly, in Grant, W., Wilson, G. K. (eds.), *The Consequences of the Global Financial Crisis: The Rhetoric of Reform and Regulation*, pp. 156–186. Oxford: Oxford University Press.

SEN, 2013. *Strategia Energetica Nazionale*. Rome: Italian Ministry of Economic Development.

Shepherd, R., Ball, J. 2006. Liquefied Natural Gas from Trinidad and Tobago: The Atlantic LNG Project, in Victor, D. G., Jaffe, A. M., Hayes, M. H. (eds.), *Natural Gas and Geopolitics: From 1970 to 2040*, pp. 268–318. Cambridge: Cambridge University Press.

Sprūds, A. 2009. Latvia's Energy Strategy: Between Structural Entrapments and Policy Choices, in Sprūds, A., Rostoks, T. (eds.), *Energy: Pulling the Baltic Sea Region Together or Apart*, pp. 223–250. Riga: Zinatne.

Sprūds, A., Rostoks, T. (eds.) 2009. *Energy: Pulling the Baltic Sea Region Together or Apart*. Riga: Zinatne.

Stern, J. 2014. The Impact of European Regulation and Policy on Russian Gas Exports and Pipelines, in Henderson, J., Pirani, S. (eds.), *The Russian Gas Matrix: How Markets Are Driving Change*, pp. 82–108. Oxford: Oxford University Press.

Stern, J., Koyama, K. 2016. Looking Back at History: The Early Development of LNG Supplies and Markets, in Corbeau, A.-S., Ledesma, D. (eds.), *LNG Markets in Transition: The Great Reconfiguration*, pp. 10–43. Oxford: Oxford University Press.

Stern, J., Rogers, H. 2012. The Transition to Hub-Based Gas Pricing in Continental Europe, in Stern, J. (ed.), *The Pricing of Internationally Traded Gas*, pp. 145–177. Oxford: Oxford University Press.

5 The Offshore Frontiers of Energy Security in the Mediterranean

Offshore hydrocarbon production, especially natural gas, represents an important indigenous energy source for the EU. In 2012, offshore crude oil production accounted for almost 9 percent of the EU's consumption of gross petroleum products, and offshore gas production covered 13.8 percent of the EU's gross energy consumption.[1] Most of the EU's current offshore hydrocarbon production is located in the North Sea, in waters belonging to the UK, Denmark and the Netherlands. In the Mediterranean, Italy has the most offshore installations (the majority of which produce gas), located mainly in the Adriatic and Ionian Seas. There are also a limited number of installations in Spanish, Greek and Croatian waters, and offshore activities also take place in the Mediterranean in the waters of non-EU member states, including Egypt, Israel, Libya, Tunisia and Turkey.

At the beginning of the 2000s, technological advances in offshore exploration, combined with high oil prices, increased energy companies' interest in the Mediterranean Sea. This development was reinforced by the 2007–08 global financial crisis and the resulting economic downturn in Southern Europe. After 2008, many EU Mediterranean countries, such as Cyprus, Croatia, Greece and Italy, formulated new plans for the exploration and exploitation of offshore hydrocarbon resources, not only to reduce energy dependence, but also to boost economic recovery by attracting foreign investments and by exploiting the oil and gas rent. The transformation of the Mediterranean into a new frontier of EU energy security has revived unresolved marine disputes between member states (e.g. Slovenia and Croatia) and between member states and non-EU countries (e.g. Croatia-Montenegro, Cyprus-Turkey) and has raised important questions about the environmental risks and negative effects of offshore energy activities on the fragile marine ecosystem of this semi-enclosed sea, especially since the 2010 BP oil disaster in the Gulf of Mexico raised public concern.

Due to the hydrocarbon resources located in the Adriatic, Ionian, Aegean and Levantine Seas, the Central and Eastern Mediterranean – which include both EU and non-EU countries – have recently attracted more interest in terms of energy development. The Levantine Basin – located along and off the coasts of Syria, Lebanon, Israel, the Gaza Strip and Egypt and extending westward into Cypriot waters – is the most promising area. According to a 2010 estimate by the US Geological Survey, this region has more than 3,000 bcm of recoverable gas reserves and 1.7 billion barrels of recoverable oil. New natural gas discoveries off the coasts of Israel and Cyprus since 2009 have already prompted new important political dynamics – both inter-state cooperation for the monetisation of the gas fields through joint infrastructures (pipelines and LNG facilities), and competition and disputes regarding sovereignty rights over seabed resources. These disputes have interacted with long-standing tensions in a region traditionally characterised by strong confrontations and recently additionally destabilised by the war in Syria and the rise of ISIS.

The Adriatic and Ionian region (which, in this chapter on offshore development, is defined as Italy, Croatia, Montenegro, Slovenia, Albania and Greece) has less than 100 bcm proven gas reserves and 0.77 of billion barrels of oil.[2] This region is therefore less significant than the Levantine Basin from an energy perspective, although its resources can help diversify Europe's gas supply, especially for the small markets of the Balkans. The most promising countries in terms of potential hydrocarbon development seem to be Italy and Croatia, followed by Albania for oil and Greece for gas reserves. Montenegro has only recently launched its first plan to develop its largely unexplored territorial sea and continental shelf. However, no major discoveries have been made recently in the Adriatic and Ionian region; instead, offshore production has declined. From the end of the 1990s to the early 2010s, offshore gas production in Italy (the main producer country in this region) fell from about 15 to 5 bcm/y (DGRME 2013). Obviously, the international and domestic situation in this region is very different than that of the Levantine Basin. After the Balkan wars and the break-up of Yugoslavia, a process of integration with the EU began, and currently the region is composed mainly of EU countries (Italy, Croatia, Slovenia and Greece) or countries in the process of joining the EU (Albania and Montenegro). However, in this case as well, the relaunch of offshore development at the end of the 2000s has revitalised unresolved marine disputes. Moreover, the Adriatic Sea has an especially fragile marine ecosystem; it is a semi-enclosed sea inside a semi-enclosed sea. It is generally considered to be the most endangered region in the Mediterranean, and important economic activities, such as fisheries and tourism, depend on its conservation (Espon 2013). Due to this fragility and the proximity among the riparian states, possible problems in the region include not only the issue of energy resource ownership – i.e. the delimitation of each state's sovereignty rights over the monetisation of gas and oil fields –, but also possible trans-boundary pollution from the normal operations of offshore installations and the risk of major incidents.

Against this background, this chapter aims to analyse the emerging politics of hydrocarbon development in the Eastern and Central Mediterranean by highlighting the main drivers and effects of the recent relaunch of offshore activities in the region and the role of the EU and EU member states. First, this chapter discusses some peculiarities of the offshore hydrocarbon sector and the main issues of international governance and politics surrounding it (i.e. ownership and environmental protection), with a special focus on the Mediterranean Sea and the EU. Then, by applying the IPE framework and the historical institutional perspective developed in the Introduction, this chapter illustrates the petroleum politics in the Eastern and Central Mediterranean, paying special attention to the Adriatic Sea and the

Levantine Basin. It is worth noting that although the IPE framework is well suited to describing the politics of energy security in these cases, the peculiarities of the offshore sector make it difficult to apply the state models described and discussed in the previous chapters. On one hand, EU-level governmental agents (i.e. the European Commission) play a minimal role in the energy diplomacy surrounding offshore politics. On the other hand, the EU's approach to external energy governance is limited in the offshore sector as well, especially in the Eastern Mediterranean region, which is outside the reach of the EU's multilateral energy frameworks.[3] However, despite these problems, empirical analysis demonstrates that recent developments in offshore politics also mirror a combination of 'old' and 'new' political dynamics, a fragmentation of national sovereignty and a reconfiguration of states' diplomatic practices, as anticipated by the network diplomacy hypothesis. The analysis also demonstrates that the politics of energy security in the EU and beyond is widely affected by the different institutional contexts in which it takes place.

Regarding environmental protection of the sea, the chapter's focus will be not the effectiveness of the governance structures at work in the Mediterranean Sea but rather how the principles, norms and arrangements formed by these structures pave the way for specific patterns of interactions among states and other actors. EU environmental and marine policies, coupled with growing public awareness about the environmental effects of offshore activities, seem to have had the most important transformative effect on the traditional international politics of offshore development. The new layers of governance created and supported by the EU have broadened the constellation of actors involved in offshore politics and promoted new transnational political dynamics. Particularly in the Adriatic and Ionian region, the development of a complex and intertwined set of institutions – or a regime complex (Keohane and Victor 2011) – has created more possibilities for non-state actors to influence offshore development. However, rather than eroding the traditional government-to-government negotiations, these dynamics have promoted a meshing of bilateral negotiations with those conducted by a wider set of public and private actors. On the other hand, more traditional inter-state interactions and security issues related to regional politics have greatly affected energy developments in the Eastern Mediterranean. That is to say, in this case, the wider security architecture – and its transformation, which is influenced by key events (e.g. the war in Syria) and the strategies of major external powers like the US and Russia – constitutes a crucial background affecting offshore politics and the international political economy of energy.[4] The EU's influence in this region has been minimal, although EU energy security strategy has interacted with national agendas in Cyprus and Greece.

Offshore Petroleum Policy and Politics in the EU

Although offshore industry maintains a close relationship with the onshore energy and hydrocarbon policies of consumer and producer states, this sector has traditionally been considered a special case, an industry *sui generis* (Goldstein

1982; Clancy 2007, 2011). One of the most important peculiarities of hydrocarbon offshore activities is that many basic governance structures and regimes are decided at the international level, especially regarding the ownership of seabed resources and, due to the inherent trans-boundary effect of marine pollution, the prevention and management of the environmental risks of offshore development activities. Other issues linked to the offshore hydrocarbon sector are managed at the intersection between the domestic and international level or mainly at the national level – e.g. the protection of investments, the contractual relationships between governments and energy companies etc. However, these two international issues (ownership of seabed resources and environmental protection) are the most likely to cause disputes or tensions among states, so they also create opportunities for international institutions that promote cooperation, which in turn structure the basic patterns of interactions among actors (Keil 2015). Regarding ownership – i.e. which state has the right to monetise energy resources under the seabed – the United Nations Convention on the Law of the Sea (UNCLOS), stemmed from the 1958 Geneva Convention on the Law of the Sea (also referred to as UNCLOS I), provides the general legal framework which governs, among other things, states' rights to the exploration and development of natural resources in their territorial seas (up to 12 nautical miles from the baseline), continental shelf (up to 200 nautical miles or 350 under certain conditions) and exclusive economic zones, or EEZ (up to 200 nautical miles). UNCLOS also provides the international legal framework and the guiding principles (e.g. 'equidistance', 'equity' and 'proportionality') for the bilateral negotiation of marine boundary delimitation when claims of different states overlap and for the involvement of third parties, such as international tribunal and arbitration panels, to help states to resolve disputes (Dundua 2007).

The delimitation of the marine areas where sovereignty rights apply is crucial to allow the effective monetisation of oil and gas resources: the political risks for energy companies investing in contested areas are generally too high. Apart from a general duty of cooperation, UNCLOS does not provide specific measures for oil and gas deposits located between the marine boundaries of two states; thus, bilateral negotiation between the states involved is necessary to find appropriate solutions. All the countries of the EU (and the EU itself) and of the Mediterranean have become parties to UNCLOS, with the important exceptions of Libya and Morocco (which have signed but not ratified the convention) and Israel, Syria and Turkey in the Eastern Mediterranean.

Concerning environmental protection in offshore development activities, especially for enclosed and semi-enclosed seas, UNCLOS has provided a framework for the development of a set of other regional institutions. The international environmental governance of specific sea regions occurs through a cluster of initiatives and regimes (at the regional, minilateral and bilateral levels) that create complex and partially overlapping institutional structures in each basin (Di Mento and Hickman 2012). In the Mediterranean, a regional governance system, the Barcelona System, was created to promote the protection of the marine environment. The Barcelona System grew out of the Mediterranean Action Plan, which was adopted in Barcelona in 1975 under the framework of the United Nations Environmental Programme. This system, which is coherent with UNCLOS, has evolved over time and is composed of a framework convention and seven specific protocols intended to promote cooperation among the states and address particular environmental risks (Scovazzi 2012). The main provisions of the Barcelona System regarding offshore activities were established with the so-called Offshore Protocol, which was signed in 1994 and entered into force in 2011.

EU environmental law and marine policy instruments and frameworks also address the environmental dimension of offshore international governance in the Mediterranean Sea. In accordance with the provision of the Lisbon Treaty on member states' right to determine the conditions for exploiting their energy resources, each member state sets its own conditions and requirements for offshore development licensing. However, since the 1990s, the EU has regulated the competitive aspects of licensing procedures, harmonising and liberalising national markets with the Directive 94/22/EC (Hydrocarbon Directive). In the wake of the 2010 BP oil disaster in the Gulf of Mexico, the EU established new specific rules for offshore activities with Directive 2013/30/EU, which improved the previous framework provided by Directive 94/22/EC, especially with regard to environmental protection. The EU has also acceded to the Offshore Protocol of the Barcelona System (although the majority of member states have not ratified it).

The EU does not have competences over the delimitation of member states' sea borders – although in the EU context there may be less of a chance to apply a unilateral approach –, so its influence is mainly manifested through rules concerning environmental protection and maritime governance (Long 2012). Directive 2001/42/CE on the Strategic Environmental Impact Assessment (SEA) and Directive 2011/92/EU (amended by Directive 2014/52/EU in 2014) on the Environmental Impact Assessment (EIA), which also cover hydrocarbon offshore activities, oblige member states to extend the consultation process for national programmes and specific projects with possible trans-boundary effects on other states. The EU is also party to both the Espoo convention and the SEA protocol, which was established in Kyiv in 2003 under the United Nations Economic Commission for Europe and lays down the general obligations of states to consult each other on all major projects that are likely to have a significant adverse environmental impact across boundaries. The SEA and EIA directives and the Espoo convention also require that states guarantee and support the participation of the public in this decision-making process. This opens another channel of potential transnational political dynamics involving local communities, subnational governments and environmental non-governmental organisations (NGOs). At the end of the 2000s, with the establishment of the Integrated Maritime Policy and the Marine Strategy Framework Directive (MSFD) (Directive 2008/56/CE), the EU took further steps to protect the sustainability of European seas. The MSFD obligates member states to cooperate in the formulation and realisation of plans with an important trans-boundary effect on the marine environment and marine activities (Long 2011, 2012). Moreover, the MSFD supported the creation of other sub-regional governance structures involved in the transnational and cooperative management of sea activities and in protecting the sea ecosystem, such as the European Union Strategy for the Baltic Sea Region (EUSBSR), established in 2009, and the European Union Strategy for the Adriatic and Ionian Region (EUSAIR), established in 2014. Finally, with Directive 2014/89/EU, the EU developed a common framework for marine spatial planning to create synergy between different activities at sea, protect the environment and increase cross-border cooperation.

The new principles and meta-frameworks for marine governance created by EU legislation have complicated the political context of offshore politics, linking offshore development activities with other marine activities (marine transport, fishing, tourism and marine conservation etc.) and establishing a new multi-level institutional context for offshore politics (Van Leeuwen, Hoof and Tatenhove 2012). Those frameworks pose a challenge to traditional 'marine national sovereignty', strengthening the supranational, subnational and transnational layers of governance in offshore development and potentially broadening the constellation of actors involved in offshore politics (Vivero, Mateos and Corral 2009).

Maritime Borders, Environmental Protection and Petroleum Politics in the Mediterranean

Petroleum politics and maritime border delimitation have traditionally interacted in the Mediterranean Sea. At first, this interaction was essentially positive, as interest in exploiting energy resources prompted governments to define their sovereignty rights and borders at sea. Later, these interactions became more negative, as resources in contested areas exacerbated long-standing existing problems.

Until the 1970s, most Mediterranean states were primarily interested in extending their territorial sea borders to the maximum 12-nautical-mile limit (smaller limits of six nautical miles have been adopted by Greece and Turkey in the Aegean Sea) (European Parliament 2010). In the following years, energy interests led to a trend among Mediterranean states to extend their control beyond their territorial waters by enacting national legislation regarding the seabed areas for exclusive exploration and production activities. Generally, this legislation did not fix the exact limits of the continental shelf, but given the size of the Mediterranean Sea, there can be no question of extending any country's continental shelf beyond the 200-mile line (even the 200-mile limit is unrealistic, since there is no point at which two coasts are more than 400 nautical miles apart) (Leanza 1993). There are only a few bilateral delimitation agreements for the continental shelves, and most of them were reached between the 1970s and the 1980s. They were also influenced by states' desire to clarify their rights in order to allow exploitation of their energy resources. Italy, in particular, took the lead in this process – partly as a consequence of its geographical position at the centre of the Mediterranean basin – establishing agreements with Yugoslavia (1968), Tunisia (1971), Spain (1974), Greece (1977) and Albania (1992). Italy had already enacted a law for granting concessions in its continental shelf in 1967, and its state-owned companies, ENI and Agip, were very active in exploration and production. Other agreements in the Southern Mediterranean, between Libya and Tunisia (1988) and

Libya and Malta (1986), were also motivated by the desire to exploit offshore energy resources (France and Monaco also signed an agreement in 1984). These agreements were negotiated according to the principles and rules established by the 1958 Geneva Convention on the Law of the Sea, i.e. the criterion of equidistance was modified to account for specific geographic circumstances (islands or the curvature of the coastline) (Annish 1993). A third party, the International Court of Justice, was involved in the agreements between Libya and Malta and Libya and Tunisia; but in the other agreements, divergences of interests were resolved through bilateral negotiations (Leanza 1993).

There have only been a few declarations of EEZs in the Mediterranean, partly due to the difficulties of delimitation. By the 1990s, only two countries had created them: Morocco in 1981 and Egypt in 1983. In the 2000s, motivated by a desire to exploit their energy resources, other countries in the Southern Mediterranean proclaimed EEZs: Syria (2003), Cyprus (2004), Tunisia (2005), Libya (2009), Lebanon (2010) and Israel (2011). In these cases, however, especially in the Levantine Sea, long-standing political disputes and the lack of an accepted common legal framework (Israel, Syria and Turkey are not parties to UNCLOS) complicated the process. At the same time, the beginning of offshore development led to new problems in the pending delimitation of other regions, such as the Adriatic Sea, where new countries emerged after the break-up of Yugoslavia.

As anticipated, apart from the general provisions of UNCLOS, two layers of regional environmental governance which apply to hydrocarbon activities are at work in the Mediterranean Sea. The first layer is the Barcelona System. The second layer, more recent and partially overlapping and interacting with the Barcelona System, stemmed from the EU's environmental and marine policy and applies primarily on EU member states. The previous section of this chapter reviewed the main EU environmental policy instruments that apply to offshore activities and their consequences for offshore politics. Here it is worth recalling that these new instruments have increased the importance of transnational dynamics in offshore development for this part of the Mediterranean, whereas in other regions, traditional inter-state dynamics – sometimes intertwined with important regional security issues such as in the Eastern Mediterranean – are still predominant.

Petroleum Politics in the Central Mediterranean[5]

Historical Background and Recent Developments

Before the recent relaunch of offshore development plans at the end of the 2000s, the history of the offshore hydrocarbon sector in the Adriatic and Ionian Seas can be divided into two main periods. In what follows, I will briefly review the main characteristics of these two periods, which constitute the background for post-2010 developments, which I will analyse in the next sections. In the first period, from the 1960s to the beginning of the 1990s, the basic domestic legislative framework and the bilateral international regime of the sector were established. At the national level in particular, the offshore sector was basically a centralised institutional structure organised around the main state-owned companies: the Italian ENI and Agip, the Croatian INA, the Greek Public Petroleum Corporation DEP and the Albanian Albpetrol (during the 1960s and the 1970s, the state-owned company Jugopetrol, in cooperation with foreign companies, also did some exploration in Montenegro, but made no important discoveries). These companies, along with the respective ministers responsible for economic development or industry, managed the sector. Externally, bilateral diplomacy and government-to-government negotiations were the instruments for solving maritime delimitation issues, under the general provision of the law of the sea. Obviously, there were differences between EU countries like Italy and Greece (after Greece joined the European Community in 1981) and non-member countries like Yugoslavia and Albania (as latter two countries were less open to foreign companies). However, the main patterns of offshore politics were characterised by the traditional partner state model, although with the peculiarities associated with this industry.

As anticipated, with regard to the delimitation of the continental shelf, Italy – the major producer country – took the lead in negotiating and defining its sea borders with Yugoslavia (1968), Greece (1977) and Albania (1992) (Blake and Topalović 1996; Symmons 1996). The Italian-Yugoslavian 1968 agreement also included provisions for cooperation in case fields were discovered between the sea borders of the two countries. During this period, there were no serious disputes that could have blocked or undermined national plans for offshore hydrocarbon development, and environmental concerns were not prominent on the political agenda, although some bilateral agreements between the states of the regions were established, and the Barcelona System began to enter into force. Italy, Yugoslavia and Greece became parties to the Barcelona Convention, while Albania did not sign the Mediterranean Action Plan and did not ratify the Barcelona Convention until 1990.

The second period, from the beginning of the 1990s to the end of the 2000s, was characterised by two opposite trends: fragmentation and integration (and homogenisation). First of all, after the Balkan wars and the break-up of Yugoslavia, the region witnessed a fragmentation of sea boundaries and a challenge to the bilateral international regime established in the previous period. Italy easily resolved the problem of new marine border delimitation since Croatia, Montenegro and Slovenia became Yugoslavia's successor states in the 1968 agreement (Slovenia became party to UNCLOS in 1995 and Montenegro in 2006 after it became independent). In 2005–06, new agreements between Italy and Croatia and between the two companies involved in the monetisation of gas resources, ENI and INA, were also signed to facilitate the common development of a gas field, the so-called 'Annamaria' gas field, discovered between the Italian and Croatian continental shelves (in 2009, Italy and Croatia signed a technical agreement for the joint exploitation of this gas field).

For the new Balkan countries, however, the situation was more complicated. In 2002, an 'interim regime' was established between Croatia and Montenegro regarding the contested coastal and sea border near the peninsula of Prevlaka. In the following years, various efforts to find a definitive solution were made through bilateral negotiations between the Croatian and Montenegrin governments. However, the dispute has proven to be very difficult to resolve, and in 2014, both governments agreed to resolve the issue of demarcation by means of international arbitration through the International Court of Justice. An agreement regarding the sea border between Croatia and Slovenia – around contested areas in the Gulf of Piran – was first negotiated in 2001, but the Croatian government did not sign the resulting treaty. No substantive negotiations took place between 2002 and 2008, but the two governments agreed to resolve the dispute with the assistance of a third party. In 2009, with the support of EU institutions and in the context of Croatia's EU accession process, the arbitration agreement was signed. The arbitral award should have been finalised by 2015, but problems emerged during the process that led to Croatia's withdrawal from the arbitration (see the next section for further details). After two years of negotiations, Greece and Albania also signed an agreement in 2009. However, in 2010, the Albanian Constitutional Court nullified the agreement due to 'procedural and substantial violations' of the constitution and of UNCLOS (Ibru 2010).

In summary, the second period is characterised by a fragmentation of the international legal regime built in the previous decades. As a result, unsettled sea borders still exist between Croatia and Slovenia, Croatia and Montenegro, and Greece and Albania, and the marine border between Montenegro and Albania has also not yet been defined (Table 5.1). So far, only Italy has signed an international agreement with all relevant parties (and Italy and Croatia have also further agreed to cooperate on the joint development of gas fields in the Adriatic Sea) (Table 5.1).

Along with this process of fragmentation, however, a parallel process of homogenisation and integration began. With EU Directive 94/22/CE, the hydrocarbon sector of member states was harmonised and opened to competition. Italy applied Directive 94/22/CE in 1996, and Greece applied it in 1995. Both countries also began a process of partial privatisation of their energy sectors and began to liberalise them as well, in accordance with internal energy market provisions. In

Table 5.1 Maritime border delimitation agreements/unresolved issues in the Adriatic and Ionian region.

	Italy	Croatia	Greece	Albania	Montenegro	Slovenia
Italy		IA/TA	IA	IA	IA	IA
Croatia	IA/TA		—	—	IR/U*	U*
Greece	IA	—		U*	—	—
Albania	IA	—	U*		No	—
Montenegro	IA	IR/U*	—	No		—
Slovenia	IA	U*	—	—	—	

Note: IA = intergovernmental agreement; TA = technical agreement; IR = interim regime; U* = unresolved issues; No = marine border/no agreement; —— = no marine border.

1993, the Albanian government transformed the state-owned energy company Alb-petrol into a public company, owned by the state, and in 1994, Albania enacted Law 7853/94 and Law 7811/94, in accordance with Directive 94/22/EC. Then, in 2006, Albania joined the Energy Community, a move which also included the transposition of the EIA directive. In Croatia, the state-owned company INA became a public company in 1993, and since 2003, it has been progressively pri-vatised. Since the mid-2010s, Croatian energy policy has focused on the liberalisa-tion and privatisation of the energy sector, and the country has gradually adopted the EU legislative energy framework, first in the context of the Energy Community and then in the process of accession, until the country joined the EU in 2013. After Montenegro gained its independence in 2006, it also started to reform its energy sector and to harmonise its laws and standards with the EU's energy legal frame-work (in 2007, Montenegro joined the Energy Community).

During the same period, the EU and Italy made important efforts to support the stabilisation and integration of the new Adriatic Balkan states. The EU-sponsored Stability Pact for South-Eastern Europe led to the creation of the Italian-sponsored Adriatic-Ionian Initiative in 2000. This initiative represented the most important inter-state, multilateral forum involving all the Southeastern European countries that aspired to join the EU (Cocco 2013). A dense network of transnational institu-tions was also created: the Forum of the Cities of the Adriatic and Ionian Basin (1999), the Forum of the Adriatic Chambers of Commerce (2001) and the Adriatic-Ionian Euro-Region (2006). This process of transnational institution-building was reinforced at the end of the 2000s when, in the context of the EU Integrated Mari-time Policy and EU Marine Strategy Framework Directive, the countries of the regions – supported by subnational governments – started a political campaign to found an EU Macro Regional Strategy for the Adriatic and Ionian Seas basin. The campaign was successful, and the European Union Strategy for the Adriatic and Ionian Region (EUSAIR) was eventually established in 2014, covering Croatia, Greece, Italy and Slovenia and four non-EU countries: Albania, Bosnia and Her-zegovina, Montenegro and Serbia. The EUSAIR strategy has an important envi-ronmental component, based on the valorisation of economic activities at sea and so-called 'blue-growth' (European Commission 2014). Also during this period, both the EU and the non-EU countries of the region ratified the Espoo and Sea Protocol, which strengthened environmental protection.

The 2010s and the Relaunch of Offshore Policies

By the end of the 2000s, offshore policies in the Adriatic and Ionian Seas had been relaunched. Albania was the first country to move to attract new investors and exploit its energy resources. Albania's national organisational structure of offshore governance was modified in 2006, when a new public agency, the National Agency of Natural Resources, was established to manage the relationships between the government and the companies involved in the hydrocarbon sector, including Alb-petrol. Currently, some areas are still unassigned, especially onshore; the only offshore blocks remaining unassigned are the 'Rodoni' north and south blocks at the marine border between Albania and Montenegro and the 'Joni-5' block at the border between Albania and Greece[6] (in both cases, as we saw, delimitation issues are still pending).

Greece's first efforts to relaunch its energy sector began in 2007, when the government took over the concessions previously granted to state-owned companies. Since the explosion of Greek's debt crisis in 2009–10, Greece has improved its energy strategy. In particular, Law 4001/2011 modified the legislative framework for granting rights for exploration and exploitation and established a new public agency (the Hellenic Hydrocarbons Management Company) in order to attract international companies. In 2014, the Greek government launched an international licensing round for 20 marine areas – 11 in the Ionian Sea and nine in the offshore area south of Crete – and an open-door invitation for two offshore areas in the Patraikos Gulf and Katakolo.[7] This plan of the Greek government in the offshore sector – along with other energy initiatives, such as the development of the Southern Gas Corridor with the Trans Adriatic Pipeline and the ITGI Poseidon project – have promoted the idea of Greece as an 'energy hub' that advances the energy security of the entire EU (Ghikas 2013).

Croatia's first attempt to improve hydrocarbon production was sketched in the policy document 'Energy Strategy of the Republic of Croatia', issued in 2009. However, it was only after 2012 that the new Croatian government began to develop a decisive strategy to expand exploration and exploitation (currently, INA is the only offshore hydrocarbon producer in the country, running five gas fields in the Northern Adriatic Sea in a joint venture with the Italian ENI). In the wake of the second Ukraine-Russia energy crisis, Croatia also decided to improve its gas supply security by promoting two new infrastructure projects, the Ionian-Adriatic-Pipeline and an LNG facility near the Island of Krk. In 2013, Croatia combined these three projects (pipeline, LNG and hydrocarbon development), with the goal of making Croatia an important energy hub for EU energy security. As for offshore activities, in 2013, the government assigned the task of conducting a seismic acquisition survey of offshore Croatia to the Norwegian Spectrum Company as a precursor to an offshore licensing round, to be held in the following years. The company estimated that Croatia could have offshore hydrocarbon reserves equivalent to 3 billion barrels of oil, enough to meet domestic demand for many decades and possibly to help supply the European market, further strengthening the government's willingness to proceed with its plans.[8] In 2013, a new regulatory framework was also enacted in order to align Croatian legislation with EU guidelines (Directive 94/22/EC) and attract foreign companies. The new 'Exploration and Exploitation of Hydrocarbons Act' established a new public agency, the Croatian Hydrocarbons Agency, to manage the licensing rounds and to help the Ministry of the Economy administrate the sector. Finally, in 2014, the government defined 29 offshore blocks in the Croatian section of the Adriatic Sea (eight blocks in the Northern Adriatic and 21 in the Middle and Southern Adriatic), and in April, it launched its first offshore bidding round.

In Italy, the relaunch of the hydrocarbon sector has been at the centre of the national energy policy agenda since the end of the 1990s. However, despite the efforts of the government, offshore activities continued to decrease during the 2000s, due in part to growing regional and local opposition to the government's plan, which was facilitated by the 2001 reform of Title V of the Italian Constitution.[9] In 2013, with the National Energy Strategy, the Italian government again decided to take action to enhance its energy security, reduce its dependence on foreign countries, and boost economic growth in the aftermath of the economic crisis. Accordingly, in September 2014, the new Italian government of Matteo Renzi enacted the so-called 'Unlock Italy' Law (Law Decree no. 133 of 12 September 2014), which introduced some changes into the governance of the upstream sector. The law simplified the procedure for obtaining concessions for exploration and production and recentralised the decision-making processes to overcome the regional and local opposition. Moreover, the new law provided for the issuance of temporary experimental concessions, designed to last five years, in the Gulf of Venice in the Northern Adriatic Sea, in order to 'preserve the national resources of hydrocarbons located in the sea and in the continental shelf in areas in the vicinity of the areas of other coastal countries which are undergoing exploration and production activities' (Law Decree no. 133 of 12 September 2014, art. 38, paragraph 10). This measure was passed in response to the new offshore Croatian plan and sought to preserve Italian resources at the marine border between the two countries.

Finally, in 2011, the government of Montenegro formulated a comprehensive energy strategy which explicitly stated that part of the government's energy policy should be based on the exploitation of domestic hydrocarbon resources and on the improvement of supply security in the gas sector. In 2010–11, Montenegro enacted two laws to establish a new legislative framework in line with Directive 94/22/CE ('Law on Exploration and Production of Hydrocarbons', no. 41/10 of 23 July 2010 and 40/11 of 8 August 2011). Then, in 2012–13, 13 offshore blocks were defined in the Adriatic Sea. And, on 7 August 2013, Montenegro launched its first international bidding round to assign the concessions for exploration and exploitation in these areas.

The New Offshore Politics in the Adriatic and Ionian Region

As we saw, the relaunch of offshore plans in the Adriatic and Ionian region has been driven by three main factors: the 2008 economic crisis, concerns about security of supply (especially in the gas sector) and intra-regional competition. On the other hand, three basic patterns of inter-state dynamics resulted from the new offshore plans: cooperation, competition and confrontations and disputes over the delimitation of states' borders at sea. Italy and Croatia have mainly cooperated, developing their shared energy resources by relying on the bilateral agreement of the 1960s and its more recent adjustments as well as on the practical cooperation between the companies involved in the development of the gas fields, i.e. ENI and INA. But while they cooperated in the joint development of gas resources, a competitive dynamic has also been at work; for example the Croatian plan provoked a 'reaction' from the Italian government to preserve possible Italian energy resources

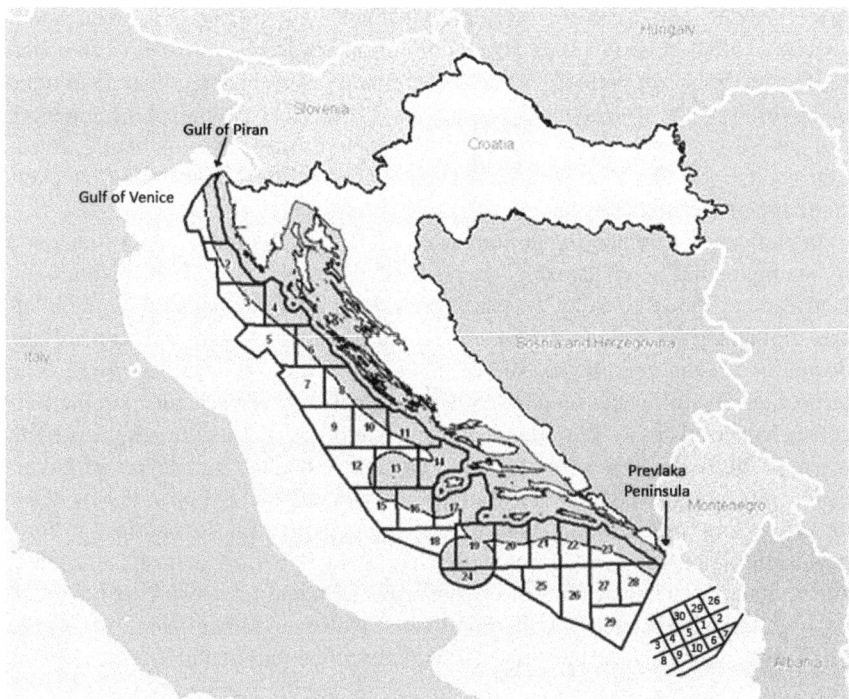

Figure 5.1 Croatian and Montenegrin offshore blocks in the Adriatic Sea.

Note: Author's elaboration for illustration.

located in the Gulf of Venice near Croatian waters (Figure 5.1). Relationships among the Balkan states have been marked primarily by confrontations and disputes, especially where the boundaries at sea were not yet defined, such as between Croatia and Slovenia (the Gulf of Piran) and between Croatia and Montenegro (the Prevlaka Peninsula) (Figure 5.1). These disputes have not prevented energy companies already active in the regional energy markets to take part in the licensing rounds launched by Croatia and Montenegro. However, in 2015, the uncertainty caused by the unresolved maritime borders, coupled with a fall in oil prices, induced some companies to review their investment decisions.

Croatia and Montenegro have also continued to support their offshore plans while trying to resolve their dispute through the traditional instruments provided by the law of the sea. The EU has indirectly supported the Balkan countries' offshore plans in the context of its wider efforts to promote the development of Southeastern Europe's energy infrastructure system. The Balkan countries have also cooperated among themselves in the area of energy infrastructures. Moreover, along these more traditional patterns of inter-state interactions, the relaunch of offshore plans has triggered a new set of national and transnational political dynamics. These dynamics are the result of two mutually reinforcing trends. The first is growing public concern about the negative environmental impact and potential risk of offshore activities and the mobilisation and opposition of environmental NGOs, generally supported by local and regional governments. The second trend is the result of the strengthened supranational and EU environmental framework that has created new bridges between offshore activities and environmental protection and has provided new institutional channels of political interactions that overcome national boundaries.

In particular, the emerging politics of offshore development in the Adriatic and Ionian region has been shaped by the progressive development of the institutional landscape. Although UNCLOS rests at the core of international politics and bilateral diplomacy with regard to the ownership of energy resources and resolving disputes over the delimitation of sea boundaries; with regard to environmental protection, an entire new set of institutions and rules have been added to the Barcelona System. The EU's environmental and marine policy instruments, along with the new sub-regional governance structures, have created new layers of governance, resulting in a complex institutional architecture that has opened new channels for actors' mobilisation (Figure 5.2). The new principles embodied in those new institutional structures, along with the growing public concern and awareness about the environmental risks of offshore development, have combined to break the traditional isolation of the offshore sector. However, rather than replacing the previous dynamics, these new transnational dynamics coexist and overlap with the

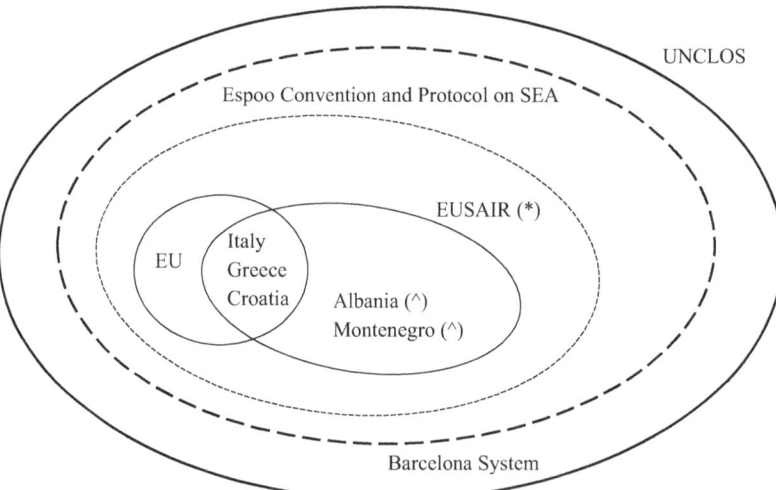

Figure 5.2 The institutional architecture of offshore international governance in the Adriatic and Ionian Region.

Note: (*) EUSAIR includes also Bosnia-Herzegovina and Serbia. (^) Albania and Montenegro are also parties to the Energy Community.

more traditional inter-state politics and bilateral diplomatic practices. In what follows, the inter-state interactions will first be further analysed, and then the transnational environmental dimension of offshore politics will be discussed.

Between Cooperation and Confrontation

Although the original 1968 agreement between Italy and Yugoslavia had already established some basic principles for cooperation in the development of joint fields, it was only in the 2009 technical agreement that the Italian and Croatian governments formally approved the programmes of gas exploitation signed by ENI and INA. The 2009 technical agreement allowed both governments to supervise and control actual production from the joint gas fields; however, in practice, its successful implementation depends on the arrangements between the companies involved in the monetisation of gas resources (Caligiuri 2015). Indeed, while ENI is responsible for production in Italian waters (Annamaria platform B), the Croatian side (Annamaria platform A) is run by a joint operating company, INAgip, owned 50 percent by INA and 50 percent by ENI. ENI, the leading operator in the Italian upstream hydrocarbon sector, was also one of the companies to take part in the 2014 Croatian offshore bidding round. The round received 10 bids for just 15 exploration areas of the 29 blocks that constitute the country's offshore zone (Table 5.1, Figure 5.1). Despite the relatively simple technical environment of the Croatian offshore – its sea depth is between 100 and 500 meters – no major international companies took part in the licensing round. Declining oil prices were one contributing factor. ENI obtained a licence in partnership with the UK-based company Medoilgas, and seven more licences were granted to a consortium consisting of Austria's OMV and the US-based Marathon Oil. The other two licences were awarded to another consortium: INA, which is co-owned by the Croatian government, and Hungary's MOL. For these companies, which were already involved in the southern and central European energy market or in the Balkans, the opportunity to find new resources and to expand their holdings in those markets were sufficient reasons to invest in the exploration of the Croatian offshore. Marathon Oil, OMV, ENI and Medoilgas also took part in the Montenegrin offshore round, as did the Russian company Novatek and the Greek company Energean. In three consortia (Marathon Oil and OMV, ENI and Novatek, and Energean and Medoilgas), these companies submitted applications for 12 of the 13 blocks offered by Montenegro (Table 5.2).

By the end of 2015, exploration had still to begin, and, notwithstanding the suggestions made by the Spectrum Company based on the seismic survey, the actual potential of the Croatian and Montenegrin offshore was not yet clear. Meanwhile, the Croatian government sought to highlight the importance of the country's resources for European energy security to bring attention to the country's offshore sector and to gain the support of EU institutions. EU institutions did not directly express support for the offshore Croatian plan, but they were supportive of the country's strategy for gas infrastructure development, which will be important

Table 5.2 Croatian and Montenegrin first offshore bidding rounds: key data and results.

	Croatia	Montenegro
Bidding round/year	2014	2013
Blocks offered (block numbers)	29 blocks (1–29)	13 blocks (1–10 and 26, 29, 30)
Bids received: companies/blocks	- Marathon Oil-OMV/7 blocks (8, 10, 11, 22, 23, 27 and 28) - ENI-Medoilgas/1block (9) - INA/2 blocks (25 and 26)	- Marathon Oil- OMV/5 blocks (1, 5, 26, 30, 29) - ENI-Novatek/4 blocks (4, 5, 10, 30) - Energean-Medoilgas/3 blocks (5, 10, 30)
Licensed issued (date): companies/blocks	(January 2015) - Marathon Oil-OMV/7 blocks (8, 10, 11, 22, 23, 27 and 28) - ENI-Medoilgas/1block (9) - INA/2 blocks (25 and 26)	(February 2016) ENI-Novatek/4 blocks (4, 5, 10, 30)
Bids retired: companies/blocks	Marathon Oil-OMV/7 blocks (blocks 23, 27 and 28 are placed in waters disputed by Croatia and Montenegro near the Prevlaka peninsula)	—
Further contracts signed	—	ENI-Novatek (Concession contract signed on 14 September 2016)

Sources: Author's compilation from press data and data available at: www.azu.hr/en-us/; www.petroleum.me/.
Note: Data and results up to November 2016.

if gas is found in the Croatian sea in sufficient quantities to allow exportation. The development of the Croatian and Montenegrin energy infrastructures (such as the Ionian-Adriatic-Pipeline) was also regarded by the energy companies involved in offshore exploration as an important guarantee that possible discoveries could be monetised in a reasonable amount of time.

Although the goal of improving Balkan energy security is supported by all the countries of the region – leading to important cooperation, such as for the realisation of the Ionian-Adriatic-Pipeline – the launch of the offshore plan has provoked new disputes. In 2014, the Montenegrin Ministry of Foreign Affairs officially filed a complaint against Croatia, arguing for the inclusion of the Prevlaka peninsula in the government-issued geographic maps that were offered to interested concessionaires for oil and gas exploration (Government of Montenegro 2014a, 2014b). In particular, Montenegro contested the Croatian plan respecting blocks 27, 28 and 29, which are located in whole or in part in a portion of the Adriatic Sea claimed by Montenegro, near the Prevlaka peninsula (Figure 5.1). Montenegro recalled that the Protocol on the Provisional Regime of 2002 obliges the two countries to refrain from unilateral actions that would prejudice determination of the common border at sea and on land. According to the Montenegrin government, Croatia's unilateral act of calling for public tenders in the southern part of the Adriatic was inconsistent with the Protocol and violated the principles set by UNCLOS (Caligiuri 2015). In January 2015, after the Croatian international offshore round was concluded, Montenegro's Ministry of Foreign Affairs and European Integration sent a formal note of protest to Croatia for the licences awarded to the consortia of INA, Marathon Oil and OMV in blocks 23, 26, 27 and 28 (Government of Montenegro 2015a). In January 2015, a formal note of protest was also sent to Marathon Oil and OMV for violating the 'letter and spirit of UNCLOS' (Government of Montenegro 2015b). But no additional actions have been taken against these companies, partly because they were also involved in the Montenegrin offshore sector. However, in July 2015, Marathon Oil and OMV decided to return the seven offshore exploration licences to Croatia, three of which were in waters disputed by the two countries (Table 5.1). This decision was also motivated by the slump in the oil prices that was forcing the energy industry to cut investments.[10]

The dispute has also gone in the opposite direction. Montenegro's offshore plan initially included a number of blocks that, according to Croatia, were in the disputed area between the two countries, violating the 2002 Protocol. Following several public exchanges with the Croatian government, the Montenegrin Government decided to exclude the disputed blocks from its first offshore round and award concessions only for the blocks in its southern waters[11] (Figure 5.1). Eventually, by the end of 2016, the Montenegrin government had approved only one oil and gas research and exploitation concession contract with the ENI-Novatek Italian-Russian consortium (the concession contract was signed by ENI-Novatek on 14 September 2016).[12] To date, this concession contract is the only deal for new drilling activities in the Montenegrin section of the Adriatic Sea, despite the bidding round that was launched in 2013, whereas in Croatia, no further steps have been taken to implement the national offshore programme since licences were issued at the beginning of 2015 (Table 5.2).

The arbitration process initiated in 2009 over the sea border between Croatia and Slovenia was not yet concluded when Croatia decided to develop its offshore plan. Therefore, in April 2014, following the launch of the Croatian bidding round, the Slovenian government presented a formal objection to Croatia for the inclusion of areas close to the contested sea border in the Gulf of Piran (Figure 5.1). The Slovenian position was soon reinforced by a declaration by the Director General for Bilateral Relations and European Affairs, reminding Croatia of its obligation to 'act in good faith' and conform to the Article 10 of the 2009 Arbitration Agreement stipulating that 'parties must refrain from any action or statement which might intensify the dispute or jeopardise the work of the Arbitral Tribunal'.[13] The final decision of the arbitration tribunal was expected by the end of 2015. However, in summer of the same year, a scandal occurred after press revelations of secret conversations between the Slovene judge on the panel and the Slovenian representative. The episode caused the Slovenian government to ask for the resignation of both persons involved, and the Croatian government began to express some unwillingness to continue the arbitration process. In the following months, despite pressure from EU institutions, Croatia decided to withdraw from the arbitration. In June 2016, the Croatian Minister of Foreign and European Affairs declared that the arbitration procedure was 'no longer relevant' for Croatia.[14]

The Transnational Environmental Dimension of Offshore Politics

In addition to the problems related to the long-standing international boundary disputes in the Balkans, the new plans for offshore development raised new concerns about the environmental protection of the Adriatic and Ionian Seas. In Italy, the new plan established by the government in 2014 prompted numerous protests by environmental NGOs, regional governments and important opposition parties such as the Five Stars Movement, which received about 25 percent of the votes in the general election of 2013, making it the second party in Italy. The strategy of offshore development in the Adriatic and Ionian Seas was also opposed by many local communities and local businesses involved in fishing and tourism. At the beginning of 2015, six Italian regions – four of which are Adriatic and Ionian coastal regions (Abruzzi, Marche, Puglia and Veneto) – appealed to the Italian Constitutional Court against Decree 'Unlock Italy', which produced a recentralisation of the decision-making process regarding onshore and offshore upstream activities. The opposition of the Italian regions reached a higher level when, in September 2015, 10 regions – Abruzzi, Basilicata, Calabria, Campania, Liguria, Marche, Molise, Puglia, Sardinia and Veneto – eight of which were led by the Democratic Party, of which the Italian Prime Minister Matteo Renzi is also the Secretary, decided to promote a referendum to halt the national government's plan in support of a proposal by environmental NGOs. In particular, the referendum aimed to abrogate some norms established by 'Unlock Italy' and other laws that had reduced the powers of regional governments in onshore and offshore development and had allowed the prorogation of oil and gas concessions within 12 nautical miles of the Italian coast until the exhaustion of the useful life of the fields[15] (in total, the referendum addressed six different issues). At the end of 2015, in response to the regions' claims and in order to avoid a referendum, the Italian government decided to review the contested norms of 'Unlock Italy' as well as other legislation targeted by the protest. New legislation was passed, eliminating five of the original six issues covered by the proposed referendum. However, on 19 January 2016, the Italian Constitutional Court approved the proposed referendum for the remaining issue, the one related to the prolongation of concessions within the 12-nautical-mile limit. The referendum was held on 17 April 2016. Many opposition parties, such as the Five Stars Movement and the Northern League, campaigned in support of regional claims, opposing the government's position. The Democratic Party campaigned for abstention as a means of defeating the referendum, since its validity was only assured with the participation of 50 percent of the voters. In the end, although approximately 85 percent of participants voted in favour of repealing the contested law, the 31 percent turnout was below the majority threshold (50 percent) required to validate the result.

Although the referendum did not ultimately reach the necessary quorum, the protest conducted by environmental NGOs and the local and regional governments had already prompted the Italian government to change its approach by reviewing the 'Unlock Italy' decree. Moreover, the domestic protest paved the way for transnational dynamics when, in the wake of the launch of the Croatian offshore plan, many environmental NGOs and regional governments called on the Italian government to ask its Croatian counterpart to participate in a Strategic Environmental Assessment, as laid out in Directive 2001/41/EC and the 2003 Kiev Protocol of the Espoo Convention. After some hesitation, the Italian Ministry of the Environment asked Croatia to participate in the process, owing to the trans-boundary dimension of the Croatian offshore plan. Along with the Italian government, five Italian Adriatic coastal regions (Marche, Puglia, Veneto, Abruzzi and Emilia Romagna) – four of which had already appealed to the Italian Constitutional Court against the Italian plan and supported the referendum against the 'Unlock Italy' decree – submitted their observations to the Croatian government, advising against the Croatian plan. Various environmental NGOs and local committees (the so-called 'No-Triv' Committees) opposing the Italian offshore development plan took part in the process, also voicing their opposition to Croatia's offshore development strategy. Italian regional governments' negative assessment of the Croatian plan was based particularly on the plan's failure to adequately consider the potential trans-boundary effects on Italy's Adriatic coastal areas, especially those that are most sensitive from an environmental point of view.[16] Moreover, regional governments raised questions about the coherence of the plan with the EU's general marine policies and environmental frameworks, such as the MSFD (Directive 2008/56/EC), Directive 2013/30/EU, and Directive 2014/89/EU on Marine Spatial Planning.

In its opinion statement, the Italian Ministry of the Environment highlighted many shortcomings in Croatia's plan and requested a number of things from its Croatian counterpart, asking that Croatian authorities consider other EU strategies, such as EUSAIR and the Marine Spatial Planning Framework. Meanwhile, Slovenia and Montenegro also requested to be and were included in the Croatian strategic environmental impact assessment. As a result, the Croatian government decided to postpone the deadline for signing the contract with companies that had received licences for offshore exploration from April to June 2015.[17]

At the same time, the Croatian government was also confronting growing domestic protest from environmental organisations and local communities. Various environmental NGOs organised public campaigns against the plan, and some political parties and businesses involved in tourism opposed and criticised the plan. In September 2015, a transnational platform of environmental NGOs, 'S.O.S. Adriatic Coalition', was established in Split in Croatia, gathering representatives of environmental organisations and initiatives opposing national offshore plans from Slovenia, Croatia, Montenegro, Albania and Italy. The socialist Croatian government emphasised that the plan was one part of its efforts to improve the country's energy security, attract investment to stimulate the Croatian economy and gain international political attention in the EU energy map. However, by the end of September 2015, in view that the general election was to be held in November 2015, it was decided to further postpone the off-shore plan. A similar decision was then made by the new centre-right govern-ment, which was formed after the election, agreeing to put offshore development on hold. Afterwards, as a result of a political crisis, a new election was held in September 2016, and it is still not clear if and when the Croatian offshore plan will be resumed.

Concluding Remarks

The recent relaunch of national plans for offshore development in the Adriatic and Ionian Seas has triggered new inter-state and transnational political dynam-ics in the region. It is too soon to determine if maritime disputes or environ-mental mobilisations will have an actual impact on states' long-term energy strategies. Furthermore, offshore development has also been negatively affected by the wider dynamics of global energy markets and the post-2015 drop in oil prices. Energy companies have been heavily cutting investments around the world, and the Adriatic and Ionian region conforms to this general trend as well. However, especially in Croatia and Italy, new offshore plans have raised many concerns about the environmental protection of this very fragile marine area, and mobilisation by local communities, subnational gov-ernments and environmental organisations has prompted national governments to review their original plans.

Traditionally, offshore policies and politics in the Adriatic and Ionian Seas have been played out by states and energy companies. International governance structures have channelled these interactions, allowing states to clarify their claims over energy resources and to construct frameworks for offshore develop-ment in the region. Environmental protection was typically managed at the inter-governmental level, while concerns about the negative effects of offshore development manifested mainly on the domestic level, especially in Italy, where the majority of hydrocarbon activities took place. Inter-state interactions – in the form of competition, disputes and cooperation – have also characterised the recent period, and energy companies continue to play an important role in off-shore development. The EU has played a very limited role in these patterns of interactions as part of its general support of the clarification of maritime borders in the Adriatic Sea and the development of energy infrastructure in the region. On the other hand, the new EU and international environmental governance structures, principles and norms have encouraged transnational dynamics. These dynamics have, in turn, challenged the traditional concept of 'marine national sovereignty', involving more and diverse players in offshore politics. However, rather than replacing traditional patterns of inter-state interactions, the new politics of offshore development have resulted in a combination of old dynamics with these new, emerging transnational trends.

Petroleum Politics in the Eastern Mediterranean

Historical Background and Recent Developments

From an historical perspective, the Eastern Mediterranean has never been of great importance in terms of energy, especially compared to its neighbouring regions: the Middle East and North Africa. The history of offshore development in the Levantine Sea and the Aegean Sea can be divided into three main periods. The first, from the 1970s to the end of the 1990s, is characterised by minor offshore activities carried out by Israel and Egypt in the Levantine Sea and by Greece and Turkey the Aegean Sea. In the Aegean Sea, these activities did not result in any major discoveries, but they provoked serious confrontations between Athens and Ankara as part of their wider conflict for the delimitation of their sea boundaries. Although Greece joined the European Community in 1981, the rivalry between Greece and Turkey was mainly handled within the NATO security framework and with the intervention of other external actors, especially the US, in the broader geopolitical context of the Cold War. Another important political development in this period was the escalation of the 'Cyprus question' and the division of Cyprus into the internationally recognised Republic of Cyprus (RoC) and the Turkish Republic of Northern Cyprus (TRNC), established in 1983 and recognised only by Turkey. This development would greatly affect Eastern Mediterranean offshore politics in the following decades. In the Levantine Sea, offshore exploration began in the late 1960s and early 1970s off the coast of Israel, but no discoveries were made that justified commercial development of the fields. The first important gas discoveries in the region were made only in the second half of the 1980s in Egyptian waters in front of the Nile Delta, north of Alessandria and Port Said (Khadduri 2012). Egypt was also the first country in the region to establish its EEZ in 1983 in accordance with UNCLOS. In the 1980s, Cyprus and Lebanon also signed the UNCLOS (in 1982 and 1984, respectively), but Israel, Syria and Turkey have not yet become parties of the convention. At the beginning of the 1990s, several important international oil companies, such as British Petroleum, ENI and British Gas, increased their investments in the Egyptian offshore. Production and domestic consumption of natural gas grew dramatically at the end of the decade after significant gas discoveries were made in 1997.

The second period (from the end of the 1990s to circa 2009) opened with a rise in offshore activities in the Levantine Sea and the discovery of some consistent natural gas fields in Egypt and off the Gaza strip. These discoveries triggered an acceleration in exploration activities to acquire more precise data on the entire Levantine Basin and in efforts to complete its international legal regime. However, these discoveries also triggered additional confrontations among states for the establishment of their sovereignty rights at sea and for the delimitation of their respective EEZs. Confrontation at sea – mainly between Cyprus and

Turkey – coexisted with cooperation on land with the realisation of the Arish-Ashkelon pipeline and the Arab Gas Pipeline, which supplied gas from Egypt to Israel, Jordan, Syria and Lebanon. More importantly, when Cyprus joined the EU in 2004, the Levantine Sea became, for all practical purposes, a sea frontier of the European Union. The EU then became active in solving the Cyprus question. In the early 2000s, the prospect of EU membership for Cyprus and Turkey increased optimism about the possibility of a breakthrough. However, the failure to reach an agreement in the 2004 UN Annan Plan referendum meant that Cyprus's prospects of EU membership decoupled from resolution of the conflict. Since then, no real progress has been made, and as the possibility of Turkey joining the EU has become more and more remote, the EU's influence over the Cyprus-Turkey dispute has decreased.

Finally, the third period began in 2009–11, when major discoveries were realised in the waters of Israel and Cyprus and the expectation of additional resources in the surrounding areas increased. These discoveries dramatically changed these countries' energy security landscape, but they also triggered more severe inter-state conflicts over the ownership of resources, especially where sea boundaries were already contested, i.e. Israel-Lebanon and Turkey-Cyprus. However, the possibility of monetising the new gas discoveries – especially after the 2013 Israeli decision to export part of its reserves – through new routes of gas export and the construction of the related infrastructures has also paved the way for new patterns of cooperation.

In the following two sub-sections the first (from the end of the 1990s to 2009) and second (beginning in 2009–11) periods will be further analysed, and the final section will focus on the international political economy of the monetisation of Levantine energy resources and on recent events (post-2015). Particular attention will be paid to the export projects involving the EU member states (Cyprus and Greece) and to the role of the EU. However, the roles of other important regional actors – mainly Israel, Turkey and Egypt, where a major gas discovery was made in 2015 (the Zohr field) – will also be addressed here. These countries' strategies influenced energy developments in Cyprus and proposed projects to export resources from the Eastern Mediterranean to Europe. Moreover, some important political events, such as the regime change in Egypt, the developments in Israeli-Turkish relations, the emergence of the Israel-Cyprus-Greece trilateral cooperation, the war in Syria and the rise of the ISIS will be considered in this section as well, because they have affected the political and economic 'game' of the monetisation of Levantine resources.

The Construction of the Levantine Sea International
Legal Regime: Developments and Contestations

Between the end of the 1990s and the beginning of the 2000s, in a context of rising oil prices, various energy companies decided to increase their investments in the Levantine Basin. Important energy discoveries were made, and international attention on the region's hydrocarbon resources definitely took off. In 1999, a consortium led by British Gas obtained a licence to explore Palestinian waters off the Gaza strip, between Israel and Egypt. In 2000, this consortium discovered a gas field (Gaza Marine) with estimated reserves of about 28 bcm. Plans to develop this resource by building a pipeline to the Gaza Strip were debated in the following years, but the deterioration of Israeli-Palestinian relations, especially after the Hamas 2006 electoral victory, prevented further discussion, and exploitation of the field came to a halt (Paraschos 2013). In 1999–2000, the first discoveries in Israeli waters were made by Noble Energy and the Delek Group, two private companies from the US and Israel, respectively. The Mari-B gas field, discovered in 2000 with about 42 bcm, changed Israel's energy security landscape when production began in 2004. This gas field allowed the country to increase its gas consumption, especially in the electricity sector, which until then had relied entirely on coal and other fuel oils (Shaffer 2012).

In the meantime, in 2005, Egypt initiated natural gas exports with the opening of two LNG liquefaction plants in Damietta and Idku. Egyptian exports increased even more when two pipelines – the Arish-Ashkelon pipeline and the Arab Gas Pipeline – came into operation and began to serve Jordan in 2003, Israel and Syria in 2008 and Lebanon in 2009. These infrastructures were very important in terms of regional energy security. In particular, the Arish-Ashkelon pipeline, a 90 km submarine gas pipeline connecting Egypt to Israel, has supplied about half of Israel's natural gas since it opened in 2008.

Hoping to explore its own hydrocarbon offshore potential, Cyprus established an EEZ in 2004, after negotiating a delimitation agreement of its southern sea borders with Egypt, which was ratified in 2003. In 2007, Cyprus signed an agreement with Lebanon for the delimitation of the Cypriot EEZ, and negotiations with Syria and Israel began. The agreement with Egypt was finalised quite easily – especially since Egypt had a practical economic interest in continuing to develop its own resources by attracting international energy companies – but with Lebanon and Syria, the process proved to be more difficult. One reason for the Syrian and Lebanese delays in reaching agreements with Cyprus was Turkish opposition. Turkey objected to these agreements – Turkey also opposed Cyprus's agreement with Egypt in 2004 – and began to strongly oppose Cypriot efforts to stabilise the legal international regime of the Levantine Sea. Indeed, maintaining that it was acting on behalf of the TRNC, Turkey repeatedly contested Cyprus's rights to declare an EEZ, to delimitate its borders with other countries and to assign areas of its EEZ to energy companies for exploration and development (Darbouche, El-Katiri and Fattouh 2012; Grigoriadis 2014). The major EU institutions, including the European Council, condemned Turkish opposition on the RoC offshore development project and sea border delimitations and supported Cyprus's plans.[18] In 2007, Cyprus enacted a new hydrocarbon law in compliance with Directive 94/22/CE and launched its first international bidding round for offshore exploration licences. In total, 11 of the 13 blocks previously defined in the Cypriot EEZ were offered; blocks 3 and 13 were excluded because of their proximity to Turkish waters or to the area administered by the Turkish Cypriot (Tziampiris 2014) (Figure 5.3).

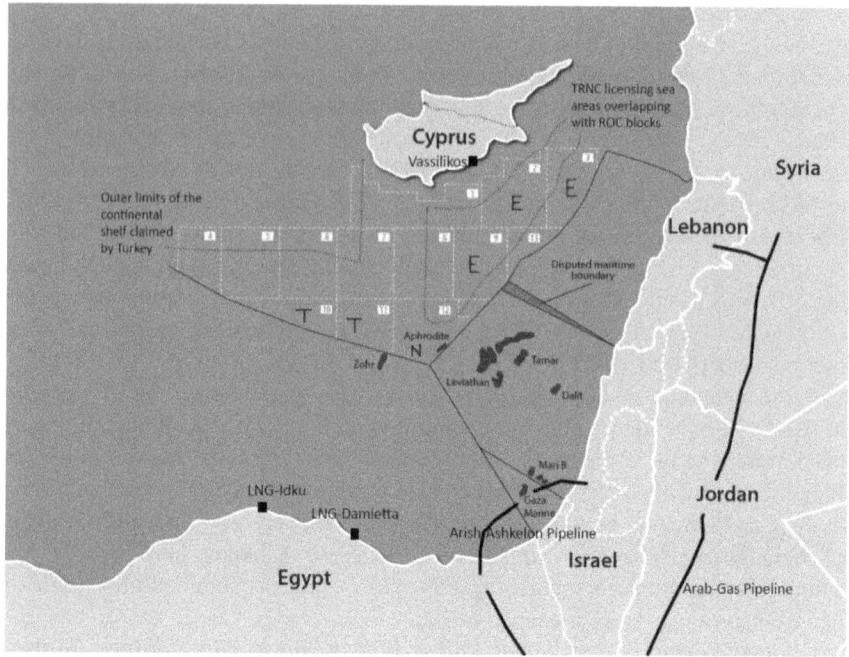

Figure 5.3 Major gas fields, delimitation issues and energy infrastructure in the Levantine basin.

Note: Author's elaboration for illustration. White dot-lines with numbers = blocks offered in the Cyprus's EEZ. Black lines = EEZs of Cyprus, Lebanon and Egypt. N = block assigned to Noble Energy and Delek Group (Cyprus's first bidding round); E = blocks assigned to the ENI-Kogas consortium (Cyprus's second bidding round); T = blocks assigned to Total (Cyprus's second bidding round). Black lines in bold = major international gas pipelines. The Zohr field was discovered by ENI in August 2015 in the Egyptian EEZ.

Between Major Discoveries and Major Contestations

Within two years, from 2009 to 2011, major gas discoveries were realised off the coasts of Israel and Cyprus. In Israel, Noble Energy and the Delek Group found two important gas fields: the Tamar gas field, in 2009, with estimated resources of 283 bcm, and a bigger field, the Leviathan, in 2010, with estimated reserves of 510 bcm. In the wake of these important discoveries (other minor discoveries were also made, see Table 5.3), it was soon clear to analysts and decision makers that Israel's reserves placed the country in the position of becoming a self-sufficient producer of natural gas for its domestic market for at least 20 years, while potentially allowing for additional natural gas exports (Darbouche, El-Katiri and Fattouh 2012). The Tamar field began production in 2013, and the Leviathan field was expected to begin production in 2017. Initially, most of this gas was intended to satisfy domestic growing demand, a critical and urgent concern for Israel. After the end

Table 5.3 The major gas discoveries in the Levantine Basin (2000–13).

Field name	Year of discovery	Country	Estimates reserves (e) (Bcm)	Main Shareholders (country of origin)
Gaza Marine	2000	Palestinian Territories	28	British Gas (UK)
Mari-B	2000	Israel	42	Noble Energy (US) Delek Group (Israel)
Dalit	2009	Israel	14	Delek Group (US) Noble Energy (Israel)
Tamar	2009	Israel	283	Delek Group (US) Noble Energy (Israel)
Leviathan	2010	Israel	510	Delek Group (US) Noble Energy (Israel)
Aphrodite	2011	Cyprus	200	Noble Energy (US) Delek Group (Israel)
Tannin	2012	Israel	34	Noble Energy (US) Delek Group (Israel)
Karish	2013	Israel	50	Noble Energy (US) Delek Group (Israel)

Sources: Author's compilation from: Darbouche, El-Katiri and Fattouh (2012), EIA (2013), and De Micco (2014).

Note: (e) estimates in 2013.

of the Mubarak regime, the Egyptian supply to Israel (and Jordan) was disrupted on a regular basis, and in 2012, the Egyptian Natural Gas Holding Company (EGAS) announced the cancellation of its supply agreement with Israel.

Due to Israel's traditional isolation in the region and its recent negative experience with the Egyptian gas supply, the debate about the development of the new gas resources was sharp and politically sensitive, especially regarding the possible exportation of part of the country's gas. Eventually, in June 2013, the government decided to allow the export of about the 40 percent of the resources and to reserve the rest for the domestic market.

The third major gas discovery in the Levantine Sea was made in 2011 in Cyprus's EEZ, after the country's first offshore licensing round, which launched in 2007 (Table 5.3). The Cypriot offshore round did not attract great interest from international energy companies, and only one block (block 12) was granted for exploration to the companies already involved in Israeli offshore development (the US company Noble Energy and the Israeli Delek Group and Ratio Oil). However, in December 2011, Noble announced a major gas discovery in the Aphrodite field, located 65 km west of Israel's Leviathan field (Figure 5.3). The Aphrodite field was estimated to have about 200 bcm and was considered sufficient to largely satisfy Cyprus domestic gas consumption for many years and to support gas export as well (Giamouridis 2012; EIA 2013).

The important discoveries made in Israel and Cyprus triggered new efforts to complete the Levantine Sea's international legal regime but caused also a new set of inter-state confrontations. Cyprus and Israel signed a bilateral agreement for the common delimitation of their EEZs in 2010 (the agreement also included provisions for cooperation in the development of cross-border resources). However, Lebanon contested this agreement because of its ongoing unresolved maritime dispute with Israel (Figure 5.3). In 2010, Lebanon established its EEZ and was planning its own offshore programme. Lebanon particularly objected to the EEZ which Israel delimitated with the RoC, as one part of it overlapped with Lebanese claims (Stocker 2012; Gürel, Mullen and Tzimitras 2013).

A second set of conflicts then emerged between Cyprus and Turkey. In response to the RoC offshore plans, TNRC (backed by Turkey) proposed its own marine energy exploration programme. In practice, this program contested the Greek Cypriot EEZ in the Eastern Mediterranean (Grigoriadis 2014). The Turkish opposition to the RoC's 'unilateral' establishment of its EEZ – which dates back to the agreement between Cyprus and Egypt – is not only related to its traditional patronage and support of the TRNC, but a by-product of the unresolved and broader issue of the delimitation of the sea borders and the continental shelf between Turkey and Greece (Ghikas 2013; Mullen 2014). Some sections of the licensed blocks (blocks 1, 4, 5, 6, 7) offered by Cyprus in the northwest section of its EEZ overlap with Turkey's claimed continental shelf area in the Eastern Mediterranean (Figure 5.3). In the wake of the Cyprus offshore round, the Turkish government declared that it would not allow companies to conduct exploration in this area 'under any circumstances' and would take 'all the necessary measures to prevent it' (Mullen 2014, 12). Furthermore, in September 2011, the Turkish government signed a bilateral agreement with the TRNC for the delineation of their continental shelves on the basis of the equitable principle of international law (only the TRNC and Turkey recognise this agreement). Then, in November of the same year, the Turkish energy company TPAO signed a contract with the TRNC to conduct exploration in the sea between Turkey and Cyprus in licensing blocks which largely overlap with those included by the RoC in its EEZ, including block 12, where the Aphrodite field was discovered (Figure 5.3).

Supported by the EU, the RoC formally protested these actions, but Turkey has continued to try to interfere with its offshore plan and to request a halt to all development activities until the Cyprus question is resolved (Tagliapietra 2013). Erdogan, the Turkish prime minister at that time, also threatened to blacklist the international firms working on Cyprus offshore exploration and to stop them from participating in energy projects in Turkey.[19] However, Turkish opposition did not prevent the RoC government from launching its second offshore international round in 2012. After the discovery of the Aphrodite field, the likelihood of additional discoveries was considered realistic, and with a growing economic and public finance crisis, the government was strongly committed to exploiting its energy resources. This time, there was a strong response from international energy companies. Fifteen companies, including international majors such as the French Total, the Italian ENI, the Malaysia's Petronas, the Korean Kogas and the Russian

Novatek, bid for contracts for nine offshore blocks south of the island. The participation of many important international energy companies showed that the threat of sanctions by Turkey – which is not a major producer country, although it has an important role as a transit country – were not very effective. The French company Total came away with blocks 10 and 11, while a consortium formed by ENI (80 percent) and Kogas (20 percent) won the bid for blocks 2, 3 and 9, all of which overlap with TRNC licensing sea areas (see Figure 5.3). It is worth noting, however, that no blocks in areas which overlap with the Turkish claim on its continental shelf west of Cyprus have been assigned (blocks 1, 4, 5, 6 and 7) (Figure 5.3). Cyprus's decision to include ENI and Total in the country's offshore activities supported its intention to strengthen its economic and political connections with other EU member states and to focus the attention of EU institutions on the potential of Cypriot resources to diversify European gas supplies.

The International Political Economy of the Levantine Energy Resources' Monetisation and the (Limited) Role of the EU

The new offshore plans in the Levantine Sea have exacerbated traditional interstate conflicts over sea boundaries. However, in the wake of the Israeli and Cypriot discoveries, it became clear that there were new, important opportunities for cooperation in this region. Israel, the first country to make a major discovery, was also the first mover in the new 'economic and political game' for the monetisation of Levantine gas resources through new export routes and infrastructures (Tsakiris 2014). In July 2010, Israeli Prime Minister Netanyahu proposed a pipeline connecting Israel to Greece via Cyprus to then Greek Prime Minister Papandreou. In that period, both governments saw energy as a cornerstone of a strategic rapprochement, especially after the collapse of the Turkish-Israeli alliance in the wake of the 2010 Mavi Marmara incident. In the following years, Israel and Greece attempted to increase their political and security cooperation by including Cyprus as well. After the discovery of the Aphrodite gas field, Cyprus was ready to play a new role in the regional energy landscape and improve its strategic position vis-à-vis Turkey (Tziarras 2016). Many of the infrastructural projects discussed were economically and technically ambitious and aimed to connect Israeli and Cypriot gas to the European energy markets. A similar solution was also backed by the EU to promote diversification of gas supply, end Cyprus's energy isolation and support the island's economic recovery. However, the EU has very limited instruments to influence regional (energy) politics, which is also affected by the wider geopolitical and security context involving other external actors like the US and Russia. The EU can provide some support to make major projects more feasible, but its effectiveness is limited if commercial realities and national preferences do not match EU strategy.

At the same time, other projects, less economically and technically ambitious but politically more difficult, were also explored. The monetisation of the new gas resources through pipeline routes could have contributed to trigger diplomatic rapprochements between Israel and Turkey and between Cyprus and Turkey.

However, all these possibilities have proved very difficult to realise. By the beginning of 2015, not one of the major projects discussed in the previous years seemed ready to materialise. On the other hand, more regionally oriented patterns of cooperation have emerged among Israel, Cyprus, Jordan and Egypt.

Proposing and Discussing Major Infrastructural Projects: 2011–14

In 2011–12, Israel, Cyprus and Greece established joint working groups to evaluate the feasibility of the main options on the table for energy cooperation (Tagliapietra 2013): i) an electricity interconnector (the EuroAsia Electricity Interconnector) from Israel and Cyprus to Greece; ii) a pipeline (East Med Pipeline) to carry Israeli and Cypriot gas to the European markets through Greece and iii) a joint Israeli-Cypriot LNG plant near Vassilikos on the southern coast of the island (Figure 5.3). However, also other projects were simultaneously evaluated according to each government's energy and security agenda and economic interests. These included an LNG or FLNG plant in Israel, an LNG in Cyprus, an Israel-Cyprus-Turkey pipeline, and an Israel-Turkey pipeline. As a result, from 2011 to 2014, various options with different technical features and price tags were competing for the monetisation of Levantine gas resources. Many of them implied cooperative efforts and political support by two or more countries (Table 5.4). Cyprus and

Table 5.4 Infrastructural projects for the monetisation of the Levantine Sea gas resources (2011–14).

Project	States involved/ EU support (*)	Main technical features	Estimated costin USD (e)	Estimated year of operation (e)
LNG plant	Cyprus (*) (^)	7 bcm/y of gas capacity	10–15 billion	2020
	Cyprus and Israel	7–14 bcm/y of gas capacity	10–15 billion	2020
Pipeline	Israel-Cyprus-Greece (*)	30–40 bcm/y of gas capacity	17–20 billion	Post 2020
	Israel-Cyprus-Turkey	5–11 bcm/y of gas capacity	5–10 billion	2023–2025
	Israel-Turkey	5–11 bcm/y of gas capacity	5–10 billion	2023–2025
Electricity interconnector	Israel-Cyprus-Greece (*)	Electrical power from gas-fired plants (2000MW duo-directional electricity cable)	2 billion	2016

Sources: Author's compilation from De Micco (2014) and press sources.

Note: The table does not include the LNG and FLNG projects discussed in Israel during this period.
(e) = estimates in 2014.
(*) = Projects included in the 2013 EU PCI list.

Greece also sought EU support for their preferred projects, including the Cyprus-Vassilikos LNG terminal attached to the so-called 'Mediterranean gas storage' concept, which was included by the European Commission on the 2013 PCI list.[20] In this period, the EU began to pay more attention to Eastern Mediterranean resources as a possible way to improve its diversification of supply.

The EuroAsia Electricity Interconnector would utilise Levantine gas resources in loci and export the electricity produced by gas power stations by linking Greek, Cypriot and Israeli power grids via a submarine cable. Since its appearance on the agenda, this project was less expensive than the other alternatives for implementing Israeli-Cypriot-Greek cooperation. However, although the project has the political support of all the governments involved and of the EU and would cost relatively little, it faces many technical challenges, since it would be world's longest subsea electricity interconnector (if built, the total length of the interconnector would be about 1,500 km, and it would lie on the seabed of the Eastern Mediterranean, reaching depths of up to 2,000 metres). Moreover, the project would be at risk of dispute since the cable would traverse contested waters due to Turkish claims and the problematic delimitation of the Egyptian and Greek EEZs (De Micco 2014).

The second option for implementing the Israeli-Cyprus-Greek energy partnership is the East Med Pipeline, which would consist of a pipeline linking Israel and Cyprus to Greece and then to the EU gas network. This project was proposed by IGI-Poseidon, a 50–50 percent joint venture of the Greek state-owned company DEPA and the Italian company Edison (part of the EDF group since 2012). It was far more ambitious and expensive than the electricity connector – the estimated costs were about 17–20 billion dollars – and it would be a viable option only if more gas were discovered in the region or if Israel decided to commit a large part of its resources to this route (Tagliapietra 2013). For Greece, which was already involved in the development of the Southern Gas Corridor, the prospect of becoming a transit country for gas supplies from the Eastern Mediterranean as well had both economic and political appeal (Tsakiris 2014). However, for Cyprus, Israel and the energy companies involved, a pipeline to Greece presented many problems due to the uncertain prospect of EU demand for gas, especially when considered against the merits of the available alternatives, such as LNG facilities to reach the more profitable Asian markets (Darbouche, El-Katiri and Fattouh 2012; Tagliapietra 2013). It is worth noting that, during this period, the appeal of LNG was also driven by the rise in LNG prices in the wake of the Fukushima nuclear accident, which forced Japan to increase its gas imports.

Politically, Cyprus and Israel also appreciated the flexibility offered by the LNG solution. This was especially true for Israel, since a pipeline would link most parts of its exports to a single route. Furthermore, this route would cross parts of the Eastern Mediterranean Sea in which Turkish claims overlapped with the Cypriot and Greek EEZs. For these reasons, Israel was evaluating the feasibility of building an LNG or FLNG facility. Meanwhile, in 2012, Cyprus made plans to build an LNG liquefaction plant with an initial capacity of almost 7 bcm/y. The terminal, which was to be built in Vassilikos, would allow Cypriot gas to reach European and Asian markets and would have initially been opened both to Israel and Lebanon.[21] However, for the LNG plant project to remain economically viable, Cyprus needed both Israeli financial support (to cover costs estimated at 10–15 billion dollars) and Israeli gas, since Cypriot resources alone were not sufficient to justify the cost of an LNG export facility (Tagliapietra 2013; De Micco 2014). Although Cyprus's preference was also supported by the energy companies involved in the development of the Leviathan and Aphrodite gas fields, political considerations persuaded Israeli policymakers to reject a similar proposal. Indeed, a potential new LNG export facility was now seen by Israeli decision makers as a 'strategic asset' that should be firmly placed under Israeli sovereignty.[22]

In the same period, a prospect of a pipeline route from Israel to Turkey also appeared on the agenda. This was in the wake of the tentative rapprochement between the two countries. In late March 2013, US President Obama persuaded Israeli Prime Minister Netanyahu to apologise to Turkish Prime Minister Erdogan for the 2010 Mavi Marmara incident. Washington – apart from its economic interests attached to the activities of the US company Noble Energy – has a wider strategic interest in assuring that new resources can promote stability in the region and provide incentives for political reconciliation in Cyprus and between Israel and Turkey (Vogler and Thompson 2015). During this period, Russia – which traditionally has close ties with Israel, Cyprus and Syria – also tried to enter the economic and political game of Levantine resource monetisation. As we saw, the Russian company Novatek took part in Cyprus's second offshore bidding round. Politically, Moscow backed Cyprus in its dispute with Turkey and offered to support Nicosia in the 2011–13 financial crisis. Gazprom expressed interest in developing and marketing the Tamar and Levantine Israeli gas fields, although without success. Russian energy companies were also involved in the development of Syrian offshore resources (Syria launched its first offshore licensing round in 2007). In late 2013, the Russian energy company SoyuzNefteGaz signed an agreement with the regime of Bashar al Assad to explore Syria's EEZ, but the deterioration of the domestic political context, the outbreak of civil war and the rise of ISIS halted further developments, limiting Russia's role in the Levantine energy sector. However, the subsequent involvement of Russia in the Syrian war and the Russia-Iran alignment has reasserted Moscow's crucial role in the Eastern Mediterranean and wider Middle Eastern international politics. This has further enhanced the Washington's strategic interest in promoting a rapprochement between the US's main regional allies (Turkey and Israel), possibly cemented by long-term energy cooperation.

From the Turkish point of view, the plan to build a pipeline from the Leviathan gas field was a useful counterbalance to Greece-Cypriot-Israeli relations. The project was also convenient from an energy perspective, since it would have supplied additional gas for the growing domestic market and supported Ankara's energy diversification strategy. Negotiations began between the Leviathan partners and important Turkish firms that showed an interest in financing this project, the estimated cost of which – 5 billion US dollars – was significantly less than the 15 billion requested for the LNG plant.[23] However, although a rapprochement between Israel and Turkey would have been realised, the political obstacles were numerous (Ghikas 2013, 7–8). There are two ways for a pipeline to reach Turkey. One crosses the Cypriot EEZ, and the other crosses the Lebanese and the Syrian EEZs (Figure 5.3). In the first case, a rapprochement between Ankara and Nicosia would be a precondition of the project. In the second case, Turkey, Syria and Lebanon would have to demarcate their territorial waters and their EEZs, something that seems very unlikely due to the conflict in Syria and the maritime boarder dispute between Israel and Lebanon, and that would present high security risks in any case.

Finally, another option appeared on the agenda. In February 2014, after the election of Nicos Anastasiades – a moderate on the Cyprus question who had previously supported the UN Annan Plan – as president of Cyprus, the ROC peace talks between the two communities of the island resumed (Grigoriadis 2014). It was hoped that the possibility of exploiting the new gas resources would make it possible to resolve the long-standing Cyprus question. In this context, a possible pipeline route from the island to Turkey would have represented a profitable and concrete solution for the monetisation of Cyprus's gas.

Towards Regional Patterns of Cooperation: 2014–15

As anticipated, by the beginning of 2015, none of the projects discussed during 2011–14 were on the point of materialising, and a variety of factors further complicated the economic and political game of monetising the Levantine resources. On one hand, in the wake of the deterioration of EU-Russia relations, the appeal of the East Med Pipeline seemed to be restored. Mainly due to the support of Cyprus and Greece, the project was confirmed in the revised EU PCI list, issued by the European Commission in January 2014. On the other hand, the prolonged economic and financial crisis in Greece added additional uncertainty to a project that was already very technically, politically and financially complex. Also, the concept of 'Mediterranean gas storage' was again included in the 2014 version of the EU PCI list. However, the prospect for the Cyprus-Vassilikos LNG terminal would soon be undermined (see the following discussion).

After the withdrawal of the Australian company Woodside from the development of the Leviathan field in May 2014, the prospect of an LNG export facility in Israel was also undermined.[24] The LNG (or FLNG) solution involved significant security risks due to the problem of fully protecting such infrastructures in the Israeli EEZ (Good 2014). Furthermore, in a market environment characterised by declining gas prices, both the government and the energy companies began to view exporting to immediate neighbours as a more viable and convenient solution. In terms of national security, Israel regarded the political stability of its immediate neighbours as a major concern, especially considering the turbulence caused in the region by the war in Syria and the rise of ISIS. In 2013, by reviewing the proposal of the Zemach Committee, the government already included exports to Jordan and Palestine in its overall estimated domestic demand, as access to energy was considered an important element for their political stability. In January 2014, Noble Energy and Delek signed the first Israeli natural gas export deal with the

Palestinian Authority's electric company (however, this agreement was cancelled in March 2015).[25] In February 2014, an initial agreement was reached for the supply of modest gas quantities from the Tamar field (0.12 bcm/y for a 15-year period) to two Jordan state-controlled companies (the Arab Potash Company and the Jordanian Bromine Company).[26] In September 2014, this agreement was followed by a major deal in the form of a 'non-binding letter of intent' for a 15-year contract with annual delivery of 3 bcm from the Leviathan field to the Jordan National Electric Power Company.[27] For Jordan, the possibility of access to Israeli's resources was particularly important from the perspective of energy security. After the disruption of Egyptian gas flow, which completely stopped in mid-2013, Jordan was forced to import expensive fuels to sustain its growing domestic demand and, in 2015, to import LNG thanks to a FSRU contracted for 10 years and moored near the Red Sea port of Aqaba (Henderson 2015).

In 2015, the energy companies involved in Israeli offshore development also signed various deals to export gas to Egypt. The supply of gas to Egypt would help meet the country's growing energy needs – which, after the turmoil of the previous years, changed from an energy exporter to an energy importer – but would also use the existing Egyptian LNG infrastructure to re-export the gas into other markets. British Gas signed a MoU with the Leviathan partner to send 7 bcm of liquefied natural gas annually for 15 years to its plant in northern Egypt at Idku. The Tamar partners signed a MoU with the Spanish company Union Fenosa to provide 4.5 bcm a year for 15 years to its LNG plant at Damietta. The Tamar partners also started talks with a private Egyptian company (Dolphinus Holdings) to supply gas to Egypt using the Arish-Ashkelon pipeline, which had formerly transported gas to Israel from Egypt.[28] However, this Israel export strategy was complicated by strong domestic political opposition to the government's gas monetisation policy, the so-called natural gas regulatory framework. This regulatory scheme was also opposed by the Israeli Antitrust Authority and Israel's High Court of Justice. It was only in May 2016 that the government was finally able to pass an amended version of the natural gas framework, paving the way for the implementation of Israel's gas export policy.

The situation in Cyprus was complex as well, although for different reasons. In 2015, the companies developing the Aphrodite field declared it commercial (with estimated reserves of about 130 bcm) and submitted a development and production plan to the government, with the intention of beginning the first gas supply from the field by 2020.[29] However, the other companies that were drilling in Cyprus's EEZ (ENI, Kogas and Total) failed to find any amount of recoverable gas. Without other reserves in the Cypriot EEZ, many of the infrastructure projects discussed in the previous years were not financially sustainable, including the LNG liquefaction terminal at Vassilikos. In 2014, the estimated bcm requirement for viable investments in the different export options was about 200 bcm for an LNG to Asia, 250 bcm for an LNG to Europe or a pipeline to Greece, and 113 bcm for a pipeline to Turkey (Mullen 2014). But, this last option was still not realistic due to the unresolved Cyprus issue. Thus, Nicosia also turned to look at its southern neighbours and less complicated projects. In September 2014, Cyprus signed a Memorandum of Understanding with Jordan for evaluating the possibilities of a LNG gas export deal, but this idea was not developed further. On the other hand, Egypt was now seen as a possible destination for Cypriot resources. In February 2015, Cyprus and Egypt signed a MoU for the use of Egypt's exporting facilities and to evaluate the possibility of building a pipeline to connect the Aphrodite gas resources to Egypt's LNG infrastructures. In June 2015, the RoC President and Ministry of Energy visited Israel to discuss the possibility of merging pipelines from Israel and Cyprus to deliver gas to Egypt, revitalising Cypriot-Israeli energy cooperation after Israel's rejection of the joint LNG facilities at Vassilikos.[30] On this occasion, the EuroAsia Electricity Interconnector project was also re-examined.

All in all, these additional agreements strengthen the regional network of political cooperation for the monetisation of the Eastern Mediterranean gas resources. However, it is only in the case of Israel that company-to-company negotiations and preliminary commercial deals have taken place; in other countries, only government-to-government energy talks have occurred (Table 5.5).

The Cypriot and Israeli plans to export gas to Egypt were eventually complicated when, at the end of August 2015, the Italian company ENI announced a huge discovery in the Egyptian offshore Zohr gas field (with 850 bcm of potential lean gas)[31] (Figure 5.3). This new discovery could potentially undermine the Israeli-Cypriot plan, especially the part that involves supplying the Egyptian market. However, both experts and Egyptian authorities forecast an important role for gas imports in Egypt until at least 2020 and possibly 2025, depending on how quickly Zohr is developed and how much domestic demand continues to grow (Tsafos 2015). In fact, after the Zohr discovery, Egypt reassured Israel and Cyprus of its intention to continue energy talks with both countries.[32] Egypt's diplomatic ties and cooperation with Israel in particular have increased amid a convergence of interests on issues ranging from support for the Saudi-initiated regional plan for brokering Arab-Israeli peace to the security of the Sinai Peninsula, in addition to their increasingly strong energy relationship.[33] Egypt is also interested in commercially exploiting its LNG facilities to allow the export of Israeli and Cypriot gas.

Table 5.5 The emerging political and commercial network for the monetisation of Eastern Mediterranean gas resources.

	Cyprus	*Egypt*	*Israel*	*Jordan*	*Greece*	*Turkey*
Cyprus		MoU	MoU	MoU	MoU	
Egypt	MoU		C-C	–	–	–
Israel	MoU	C-C		C-C	MoU	C-C
Jordan	MoU	–	C-C		–	–
Greece	MoU	–	MoU	–		–
Turkey	–	–	C-C	–	–	

Note: MoU = Memorandum of Understanding for government-to-government energy cooperation; C-C = Company-to-Company negotiations and/or preliminary gas deals.

In sum, since 2014, regional patterns of energy cooperation have been strengthened among the Eastern Mediterranean countries. However, it is worth noting that owing to the long-term perspective of gas infrastructure – i.e. the time frame to recoup investments extends over many years – the actual prospect for realising the projects discussed in this period remain complicated. Despite the intensification of energy talks and dialogues, companies can be discouraged by the unstable regional security context and the historical records of abrupt changes in the status of bilateral relations among the Eastern Mediterranean countries.

Post-2015 Developments

After the clarification of the regulatory framework in Israel, Jordanian talks with the Leviathan partners were relaunched. Despite some political resistance, the Jordanian parliament passed a law in May 2016 authorising Israeli companies to participate in national projects administrated by the Jordanian Investment Fund.[34] And in summer 2016, the newly appointed Jordanian Prime Minister, Hani Al-Muki, met a senior Israeli delegation to discuss common infrastructure projects, paving the way for the implementation of the gas deal.[35]

After the approval of the natural gas framework, negotiations for the Israel-Turkey pipeline were relaunched, parallel to the ongoing process of normalising Tel Aviv-Ankara relations. An Israel-Turkey rapprochement must be placed in the broad context of the reconfiguration of the Eastern Mediterranean security structure, which includes the war in Syria and the growing role of Iran in the Middle East since the nuclear deal. But energy relations can play an important role in this process, along with Turkey's willingness to diversify its gas suppliers and reduce its dependence on Russia (a problem that was particularly exposed during the Moscow-Ankara crisis after a Russian jet was shot down over the Syrian border). However, for the Israeli-Turkish pipeline to be realised, Tel Aviv will need approval from Cyprus as well.

In January 2016, a trilateral summit was held in Nicosia. Israeli Prime Minister Netanyahu, Greek Prime Minister Alex Tsipras and Cypriot President Nicos Anastasiades discussed strengthening their political and economic cooperation. A Trilateral Committee was established to relaunch consideration of the East Med Pipeline. With support from Greece, Cyprus and Italy, the pipeline was included in the 2015 EU PCI list (the East Med pipeline was also awarded a grant of two million euro through the Connecting Europe Facility to co-finance feasibility studies). At this summit, however, Netanyahu stressed that Israel's current 'gas capabilities' could supply pipelines to both Egypt and Turkey, while a possible pipeline to Europe through Cyprus and Greece would depend on the development of additional gas fields.[36] Cyprus and Greece support a similar solution. In particular, Athens, which cannot directly influence monetisation decisions, hopes to use instrumental energy-related projects to strengthen its regional role, increase its influence and, in the medium- to long-term, support its economy (Dokos 2016). Moreover, although the projects discussed may not actually be realised in the near future, energy resources have already helped strengthen Israel-Cyprus-Greek international relations. As correctly pointed out by Tziarras (2016), this recent trilateral cooperation can be defined a 'comfortable quasi-alliance': it lacks the more formal and substantive military-oriented character found in a formal alliance; and it does not necessitate mutual exclusiveness with regard to the bilateral relations between Athens, Nicosia, Tel Aviv and Ankara. That it is to say, the nature of this cooperation allows the three countries to manoeuvre politically so as not to exclude future parallel relations with Ankara. But, at the same time, the partnership can give the three states some leverage vis-à-vis Turkey and accommodate their specific economic and political interests.

In this context, the Israeli-Cyprus energy and political dialogue continued hand in hand with the Israeli-Turkey rapprochement, eventually announced on 27 June 2016. After this event, Israel resumed energy talks with Cyprus for a unitisation agreement to delimitate the Aphrodite gas field and hasten the development of Leviathan in conjunction with Aphrodite.[37] Israel's position towards a rapprochement with Ankara did not change after the failed Turkish coup of 15 July. On the other hand, after the coup, Turkey also reaffirmed its commitment to a rapprochement with Israel and to continuing to pursue an energy diversification agenda, including the possibility of an Israel-Turkey pipeline.

Meanwhile, after the discovery of the Zohr field, interest in the Eastern Mediterranean resources has risen again. When, in March 2016, Cyprus launched its third licensing round for offshore exploration, offering three blocks in its EEZ, applications were submitted by major oil companies like ENI, Total, Exxon-Mobil, Qatar Petroleum and Statoil.[38] Cyprus's third licensing round was supported by the European Commission. Cypriot President Nicos Anastasiades stressed that the construction of an LNG export terminal depends on the possible new discoveries that could result from this round.[39] However, Cyprus has also continued to work with Egypt. In September 2016, Cyprus and Egypt signed a new political agreement for the transport of Cypriot natural gas to Egypt and to support possible company-to-company deals in the future. However, such deals are still complicated because of low gas prices, which are currently halting major investment plans.[40] Besides, as for the other projects in the Eastern Mediterranean, also in this case energy companies can be discouraged by security issues, regional instability and concerns related to possible changes in inter-state political relations.

Concluding Remarks

As illustrated in this chapter, recent energy developments in the Eastern Mediterranean are very complex. The international political economy of Levantine offshore exploration and gas monetisation is intricately intertwined with broader security and foreign policy implications, reaching into the regional politics of the entire Middle East and involving major powers. Although the IPE approach developed in the book has been useful for highlighting the interactions between the main economic and political dynamics in this case as well, the conceptual framework based on the notion of forms of state encounters some limits. To be sure, regional energy developments have been widely affected by national interests, energy security agendas and government-to-government, government-to-company and company-to-company patterns of interactions. However, the case of Cyprus, a very small island physically separated from the EU network and without any previous experience in the energy sector, can hardly be framed in the traditional partner state model (and a similar discourse applies to Israel as well). At first glance, the image of the associational state – with governments supporting private companies and offering security (including military) and diplomatic cover to investment projects – could be extended to describe some elements of the politics of Eastern Mediterranean energy security (especially considering the serious security issues surrounding offshore development and monetisation alternatives). On the other hand, in the cases of Cyprus and Greece, findings in line with the catalytic state model and its network diplomacy can be discerned. These member states have tried to create inter-state coalitions to support the projects proposed by energy companies and involve the EU institutions in the export plans for the monetisation of Levantine gas resources: the Vassilikos LNG and the East Med Pipeline. However, this case also demonstrates the EU's limits; it has very minimal influence over export routes when its preferences are not supported by commercial fundamentals or when wider national security interests drive energy policymaking in non-EU countries, such as Israel. Besides, as we saw, the influence of the EU on offshore governance and delimitation issues has been very minimal as well. All in all, the study of the Eastern Mediterranean gas development has additionally confirmed how the politics of energy security in the EU and beyond – and the potential effectiveness of the EU strategy – are shaped by and highly dependent on the specific contextual conditions in which they take place.

Notes

1 See the data provided by the EU Offshore Authorities Group, available at: http://euoag.jrc.ec.europa.eu/node/63 [accessed 13 June 2016].
2 Author's elaboration from US Energy Information Administration statistics, available at: www.eia.gov/ [accessed 15 January 2016].
3 For a discussion of the limits of the EU external governance approach in the non-EU countries in the Southern Mediterranean, see Chapter 2.
4 For a brief review of the 'security architecture' in the Eastern Mediterranean and its major transformation in recent years, see Alterman and Malka (2012).
5 This section is adapted from Prontera (2016).
6 See data available at: www.akbn.gov.al/wp-content/uploads/2015/06/Albanian-exploration-blocks-and-respective-coordinates.pdf [accessed 10 September 2016].
7 Data concerning procedures and results of the Greek international licensing round and open-door invitation are available at: www.ypeka.gr/Default.aspx?tabid=765&language=en-US [accessed 20 April 2016].
8 See 'Faltering Croatia seeks oil bonanza', 29 September 2013, available at: www.thesundaytimes.co.uk/sto/news/world_news/Europe/article1320454.ece?CMP=OTH-gnws-standard-2013_09_28 [accessed 22 June 2016].
9 On April 2016, the Italian Parliament passed a new law to reform the Italian Constitution. The new law also provides for a recentralisation of decision-making power on energy issues (reforming Title V of the Italian Constitution). The reform proposal was subject to a referendum that was held on 4 December 2016. However, the Italian voters rejected the reform and these constitutional changes.

10 See 'Marathon, OMV hand back Croatia oil exploration licences', 29 July 2015, available at: www.reuters.com/article/2015/07/29/marathon-omv-croatia-idUSL5N1091Z120150729 [accessed 29 June 2016].

11 See 'Offshore exploration and exploitation of hydrocarbons in Montenegro', 29 April 2015, available at: www.ceelegalmatters.com/index.php/legal-analysis-energy/item/2425-offshore-exploration-and-exploitation-of-hydrocarbons-in-montenegro [accessed 1 July 2016].

12 See 'Novatek, ENI to explore for oil and gas offshore Montnegro', 14 September 2016, available at: www.lngworldnews.com/novatek-eni-to-explore-for-oil-and-gas-offshore-montenegro/ [accessed 18 September 2016].

13 See 'Slovenia fears Croatia's bidding round launch would jeopardise maritime dispute', 17 April 2014, available at: www.naturalgaseurope.com/croatia-slovenia-maritime-dispute [accessed 28 August 2016].

14 A chronological account of the main events regarding the arbitration process can be found at: www.mvep.hr/en/other/termination-of-the-arbitration-process/ [accessed 3 September 2016].

15 In January 2016, Abruzzi reviewed its position and decided to not support the referendum further.

16 All the reports included in the Italian trans-boundary Strategic Environmental Assessment can be consulted at: www.va.minambiente.it/it-IT/Oggetti/Documentazione/1540/2484?pagina=1#form-cercaDocumentazione [accessed from 15 April to 5 May 2016].

17 See the interview with the Croatian Ministry of Economy, 'Offshore exploration will not endanger Croatia's tourism, Minister of Economy says', 2 April 2015, available at: www.offshoreenergytoday.com/interview-offshore-exploration-will-not-endanger-croatias-tourism-minister-of-economy-says/ [accessed 2 June 2016].

18 For a detailed review of the EU's position, the major EU member states and other international actors on the issue, see Gürel, Mullen and Tzimitras (2013).

19 See 'Erdogan threatens blacklist for oil firms drilling in Cyprus', 22 September 2011, available at: www.bloomberg.com/news/articles/2011–09–22/erdogan-threatens-to-blacklist-companies-working-with-cyprus-on-oil-gas [accessed 3 June 2016].

20 The 'Mediterranean gas storage' concept included in the 2013 EU PCI list refers to a 'storage facility associated with the LNG terminal in Vassilikos aiming at the storage of gas from the Levantine Basin (Israel and Cyprus) in liquefied form onshore Cyprus, for further transport namely to LNG Receiving and Regasification Terminals located in the Mediterranean Sea' (European Commission 2013).

21 See 'Cyprus' LNG project continues despite complicating factors', 21 January 2014, available at: www.naturalgaseurope.com/cyprus-lng-project-continues [accessed 3 August 2016].

22 See, in particular, the positions expressed by the so-called 'Zemach Committee' (*The Recommendations of the Inter-Ministerial Committee to Examine the Government's Policy Regarding Natural Gas in Israel*, September 2012).

23 See 'Turkey and Israel may reconcile after years of tension', 4 April 2014, available at: www.naturalgaseurope.com/turkey-israel-may-reconcile-after-years-of-tension [accessed 12 September 2016].

24 See 'Noble, Woodside terminate $2.5 billion MOU for Leviathan', 21 May 2014, available at: www.ogj.com/articles/2014/05/noble-woodside-terminate-2–5-billion-mou-for-leviathan.html [accessed 18 August 2016].

25 See 'Palestinian power company nixing Leviathan gas import deal', 3 November 2015, available at: www.jpost.com/Business/Palestinian-Power-Generation-Company-nixing-Leviathan-gas-import-deal-393570 [accessed 13 September 2016].

26 See 'Jordan's energy decision: Go with Israel', 3 September 2014, available at: www.washingtoninstitute.org/policy-analysis/view/jordans-energy-decision-go-with-israel [accessed 16 August 2016].

27 Ibid.
28 See 'Israel's Tamar group looks to sell gas to Egypt via EMG pipeline', 19 October 2014, available at: www.reuters.com/article/2014/10/19/israel-natgas-egypt-idUSL6 N0SE03G20141019 [accessed 27 November 2016].
29 See 'The Eastern Mediterranean's natural gas struggles', Natural Gas Europe, 13 July 2015, available at: www.naturalgaseurope.com/eastern-mediterraneans-natural-gas-struggles-24591 [accessed 29 November 2016].
30 See 'Cyprus and Israel pledge long term energy cooperation', Natural Gas Europe, 23 June 2015, available at: www.naturalgaseurope.com/cyprus-and-israel-pledge-long-term-energy-cooperation-24311 [accessed 30 June 2016].
31 See 'Eni discovers a supergiant gas field in the Egyptian offshore, the largest ever found in the Mediterranean Sea', available at: www.eni.com/en_IT/media/2015/08/eni-discovers-a-supergiant-gas-field-in-the-egyptian-offshore-the-largest-ever-found-in-the-mediterranean-sea [accessed 8 June 2016].
32 See 'Interview-Egypt says Zohr gas find will not undermine talks on imports from Israel', 2 September 2015, available at: http://uk.reuters.com/article/egypt-energy-israel-idUKL4N11834820150902 [accessed 28 May 2016].
33 See 'Old Mideast foes unite over gas deals and fighting militants', 11 July 2016, available at: www.bloomberg.com/news/articles/2016-07-10/old-middle-east-foes-unite-over-gas-deals-and-fighting-militants [accessed 28 July 2016]; and 'Netanyahu, Sisi and zero problems diplomacy', 6 June 2016, available at: www.aljazeera.com/indepth/opinion/2016/06/netanyahu-sisi-problems-diplomacy-160605061312495.html [accessed 24 July 2016].
34 See 'In blow to BDS, Jordan authorises Israel's participation in national investment fund', 23 May 2016, available at: www.jpost.com/Arab-Israeli-Conflict/In-blow-to-BDS-Jordan-authorizes-Israels-participation-in-national-investment-fund-454758 [accessed 10 June 2016].
35 See 'Israel and Jordan working towards closer relations', 25 July 2016, available at: www.globes.co.il/en/article-israel-and-jordan-working-towards-closer-relations-1001141927 [accessed 2 August 2016].
36 See 'Gas pipeline focus of "historic" talks between Israeli, Greek and Cypriot leaders', 28 January 2016, available at: www.jpost.com/Israel-News/Politics-And-Diplomacy/Gas-pipeline-focus-of-historic-talks-between-Israeli-Greek-and-Cypriot-leaders-443120 [accessed 27 May 2016].
37 See 'Israel, Cyprus work on cross-border agreement', 25 July 2016, available at: www.naturalgaseurope.com/israel-cyprus-to-seek-unitization-agreement-by-september-30745 [accessed 3 August 2016].
38 In November 2015, British Gas had acquired a 35 percent of the Aphrodite reservoir from Noble Energy. This commercial deal was approved by the Cypriot government in January 2016.
39 See 'Cyprus LNG terminal non-starter?', 21 April 2016, available at: www.marinelink.com/news/nonstarter-terminal408479.aspx [accessed 16 September 2016].
40 See 'Cyprus, Egypt start gas trade talks process', 31 August 2016, available at: www.naturalgaseurope.com/cyprus-egypt-start-gas-trade-process-31361 [accessed 9 September 2016]; and 'Cyprus and Egypt sign gas agreement', 7 September 2016, available at: www.naturalgaseurope.com/cyprus-and-egypt-sign-gas-agreement-31487 [accessed 10 September 2016].

References

Alterman, J. B., Malka, H. 2012. Shifting Eastern Mediterranean Geometry. *The Washington Quarterly* 35(3): 111–125.
Annish, F. A. 1993. *The International Law of Maritime Boundaries and the Practice of States in the Mediterranean Sea.* Oxford: Oxford University Press.

Blake, G., Topalović, D. 1996. The Maritime Boundaries of the Adriatic Sea. *IBRU Maritime Briefing* 1(8): 76–94.

Caligiuri, A. 2015. Offshore Shared Natural Resources and the Duty to Cooperate in a Semi-Enclosed Sea, in Caligiuri, A. (ed.), *Offshore Oil and Gas Exploration and Exploitation in the Adriatic and Ionian Seas*, pp. 1–5. Naples: Editoriale Scientifica.

Clancy, P. 2007. Offshore Petroleum Politics: A Changing Frontier in a Global System. *Policy and Society* 26(1): 113–134.

Clancy, P. 2011. *Offshore Petroleum Politics: Regulation and Risk in the Scotian Basin.* Toronto: UBC Press.

Cocco, E. 2013. *The Evolving Role of the Adriatic Space in the Mediterranean: Challenges and Opportunities.* Mediterranean Paper Series, The German Marshall Fund of the United States.

Darbouche, H., El-Katiri, L., Fattouh, B. 2012. *East Mediterranean Gas: What Kind of a Game-Changer?* Oxford Institute for Energy Studies, NG-71, December 2012.

De Micco, P. 2014. *The Prospect of Eastern Mediterranean Gas Production: An Alternative Energy Suppliers for the EU?* European Parliament, DG External Policies, Policy Department, April 2014.

DGRME, 2013. *The Sea: Supplement to Hydrocarbons and Geothermal Resources Official Bulletin.* Directorate-General for Mineral and Energy Resources, Rome.

Di Mento, J. F., Hickman, A. J. 2012. *Environmental Governance of the Great Seas: Law and Effect.* Cheltenham, UK: Edward Elgar Publishing.

Dokos, T. 2016. Energy Geopolitics in the Eastern Mediterranean: The Role of Greece, in Giannakopoulos, A. (ed.), *Energy Cooperation and Security in the Eastern Mediterranean: A Seismic Shift towards Peace or Conflict?*, pp. 37–47. Tel Aviv: SDAC, Research Paper No. 8.

Dundua, N. 2007. *Delimitation of Maritime Boundaries between Adjacent States.* United Nations, Division for Oceans Affairs and the Law of the Sea. Research report under the UN-Nippon Fellowship Programme 2006-2007. Available at: http://www.un.org/depts/los/nippon/unnff_programme_home/fellows_pages/fellows_papers/dundua_0607_georgia.pdf (accessed 12 May 2016).

EIA, 2013. *Eastern Mediterranean Region, Full Report.* US Energy Information Administration, 15 August 2013.

Espon, 2013. *European Seas and Territorial Development, Opportunities and Risks: Annex 12 to the Scientific Report Governance Case Studies: Mediterranean Sea.* European Observation Network Territorial Development and Cohesion, Espon, 16 January 2013.

European Commission, 2013. Commission delegated regulation n. 1391/2013 of 14 October 2013 amending regulation n. 347/2013 of the European Parliament and of the Council on guidelines for trans-European energy infrastructure as regards the union list of Projects of Common Interest. Official Journal of the European Union, 21.12.2013.

European Commission, 2014. *Action Plan: European Union Strategy for the Adriatic and Ionian Region.* Brussels, SWD(2014) 190 final.

European Parliament, 2010. *Jurisdictional Waters in the Mediterranean and Black Seas.* Brussels: Policy Department, Structural and Cohesion Policy.

Ghikas, P. 2013. Petroleum Resources in South Eastern Mediterranean: A Deus ex Machina for EU Supply Security? *Oil, Gas & Energy Law Intelligence* 11(3): 1–22.

Giamouridis, A. 2012. *The Offshore Discovery in the Republic of Cyprus: Monetisation Prospects and Challenges.* Oxford Institute for Energy Studies, NG-65, July 2012.

Goldstein, J. 1982. *The Politics of Offshore Oil.* New York: Praeger.

Good, A. 2014. *Defending Israel's Natural Gas.* Middle East and African Foreign Policy, 13 January 2014. Available at: http://foreignpolicy.com/2014/01/13/defending-israels-natural-gas/ [accessed 12 August 2016].

Government of Montenegro, 2014a. *Communication from the Government of Montenegro, Dated 2 July 2014, Concerning Exploration and Exploitation of Resources in the Adriatic Sea by the Republic of Croatia.* Available at: www.un.org/Depts/los/LEGISLATION ANDTREATIES/STATEFILES/MNG.htm [accessed 30 May 2016].

Government of Montenegro, 2014b. *Communication from the Government of Montenegro, Dated 1 December 2014, Concerning Exploration and Exploitation of Resources in the Adriatic Sea by the Republic of Croatia.* Available at: www.un.org/Depts/los/LEGISLATION ANDTREATIES/STATEFILES/MNG.htm [accessed 3 June 2016].

Government of Montenegro, 2015a. *Note of Protest of Montenegro's Ministry of Foreign Affairs and European Integration to the Government of Croatia, No. 09/16-109/1, Dated January 5, 2015.* Available at: http://www.un.org/depts/los/LEGISLATIONAND TREATIES/PDFFILES/communications/MNG_note20150619en.pdf (accessed 24 June 2016).

Government of Montenegro, 2015b. *Note of Protest of Montenegro's Ministry of Foreign Affairs and European Integration to Marathon Oil Netherland OMV Croatia, No. 09-16-109/10, Dated January 27 2015.* Available at: http://www.un.org/depts/los/ LEGISLATIONANDTREATIES/PDFFILES/communications/MNG_note20150619en. pdf (accessed 24 June 2016).

Grigoriadis, I. N. 2014. Energy Discoveries in the Eastern Mediterranean: Conflict or Cooperation? *Middle East Policy* 21(3): 124–133.

Gürel, A., Mullen, F., Tzimitras, H. 2013. *The Cyprus Hydrocarbon Issue: Context, Positions and Future Scenarios.* Peace Research Institute Oslo, PRIO, PCC Report, 1/2013.

Henderson, S. 2015. *Jordan's Energy Supply Options: The Prospect of Gas Imports from Israel.* GMF, Foreign and Security Policy Paper Series, October 2015.

Ibru, 2010. *Albanian Constitutional Court Nullifies Maritime Boundary Agreement with Greece,* 10 February 2010. Available at: www.dur.ac.uk/ibru/news/boundary_ news/?itemno=9534 [accessed 22 June 2016].

Keil, K. 2015. Spreading Oil, Spreading Conflict? Institutions Regulating Arctic Oil and Gas Activities. *The International Spectator* 50(1): 85–110.

Keohane, R. O., Victor, D. G. 2011. The Regime Complex for Climate Change. *Perspectives on Politics* 9(1): 7–23.

Khadduri, W. 2012. East Mediterranean Gas: Opportunities and Challenges. *Mediterranean Politics* 17(1): 111–117.

Leanza, U. 1993. The Delimitation of the Continental Shelf of the Mediterranean Sea. *The International Journal of Marine and Coastal Law* 8(3): 373–395.

Long, R. 2011. Marine Strategy Framework Directive: A New European Approach to the Regulation of the Marine Environment, Marine Natural Resources and Marine Ecological Services. *The Journal of Energy & Natural Resources Law* 29(1): 12–31.

Long, R. 2012. Stepping over Maritime Boundaries to Apply New Normative Tools in EU Law and Policy, in Nordquist, M., Moore, J. N., Beckman, R., Djalal, H. (eds.), *Maritime Border Diplomacy*, pp. 213–264. Boston/Leiden: Martinus Nijhoff Publishers.

Mullen, F. 2014. Cyprus Gas: Positions on Sovereignty and Latest Market Developments, in Gürel, A., Tzimitras, H., Faustmann, H. (eds.), *East Mediterranean Hydrocarbons Geopolitical Perspectives, Markets, and Regional Cooperation*, pp. 7–19. PCC Report, 3/2014.

Paraschos, P. 2013. Offshore Energy in the Levant Basin: Leaders, Laggards, and Spoilers. *Mediterranean Quarterly* 24(1): 38–56.

Prontera, A. 2016. The New Offshore Frontiers of EU Energy Security in the Mediterranean: The Politics of Hydrocarbon Development in the Adriatic and Ionian Seas. *Mediterranean Politics*, advanced online publication, 5 July 2016, http://dx.doi.org/10.1080/ 13629395.2016.1199460.

Scovazzi, T. 2012. The Mediterranean Sea, in Di Mento, J. F., Hickman, A. J. (eds.), *Environmental Governance of the Great Seas: Law and Effect*, pp. 89–115. Cheltenham, UK: Edward Elgar Publishing.

Shaffer, B. 2012. *Energy Resources and Markets in the Eastern Mediterranean Region.* GMF Policy Brief, June 2012.

Stocker, J. 2012. No EEZ Solution: The Politics of Oil and Gas in the Eastern Mediterranean. *Middle East Journal* 66(4): 579–597.

Symmons, C. R. 1996. Albania and the Law of the Sea: An Analysis of Recent Practice. *International Journal of Marine and Coastal Law* 11(1): 69–78.

Tagliapietra, S. 2013. *Towards a New Eastern Mediterranean Energy Corridor? Natural Gas Developments between Market Opportunities and Geopolitical Risks.* Fondazione ENI Enrico Mattei, n. 12/2013.

Tsafos, N. 2015. *Egypt: A Market for Natural Gas from Cyprus and Israel?* GMF, Foreign and Security Policy Paper Series, October 2015.

Tsakiris, T. 2014. *Greece and the Energy Geopolitics of the Eastern Mediterranean.* LSE IDEAS, Strategic Update, June 2014, London.

Tziampiris, A. 2014. *The Emergence of Israeli-Greek Cooperation.* Cham, Switzerland: Springer.

Tziarras, Z. 2016. Israel-Cyprus-Greece: A 'Comfortable' Quasi-Alliance. *Mediterranean Politics*, online publication, 20 January 2016, pp. 1–21.

Van Leeuwen, J., Hoof, L. van, Tatenhove, J. van 2012. Institutional Ambiguity in Implementing the European Union Marine Strategy Framework Directive. *Marine Policy* 36(3): 636–643.

Vivero, J. L. S. de, Mateos, J. C., Corral, D. F. del 2009. Geopolitical Factors of Maritime Policies and Marine Spatial Planning: State, Regions, and Geographical Planning Scope. *Marine Policy* 33(4): 624–634.

Vogler, S., Thompson, E. V. 2015. *Gas Discoveries in the Eastern Mediterranean: Implications for Regional Maritime Security.* GMF, Policy Brief, March 2015.

6   Conclusion

During our long journey through the politics of energy security in the EU and beyond, we have analysed various policy areas and issues in detail. The IPE framework applied, and the conceptual analysis based on the notion of forms of state, have been crucial in making sense of such complex and fluid subject matter, in appreciating the emerging reconfiguration of the state-market nexus and in finding a comparative viewpoint from which to study the current dynamics. The historical institutional perspective, on the other hand, has been essential in outlining the extent, pace and degree of the changes observed in recent years and in placing them into a wider and more long-term context. This conclusive chapter briefly recalls and reviews the main overarching themes and theses of the book: the fundamental role that states still play in the practice of EU energy security governance; the inescapable political significance that energy resources have, even in the liberalised EU market structure; the need to put the interactions between states, markets and institutions into specific, national and regional contexts for a true understanding of energy security politics; and the meshing, in the current politics of energy security in the EU and beyond, of old and new dynamics.

Energy Security and the False Promise of 'Depoliticisation'

The goal of this book has been, by applying an IPE framework, to overcome the false dichotomy between 'high' and 'low' politics in the current practice of European energy security and to highlight the large portion of political dynamics that take place in the 'middle' zone between these two opposite poles – a zone where politics, security and economics intertwine. As we saw, the construction of the internal energy market (along with other global developments, especially in the gas sector) has shifted the previous balance between states and markets in favour of the latter. However, the result of this process is far from a linear retrenchment of the state. The empirical findings do not support the idea that energy security in a liberalised market structure means a depoliticisation of energy dependence and energy affairs. On the contrary, the evidence points to a general and widely accepted awareness among European governments and policymakers of the political significance of those issues that continue to require direct intervention by public authorities. In other words, the thesis that market dynamics would lead towards an 'economisation' of energy security has resulted in false expectations.

A similar outcome is not only evident in those EU member states where energy dependence is imbued with highly political symbolism and intertwined with the past legacy of Soviet dominance, such as in the Baltic States or other 'new' EU members in Eastern Europe; it also manifests among the 'old' member states, which continue to pursue various strategies to influence energy affairs. Rather than limiting their actions in 'setting the stage' for market actors to operate or designing the rules of the game to prevent and avoid market failures, governmental agents are well placed inside the field and ready to play according to their own agenda.

The fundamental role that states still play in the practice of EU energy security governance does not mean that nothing has changed in the EU's newly liberalised and de-monopolized market environment. National governments have lost many of their previous means of influence. Additionally, the shift toward the market has reduced their ability to manage their energy dependency and foreign energy relations with producers. As a result, governments are trying to find new strategies with which to achieve their objectives. They combine old and new policy instruments to address traditional energy security concerns, interact with state and non-state actors and pursue other policy goals in such areas as industrial and foreign policy.

The EU's liberalised market structure and the progressive integration of the European energy policy has also paved the way for new political dynamics. National governments compete and/or create coalitions to 'upload' their own preferences and agendas at the EU level and try to use the EU policy toolbox to achieve their goals. Governments also compete to increase the 'gains' offered by an integrated continental energy market. Examples range from their support of the energy companies that they host – or the many national champions, partially state-owned, still operating in the EU – to the competition to become 'energy hubs' that serve the wider European market. At the same time, national governments and EU-level governmental agents compete to assert their competences and views on energy security affairs.

As widely illustrated, the current situation represents the opposite of a depoliticisation of energy security. This can be seen on the EU level, specifically in the actions of the European Commission, once considered the champion of the market approach. Obviously, the main cases in point are relations with Russia and the EU's approach to diversification of gas supply and pipeline politics (e.g. the South Stream, Nord Stream 2 or the Southern Gas Corridor). However, it is worth noting that this more direct approach to energy security by the EU cannot be solely explained as a reaction to external events. To be sure, the Russia-Ukraine gas crisis, the deterioration of EU-Russia relations and the low level of trust after the war in Eastern Ukraine and the annexation of the Crimea have greatly contributed to Brussels's more proactive approach to diversification of gas supply. And in the future, the status of EU-Russia relations will continue to affect energy security strategy in Brussels and national capitals in both Western and Eastern Europe. But the important point here is that, from a historical perspective, it is common for the pendulum of energy policy to swing back and forth from states to markets in reaction to different market-related or geopolitical developments. The actual novelty is that the competences the EU has acquired during the last two decades – both with regard to the oversight of the internal energy market, where the European Commission makes *political decisions*, and external energy relations – have firmly placed the EU governmental agents into the day-to-day European politics of energy security. This politics now takes place in a truly multi-level political and diplomatic environment, although with differences and peculiarities related to the context in which it is embedded.

Putting States, Markets and Institutions into Contexts

The second thesis proposed in this book concerned the need to put the interactions between states, markets and institutions into specific national and regional contexts. This need is particularly evident in the EU. Not only, as demonstrated in the previous chapters, do the politics of energy security tends to assume specific features in different policy sectors (e.g. pipeline politics, LNG politics and offshore politics), but it also tends to change according to specific geographical and historical contexts. Neither global nor EU-level developments can explain the patterns of transformation illustrated in the case studies, which are shaped by the combination of these developments with the specific nature and meaning that energy security challenges assume in different sectors and national and local contexts. Moreover, the interactions between supranational dynamics and regional and domestic dynamics are also crucial to understanding the effectiveness of the EU energy security strategy.

In other words, the 'reconfiguration' of the politics of energy security in the EU and beyond cannot easily be summarised in a catch-all formula. With this in mind, scholars must be very cautious in considering single aspects of European energy security as indicative of the EU's overall pattern of evolution. Although the literature review presented in the first chapter has revealed that this is a common practice – which, among other things, tends to reproduce an idea of the current situation based on oversimplified dichotomies (e.g. 'geopolitics vs. the market', 'member states vs. the European Commission' or 'supranational vs national dynamics') – it is important to resist this temptation. As our journey from the Baltics to the Eastern Mediterranean Sea and from Western Europe to Central Asia has witnessed, context matters. On one hand, many member states have resisted the EU's intrusion into their national energy businesses and have backed their companies both domestically and abroad. On the other hand, the European Commission has, in some cases, been directly invited by national governments into the traditional *domaine reservé* of energy diplomacy and government-to-company negotiations. While member states have continued to develop their bilateral energy diplomacy, they have also delegated to the European Commission the power to develop EU-level energy diplomacy and have supported the EU's promotion of multilateral governance structures. The EU has favoured the spread and incorporation of environmental and sustainable development principles throughout the European system of governance; however, those principles have complicated the EU's and member states' energy security strategies. The list of such apparently opposed but coexisting dynamics is long.

In summary, when studying EU energy security, scholars must be very careful in generalising based on analyses of a single region, country, sector or actor. The politics of energy security in Lithuania have unique characteristics, and the same is true for Cyprus, Italy, Spain, France, Germany, Latvia and the rest. Similarly, the politics of offshore hydrocarbon development have specific features which differ from those of LNG or pipeline politics. In addition, the politics of offshore hydrocarbon development change if we move from the Adriatic and Ionian Seas to the Eastern Mediterranean Sea, and the politics of pipelines change if we move from the East-West corridor to the South-North corridor. These differences are not only related to the diverse conditions of energy markets, geography or resource endowments. They are strictly associated with the very meaning that energy security and energy politics assumes in different cases, often as a result of historical trajectories. This way, it is not possible to really understand the politics of energy security in the Baltic States without considering the way in which their energy relations with Moscow are imbued with a specific legacy related to the Soviet period. Similarly, looking at the opposite borders of the EU, it is crucial, for a true understanding of energy security politics in the Levantine Sea, to consider the way in which Cyprus-Turkey or Greece-Turkey energy disputes incorporate long-term, wider confrontations over national sovereignty, identity and status.

It is worth noting that accepting this argument also means accepting that, even if the EU is able to reach a full integration of its energy markets, it will not overcome its regional and national peculiarities. The promise of depoliticisation of energy security, in parallel with the move towards the market, is false. Also, the expectation that a more integrated EU energy market will automatically lead to a more common approach to energy security underestimates the important differences embedded in the very political meanings that energy security issues have in those specific contexts.

Obviously, the same argument can be applied on the EU level, where the approach to EU-Russia relations is shaped by the different perceptions and considerations of Moscow's foreign and energy policies among Western and Eastern EU member states. But energy issues also tend to incorporate specific features at the local level, where the politics of energy security is affected by the relations between the centre and the periphery and/or the interactions between energy and environmental concerns. This local, environmental dimension has gained importance hand-in-hand with the spread of the new principles and ideas contesting the preceding connection between large energy infrastructures and notions of economic 'development' or 'progress'.

Putting states, markets and institutions into contexts and focusing on the interactions between supranational dynamics and regional and domestic dynamics is also crucial for a true understanding of the limits and potential of the EU's energy security strategy. The effectiveness of the EU's approach is widely shaped by the context in which EU policies and institutional structures are embedded.

This means that the study of the success or failure of the EU's energy security strategy must consider both the features of the EU policy tools (and the relations among them) and the way in which they interact with policy tools, institutional structures, goals and principles promoted by other international actors as well as with domestic political and energy circumstances.

Finally, owing to the inherent complexity and context-dependence of energy security politics, it is important to pay attention to the different manifestations of the 'EU' in the energy realm. Depending on the context and issue under consideration, the EU can exercise its influence in multiple ways: as an actor, by directly using its organisational, financial and diplomatic resources; as a set of institutions and principles which reinforce or compete with other institutions and principles to influence actors' behaviours; or by virtue of its energy market. This tripartite aspect of the EU's role in energy security politics partially mirrors the traditional debate over the quality of the EU as an international actor. However, rather than assuming that one particular dimension can best represent the overall impact of the EU on energy affairs, it is important to consider which dimension, or which combination of dimensions, contributes to the transformation of the politics of energy security with regard to specific issues and regions.

EU Energy Security: Something 'Old' Something 'New'

Recognising the inherent complexity of energy matters and the crucial role of contexts obviously does not mean that it is impossible to elaborate and apply conceptual frameworks to cope with these problems. The opposite is true. The IPE framework that has been developed, along with the historical and comparative analysis undertaken based on the concept of forms of state, have precisely served this set of issues. In particular, by using this framework and concepts to provide an empirical analysis of various sectors and regions, this book has demonstrated how the developments of recent decades have led to a 'reconfiguration' of the politics of energy security in the EU and beyond. But, in contrast to the approaches that envisage the emergence of an entire new politics of energy security – due to the recent economic and institutional transformations at the international and EU levels – and the approaches that, instead, emphasise a substantial continuity with past experiences, the book has demonstrated that the current situation is better mirrored by a particular and context-dependent combination of 'new' and 'old' dynamics. The process of transformation triggered by the construction of the internal energy market and the deepening of European integration in energy affairs has only gradually challenged the previous institutional structures and political dynamics. Once again, they have not disappeared; nor have they simply been replaced by the new structures and dynamics. That it is to say, by stressing that the politics of energy security in the EU and beyond combines something 'old' and something 'new', this book does not suggest that the current phase is only a period of transition towards a different and definitive stage represented by the full accomplishment of all the new elements. Such a conclusion would be similar to the traditional view expressed in the literature, which places EU energy security 'in between' two opposite poles and inevitably 'lost in transition'. On the contrary, pointing to this combination of 'old' and 'new' dynamics has served to demonstrate that a specific state-market nexus and equilibrium has already emerged and that original concepts, such as the notion of the catalytic state, must be elaborated upon to cope with this situation.

The concept of the catalytic state, in particular, has been very useful for highlighting this emerging trend. On one hand, this concept has been sensitive to the particular national legacies and ideational context which have affected the complex transformations in the state-market nexus. The move towards the catalytic state has shown different pace and timing and future research should focus on the varieties of catalytic states, mirroring the existing literature on the varieties of regulatory states in the EU (e.g. Lodge 2002). On the other hand, through this concept it has been possible to stress some common tendencies: the practice of combining market-based policy tools with more direct forms of state intervention; the development of new modes of public involvement in ownership (including the establishment of public-private partnership); the persistence of the bilateral diplomacy and foreign energy policy promoted by the member states along with the new role played by the European Commission; and the coexistence of new principles and goals attached to the market paradigm of energy policy with the traditional attention national governments place on energy business as a sensitive area with important ramifications for domestic politics and foreign affairs. The notions of network and hexagonal diplomacy have also offered a privileged perspective for understanding the emerging patterns of interactions among state and non-sate actors in the EU's multi-layered political and diplomatic environment. Government-to-government, government-to-company and company-to-company relations are still crucial today, but new patterns of interactions involving the supranational and subnational levels are becoming increasingly important. Energy security in Europe is still the product of interactions between public authorities and market players, but the fragmentation of the state, along with the spread of new business models, has greatly complicated the picture. With this in mind, it is possible to rethink the main problems affecting the EU's energy security strategy. They are not related to fact that the EU is (to paraphrase the title of a recent and important book on the subject) 'a liberal actor in a realist world' (Goldthau and Sitter 2015) but, rather, to the fact that EU energy security suffers from well-known problems of vertical and horizontal coordination and coherence (e.g. Gebhard 2011; Peters 2012). To be sure, these problems are common in other policy fields and are structural features of the EU's complex, multi-layered institutional and political system. However, particularly in the energy security realm – due to its ramifications into the core of domestic and foreign affairs and to the long-term perspective needed to address such problems – without political agreement and common understanding about the main goals and direction of the European integration process, it will continue to be difficult to coordinate actors' strategies and promote coherent and effective policy responses to the current challenges.

References

Gebhard, C. 2011. Coherence, in Hill, C., Smith, M. (eds.), *International Relations and the European Union*, pp. 101–127. Oxford: Oxford University Press.

Goldthau, A., Sitter, N. 2015. *A Liberal Actor in a Realist World: The European Union Regulatory State and the Global Political Economy of Energy*. Oxford: Oxford University Press.

Lodge, M. 2002. Varieties of Europeanisation and the National Regulatory State. *Public Policy and Administration* 17(2): 43–67.

Peters, G. B. 2012. Coordination in the EU, in Jones, E., Menon, A., Weatherill, S. (eds.), *The Oxford Handbook of the European Union*, pp. 795–810. Oxford: Oxford University Press.

Index